Undeniable
Biblical
Proof

JESUS CHRIST

Will
Return
To
Planet
Earth
Exactly
2,000
Years
After
The
Year
Of
His
Death

What you MUST <u>DO</u> to be ready!!!

Undeniable
Biblical
Proof

JESUS CHRIST

Will
Return
To
Planet
Earth
Exactly
2,000
Years
After
The
Year
Of
His
Death

What you MUST _DO_ to be ready!!!

Gabriel Ansley

Mill City Press, Inc.
212 3rd Avenue North, Suite 290
Minneapolis, MN 55401
612.455.2294
www.millcitypublishing.com

ISBN - 978-1-936107-44-5
ISBN - 1-936107-44-9
LCCN - 2009941836

Cover Design by Wes Moore
Typeset by Peggy LeTrent

Printed in the United States of America

UndeniableBiblicalProof.com

Table of Contents

Foreword

This book could have just as easily begun with chapter 1 *"God's Master Time Plan"*, but I have been moved by God's Spirit to include an Introduction. It reads more like an autobiography of the amazing miracles, manifestations, and revelations God has performed in my life—and yet, it is only SOME of them! I have written about them NOT to boast of myself or to imply that I am something special, for I am nothing but a servant of God. I am simply one of God's spirit children, just like you. But I HAVE written the Introduction for your benefit, so that you would absolutely, positively KNOW God has a prophetic call on my life, thereby being convinced you can trust the words God has written through me in this book.

God told Moses: *"IF there be a prophet among you, I the LORD will make myself known unto him in a vision, and will speak unto him in a dream" (Numbers 12:6)*. The word "dream" was translated from the Hebrew word *"hªlôm"* meaning: dream; this can refer to a supernatural revelation by God by words and IMAGES. Though it took me awhile, I now understand I am one of God's prophets, and I humbly believe you will agree with me on this fact after reading the Introduction and contents of this book. Thus, I have been born on Earth for your benefit, and you would do extremely well to heed the words I have written: *"(for) surely the LORD God will do nothing but he (first) revealeth his SECRET unto his servants the prophets" (Amos 3:7)*.

Introduction

I, Gabriel, was born December 25, 1970. At 10 years of age in front of a church altar, I was <u>instantaneously</u> healed by God of acute bronchial asthma—which I had suffered immensely from for over 2 years!—and I fell in love with the God who created heaven and Earth. I did not know much about Him as a small boy, but I <u>knew</u> He must have loved me dearly to take away all my hurting. And my heart has been His ever since.

Two years later, when I was 12 years old, my father noticed an ad in the local newspaper about a traveling prophet who was coming to a church in a nearby town. Intrigued, dad decided our family should go. Now we had <u>never</u> stepped foot in the church and did not know anyone there, but near the end of the prophet's preaching, he walked back the central aisle, pointed at me and said, "Stand up, son. Do you know God gave you your name? For your name is Gabriel! And God's placed the creativity of 4 men inside of you. Son, you will be like John the Baptist in the last days preparing the people to meet the Lord, for God is going to place you in a position to be able to influence multitudes of people." I sat back down in my pew in a state of bewilderment. I was still wondering how the prophet knew my name! It has been 25 years since that night and I have never forgotten the words that prophet spoke over my life.

I watched my father die January 2, 1992, 8 days after I had turned 21 years of age. In the fall of that same year, I was lying in bed one Sunday morning viewing a television evangelist program. While the show was still in the music portion, I noticed my dad's Bible—which

1

my mother had given me after he passed away—lying in the middle of the bedroom floor. For no particular reason, I got out of bed, picked it up, and tossed it gently on my bed. (I guess I wanted it nearby so I could read along with the evangelist when he began preaching.)

About 15 minutes later, commenced to preaching, the evangelist directed us to Mark 16:15-18. When I turned to look up the passage in my Bible, I was dumbfounded to find it lying open to the EXACT page of those verses! Then, for the first time in my life I heard the voice of the Lord speak to me in my spirit, "Listen to this message, son, for it is for you!" The weighty verses read: *"And he (Jesus) said unto them, **Go ye into all the world, and preach the gospel to every creature**. He that believeth and is baptized shall be saved; but he that believeth not shall be damned. And these signs shall follow them that believe; In my name shall they cast out devils; they shall speak with new tongues; They shall take up serpents; and if they drink any deadly thing, it shall not hurt them; they shall lay hands on the sick, and they shall recover." (Mark 16:15-18)*. I was astonished: It was the great commission! "How in the world am I ever going to fulfill THAT," I mused. "I'm just a kid!" Since I had no clue how I was to proceed, I left the years pass without giving it much consideration.

Then, 13 years later at the age of 34, God dropped a supernatural bomb on me. For on a Friday night around 10:45 p.m. May 6, 2005, an angel of the Lord visited me in the most miraculous way. Amanda—my girlfriend at the time—and I had just finished watching a Robin Williams movie about dead people called *"The Final Cut"*. The movie was extremely somber, so to lighten the air in my apartment after it was over I decided to play some music. The choice was easy for Amanda had finally remembered that night to bring over a Joe Diffie cassette for me to listen to. (I had been asking her for months to bring it!) Seeing it sitting on top of the entertainment center, I grabbed it, sat down, and then placed it in my karaoke box tape deck and hit play.

The first song on the album was the one I had been dying to hear. It was entitled *"In another world"*. As the song neared the end, Joe Diffie was wailing the lyric, *"That's another place in time, back when you were mine, in another world, in another world, in another world!"* At that very moment, I looked up and 18 feet in front of me—yes, I

2

measured it!—on my refrigerator door, perfectly centered, was a 32 inch tall shadowed profile of my deceased father's face. The very second my eyes beheld the darkened profile I knew it was him! My mind started spinning in amazement, but somehow I collected my thoughts enough to stammer to Amanda, "My dad's here now!"

I did not move. I just sat there riveted to the floor, staring at the face on the refrigerator door. The words I had just spoken hung hauntingly in the air. "Why did I say THAT?" I thought. "Why did I not just point and say, 'Hey, that looks like my dad'? But to declare, 'My dad's <u>HERE</u> now'…that was spooky!" Trapped in my own swirling fog of shock and confusion, I heard Amanda's inquiring words cut through my mental haze like a knife, "Isn't today his birthday?" "Is today May 6th?" I replied! Oh, my goodness!!! It would be impossible to accurately describe to you the overwhelming feeling of awe that coursed through my body when I realized what she asked was correct, but cold chills ran up and down my body like a rollercoaster, forming goose bumps on top of goose bumps until every hair on my body was at attention. It was extremely hard to grasp the fact that I had forgotten my father's birthday, yet there he was! It was miraculous enough just seeing my father's profiled face, but to be <u>ON</u> his birthday…well, that was almost too much to mentally process.

I can only guess the shock Moses experienced in the desert when he witnessed a bush burning yet not being consumed, but I understand perfectly well his reaction to the miracle: *"And <u>the angel of the LORD appeared unto him (Moses)</u> in a flame of fire out of the midst of a bush: and he looked, and, behold, the bush burned with fire, and the bush was not consumed. And Moses said, **<u>I will now turn aside, and see this great sight</u>**, <u>why the bush is not burnt</u>" (Exodus 3:2, 3)*. I, too, having witnessed a great miracle, turned aside to investigate how the shadowy image of my father's face was being made. But I must back up in time (a little) to fully relate to you the miraculous account.

About a month earlier, I became infatuated with putting Big Ben 1,000 piece puzzles together—yeah, go figure!—and I had moved a set of saw horses into my living room with a piece of plywood across them for a puzzle table: My seat was a swiveling barstool. Since my 1 bedroom apartment was/is VERY small, this cramped "set up" sat beside my entertainment center, hogging up most of the living room floor. Then, days before the miracle, I attached a clip-on, aluminum floodlight to a CD rack hanging on the wall above the puzzle table for better light. Alright, so here is what happened the night of May 6, 2005.

Upon returning home from Blockbuster with the Robin Williams movie, I haphazardly grabbed the puzzle barstool and sat it nonchalantly in the "middle" of the kitchen, clearing room to sit on the living room floor. (The living room & kitchen are all one small combined room.) Then, after turning out ALL the lights and starting the movie, I sat down on the living room carpet and Amanda lay down on the couch to watch. When the gloomy movie was over, I got up in the darkness and clicked on <u>ONLY</u> the floodlight above the puzzle table to be able to see to get the Joe Diffie cassette. The rest proceeded as I have written above!

So how was the profiled image of my father's face being formed? It was a perfect combination of the shapes being created by Amanda's tasseled pocketbook sitting on the T-shirt toting, V-backed barstool I had randomly sat in the kitchen, which was casting a shadow from the floodlight's light onto the refrigerator door! Like an inquisitive child hunched over an ant on the sidewalk, I detected the chair's leather seat made his chin, the pocketbook's tassels made his lips, the top of the pocketbook made his nose, the chair's acutely-angled metal back made his glasses, and the gathered T-shirt hanging over the middle of the chair's back made his hair lines. All of these things were perfectly proportioned with respect to each other to create my father's profiled head. If anything was moved even slightly, the face was gone!

I stumbled around my apartment looking for a piece of poster-board big enough to trace the profile. Finally finding a piece in the garage, I captured the face! And it now hangs on the wall in my hallway as a permanent reminder of God's miraculous power! See, Moses' "burning bush" miracle was created by God simply using natural "things"—namely, a bush and fire. But it was what God <u>DID</u> with those "things" that was supernatural! Likewise, it was what God <u>DID</u> with the "things" in my apartment that created the miracle He performed for me. (Incidentally, my father loved profiles so much so that he sat my brother and me down sideways in chairs when we were small boys in grade school, clicked a floodlight on beside us, and drew our shadowed profiles on poster-board tacked to the wall. He then cut them out, traced them on plywood, and sawed out wooden replicas that he hung on our respective bedroom doors for years! Who knew one day I would be doing the same of him?)

After the incredible miracle, I turned aside from my life and desires and began drawing nigh unto God. I fashioned myself after Solomon: *"I applied mine heart to know and to search, and to seek out wisdom, and the REASON of THINGS, and to know the wickedness of folly, even of foolishness and madness" (Ecclesiastes 7:25).* For the first time in my life I was now <u>driven</u> to know the historical, archaeological, and scientific proof of the Bible's validity. I had to know the cold, hard evidence! I HAD to know if God wanted people to believe in Him without a single shred of evidence or if the Bible was something more.

The wondrous appearance of my deceased father's face was so overwhelming to me, considering the synergy of the song lyric, movie's theme, cold refrigerator location—dead people are said to be on ice!—and birthday, that it haunted my thoughts for months as to how God setup such an astonishing miracle. Did God place the desire in me to put puzzles together? Did God plant the notion in me to install a floodlight above the puzzle table? Did God stir Amanda to <u>finally</u> bring over the Joe Diffie cassette <u>that</u> night? Did God put the longing in me to purchase a particular style barstool, a year earlier, for a kitchen island I never built anyway? Did Amanda sit her pocketbook on that barstool, for like she said, she <u>always</u> sat it on the carpet beside the couch? How long had God been planning this miracle anyway? And on and on the unanswered questions rolled…tormenting my mind!)

I realize now it was all part of a divine plan for my life, because God recaptured center stage in my heart. He had my full and undivided attention! I thought about Him constantly, day and night. I so desperately wanted to read His Bible that it actually pained my spirit—thoughts, desires, & emotions—to have to go to work! I could hardly wait for the work day to end, so I could get home to read. Eventually, I devised a cure for my predicament; I carried a pocket Bible around with me at work and would sneak a peek whenever I could. (I even read the Bible lying in the dirt under a house foundation with a Bic lighter!)

I have experienced the full truth of the Bible verse: *"he (God) is* a _rewarder_ of them that **_diligently_** _seek him" (Hebrews 11:6)._ Because the last 3 years of my life have been a whirlwind of manifestations and revelations from God. I will share many of these experiences in this book. God has become my closest companion. He is the reason I am breathing, and He is the joy of my life! He is my protector and my provider. And I love obeying His laws, because I love Him. I can truly sing with the psalmist: _"**With my whole heart have I sought thee**...And I will DELIGHT myself in thy commandments, which I have loved...Teach me good judgment and knowledge: for I have believed thy commandments...The law of thy mouth is better unto me than thousands of gold and silver...**O how love I thy law**! IT is my meditation all the day...Depart from me, ye evildoers: for **I will keep the commandments of my God**...I love thy commandments above gold; yea, above fine gold...I opened my mouth, and panted: for I longed for thy commandments...LORD, **I have hoped for thy salvation, and DONE thy commandments**...My tongue shall speak of thy word: for ALL thy commandments are righteousness...I have longed for thy salvation, O LORD; and thy law is my delight"_ (Psalms 119:10, 47, 66, 72, 97, 115, 127, 131, 166, 172, 174).

Two years later, during May of 2007, while watching TV one night, God asked me to give $2,007 to a specific Christian ministry. After I said yes, I distinctly heard God's voice ask, "What do you want in return?" Now God had taught me to be a generous man long before that night, but I never once considered asking Him for something in return. (When I give to God, I am just elated to be of service to Him.) Thus, God's question startled me! But I could feel His heavy presence awaiting my answer, so I thought about it briefly and instantly knew what I wanted. I said, "Father, God, I want to KNOW the true meaning of your Bible. I want to really know what it is ALL about. For there are many stories I don't understand and verses that seem contradictory. So please teach me the absolute truth of your Word!" Once I made my request known, I did not hear a reply: His voice was gone!

Days later, while surfing on the internet, His voice was back! This time He asked, "Will you fast 40 days for me?" He told me when to begin the fast (Tuesday, May 29th) and when to end it (Saturday, July 7th). He even informed me specifically on how to observe it, because I

6

worked as a carpenter Monday through Friday and would have to eat something on those days for strength. Explicitly, I was to eat during a 10 hour window each day—6am to 4pm—and fast the other 14 hours of the day. Well, since my carpentry job ran from 7:30am to 4pm, I knew the week days were going to be difficult. During those days, I would only get breakfast at 9am and lunch at 12pm. Trust me, after carpentering all day, by 7 o'clock in the evening I was real hungry! And I cherished my evening meal and late night snack before bedtime. So I knew this was going to be a HUGE sacrifice for me: Going to bed hungry every night for 40 days was not something to look forward to! Thus, I was extremely tentative about committing to the fast, but with the wind knocked out of my sails, I answered God with a hesitant, half-hearted, "Ok…I'll do it."

As the day to begin fasting approached, I desperately tried to convince myself maybe God was not so serious about this fasting "thing" anyway. Boy, I could not have been more wrong!!! When Tuesday May 29th arrived I was still battling indecision, but I obeyed God. The next night I had my first opportunity to disobey, for I went bowling with a good friend of mine and her niece and afterward they wanted to go to Captain D's to get something to eat. I could hear a voice in my spirit say, "Don't do it, son!" But stupid me, I went and ate with them. That VERY night I was awakened around 3am by a tremendous pain in my mouth! I thought, "My God, what is this?" Standing in front of the bathroom mirror with a flashlight shining into my mouth, I noticed a dime-sized section of flesh behind my lower left, back molar had turned ghost white. It looked like leprosy!!! Horrified that I could barely open my mouth because of the severe pain, I slowly became conscious of God's presence watching me.

Then in a moment, I knew the strange sore was a result of my disobedience to the fast and I asked God how long it would last. Immediately, I heard, "Your suffering will pass in 7 days, but I avidly desire your completion of the 40 day fast I asked you to carry out." Well, needless to say, I jumped on board His way of thinking real quick! The next 7 days were hell on Earth. Even during the time I was allowed to eat, I ate very little because of the excruciating pain of opening my mouth. I would try to push food between my almost closed teeth,

7

crying in pain. It was pitiful. I hardly slept either, because my entire head and neck throbbed continuously from the pain. I downed Tylenol like it was candy—and I despise taking pain medication!—yet it only mildly reduced the agony. Nothing could mask the brutal, gnawing pain. The only reason I stayed calm and sane during those 7 days was I KNEW when the supernatural plaque would end. And sure enough, like clockwork, the 7th day the affliction was gone!

I dropped over 10 pounds that first week! To be sure, I was fasting now! But I never once thought evil of God. I was happy to suffer for Him, because I knew the Scripture verse: *"My son, despise NOT thou the chastening of the Lord, nor faint when thou art rebuked of him: **For whom the Lord loveth he chasteneth, and scourgeth every son whom he receiveth**. If ye endure chastening, God dealeth with you as with sons; for what son is he whom the father chasteneth not?" (Hebrews 12:5-7)*. Deep in my heart, I knew God had some higher purpose for wanting me to fast 40 days. Even though I did not know why, I knew all He wanted out of me at the time was my obedience. I lost over 25 pounds during those 40 wearisome days, but I obeyed my Father God.

My fast came to an end on a Sabbath Saturday, July 7th, 2007, with a required ALL day fast! I diligently and fearfully obeyed, but I spent the last half hour feebly pacing my kitchen floor, counting the minutes down to midnight till I could eat a little something. Lying in bed that night enduring my final hunger headache, I was completely exhausted, scrawny, and very thankful the fast was over. By this time, I had pretty much forgotten my humble request a few months earlier to know the true meaning of the Bible. Little did I know; God had not!!!

Exactly 5 months to the day after my fast ended, I lit a Sabbath candle as the sun was setting in the sky on Friday evening, December 7, 2007. Holding the flickering light up high, I offered up a prayer of thankfulness to God for the beautiful world He created and the opportunity to live in it and work for Him. Then I welcomed the Holy Spirit and asked Him to uncover deeper things concerning God's Word to me. Later that evening, I was stirred to randomly search for Biblical knowledge online. I stumbled across a website touting physical evidence of the Israelite's Exodus out of Egypt and, subsequent, Red Sea crossing. The site displayed ancient Hebrew inscriptions on cliffs in the Sinai area collaborating Moses' Biblical account of the Exodus, coral encrusted chariot wheels at the bottom of the Red Sea, sandstone inscriptions supporting Biblical happenings of the Israelites 40 year wilderness journey, and writings by ancient historians of great Egyptian plagues with a belief that some God was punishing them because of strangers in their land. By this time it was late at night; so I turned off the computer, blew out my candle, and went to sleep.

Around 8am Sabbath morning, I awoke to the presence of the Spirit of the Lord!!! As I lay in bed, He began explaining the real meaning behind the Israelite's story. I was told their 400 years of bondage in Egypt, escape into the wilderness, and 40 year journey to the Promise Land was all planned by Him! It was ALL a massive, detailed, PROPHETIC parable explaining EVERYTHING concerning God's plan of salvation for mankind's souls—e.g. mankind's souls were in bondage, mankind's souls needed to be delivered, etc. Then, God began walking me through New Testament Scriptures, verse by verse, explaining how they related to the Israelite's story. I was floored! All seemingly conflicting passages in Paul's New Testament letters—concerning what mankind must DO to obtain eternal life—were now crystal clear. And there was NOTHING conflicting at all!!!

Thus, on a Sabbath morning, Saturday December 8, 2007, the Lord first revealed the true meaning of the Bible to me. Oh, but that was not the end of it, for more revelations continued to happen. For months it was like God sat down with me, wrapped his right arm around my shoulders, and carefully explained the meaning behind every detail of the ancient Bible stories. Friend, the ancient Bible stories are ALL prophecy: God caused and controlled every detail in them to happen to foretell the future!!! In due time, the entire purpose and significance of the Bible was made clear to me. Knowing the true implications behind the details, I voraciously reread the first 5 books of the Old Testament and the whole Bible sprang to life! The verses literally leapt off the pages with spiritual prophetic value! The Bible's true significance is flabbergasting, and I bowed on my knees in reverence to God many times for what He was revealing to me.

Then, during February of 2008, God asked me to quit my carpentry job to write a book on what He taught me. This is that book!

9

If you have a thirst to know why God wrote the Bible; please read this book. If you really want to know what it is ALL about; please read this book. You will learn the stunning secrets behind the "wording" in the 7 day Creation story, what really died the day Adam & Eve ate the forbidden fruit, why God destroyed the Earth with a flood while having Noah build an ark to save his house, why God created a people called Israel and put them in bondage 400 years, why God sent 10 plagues on Pharaoh, why God picked the 10th & 14th days of a lunar month for the "choosing & killing" days of Israel's Passover lamb, respectively, why God wanted Joshua's army to walk around Jericho for 7 days, and a whole HOST of other things in the pages of this book! Once the true meaning and purpose behind the ancient Bible stories is realized, many details undeniably reveal Jesus' 2nd Coming will take place exactly 2,000 years after the year of his death, resurrection, and ascension! But more importantly, in this age of Biblical confusion and deception caused by Satan, you will learn the undiluted Biblical Truth of what EVERY mankind's soul—no matter when or where they were born on Earth!—has had and still needs to DO to obtain eternal life. And this is the REAL purpose of this book! For it is useless to know the approximate time of Christ's 2nd Coming, if you are not properly prepared to meet Him.

I can tell you from the outset, the overall reason God wrote the Bible was simply to increase mankind's faith in Him. Paul wrote: *"So then faith cometh by hearing, and hearing by the word of God"* *(Romans 10:17).* As you read this book and learn the amazing prophetic truth behind the ancient Bible stories, your belief in God is going to soar! It will become obvious mere mankind could not have secretly concealed the breadth of prophetic information contained in the details of the Old Testament stories. Thus, the Bible proves God's existence! So I am inviting you to take a journey with me through God's written Word for the amazing Truth contained in its pages. I believe you will be astonished at the magnificence of what God did and said in "It".

Chapter 1

God's Master Time Plan

"For I am God...and there is NONE like me,
Declaring the END from the BEGINNING"
(Isaiah 46:9, 10)

Taken at face value, it is no secret the Bible asserts planet Earth was created around 4000 BC. (I realize today this belief is by far in the minority, but keep reading this chapter and entire book for evidence it is true!) A simple computation of the ages given in Genesis for the first 22 fathers from Adam in the genealogy of Jesus Christ accounts for <u>every</u> year right down to the entrance of Jacob (Israel) into Egypt. Adding to that total the 400 years the Israelites spent in Egypt, you will learn <u>the Biblical Exodus occurred 2,638 years after Creation</u> [See Figure #1]. And since historians—referencing the historical record of the Pharaohs—maintain the Exodus occurred around <u>1300 BC</u>, the Bible clearly, yet tacitly, alleges a Creation date of around 4000 BC.

Now before AD 1600 and the dawn of science, the age of Earth was hardly questioned. Educated Europeans accepted the Biblical Creation account along with Noah's worldwide flood as Gospel truth. Thus, in AD 1640, Ussher unveiled his famous Biblical calculation of <u>4004 BC</u> for the Creation of the world. (I still remember learning this date as a child in Sunday school class!) But there were other prominent

Figure # 1
Year of Israelite's Exodus from Egypt

Father #	Information	Year after Creation
1. Adam	birth (Gen. 5:1, 2)	0
2. Seth	birth (Gen. 5:3)	130
3. Enos	birth (Gen. 5:6)	235
4. Cainan	birth (Gen. 5:9)	325
5. Mahalaleel	birth (Gen. 5:12)	395
6. Jared	birth (Gen. 5:15)	460
7. Enoch	birth (Gen. 5:18)	622
8. Methuselah	birth (Gen. 5:21)	687
9. Lamech	birth (Gen. 5:25)	874
10. Noah	birth (Gen. 5:28, 29)	1056
11. Shem	birth (Gen. 5:32)	1556
	Flood (Gen. 7:6)	1656
12. Arphaxad	birth (Gen. 11:10)	1658
13. Salah	birth (Gen. 11:12)	1693
14. Eber	birth (Gen. 11:14)	1723
15. Peleg	birth (Gen. 11:16)	1757
16. Reu	birth (Gen. 11:18)	1787
17. Serug	birth (Gen. 11:20)	1819
18. Nahor	birth (Gen. 11:22)	1849
19. Terah	birth (Gen. 11:24)	1878
20. Abraham	birth (Gen. 11:27)	1948
21. Isaac	birth (Gen. 21:5)	2048
22. Jacob (Israel)	birth (Gen. 25:26)	2108
	Joseph enters Egypt (Exo. 12:40)	2208
	Jacob moves to Egypt (Gen 47:28)	2238
	Exodus (Gen. 15:13)	2638

dates calculated, too. For instance, Lightfoot, in AD 1644, calculated the Biblical Creation at <u>3928 BC</u>. But no matter whom the Bible believing person in the 1600's, the date for the creation of the universe & Earth was plainly and obviously accepted as near 4000 BC. (It is important you wrestle with the understanding that these "Biblical Creation dates" were determined in/at a time LONG before mankind invented cars, planes, computers, satellites, atomic bombs, or knew <u>when</u> Israel would be reborn as a nation. In other words, I am not "making-up" some false assertion after the fact; mankind has known Earth's genesis was around 4000 BC for centuries!)

But, today, knowing Israel became a nation again in AD 1948—for Scripture <u>unmistakably</u> prophesied of her rebirth right before Jesus' 2nd Coming!—combined with other Biblical secrets the Lord has revealed to me (that I will disclose in this book), I now have the benefit of working backwards (I will explain soon) and am able to now, much more precisely, calculate a date of <u>3972 BC</u> for the Creation. How about that? My date is hitting all over the bulls eye of the two famous dates I cited in the paragraph above from 4 centuries ago! In other words, even what God has done in the last century in fulfilling "end-time" Biblical prophecy does <u>NOT</u> contradict the Bible's assertion of a Creation date around 4000 BC. In fact, it does the very opposite; the evidence farther validates and <u>strongly</u> supports the truth of the Bible's claim. Therefore, with all things considered, it is irrefutable the Bible maintains the Creation of the world is somewhere around 4000 BC, <u>which means we are obviously living today in the time surrounding 6,000 years of history on planet Earth</u>!!!

But who cares, right? What is the big deal concerning 6,000 years of mankind's history? Did God give us any clues in the Bible that the <u>END</u> of 6,000 years on planet Earth would be a significant time period? **The answer is an overwhelming…YES**!!! The dazzling fact is <u>God incorporated His master TIME plan for mankind on Earth IN the Bible's 7 day Creation story</u>! Did you ever sit down and wonder why the Bible records God created the world in <u>6</u> days and <u>rested</u> on the 7th? Why did it not take Him 3, 8, 11, 15, or any other number of days? And what is up with God resting on the 7th day? God does not need to rest!!! So why is a "day of rest" part of the Creation story? I mean, seriously, who made this stuff up? I can understand perfectly well why someone would think the Bible's Creation story is just a silly fable.

Ah, but if you take a spiritual lens and zoom in a little closer on the <u>exact</u> <u>words</u> used in the Bible's 7 day Creation story, you will be astonished at what you find! Soon, it becomes apparent the story is not stupid at all as God's infinite wisdom and foresight come into perfect focus: For the Creation story was/is actually a terse PROPHETIC synopsis of God's plans for mankind's time on planet Earth!!! God told the prophet Isaiah: *"For I am God, and there is NONE else; I am God, and there is NONE like me, **Declaring the END from the BEGINNING, and from ancient times the things that are not yet done**, saying, My counsel shall stand, and I WILL DO all my pleasure…Hearken unto me, ye stouthearted, that are far from righteousness" (Isaiah 46:9-12).* In other words, God is clearly saying here that He told WHEN the END would occur from the beginning, and also "things" that would happen in the future. Now seriously… HOW did God do all THAT from the beginning, which was the Creation? Friend, it was ALL stunningly contained in the 7 day Creation story's verbiage!!!

HOW did God *"declare the END"* from the beginning? He clandestinely concealed it in the fact that the Creation "event" concluded in 7 days. Say what? Look, the only thing missing initially to mankind was God's "prophetic time key" for the length of a day. God's first Biblical revelation of this time comparison came to us through Moses in the 14th Century BC: *"**For a thousand years in thy (God's) sight are but as yesterDAY**" (Psalms 90:4).* In other words, in God's eyes, 1 day = 1,000 years! Most people whimsically gloss over this verse to simply mean "time is irrelevant to God", but these people are severely mistaken for NOTHING could be any farther from the truth!!! This Scripture was given to mankind to really, truly, prophetically declare 1 day = 1,000 years in God's sight. Consequently, this little innocuous Bible verse actually contained God's "prophetic master time key" for His complete plan for mankind on Earth. In short (as you will soon see) the 7 day Creation story actually represented and foretold of an absolutely fixed 7 day (7,000 year) plan for mankind's time on planet Earth. Therefore, God HAD told when the END would occur from the beginning…in 7 days!

Incidentally, realize "time" was also created by God, for the length of our year is simply the time it takes planet Earth to orbit the sun once. Thus, this "length of time" is something God arbitrarily determined as part of His Creation. Subsequently, God's master Time plan for mankind was/is to be completed after planet Earth makes 7,000 trips around the sun! Friend, if you have not figured it out yet, God is running this show and He has been ever since the beginning! He will surely do ALL His pleasure, and He has a set time, place, and purpose for everything.

In the Bible, God uses numbers to communicate things to mankind. (Note: numbers are also just a natural byproduct of God's created, seeable, physical world—which means He created them, too!) So, since God's master TIME plan for mankind on Earth was/is fashioned around a factor of 7, He instituted the 7 day week—which is 7 revolutions of Earth on its axis—from Creation as a continual, mini-glimpse of His overall 7 day (7,000 year) plan for mankind! In other words, EVERY 7 day week that passes mankind (most unknowingly) pays tribute to the Creator God's Master Time Plan!!! Is that not awesomely incredible? Friend, the TIMING of God's master plan for mankind on Earth is written into His Creation: The revolutions and orbits of the celestial bodies are like the interior workings of a giant grandfather clock, ticking off the seconds of His amazingly precise plan.

During the 1st century AD, the Apostle Peter wrote about what people would say in the "last days" right before Jesus' 2nd Coming: *"**there shall come in the last days scoffers,** walking after their own lusts, And saying, Where is the promise of his (Jesus 2nd) coming?" (II Peter 3:3, 4)*. Have you heard someone hiss like this recently? Maybe you even said it with your own tongue! Did you notice in the verse above why people scoff at the idea of Jesus' 2nd Coming? It is because they live in lustful sins and do not want to change! They willingly want to believe the Bible is a fairy tale. Oh, but then Peter makes an amazing statement right in the middle of his discussion on the timing of Jesus' 2nd Coming: *"But, beloved, **be not IGNORANT of this one thing**, that one day is with the Lord as a thousand years, and a thousand years as one day" (II Peter 3:8)*. Wow, are you kidding me? Why would the Holy Spirit lead Peter to write THAT in the middle of a talk concerning the timing of Jesus' 2nd Coming? Friend, the Holy Spirit (writing through Peter) KNEW the time comparison of 1 day = 1,000 years is God's "prophetic master Time key" for discovering when Jesus will return to Earth! And if we "last days" people would recognize what "time" it is, we would not be scoffing right now!!!

Armed with the divine PROPHETIC knowledge that 1 day = 1,000 years, let us now take a closer look at the astonishing Creation narrative found in chapter 1 of the book of Genesis. Be prepared to be dumbfounded for God not only told WHEN the end would occur from the beginning by utilizing 7 days for the Creation, but He also prophesied remarkably about "things" in between, for in the 7 day Creation story's narrative, EACH day's activities prophetically mirrored the "major spiritual occurrence" of THAT particular 1,000 year period of mankind's history!!! Do you understand? In other words, the language used to describe the "events" of each of the 7 Creation days actually foreshadowed the most important spiritual event(s) of that particular millennial day [See Figure #2]. Let us take a look at this mind-boggling revelation.

Day 1 represented the first 1,000 year period of mankind on Earth, which would run from 3972 BC to 2972 BC on our current Gregorian calendar (I'll explain shortly how I arrived at my date of 3972 BC for the Creation). This millennial day's most momentous spiritual event was to be the "spiritual fall" of Adam & Eve after they sinned in the Garden of Eden. Having eaten the forbidden fruit from the "*tree of the knowledge of good & evil*", mankind instantly learned the difference between good & evil—which is to say "light & dark". Consequently, we read on the first day of Creation that God made light and SEPARATED the light from the dark: "*...God saw the light, that it was GOOD: and God DIVIDED the light from the darkness*" *(Genesis 1:4)*. The Bible would later go on to refer to good as light and evil as darkness. Jesus said, "*...and men loved darkness rather than light, because their deeds were evil. For every one that doeth evil hateth the light*" *(John 3:19, 20)*. Do you see? In short, the spiritual watershed moment of the 1st millennial day on planet Earth was when good & evil (light & dark) became discernible (separated) in mankind's hearts. And God had prophetically declared the "event" and its "timing", albeit secretly, in the Creation story's 1st day narrative!

Day 2 represented the second 1,000 year period of mankind on Earth, which would run from 2972 BC to 1972 BC. This was to be the millennial day when the worldwide flood of Noah would devastate planet Earth. Friend, the story of Noah is actually a detailed prophetic

Figure # 2
God's 7 day (7,000 year) Master Plan

Day	Year	Calendar	Event
1	0	3972 BC	Creation
	?	?	**Fall in Garden of Eden**
2	1056	2916 BC	Noah born
	1656	2316 BC	**Noah's flood**
	1948	2024 BC	Abraham born
3	2023	1949 BC	Abraham leaves his father
	2048	1924 BC	Isaac born
	2108	1864 BC	Jacob (Israel) & Esau born
	2208	1764 BC	Joseph enters Egypt
	2238	1734 BC	Jacob (Israel) enters Egypt
	2558	1414 BC	Moses born
	2638	1334 BC	**Exodus (Moses 80 yrs. old)**
	2678	1294 BC	Israel enters Promise Land
4	3967?	5 BC?	John Baptist & Jesus born
	4000	28 AD	**Jesus crucified**
5			
6	5920	1948 AD	Israel nation reborn
	5993	2021 AD	**Antichrist**
	6000	2028 AD	**Jesus Christ's 2nd Coming**
7	6000	2028 AD	Millennial reign begins
	7000	3028 AD	Millennial reign ends

picture of Jesus' 2nd Coming!!! It contains more truth about what will take place during Christ's return then you could ever have possibly imagined. (Read ahead in the chapter on "*Noah*" if you cannot wait! But I wish you would wait and do not skip ANY of this book's message, or you will miss very important information.) Adding up the ages of the Patriarchs from Genesis chapter 5 along with the age of Noah when the flood occurred in Genesis 7:11, the Bible clearly records the global flood took place 1,656 years after Creation. Thus, you see, it happened during the 2nd millennial day of mankind's history! And the Bible's second day Creation narrative had secretly foretold: *"And God made the firmament, and **divided the waters which were under the firmament from the waters which were above the firmament**" (Genesis 1:7).* Friend, this is flood talk! These words foreshadowed the great flood! Watch how closely the language mirrors Peter's later words describing Noah's flood: *"...and the earth standing out of the water and in the water: Whereby the world that then was, being overflowed with water, perished" (II Peter 3:5, 6).* I postulate the Great flood covered planet Earth during year 2316 BC (3972 BC – 1,656 years).

Day 3 represented the third 1,000 year period of mankind on Earth, which would run from 1972 BC to 972 BC. This was the millennial day when God would create and direct the 440 year long "tell-all" Israelite "bondage-to-freedom" story (from the 2238th year till 2678th year) which secretly foretold everything concerning His plan for the souls of mankind's salvation (freedom) and confirmed what they must <u>DO</u> to obtain eternal life. (This will all be explained in the *"Moses"* & *"Wilderness"* chapters!) The climax of God's parable (which revealed how He would deliver mankind's souls out of bondage to sin) was when He delivered the Israelites out of Egypt's bondage at the Red Sea. As you know, God <u>supernaturally</u> rolled back the impassable waters so the Israelites could cross on dry land: *"And Moses stretched out his hand over the Sea; and the LORD caused the sea to go back by a strong east wind all that night, **and made the sea dry land, and the waters were divided**. And the children of Israel went into the midst of the sea upon the dry ground: and the waters were a wall unto them on their right hand, and on their left" (Exodus 14:21, 22).* And what does the Bible prophetically record happened on the third day of Creation? It says: *"And God said, **Let the waters under the heaven be gathered together unto one place, and let the dry land appear**....And God called the dry land Earth; and the gathering together of the waters called he Seas" (Genesis 1:9, 10).* Are you stunned yet? God's 7 day Creation story's narrative was perfectly foreshadowing *"things not yet done"* for mankind!

18

Day 4 represented the fourth 1,000 year period of mankind on Earth, which would run from 972 BC to AD 28. This was the millennial day when God planned to send forth His Son, the Messiah, into the world to atone for mankind's sin, effectively freeing them from their spiritual bondage to sin & death. (It is now believed Jesus was born somewhere between 4 BC & 6 BC.) Jesus was/is the true light of the world! Like the physical Earth would die without the sun's light, so too mankind would be forever spiritually dead without Christ's light! The Apostle John wrote about Jesus: *"**that (Jesus) was the true Light, which lighteth every man that cometh into the world**. He was in the world, and the world was made by him, and the world knew him not"* (John 1:9, 10). Jesus declared, *"As long as I am in the world, **I am the light of the world**"* (John 9:5). And what do we read was created on the fourth day of Creation? The LIGHT sources—i.e. the sun and the moon!!! Genesis chronicles: *"And **God made two great lights; the greater light to rule the day, and the lesser light to rule the night**: he made the stars also"* (Genesis 1:16). Biblically undeniably (as you will soon learn) the YEAR of Jesus' death, resurrection, and ascension absolutely, positively occurred during mankind's 4,000th year of history, which means he lived on Earth DURING mankind's 4th millennial day! But not only did Jesus live on Earth during the 4th millennial day, so did John the Baptist: He was the "lesser light"!!! Just like the moon reflects (or bears witness of) the true light of the sun, so John the Baptist merely bore witness of Christ's light. The Apostle John wrote: *"He (John the Baptist) was not that Light, **but was sent to bear witness of that Light**"* (John 1:8). See, John the Baptist was like the moon! Is that not incredible? Yes, friend, God's creation of the "greater and lesser lights" on the fourth day of Creation foretold the coming of John the Baptist & Jesus Christ during mankind's 4th millennial day.

Day 5 represented the fifth 1,000 year period of mankind on Earth, which would run from AD 28 to AD 1028. At this time, I have not been given the spiritual interpretation of the relationship of the Creation narrative to the actual events of this millennial day of mankind's history.

Day 6 represents the sixth 1,000 year period of mankind on Earth, which runs from AD 1028 to AD 2028! You are living in the

19

last score of this millennial day right now!!! During this millennium, mankind fully inhabited planet Earth. This period contains the great explorers who circumnavigated the globe on the high seas—e.g. Marco Polo (AD 1254 – AD 1324), Ferdinand Magellan (AD 1480 – AD 1521), Christopher Columbus (AD 1451 – AD 1506), and Sir Francis Drake (AD 1540 – AD 1597). Furthermore, human population has exploded in the last 1,000 years to incredibly massive numbers—500 million to almost 7 billion now! God would later prophecy in the Bible that this millennial day will <u>end</u> with a MAN, an Antichrist, <u>subduing</u> ALL of mankind on Earth: *"And **<u>he (Antichrist) causeth ALL</u>**, both <u>small and great, rich and poor, free and bond, to receive a mark in their right hand, or in their foreheads</u>: And that no man might buy or sell, save he that had the mark, or the name of the beast, or the number of his name...<u>Let him that hath understanding count the NUMBER of the beast: for it is the number of a **MAN**; and his number is Six hundred threescore and six"* (Revelation 13:16, 17)*.* And what do we read God created on the <u>sixth</u> day of Creation? He made man: *"God created <u>man</u> in his own image...And <u>God blessed them</u>, and God said unto them, **<u>Be fruitful, and multiply, and replenish the earth, and SUBDUE it</u>**" (Genesis 1:27, 28)*. I could not think of more pertinent <u>prophetic</u> words to perfectly sum up the happenings of the past 1,000 years, for <u>man</u>kind has truly mapped, populated—and Antichrist will soon subdue!—the entire globe during this 6th millennial day!

Now, **<u>Day 7</u>** represents the coming seventh 1,000 year period of mankind on Earth, which will run from AD 2028 to AD 3028! This millennial day will be ushered in with the fiery RETURN of Jesus Christ to planet Earth during year 6,000, or the <u>END</u> of the sixth day! So, on the seventh day in the Creation story, we find God <u>rested</u> after <u>ENDING</u> all His created work: *"And on the seventh day God <u>ENDED</u> his work which he had made; and **<u>he rested on the seventh day from all his work</u>**" (Genesis 2:2)*. God waited for over 4,000 years until He first revealed to mankind in the Biblical book "The Revelation"—written by John the Revelator on the Isle of Patmos around 90 AD—about a coming 1,000 year peaceful, <u>restful</u> kingdom reign of Christ on Earth: *"And he laid hold on the dragon, that old serpent, which is the Devil, and Satan, and bound him a <u>thousand years</u>...and **<u>they (the saints)</u>***

20

**lived and reigned with Christ a thousand years**" _(Revelation 20:2, 4)._ Do you see? During this millennial day, Satan will be locked up and only all the <u>resurrected</u> righteous will live on a NEW, regenerated Earth: _"he (Jesus) shall judge among many people...and they shall beat their swords into plowshares, and their spears into pruninghooks: nation shall not lift up a sword against nation, neither shall they learn war any more" (Micah 4:3)._ In other words, it will be a millennial day of <u>REST</u> on planet Earth! <u>THAT</u> is why God included a 7th day of rest in the Creation story: It foretold of the coming 1,000 year Sabbath reign of Jesus Christ on planet Earth, which will commence during mankind's 6,000th year. (The hidden truth behind the details in the story of Noah will <u>absolutely</u> confirm Jesus' 2nd Coming will occur during mankind's 6,000th year!)

Are you shocked? God's <u>complete</u> master plan for mankind's TIME on Earth was prophetically contained in His <u>7</u> day Creation story! Talk about a reason to believe in God and His Bible. Friend, we are undisputedly on the verge of closing out the 6th millennial day (6,000 years) on Earth and watching Jesus Christ burst through the darkened clouds to set up his Earthly, restful, millennial Kingdom. It is an inescapable, unavoidable fact!!! The Bible is sprinkled from front to back cover with prophetic clues about how this 6th millennial day will come to an end, and we would be extremely naïve to not be able to look around and see what is happening on planet Earth today and recognize the signs of his imminent return. I cannot say it any clearer or louder: <u>JESUS CHRIST IS COMING VERY SOON</u>!!! Are you ready to meet him? Are you ready to meet the man who loved you enough to die on a cross for you? Do you love him? Are you excited to see him? Well, ready or not, his fierce coming is unstoppable, and I pray for your sake you are ready!

To further prove God is real and the Bible is His divinely inspired Word, I want to now shed light on just a few "end time" Biblical prophecies. Realize these prophecies were written in the Bible over 2,000 to 3,000 years ago! Imagine living back then trying to make predictions about the distant future: It would have been impossible to tell what would happen, let alone when. But the Bible has done just that! All the Bible's "end time" prophecies are coming to fruition right now at the close of 6,000 years! That is the shocking reality!!! Like clockwork, they are setting up for the END of God's 6th millennial day. Thus, they further prove God is real, His 7 day (7,000 year) plan is real, and the world (Earth) is truly not quite 6,000 years old! Sit back and mull over a brief inspection of some of these stunning prophecies.

First, ponder the exponential human population growth of the last 100 years. Who could have known 2,000 years ago that the human population would explode during the 20th century AD? It would have been impossible to predict back then. Yet here we are, and it has just happened right now before the end of 6,000 years. When Jesus walked on Earth the world population was roughly 250 million (1/4 billion). It took mankind another 1,800 years to reach 1 billion. Therefore, it took over 4,000 years from Noah's flood (2316 BC) to reach 1 billion people on the face of Earth by AD 1800. We hit 2 billion by 1930, 3 billion by 1962, 4 billion by 1977, 5 billion by 1985, 6 billion by 2000, and now were closing in on 7 billion! Are you kidding me? I ask again, "WHO could have known WHEN this crazy population explosion would occur some 2,000 years ago?" Friend, only an "all-knowing" God could have! And, yet, it had to occur to fulfill a 1st century AD, Biblical "end time" prophecy mentioning a great Eastern army of 200 million men: *"And the number of the army of the horsemen were **two hundred thousand thousand**: and I heard the number of them...and the heads of the horses were as the heads of lions; and out of their mouths issued fire and smoke and brimstone. <u>By these three was the third part of men killed</u>" (Revelation 9:16-18)*. This is horrifying, but it will happen soon! China, from the East, has become the most populated country on Earth, and now touts an army of this size. Only a freakish 20th century human population upsurge has made fulfillment of this prophecy possible.

Next, there is the "knowledge explosion" to consider. It took almost 2,000 years (from Jesus' day to AD 1800) to double the amount of information we know. Now we are doubling our knowledge base quicker then every 2 years! That is a mind-blowing rate. Yet, God told the prophet Daniel in the 6th century BC, concerning the "last days" right before Jesus returned to set up his Earthly Kingdom: *"**There shall be a time of trouble, such as never was since there was a nation**"* *even to that same time: and at that time thy people shall be delivered, every one that shall be found written in the book. And many of them that sleep in the dust of the earth shall awake, some to everlasting life, and some to shame and everlasting contempt…even to the time of the end: many shall RUN to and fro, and KNOWLEDGE SHALL BE INCREASED" (Daniel 12:1-4).* No one living in Daniel's day could have known when mankind's "knowledge explosion" would take place on Earth, but GOD KNEW it would occur during the final century right before 6,000 years expired!

Then, we must contemplate the increased speed of travel made possible by the invention of trains, planes, and automobiles in the past few centuries. Did you notice Daniel's prophetic phrase *"many (people) shall RUN to and fro,"* in the paragraph above? I doubt Daniel had a clue what God really meant by that phrase, for it would have been impossible to foresee cars and planes running on fossil fuels 2,500 years ago! However, today on planet Earth mankind hectically rushes "this way and that" like a bunch of crazed bees. Written in the only words available back then, God gave the 8th century BC prophet Nahum a graphic vision of "last days" transportation: *"The chariots shall rage in the streets, they shall justle one against another in the broad ways: they shall seem like torches, they shall run like the lightnings" (Nahum 2:4).* What an impeccable depiction of today's vehicular road rage, car crashes, wide highways, electric headlights, and traveling speed faster than a cheetah! No one but an Almighty God could have prognosticated our modern means of transportation and known when it would occur on Earth. But here it is, just like magic, taking place at the end of 6,000 years!

Next, we should marvel at the incredible "globalization" taking place. The last century has witnessed planet Earth become universally connected through telephone, television, satellite, and internet. Today, we simultaneously bounce information, news, and entertainment around the globe. Have you noticed planet Earth has become totally connected? How could anyone living thousands of years ago possess the foreknowledge to predict this kind of colossal globalization, let alone know when it would occur? Yet, here we are right on cue at the close of 6,000 years! And globalization had to arrive to fulfill Jesus' words: *"And this gospel of the kingdom shall be preached in ALL the* *world for a witness unto ALL nations; and **then the END shall come***" *(Matthew 24:14)*. Today, a single preacher's words can bounce off satellites, blanketing the entire planet, concurrently. Jesus knew this would happen RIGHT before his return to planet Earth!

Moreover, reflect again on the antichrist's mission: "*He causeth ALL, both small and great, rich and poor, free and bond, to receive a mark in their right hand, or in their foreheads: And **that no man might buy or sell, save he that had the mark**, or the name of the beast, or the number of his name*" *(Revelation 13:16, 17)*. Do you understand economic and technological globalization had to arrive first, before some maniac could make ALL people on Earth take a mark for commerce? There is no way John the revelator could have surmised how this verse might be fulfilled, but today the technology exists in the world to satisfy this prophecy! It is called Radio frequency identification (RFID). Data can be stored and received on a device the size of a grain of rice and implanted under the skin. These devices are already in use for animal identification and a host of other things. Yes, the fulfillment of this prophecy is inevitably coming very soon!

Do you really need to hear more "end time" Bible prophecies to believe in the Bible? If so, then brood over the terrifying weapons of mass destruction developed in the last century. Mankind has created a device (a nuclear bomb) that can singularly kill over 1 million people! How could anyone have dreamed of such technology over 2,000 years ago? Yet, God showed the 6th century BC prophet Zechariah a shocking and appalling "end time" event: "*And this shall be the plague wherewith the LORD will smite all the people that have fought against Jerusalem; **Their flesh shall consume away WHILE THEY STAND UPON THEIR FEET, and their eyes shall consume away in their holes, and their tongue shall consume away in their mouth**" (Zechariah 14:12).* Alright, let us take a deep breath and say, "Wow"!!! The English word "plague" was translated from the original Hebrew word "*maggēpâ*" meaning: plague; blow, strike, or slaughter. I am sure the fulfillment of this verse puzzled Bible scholars throughout the centuries. But not now! For this is a precise, detailed description of the effects caused by a nuclear blast from an atomic or neutron bomb. What else could vaporize a human being's flesh, eyes, and tongue before their skeleton even had a chance to fall to the ground? Only God alone could have presaged this horrifying feat of human engineering! Yet, here it is conceived, designed, and ready to be implemented at the close of 6,000 years. Zechariah's prophecy will be fulfilled very shortly!

I could go on and on discussing hundreds of Biblical "end time" prophecies that are all being perfectly positioned for fulfillment at the same time and place (the conclusion of 6,000 years of mankind's history on planet Earth!), which gives massive credence to the Bible's assertion that planet Earth is not quiet 6,000 years old. So how did an entire generation of billions of people today come to universally accept planet Earth as being 4.6 billion years old? The answer is simple: It is because most people just believe what they are told, and errant scientists have crammed their guesswork down their throats. Today, we are inundated daily with newspapers, magazines, newscasters, and schoolteachers regurgitating scientist's theories. But, friend, let us call a spade a spade; a theory is a guess! Therefore, the theory of macroevolution and the big bang theory are nothing more than speculation. And these two theories demand a very old Earth and universe to be true, so scientist—without definitive evidence—falsely assume they are! And, unfortunately, their guesses are being taught as truth to our children in schools. Thus, we have the perfect storm for festering evil: A generation of Biblically illiterate kids are growing up believing whatever their teachers teach them in school, which contradicts the Bible's trueness!

Friend, the great "end time" deception is in full force! Paul wrote about it: *"evil men and seducers shall wax worse and worse, deceiving, and being deceived. But continue thou in the things which thou hast learned and hast been assured of...And that from a child thou hast known the Holy Scriptures" (II Timothy 3:13-15).* As a 3 year Chemistry/Biochemistry majored collegiate student with a 3.84 GPA, let me assure you there is not a single test a scientist can perform to absolutely, positively verify the age of something! The tests all involve assumptions—including radiometric dating—and therein lay the error. Are you really going to throw away hard, cold, ancient, Biblical "end times" prophetic evidence, including the 7 day Creation story's amazing prophetic verbiage, all of which support the truth of a 6,000 year old Earth, to believe in mankind's scientific guesses?

25

Allow me to tell you first <u>HOW</u> the world was created, for the answer is in Scripture! Then we will investigate how the great "end-time" deceptive theories like macroevolution & the big bang arrived, claiming a very old universe. Friend, the method God used to create the world is blatantly flaunted in a miracle Jesus performed twice. I want you to seriously consider the miracle, for it appears God wanted the miracle to be remembered above ALL other miracles, because it is the <u>ONLY</u> one contained in <u>ALL</u> 4 Gospels. And rightly so, for it should be contemplated by all: The miracle is the feeding of around 5,000 men one time and close to 4,000 men another time with little food.

The miracle of feeding around 5,000 men—plus all their women and children!—occurs in Matthew 14, Mark 6, Luke 9, & John 6. After Jesus found five loaves and two fish among thousands of people listening to him speak, Matthew records: *"And he (Jesus) commanded the multitude to sit down on the grass, and took the **five loaves, and the two fishes**, and looking up to heaven, he blessed, and brake, and gave the loaves to his disciples, and the disciples to the multitude. <u>And **they did ALL eat, and were filled**: and they took up of the fragments that remained twelve baskets full</u>. And they that had eaten were <u>about five thousand men, beside women and children</u>"* (Matthew 14:19-21). Do you see it? Thousands of fish and loaves of bread were just popping into existence out of the clear, thin air!!!

"Scientifically" this is impossible, but not with God. I do not claim to understand how He did it, but the miracle proves He can <u>instantly</u> form an elephant, tiger, or the entire universe if He so desires! Do you understand? I believe whole-heartedly Jesus performed this miracle to prove the <u>Creator</u> God's Spirit, who brought everything into existence, was inside him. Now think about this; if today's scientists lived back in Jesus' day and got a hold of one of the fish he popped into existence, they would have analyzed its size, run radiometric dating on its carbon 14 atoms, and proclaimed the fish was 2, 3, 4, or however many years old. But would they be right? Nope!!! The fish would only have been seconds old, and they would be dead wrong! Likewise, scientists today can run tests until their faces turn blue, but they will still be dead wrong about the age of the universe and Earth, because it is only now approaching 6,000 years old! Friend, God popped this world into existence just like He popped those fish's eyes, hearts, mouths, gills, etc. into existence back then! It did not take billions of years of cosmic evolution followed by millions of years of biological macroevolution to create a fish from nothing. It took only a split second!!!

Let us now take a look at how the scientific "old Earth" deception began. (Remember, in AD 1600, most educated people still correctly believed the Bible's assertion of an approximately 6,000 year old Earth.) Regrettably, the 17th century AD saw the "scientific age" commence. During it, speculative cosmogonies arose seeking "rational" explanations for the universe's existence and Earth's physical features. These cosmogony theories were nothing more than armchair speculations—the Devil whispering lies in their ears!—but they got the ball rolling towards getting mankind to doubt the Bible.

The 18th century AD ushered in the "science" of field geology, where scientists studied earth's sedimentary rock layers (strata) and observed rain, wind, and sea erosion rates. In short, mankind scratched around in the dirt and made more guesses concerning how long it might have taken mountains and valleys to form, assuming they were created by slow wind and water erosion. Using these physical considerations, in AD 1774 Buffon supposed planet Earth was 75,000 years old. Then, in 1795 James Hutton wrote his book "*Theory of the Earth*", which greatly encouraged people to doubt a 6,000 year old Earth. Thus, by AD 1800 it was already widely accepted among scientists planet Earth had a long history, even though there was no hard proof!

From AD 1780 to AD 1850, two major contrasting scientific theories (both working from the assumption of an old Earth) battled it out for acceptance to explain the formation of Earth's geological layers. In one corner there were "catastrophists" who maintained Earth's features were shaped by catastrophic events over its long history. In the other corner were "uniformitists" who surmised Earth's features were shaped by slow, relatively uniform changes throughout its very long history. Since by now scientists had garnered respect among the common man, whatever they conjured up was written down and for the most part believed, even though, again, it was all guesswork! Feeling a need to reconcile the scientist's "old Earth" claims with the Bible, in 1814 Thomas Chalmers popularized the unnecessary, unscriptural "Gap

Theory" for the church crowd, which allowed for millions or billions of years between Genesis 1:1 and 1:2.

Then, AD 1859 saw the publication of Charles Darwin's theory of evolution entitled *"On the Origin of Species"*. This useless theory <u>demanded</u> the acceptance of a very old Earth to give time for macroevolution to occur. Darwin maintained the "fossil record" would eventually show thousands and thousands of intermediate transitional life forms if his guess were true: NONE have ever been found! THIS is evidence enough his theory is false! Yet, today, "macro-<u>evil</u>-lutionary" theory graces the pages of colorful textbooks, masquerading as truth, while "pack-following" teachers corrupt little children's innocent minds with its lies. Eventually, in support of macroevolution, during the tail end of the 19th century <u>uniformitarianism won the great debate (deception), and today it is the leading theory among scientists for how Earth's geological formations came into existence</u>.

Amazingly, God prophesied 2,000 years ago in the Bible about today's scientific "uniformitarianism" theory: *"Knowing this first, that <u>there shall come in the last days scoffers</u>, walking after their own lusts, And saying, 'Where is the promise of his (Jesus 2nd) coming? For since the fathers fell asleep, **<u>all things continue as they were from the beginning of the creation</u>**.' <u>For this they willingly are ignorant of...the world that then was, being overflowed with water, perished"</u> (II Peter 3:3-6)*. Do you see? God knew "science" would arise in the last days, <u>willingly rejecting the decimation of an amazingly different world on planet Earth by a global flood!</u> *"All things continue as they were from the beginning of creation"* is practically, verbatim, the definition of the uniformitarian theory! (Read its definition again two paragraphs above.) Yet, Earth's physical evidence for a massive global flood is enormous— e.g. marine fossils atop every major mountain range in the world, global prevalence of sedimentary rock, and hundreds of corroborative flood legends from isolated indigenous cultures. In the *"Noah"* chapter, I will reveal God's secret, prophetic intent behind every detail of Noah's story, fully cementing your belief in the worldwide flood: In other words, when you learn the hidden truth of what the story was <u>REALLY</u> all about; you will absolutely, positively believe it occurred!

Returning to our chronological lesson on the history of the

"scientific age" of planet Earth, in AD 1862 physicist Lord Kelvin proposed Earth was 98 million years old by—get this absurdity!—calculating the rate of cooling of Earth's inner core. (Stop, stop, my sides are hurting!) Who in their right mind has any idea how hot Earth's inner core was when it formed? I just have to laugh at this kind of idiocy. But anyway, 35 years later in AD 1897 Lord Kelvin said he miscalculated and Earth was really only between 20 or 40 million years old! Are you kidding me? Ah, what the heck, what is 60 or 80 million years of error among buddies? Gather the children so we can start lying to them! Of course, macro-evolutionists could not accept Kelvin's date because it was far too young to support their theory. Are you getting a sense for scientist's madness and senselessness?

Today, scientists tell us they use radiometric dating techniques to obtain the age of Earth. But what they hide from you is the assumptions they must first make to get their results. They have to assume they know the quantity of the radiometric element originally contained in a sample, but there is no way to know that! They have to assume the rate of decay they detect today has always been the same, but there is no way to know that either! And on and on it goes. Scientists say they radiometric dated Precambrian basement granite to 1.5 billion years old, yet the quantity of helium—the radioactively formed intermediate element of decay—is still mostly all in the rock! We can detect today the diffusion rate of helium atoms out of Precambrian rock, and with the quantity of helium still left in the rock it verifies the rock is only between 5,680 (+/- 2,000) years old! Friend, an extremely old Earth is nothing but a lie. Planet Earth is only now bearing down on finishing 6,000 years of history, and God's 7 day (7,000 year) plan is true and intact! Remember who wrote the Bible: *"Let God be true, but every man a liar" (Romans 3:4).*

The disciples asked Jesus one day, *"what shall be the sign of thy coming, and of the end of the world (age or time period)?" (Matthew 24:3).* I have to give the Disciples a "shout-out" for asking such a great question, because Jesus' answer in the Bible fills my heart with hope for his imminent return. The signs Jesus gave preceding his 2nd Coming are like a play by play of the last century. Jesus foresaw WW I & WW II of the first half of the 20th century, when he said, *"**nation shall rise against***

29

nation, and kingdom against kingdom: and there shall be famines, and pestilences, and earthquakes, in diverse places. All these are the beginning of sorrows" (Matthew 24:7, 8). Since Jesus was talking to his Jewish Disciples, he warned them of what would befall their people during World War II: *"Then shall they deliver you up to be afflicted, and shall kill you: and ye shall be hated of all nations for my name's sake" (Matthew 24:9)*. Jesus foresaw the holocaust!!! Hitler afflicted the Jews by performing horrendous scientific medical experiments on them and killed them in masses by gas chambers and firing squads. Now the world hates the fact that the Jewish people have gotten their homeland back.

Jesus went on to explain that wickedness will abound, while people hate one another and deceiving false prophets arise. He said most people will not know how to love—you will learn what "to love" truly means in the *"love"* chapter. Then Jesus proclaimed the Gospel of the Kingdom will be preached in the entire world—which foretold of television, internet, and satellite technology by the 1980's. He mentioned the Beast (Antichrist) sitting in Jerusalem at the very end, and said, *"then shall be great tribulation, such as was not since the beginning of the world to this time, no, nor ever shall be" (Matthew 24:21)*. Friend, there is a time of horror coming to this planet you cannot begin to envisage! Jesus said, *"except those days should be shortened, there should no flesh be saved" (Matthew 24:22)*. In other words, the killing will be so terrible that if Jesus did not return to planet Earth, all mankind would literally perish off the face of Earth!

Oh, but right then Jesus' 2nd Coming will occur, for he declared, *"Immediately after the tribulation of those days...they shall see the Son of man coming in the clouds of heaven with power and great glory. And he shall send his angels with a great sound of a trumpet, and they shall gather together his elect from the four winds, from one end of heaven to the other" (Matthew 24:29-31)*. He proclaimed the sun, moon, and stars will be darkened at this time, while the powers of heaven are shaking! This seems to suggest massive amounts of pollution in the Earth's atmosphere from war or a possible asteroid strike, smothering out the celestial lights. Can you picture the ghastly scene? Then, all of a sudden, out of seemingly nowhere a blinding white light appears

30

as Jesus Christ pierces through the darkened atmosphere, illuminating planet Earth! Unbelievers will beat their chests in anguish, wailing out loud, but it will be too late. The angels will only swoop up those who loved God, and the rest of human flesh will perish in the ensuing fiery destruction of God's wrath! I get goose bumps even thinking about this soon coming day.

Still answering, Jesus then uttered an enlightening parable to his Disciples, providing a huge clue into knowing <u>WHEN</u> his 2nd Coming will take place: *"Now learn a **parable of the FIG TREE**; When his branch is yet tender, and putteth forth leaves, ye know that summer is nigh: So likewise ye, when ye shall see ALL these things, KNOW that it is near, even at the doors. Verily I say unto you, **THIS GENERATION shall not pass, till ALL THESE THINGS BE FULFILLED**"* (Matthew 24:32-34). In a parable, a physical "thing" always represents something else. Well, any honest student of the Holy Scriptures knows the "fig tree" represents Israel! God referred to them as a "fig tree" throughout Scripture: *"I found Israel like grapes in the wilderness; I saw your fathers as the firstripe in the fig tree at her first time"* (Hosea 9:10). God was referring here to when he first led the children of Jacob (Israel) out of Egyptian bondage into the wilderness. It was then that the Israelites first became an independent people, and God saw them as the first ripe figs on a fig tree.

Furthermore, after ministering for 3 years all throughout Israel, Jesus told this parable: *"A certain man had a fig tree planted in his vineyard; and he came and sought fruit thereon, and found none. Then said he unto the dresser of his vineyard, Behold, these **THREE years I come seeking fruit on this FIG TREE** and find none: cut it down; why cumbereth it the ground? And he answering said unto him, Lord, let it alone this year also, till I dig about it, and dung it: And if it bear fruit, well: and if not, then after that thou shalt cut it down"* (Luke 13:6-9). Undeniably, in this parable, the fig tree again represented Israel! Jesus had preached to Israel for 3 years and knew he had under 1 year left to minister to them before being crucified! God was the certain man who planted a fig tree (nation of Israel) in his vineyard (planet Earth), but they would not repent (bear the fruit of love) even after the dresser (Jesus) had ministered to them for 3 years! I say it again; God

31

has always referred to Israel as the fig tree.

Stunningly, only <u>days</u> before his crucifixion, Jesus finished the above parable of the fig tree (Israel) by cursing a literal fig tree: *"And <u>seeing a fig tree afar off having leaves</u>, he came, if haply he might find anything thereon: and when he came to it, <u>he found nothing but leaves</u>... And Jesus answered and said unto it, <u>No man eat fruit of thee hereafter</u>... And in the morning, as they passed by, **<u>they saw the fig tree dried up from the roots</u>"** (Mark 11:13, 14, 20)*. This symbolized Israel's time had come and gone, for they did not recognize Christ as their Messiah and repent of their wickedness; thus, by AD 70 the Temple was destroyed, Jerusalem burned, and the Israelites expelled and dispersed throughout the world. The fig tree (nation of Israel) had dried up!

Now take note, the SAME day the Disciples witnessed the fig tree dried up from the roots was the <u>very</u> day they later asked Jesus <u>what the signs of his 2nd Coming would be</u>! NOW do you see the relevance of Christ's "parable of the fig tree" at the conclusion of his answer to their question? The parable meant when mankind sees the fig tree (nation of Israel) put forth her leaves—meaning become a nation again!—his return would happen before THAT generation of people all die. (Read the parable again three paragraphs above.) Now THAT is an <u>ironclad</u> sign of when Christ's 2nd Coming will occur!!! And, sure enough, against all odds Israel became a nation again May 14, 1948! After almost 2,000 years of non-existence, her branches became tender again and put forth their leaves. Therefore, <u>the generation of people born in 1948 ARE the final generation</u>, and THEY will not all pass away (die off Earth) before Jesus Christ returns in the clouds to establish his Earthly millennial Kingdom! Who could have known "Israel" would come back on the map over 1,800 year later? The event is as astonishing as if the Inca or Aztec civilizations arose again! The Jews should have long since been assimilated into other cultures and died out as a people. But nope, "Israel" is back on the map just like Jesus remarkably prophesied they would be, perfectly positioned for the culmination of 6,000 years!

The million dollar question then is how LONG is a <u>Biblical</u> generation of people? Astonishingly, the answer is found in the very SAME Psalm of Moses that first gave us God's time Key of 1 day = 1,000 years! How about that? Do you think that is just a coincidence?

Moses wrote: *"The days of our years are threescore years and ten (70); and if by reason of strength they be fourscore years (80)"* (Psalms 90:10). Moses wrote this Psalm in the 14th Century BC! How could he have possibly known over 3,300 years later, with the advent and advancements of modern medicine, the average lifespan of men and women would still be between 70 & 80 years? It is astounding that Moses' words are precisely true today! Therefore, AD 2028 (AD 1948 + 80 years) is the latest possible year that would still fulfill Jesus' parable!

Why do I believe AD 2028 is THE year of Christ's 2nd Coming? Because there is a HUGE Biblical secret the Spirit of the Lord revealed to me in AD 2008 (that I have already alluded to in this chapter) which points like a neon sign to AD 2028 as the 6,000th year of mankind's history! The amazing secret is Jesus' death, burial, & resurrection absolutely occurred during mankind's 4,000th year of history on Earth! The proof of this secret is contained in the details of an ancient Bible story and will be clearly revealed in the *"Moses"* Chapter. But this truth is also contained in other Biblical details that I will reveal. After you learn them, you will know without a shadow of a doubt this fact is truth! When God revealed these "things" to me I was stunned. For the truth is glaring, yet I know of NOBODY who ever understood the meaning behind the Biblical details that prove this truth! And I never would have either, except for God's Spirit revealing it to me.

Knowing Jesus' death occurred during year 4,000 allows me to say with certainty he will come back EXACTLY 2,000 years from that year, because he WILL return to Earth during year 6,000! (Remember, the story of Noah will absolutely prove this.) Thus, if we knew definitively what year Jesus died, I could tell you with absolute certainty what year he will return! Do you understand? So, DO we know the year of Jesus' death? Well, not positively, but the respected dates are from AD 26 to AD 30. Therefore, Jesus' 2nd Coming could be anywhere from AD 2026 to AD 2030. But wait! We know the fig tree (Israel) budded in AD 1948 and the "80 year generational time limit" from Christ's parable runs out in AD 2028. Consequently, I can farther limit the date of Jesus' 2nd Coming from AD 2026 to AD 2028!

So, why do I believe AD 2028 is THE year and not AD 2026 or

2027? Because I have acquired a keen appreciation for God's perfection with numbers! (And after reading this book, you will too!) Friend, it would not be like God to have Christ return during Israel's 78th or 79th national birthday, for the numbers do not mean anything. But the number 80? Oh, that is a whole different ballgame!!! God sent Moses to lead the Israelites out of their Egyptian troubles when he was 80 years old. Thus, it seems very fitting that God will send Jesus Christ to Earth to save Israel out of their current day troubles—when the Antichrist is sitting in their temple proclaiming himself to be God!—during Israel's 80th Birthday. Consequently, my spirit believes Jesus' 2nd Coming will occur in the year AD 2028, which places his death in AD 28. And now you know how I calculated 3972 BC (AD 2028 – 6,000 years) as the year of Creation!

Well, I have only introduced you to God's 7 day (7,000 year) Earthly master Time plan in this chapter, but throughout this book I will show you how God continued to verify it by controlling the details of ancient Bible stories. I will even show you how God further confirmed it, mind-bogglingly, by reproducing it the actual "7 day week" of Jesus' death, burial, and resurrection (this information is contained in the "*Moses*" chapter). But for now, with respect to God's 7 millennial day master Time plan for mankind on planet Earth, I can tell you with absolute certainty Jesus Christ will return to planet Earth exactly 2,000 years after the year of his death, resurrection, and ascension! (The full weight of this sobering TRUTH will only hit you after you mentally digest the Biblical secrets contained in the rest of this book.)

Chapter 2

Physical / Spiritual

*"And the Lord God formed man of the dust of the ground,
and breathed into his nostrils the BREATH OF LIFE;
and man became a living SOUL"
(Genesis 2:7)*

Before I go any further in revealing what the Bible is all about and God's purpose for writing it, it is imperative you first have a firm mental grasp of two very real realms—namely, the physical realm and the spiritual realm. For without a clear realization and understanding of these two factual realms and how they relate to the makeup of a human being, it is impossible to understand the true meaning of the Bible. Therefore, I will delve into a fairly detailed analysis of these two realms in this chapter. Please do not skip over this chapter, because internalization of these concepts has power to change your life, which in turn will change your eternal destiny!

As a brief and very general introduction, the physical realm is made up of "material" that we <u>can</u> currently see, touch, taste, smell, and hear. Scientists call this material "matter", and matter is made up of "atoms". On the other hand, the spiritual realm is made up of "material" that we <u>cannot</u> currently see, touch, taste, or smell. It is like an invisible dimension existing all around us, in us, and throughout the entire physical universe! The Bible reveals God <u>created</u> the physical realm and much—if not all—of the spiritual realm. As human beings, we live on planet Earth consciously interacting with the physical realm. But the crucial concept to comprehend is "what" we REALLY are! <u>We are spiritual beings housed in physical bodies!</u> In other words, human beings are made of both realms—physical & spiritual!!! Our physical material is our flesh, which is made up of Earthly atoms, but our spirit "material" is our soul, which contains our thoughts, desires, & emotions. Are you confused? Well, let us dig Biblically deeper into each of these two realms; physical first, then spiritual.

The first sentence in the Bible is powerfully complete, yet impressively concise, in describing God's created physical realm known as the "universe", which consists of time, space, and matter. God the Father, Son, & Holy Ghost simultaneously brought these three characteristics into co-existence at the genesis of Creation: *"In the beginning (time) God created the heaven (space) and the earth (matter)" (Gen 1:1).* Astonishingly symmetric and poetic, these three dimensions each have their OWN respective trinities: <u>Time</u> consists of past, present, & future; <u>space</u> contains length, width, & height; and <u>matter</u> exists as solid, liquid, & gas. This trinity of trinities was all conjured up and designed by God and makes up the PHYSICAL realm (world).

We owe our five sense "experience" to the creativity God bestowed upon the physical world. Mankind would not have a clue what a star is or looks like if God had not created one. And who could have dreamed of an elephant's size, shape, and color if God had not made one? And no one would have conceived of the splendid color, texture, and fragrance of a flower's bloom without God's handiwork. All of these physical wonders are part of God's impressively created physical world. The Bible says it best: *"The <u>heavens are telling the glory of God; they are a marvelous display of his craftsmanship. Day and night they keep on telling about God. Without a sound or word, silent in the skies, their message reaches out to all the world</u>. The sun lives in the heavens where God placed it and moves out across the skies as radiant as a bridegroom going to his wedding" (Psalms 19:1-5, Living Bible).*

Step outside some full moon night and watch in admiration as wind-driven, translucent, angelic-shaped clouds whisk past its white reflected light. Gaze in awe at a morning sky splayed in shades of orange and red, as the burning sun crests the horizon. Watch our circular sun black out perfectly for a few breathtaking seconds by our eclipsing circular moon during a solar eclipse, and reason at the precision of God's handiwork in calculating the sizes, shapes, and distances between these heavenly bodies to afford us such a spectacular physical event! Marvel at the fact our moon orbits planet Earth, fully, every 27½ days but appears to take 29½ days because planet Earth is traveling 66,000 miles an hour in its orbit around the sun and has moved so far along its arc that from our perspective it takes an extra two days for the moon to go from one full moon to another. Then wonder at the magnificence and meticulousness of God for creating our moon to revolve <u>once</u> on its axis every 29½ days; thus, we continuously see the same side of the moon! Yes, my friend, the heavens are truly declaring the existence, precision, and glory of God!

But what about mankind's physical body? How did God conjure up the physical features of a human being? Friend, He patterned us after himself!!! *"And God said, <u>Let US make man</u>...<u>after our likeness"</u> (Genesis 1:26).* The original Hebrew word translated *"likeness"* is *"dᵉmûṭ"*, meaning: <u>likeness, figure, image, form</u>. In a nutshell, we were fashioned to look like God! Thus, the physical concept of a human being having legs to walk, arms to hold, torso to twist, eyes to see, mouth to taste, nose to smell, and ears to hear was not the product of millions of years of random, evolutionary chance: It was God making us "like Him"! It is insanity to believe mindless spontaneity created the physical features of a human being, yet macro-evolutionary theory proposes such a ridiculous idea.

Scientists, if you want to know where the ear and the eye came from, study the Scriptures: *"<u>Understand, ye brutish among the people: and ye fools, when will you be wise?</u> **<u>He (God) that planted the ear</u>**, shall he not hear? **<u>He (God) that formed the eye</u>**, shall he not see?" (Psalms 94:8, 9).* Scientists are still trying to understand "light", for it is an extremely complex phenomenon, having the properties of both waves and particles. Yet, macro-evolutionists want us to believe good-old random "nothingness" new exactly what light is, designing an eye to "capture <u>it</u>", optic nerve to "transmit <u>it</u>", and brain to "process <u>it</u>" into sight? Are you kidding me? Only a lunatic would believe that! Friend, when you look at your physical body in the mirror, you are looking at God's creation.

Allow me now to get technical about the physical realm for your benefit. What <u>EXACTLY</u> makes up the physical world? Friend, it is all made of atoms! An atom is the basic building block for the entire physical universe. To understand this concept, let me simplify it for you with an analogy. There are approximately 100 DIFFERENT atoms— <u>called elements</u>—that make up everything in the physical universe. This is not unlike there are 26 different sounds—<u>called letters</u>—that make up the English Language. If we name each sound we say that is letter "m", or "t", or "a", etc. Likewise, if we name each different atom we say that is an element of "carbon", or "hydrogen, or "oxygen", etc. In other words, a study of the *Periodic Table of the Elements* in Chemistry is like studying the alphabet in English.

Then, in the same way one picks and groups certain of these 26 different letters together to make <u>words</u> such as "d-o-g" or "a-n-g-r-y", so, too, in the physical world God has picked and grouped certain of these approximately 100 different elements together to make <u>molecules</u>, such as "Hydrogen-Oxygen-Hydrogen" (water) or "Sodium-Chlorine" (table salt). Words are then combined to make sentences like molecules are combined to make cells. Sentences are combined to make paragraphs like cells are combined to make organs. And, finally, paragraphs are combined to make complete documents like organs are combined to make complete organisms, such as a physical human being!

But here is what I want you to mull over; <u>the atoms making up the physical world DO NOT wear out</u>! In other words, <u>THE SAME ONES HAVE ALL BEEN HERE SINCE THE BEGINNING OF CREATION</u>!!! So think about this; <u>all</u> that has been happening in the physical realm on Earth, since the beginning of time, is the EXACT SAME atoms are being continually shuffled around from one location to another! Do you understand? No new atoms are being created and none are being destroyed. Thus, the atoms making up your physical body right now have always existed on planet Earth since Creation! (Would you not like to know where they have all been throughout history?)

See, you might have a carbon atom in you that existed inside Jesus' body 2,000 years ago! After he breathed it out in a carbon dioxide molecule, maybe it eventually ended up trapped in a spinach leaf that you ate, and now is part of a fat molecule in an epidermal cell on your right thigh! I know this all sounds silly to ponder, but I wish you would give it much thought, for it would teach you the relative worthlessness of your physical body and ALL materialistic things on Earth. See, all the possessions you "think you own" are merely atoms that have existed on planet Earth for thousands of years long before YOU were ever born, and they will all be here after YOU are gone!!! Do you recognize the folly in desiring those things? The Bible states clearly who owns the atoms of planet Earth: *"LET NO MAN SEEK HIS OWN... **For the earth is the Lord's**, and the fullness thereof" (I Corinthians 10:24, 26).* The truth is no one owns ANYTHING on planet Earth! You do not even own the atoms making up your own physical body!!! The Bible (speaking of our physical bodies) clearly states: *"...till thou return unto the ground; for out of it wast thou taken: for dust thou art, and unto dust shalt thou return" (Genesis 3:19).*

As you look at your physical body in the mirror tonight, I want you to contemplate how you accumulated that pile of atoms. Where did they all come from? The answer is they came from a lifetime of food consumption, skin absorption, and air inhalation. Think about it; at conception you were a 1 celled organism made up of atoms from your father's sperm and mother's egg. As your mom ate food made of atoms and breathed air full of atoms, you acquired millions and millions of those atoms and grew in size. Then, when you were born you breathed and ate your own atoms and got bigger and bigger. So, on a mere physical plane you are nothing more than the atoms you have consumed and retained in your lifetime! Today we know every atom in a human body is, on average, replaced every 7 years! Some are replaced a lot quicker and some take longer. Consequently, your physical body is mostly made up of atoms you amassed in just the last 7 years!

Cognizant of this, I pose a question to those of you who do not believe in a spiritual realm: If you are ONLY made up of atoms acquired from food, water, & air, then how or when did those atoms start thinking and feeling? In other words, which can of beans did you eat that has you hating your brother? Which sprig of asparagus did you consume that now retains a memory from your childhood? For that matter, what atoms or molecules hold memories, and how do they continue to retain a thirty year old memory while your atoms are being replaced? What molecule emits depression? Which atoms think thoughts of suicide? Can we avoid eating the suicide molecule? Do you see how absurd these questions are? There <u>HAS</u> to be something more to a human being than just physical atoms. And there absolutely is; it is called our spirit or soul, and it is part of the spiritual realm!

So what IS the spiritual realm? What are its basic building blocks, and where is it located? These are very good questions, but we do not know the answers because the spiritual realm is currently invisible to us, and it is difficult to define something when you cannot see it! But from what we learn in the Bible, it seems logical the spirit realm's "material" is all around us and inside of us like some other dimension. Let us investigate.

We know angels exist in the spirit world, for the Bible affirms God CREATED—which means <u>during</u> the 6 day CREATION—an innumerable host of supernatural angelic beings to serve Him and minister to us in the spirit realm! The Bible declares: *"Are they (angels) not <u>ALL</u> ministering <u>spirits</u>" (Hebrews 1:14)*. Furthermore, Paul wrote: ***"<u>For by him were ALL things created, that are IN heaven, and that are IN earth, visible and invisible</u>**, whether they be <u>thrones, or dominions, or principalities, or powers</u>: <u>ALL</u> things were created by him, and for him: And he is BEFORE all things, and <u>by him all things consist</u>" (Colossians 1:16, 17)*. Do you remember the first verse in the Bible: *"<u>In the beginning God created the heaven and the earth</u> ... And the evening and the morning were the first day" (Genesis 1:1-5)*? If God created heaven (space) and earth (matter) on the first day, it follows logically that it was sometime after that when He created <u>ALL</u> the perceptible and imperceptible things that exist <u>IN</u> heaven and earth, like human beings and angels. Do you see? (I point this out merely to debunk the false belief people have that angels have existed with God long before the Creation. This is a lie! Angels were created DURING the 6 day Creation period.)

40

But what is the relationship of "spirit material" to a human being? Does the Bible claim "spirit material" is <u>inside</u> of a human being? Yes, yes, yes!!! The Bible says: *"And the Lord God formed man of the dust of the ground, and <u>breathed into his nostrils the BREATH OF LIFE; and</u> **<u>man became a living soul</u>**" (Genesis 2:7)*. See, mankind has a physical body and a spiritual soul! Our physical body came from the dirt of the ground and is made up of lifeless atoms, but our soul is made up of "spirit material" invisible to us right now but FULL of LIFE. (Note: our "spirit material" is called our "<u>living</u> soul".) Jesus fixedly declared: **"<u>God IS a Spirit</u>"** *(John 4:24)*. And he also affirmed: *"<u>The Father (God) hath LIFE IN HIMSELF</u>" (John 5:26)*. This means <u>God IS the Spirit of Life</u>, and <u>ALL</u> life comes from Him. Subsequently, on day 6 of Creation, what really happened was God breathed a portion of His "Spirit material" INTO mankind's physical atoms of dirt, <u>giving</u> us life! In other words, when God breathed into the nostrils of Adam <u>He gave him a part of His Spirit</u> and his lifeless lump of atoms sprang forth with movement. See, only "spirit material" gives life. James wrote: *"For as **<u>the (physical) body without the spirit is dead</u>**, so faith without works is dead also" (James 2:26)*.

Be acutely aware that every time you interact with another human being you are really interacting with God, because the "spirit material" inside each of us came from Him! Subsequently, we are all called His "spirit children"!!! The Bible says: *"Furthermore we have had fathers of our flesh which corrected us, and we gave them reverence: <u>shall we not much rather be in subjection unto the</u> **<u>Father of spirits</u>**, and live?" (Hebrews 12:9)*. Do you see? God is our TRUE Father, and we are <u>ALL</u> His spirit children; thus, He is known as the "Father of spirits". Again, the Bible writes: *"Let the Lord, the **<u>God of the spirits of all flesh</u>**" (Numbers 27:16)*. In other words, we are ALL brothers and sisters of our Father God! See, your brothers & sisters are not just the few in your immediate, physically born family; <u>THEY are EVERYONE on Earth</u>!!! If you can remember this (every human being is God's spirit child), it should help you treat everyone with dignity, fairness, and kindness, for one day you will answer to God for how you treated HIM through His children—YOUR brothers & sisters! And, friend, God loves <u>ALL</u> His spirit children, and you better, too!

So what do we know about this life-giving spirit (soul) in us? Listen up, because this point is colossal: <u>Our spirit is the part of us that contains our thoughts (mind), desires (will), & emotions (feelings)</u>. See, these "things" come out of our spirit! It is the spirit that can retain a lifetime of memories, house wants and desires, and feel emotions ranging from joy to pain. Friend, "spirit" is amazing stuff! "Spirit" can give and receive love. In fact, God is not only the Spirit of Life; He is also the Spirit of Love! John wrote: *"<u>He that loveth not knoweth not God; for</u> **<u>God IS Love</u>**" (I John 4:8)*. These truths are simple, yet incredibly central to understanding what a soul MUST <u>DO</u> to obtain eternal life!!! Therefore, please remember and internalize these vital points; <u>God = Spirit of Life and God = Spirit of Love</u>, and y<u>our spirit is where your thoughts, desires, & emotions exist</u>!

The Apostle Paul understood clearly a human being's pile of physical Earthly atoms move around ONLY because God's spirit (breath of life) is inside it! He addressed the men of Athens saying; *"<u>God that made the world and all things therein</u>, seeing that he is Lord of heaven and earth, dwelleth not in temples (church buildings) made with hands...<u>seeing he giveth to all life, and breath</u>...**<u>For in him we live, and move, and have our being</u>**...For we are also his offspring"* *(Acts 17:24-28)*. See, we live, move, and have our being because God's "spirit material" is inside us—which again confirms we are <u>all</u> His spirit children (offspring).

Allow me to break this down further, showing you exactly how "spirit" moves a physical dirt body around. (Remember, our spirit (soul) contains our thoughts, desires, & emotions!) Watch how simple this is...If a <u>thought</u> of hunger arises in your spirit and you <u>decide</u> you want a sandwich, what happens? Your pile of Earthly atoms gets up and moves toward the refrigerator, opens the door, and starts assembling the ingredients for a sandwich. Do you understand what just happened? <u>Your spirit moved your physical body</u>!!! If you ever cease having thoughts, your physical body will lie motionless on the ground like a vegetable. Elihu wisely fomented to Job: *"<u>If God were to withdraw his Spirit, ALL life would disappear and mankind would turn again to dust</u>" (Job 34:14, 15, Living Bible)*. Friend, the Bible is truth; it is God's spirit that gives life to our physical bodies. Thus, *"we live, and* *move, and have our being"* only because of "spirit material" in us that came from God. It is not a small matter to ponder: YOU are housing a part of God inside of you!!!

Let us talk about speech. Where do the words pouring out of our mouth originate? They, too, come from our spirit! Think about it; after a thought forms in your spirit, air atoms move out of the lungs, pass over the larynx's atoms, and begin vibrating upward until the tongue atoms expel them intermittently out of the mouth cavity in the form of words. Jesus said this (not so technically) in the passage: *"O generation of vipers, how can ye, being evil, speak good things?* ***For out of the abundance of the heart (spirit) the mouth speaketh"*** *(Matthew 12:34).* A great deal can be learned about the condition of someone's spirit (soul) simply by listening to them talk! "Spirit" can spew forth words of hate, greed, & pride, or love, compassion, & humility. But "language communication" is ALWAYS a "spirit to spirit interaction".

Think about communication, scientifically...what physically takes place when you converse with someone? Do you pass atoms to them? If you whisper in someone's ear, maybe your breath does, but what if you yell at someone 500 feet away? Then you do not! In that case, all "words" do are vibrate the already densely packed air atoms existing between the two people, transferring intermittent waves, which vibrate the listener's ear drum atoms. Thus, no physical atoms are exchanged between the speaker and the listener. So, in the physical realm it is almost as if nothing happened, and yet you could say the wrong words to someone and be killed! That is because words are powerful because they are "spirit". Jesus knew all of this: *"It is the spirit that quickeneth; the flesh (atoms) profiteth nothing: **the words that I speak unto you, they are spirit**, and they are life" (John 6:63).* Clearly, even in speech, the spirit simply moves physical atoms around!

Incidentally, THIS is how God created the physical universe: *"And the earth (atoms) was without form, and void; and darkness was upon the face of the deep. And the Spirit of God moved upon the face of the waters" (Genesis 1:2).* Listen, when the "Spirit of God" began moving, thoughts formed and He spoke, and a formless sea of atoms in a chasm of darkness began to move, aligning themselves into the "things" we see and love today. Scientists know nothing moves in the

43

physical universe unless acted upon by a force, so initially there HAD to be a force that got everything (the atoms) moving at the genesis of Creation. THAT force was/is the Spirit of God (life)!!! That is why Jesus said my words are SPIRIT AND LIFE. Creation began as words flowed out of the Holy Spirit of God and every atom moved in perfect obedience to the sound of His voice. Hallelujah! *"And God SAID, Let there be light: and there WAS light" (Genesis 1:3).*

So here now is a good question…can we see God? No, but we can observe the movement of physical dirt atoms that have His life giving spirit inside them! In other words, we can see God by observing His creation!!! This is what Paul meant when he wrote: *"For the invisible things of him (God) from the creation of the world are clearly seen, being understood by the things that are made" (Romans 1:20).* Do you see? The other day I surreptitiously peeked through my window blinds to watch a male and female cardinal couple eating worms in my front yard. Since the female cardinal was not having much luck finding any worms, every third or fourth worm the male cardinal would find he would teeter-totter over to his honey and give it to her to eat. It was the sweetest thing to witness, and then I realized…I was seeing love!!! I saw and understood the *"invisible things of God"*—namely, His Spirit of Love—by watching two piles of atoms God had formed into birds move around. You can see God in a baby's smile, a mother's kiss, and a tail-wagging puppy licking a little boys face. Yes, as Paul wrote, the invisible things of God can clearly be seen!

You can acquire an appreciation of God's love for His spirit children by watching an Earthly dad's pile of atoms interact with his child's pile of atoms. Watch him protect his child from harm; watch him diligently teach him things; and watch him sit back and chuckle in amusement at his playing. These things are happening on a spiritual plane, for it is "spirit" that lives, laughs, learns, and loves. Never forget: God loves YOU immensely because He IS Love and you ARE His child.

So what really happens when we "die" on Earth? Friend, it is not death at all!!! "Death" on Earth occurs when our spirit leaves our physical body. The REAL us (our spirit) is still living! Jesus vociferated on the cross: *"Father, into thy hands I commend my SPIRIT: and* *having said thus, **he gave up the ghost (spirit)**" (Luke 23:46)*. At that point, Christ's spirit left and his physical body went limp and became motionless. All the atoms making up his physical body were still hanging on the cross, but his spirit was gone! See, physical death on Earth is just a "relocating" of our spirit to another location (dimension). When Jacob's wife, Rachel, died the Bible explains: *"And it came to pass, as **her SOUL was in departing**, (for she died)" (Genesis 35:18)*. When Jesus resurrected Jarius' 12 year old dead daughter, listen to what happened: *"And he (Jesus)...took her by the hand, and called, saying, Maid, arise. And her SPIRIT came again, and she arose straightway" (Luke 8:54, 55)*. See, if the spirit <u>returns</u> to the physical body, then it is alive again! So please understand "death" as we know it on Earth is simply a separation of our spirit (soul) from our physical body: *"Then shall the dust return to the earth as it was: and **the spirit shall return unto God who gave it**" (Ecclesiastes 12:7)*.

Moreover, since our spirit <u>contains</u> our thoughts, desires, & emotions, when IT leaves our physical body we take those "things" with us! In other words, after exiting your physical body your spirit will still remember <u>EVERYTHING</u> you ever did on Earth. Do you understand? If you harbored un-forgiveness and hatred towards your Earthly father during your days on Earth, you will still have those feelings toward him when your spirit transfers into the spirit world. If your favorite color was blue, it will still be blue. If you got shot robbing a bank when you "died", you will recall how it went down! I am just confirming your spirit is the REAL YOU!!! Subsequently, the "condition" of your spirit (soul) will not change when it leaves your physical body.

In this regard, the Bible has a far better "term" that more accurately describes (from mankind's perspective on Earth) what condition someone is IN who "died" on Earth; it says they are "ASLEEP"! See, Lazarus' spirit (soul) had left his physical body and his sisters had buried his cold flesh in a tomb for 4 days, but Jesus simply told his disciples: *"<u>Our friend Lazarus sleepeth</u>; but I go, <u>that I may awake him out of sleep</u>" (John 11:11)*. Do you understand? With stones pelting his body and head, listen to the Bible's conclusion of Stephen's death: *"<u>And he kneeled down</u>, and cried with a loud voice, Lord, lay not this sin to their charge. <u>And when he said this</u>, **he fell asleep**" (Acts 7:60)*. In other

45

words, he died! Now listen, when someone is <u>sleeping</u> on Earth their spirit is FULLY alive for it is still having thoughts (dreams); the only problem…YOU CANNOT COMMUNICATE WITH THEM!!! <u>THIS</u> is <u>precisely</u> how it is with <u>everyone</u> who has ever "passed on" or "died" on Earth: Their spirits are fully alive; we just cannot communicate with them. Consequently, (from our perspective) a "dead" person is merely SLEEPING!

Today, there is a massive body of evidence supporting the fact that human beings are really "spirit beings" housed inside physical bodies, for there are literally millions of people who have had "out-of-body" experiences! These incidents are called near-death-experiences (NDE). During these encounters, the spirit exits the physical body, leaving it motionless and unresponsive. The person is deemed clinically dead—no heartbeat, no breathing, and no electrical brain activity—for a period of time, until their spirit returns to their physical body, reviving them to life. When studying these NDE cases it is remarkable how similar the experiences are! Although out of the physical body, initially the spirit remains conscience of the Earthly location it just left—a hospital room, a mangled car wreck, or wherever "death" found them. Then, depending on how long the NDE lasts, the surroundings start to change as spiritual beings come to "interact" with them! Some are taken to hellish places, while others are taken to heavenly places. But always, in their spirit body, they realize they have the same thoughts, feelings, & desires they had when in their physical body, remembering everything they ever did or experienced—e.g. they know their parents, marriage partner, kids, etc.

NDE's are nothing new, though, for the Bible mentions such a case almost 2,000 years ago: *"I (Paul) knew a man in Christ above fourteen years ago, (**whether in the body, I cannot tell; or whether out of the body, I cannot tell**: <u>God knoweth;</u>) such an one caught up to the third heaven" (II Corinthians 12:2).* See, truth is truth. Consequently, indubitably people have been having NDE's all throughout mankind's history. In the 1980's a lady "died" in a hospital room and her spirit body floated up through the ceiling to the flat roof of the hospital, where she saw a pair of sneakers lying there. When she revived (her spirit returned to her physical body) she told the doctors what she had experienced and

46

seen. They were stunned, having gone up onto the roof, to find what she saw was real! Friend, this NDE proved "out-of-body" experiences are NOT hallucinations: They are reality!!! Frankly, it is silly to deny the truthfulness of these people's encounters after witnessing the profound change it makes in their lives afterwards! I greatly encourage you to go online and read some notable NDE accounts—e.g. Howard Storm, Ned Dougherty, Ricky Randolph, etc—for the lessons they learned during their ordeals sum up the TRUTH of the Bible's message.

A mystery is how our spirit is intermeshed or intertwined with our physical body. In other words, where in the physical body does the spirit reside? The Bible seems to hint the answer as being "in the blood": *"For the **life of the flesh is in the blood**" (Leviticus 17:11).* Since the blood is in contact with every cell of our physical body, it stands to reason the "spirit of life" might reside there—i.e. the spirit gives life to the flesh and the flesh's life is in the blood! Supporting this likelihood are the words God spoke to Cain after he slew his brother, Abel: *"What hast thou done? The VOICE of thy brother's BLOOD crieth unto me from the ground" (Genesis 4:10).* Since we know words form in the spirit, this verse also suggests the spirit resides in the blood.

Another mystery is when does a spirit (soul) become lodged into a multiplying group of cells in a mother's womb after insemination? Solomon wrote: *"God's ways are as mysterious as the pathway of the wind, and as the manner in which a human spirit is infused into the little body of a baby while it is yet in its mother's womb" (Ecclesiastes 11:5 Living Bible).* At least we know the spirit (soul) is placed inside the physical body while the fetus is still inside its mother's womb!

In the Bible, synonymous terms for a human being's spirit are: soul, heart, ghost, and inner man; and the synonymous terms for a human being's physical body are: body, flesh, and outer man. The Bible is replete with verses that juxtaposition these two entities. For example: *"For bodily (fleshly or atom) exercise profiteth little: but **GODLINESS (spiritual exercise) is profitable unto all things**, having promise of the life that now is, and of that which is to come" (I Timothy 4:8).* Here we learn the relative value between the two: Conditioning our physical body is relatively worthless because the atoms making it up just go back to the dirt to be recycled, but conditioning our spirit to godliness is priceless for that has to do with forsaking sin and aligning our thoughts, desires, & emotions up to right (righteous) living, which will then allow our spirit (soul) to live eternally!

Jesus confirmed the immense worth of our spirit when he said, *"For what is a man profited, if he shall gain the whole world (atoms), and lose his own soul? Or what shall a man give in exchange for his soul?" (Matthew 16:26)*. Here, Jesus makes it abundantly clear that we can *"lose our soul"*, meaning forfeit it for all eternity! Now, here is wisdom of the highest degree—and I will only introduce you to this concept here, but it is SO important that throughout this book I must Biblically develop it—do you know what is the MAJOR desire (which means it comes out of one's spirit) fighting against your soul's chance at eternal life? IT IS YOUR SOUL'S LUST FOR WORTHLESS EARTHLY ATOMS!!! (Did it feel like I just drove a knife into your heart? If so, that is serious cause for concern! And if you care at all about your soul's eternal destiny, I beg you to finish this book.) THAT is why Christ lamented even if you gain control of every atom on Earth (in the form of land, houses, & possessions) during your brief tenure on planet Earth, it will not be worth the price of "losing your soul" for all eternity. In other words, your 1 soul is worth more than ALL the atoms making up planet Earth!!!

Well, an entire book is needed to truly do the subject of the physical realm versus the spiritual realm justice, but I pray in reading this chapter you now have an inkling of the difference between the two. But most importantly, I hope you understand YOU (and all mankind) are God's "spirit children" housed inside physical dirt bodies made of Earthly atoms. And you should realize the REAL YOU is your spirit (soul), which contains your thoughts, desires, & emotions. With this important insight into the "makeup of man", we can now proceed with understanding the Bible, for it is truly a book about God's plans for mankind's souls!

48

Chapter 3

Adam & Eve

"Behold, the man is become as one of us,
to KNOW GOOD and EVIL"
(Genesis 3:22)

The most important thing to understand after reading this chapter is PRECISELY what happened to Adam & Eve's spirits (souls) AFTER they sinned in the Garden of Eden, for this truth sets up a particular "theme" God will employ over and over again in the Old Testament Bible stories. In other words, clearly grasping what occurred TO & IN Adam & Eve's spirits after they sinned is the key to understanding the entire Bible, because what happened to them was automatically passed on to every single human being's soul that lived thereafter. But most importantly, comprehension of this truth will lead you to the plain truth of exactly what EVERY soul has/had to DO to obtain eternal life.

But before we analyze Adam & Eve's fiasco, allow me to digress a moment and explain God's motive for creating everything: The Bible says: *"Thou art worthy, O Lord, to receive glory and honour and power: for thou hast created all things, and for thy PLEASURE they are and were created"* (Revelation 4:11). This word "pleasure" is translated from the Greek word *"thelēma"* meaning: will, decision, desire. Thus, God created the universe, stars, angels, planet Earth, animals, mankind (spirit children), and everything existing for His pleasure!

You might ask; how does God receive pleasure from the things He created? The answer is because He set up creation like a game!!! I will explain with an analogy: It is like mankind "creating" the game of football for his pleasure. The game has a playing field, a beginning an ending time, rules, and players that can win or lose. As mankind watches a football game being played, he receives great enjoyment out of it. Every detail of every play is fun to watch. Pleasure is manifested by spirits screaming, chanting, crying, and shouting as they root on who they want to win! Do you understand? This is a picture of God's excitement, rooting us on to win in the Game of Life He created. Jesus said, *"I say unto you there is JOY in the presence of the angels of God over one sinner that REPENTETH" (Luke 15:10).* Yes, friend, God is receiving great pleasure from His Creation.

Digressing further, allow me to say a few pertinent words about the Creator God himself. He is a KING that has ALWAYS existed! I know that is hard to cogitate, but Paul wrote: *"Now unto the King eternal, immortal, invisible, the only wise God, be honour and glory for ever and ever" (I Timothy 1:17).* Since He created everything, He is God. In fact, He is the only God: *"I am the LORD, and there is NONE else, there is no God beside me" (Isaiah 45:5).* He is perfect in wisdom, power, and might, and deserving of us bowing on our knees with heads low, worshiping Him like the God He is! Jeremiah declared: *"But the LORD is the true God, he is the living God, and an everlasting king: at his wrath the earth shall tremble, and the nations shall not be able to abide his indignation…**He hath made the earth by his power, he hath established the world by his wisdom, and hath stretched out the heavens by his discretion**" (Jeremiah 10:10, 12).* Thankfully, He is a good God! Hundreds of times the Bible claims such: *"Good and upright is the LORD" (Psalms 25:8).* Rest assured the Creator God is good, for He IS Love!

Let us now examine the components making up the Game of Life God has created for His pleasure: The playing field is planet Earth, the length of the Game is 7,000 Earth trips around the sun, the rules are the 10 Commandments, the players are His spirit children, and the Bible is the Game's handbook. The object of the Game is for God's

50

spirit children (mankind) to obtain eternal life for their soul. THAT is how we win!!! To lose the game is to lose your soul for all eternity, being cast into outer darkness. (A sobering Biblical fact…most people will lose, but more about that later!) To win the game and receive ETERNAL life, all WE have to **DO** is OBEY the rules! Paul wisely wrote: *"**Follow the Lord's rules for doing his work**, just as an athlete either follows the rules or is disqualified and wins no prize" (II Timothy 2:5 Living Bible).* (I have much more to say about all this, so do not stop reading!) But let us turn now to the heartbreaking story of Adam & Eve, for their account is the tale of how the "option to lose" was initiated; thus, completing the setup of God's Game of Life.

After God created the physical universe and the invisible spiritual realm in 6 days, along with mankind (spirit children) and the angels, He honed in on planet Earth. Earth was already hurling 66,000 miles an hour toward completing its first loop around the sun and counting off the 1st year of His 7,000 year plan. (The year was likely 3972 BC on our current Gregorian calendar, but back then it was year #1.) The locale on planet Earth was the place we today call the Middle East. In that area, God created a lush garden called Eden, where He placed his first spirit child, Adam: *"And the Lord God planted a garden eastward in Eden; and there he put the man whom he had formed. And out of the ground made the Lord God to grow every tree that is pleasant to the sight, and good for food; the tree of life also in the midst of the garden, and the tree of the knowledge of good and evil" (Genesis 2:8, 9).*

God then caused Adam to fall into a deep sleep, took a rib from his side, and made him a woman companion. (It is now known the lower rib is the only bone in the human body that can regenerate itself if taken out! Think God knew what he was doing?) Note: when I use the term "mankind" in this book, I am referring to "woman" as well, because she was taken out of man. Adam said: *"This is now bone of my bones, and flesh of my flesh: she shall be called Woman, because she was taken out of Man" (Genesis 2:23).* Eventually, Adam named his companion "Eve" meaning "life", for she was to be the mother of all humans.

Now, in the Garden of Eden, please understand Adam & Eve's souls were initially in PERFECT UNION with God's Spirit of Life. This is symbolized in the story by a *"tree of life"* being IN the Garden. And since Adam & Eve lived IN the Garden, obviously, they had access and right to partake of that tree whenever and as often as they liked. What a beautiful picture of the wonderful, joyous connection that existed between God's Spirit of Life and Adam & Eve's spirits.

God then gave them 1 Commandment (Law) to test their faithfulness to Him: *"Of the tree of the knowledge of good and evil, THOU SHALT NOT eat of it: for in the day that thou eatest thereof thou shalt surely DIE"* (Genesis 2:17). One Law was all God needed to prove mankind's belief and trust in Him—which is actually LOVE shown towards Him! See, God could RECEIVE pleasure (love) from His spirit children simply by providing them with a choice to obey or disobey Him. Do you see? If they obeyed Him, they loved Him!!! This is like the pleasure you receive when a love interest chooses you over someone else: If you were the only person on Earth there would be no choice, making that pleasure nonexistent! In other words, without a choice to disobey Him, mankind's souls would have been like boring robots. But once a choice existed, a choice was always being made to obey or to disobey—i.e. to love or to not love!

So who else was in the Garden of Eden? An angel, Lucifer! God declared: ***"Thou (Lucifer) hast been in Eden the garden of God;*** *every precious stone was thy covering…Thou art the anointed cherub that covereth; and I (God) have set thee so: thou wast upon the holy mountain of God…Thou wast perfect in thy ways from the day that thou was created, till iniquity was found in thee"* (Ezekiel 28:13-15). Thus, Lucifer (a created, angelic, ministering spirit) was in God's created Garden of Eden as a perfect, sinless being! God's words of summation closing out the 6th Creation day verify this: *"And God saw **EVERY THING** that he had made, and, behold, it was VERY GOOD. And the evening and the morning were the sixth day"* (Genesis 1:31). How could everything created be "very good" if rebellion had already occurred? Friend, listen, ALL God's Creation (Adam & Eve, the animals, the angels, etc) was getting along just fine after God's 6 days of Creation.

Oh, but then something terrible happened!!! "Iniquity" was found in Lucifer! The Hebrew word is *"āwel"* meaning: wrong, evil, sin, injustice, what is morally perverted, warped, and twisted. But when did this happen? Well, obviously, sometime after the initial 6 day Creation, and once the scattered Biblical passages relating to the incident are collected, it becomes apparent from the verbiage that the <u>fateful day Lucifer coerced Eve to eat the forbidden fruit from the tree of the knowledge of good & evil is the SAME day God first found iniquity in him</u>! In other words, yes, the two events happened simultaneously— mankind's "fall" and Lucifer's "fall"! Let us investigate.

First, what prompted Lucifer to sin? Friend, one word, "GREED"!!! Ezekiel writes about Lucifer: *"<u>every precious STONE was thy covering</u>, the sardius, topaz, and the diamond, the beryl, the onyx, and the jasper, the sapphire, the emerald, and the carbuncle, and gold...the day that thou was created...**<u>BY the MULTITUDE of thy MERCHANDISE</u>** <u>they have filled the midst of thee with violence, and</u> **<u>THOU HAST SINNED</u>**...<u>Thine heart was LIFTED UP because of thy beauty, thou hast corrupted thy wisdom by reason of thy brightness</u>"* (Ezekiel 28:13-17). Do you see? God had bestowed upon Lucifer an "abundance of materialism". And what happened? It puffed-up his heart and corrupted his mind with greed, which led him to sin!

In his prideful, arrogant state, what did Lucifer's greedy spirit now want? He wanted MORE materialism and power! He wanted complete control over God's beautiful creation. He wanted to call the shots. He wanted to be God! Isaiah writes about him: *"For thou hast said in thine heart (spirit), **I** <u>will ascend</u> into heaven, **I** <u>will exalt</u> my throne above the stars of God...**I** <u>will ascend</u> above the heights of the clouds; **<u>I will be like the most High</u>**"* (Isaiah 14:13, 14). Do you see what the "acquisition of materialism (atoms)" does to a spirit being's thoughts, desires, & emotions? It swells it with the "I" syndrome. What is that? Selfishness, my friend—which is pride! See, pride can only grow out of the soil of self-centeredness. And an "I-me-myself" attitude is the spiritual mindset in one's thoughts, desires, & emotions that produces sin. (Take notice of the middle "letter" in the words "pr-**I**-de" & "s-**I**-n".) When our thoughts are focused entirely on our self, our life, and our ambitions, we do not know God (love) and are headed for a disastrous fall!

The Holy Spirit of God will bluntly reveal later in the Bible that "greed" is the <u>root</u> of ALL sin by saying: *"the <u>LOVE OF MONEY is the</u>*

root of ALL evil" (I Timothy 6:10). See, mankind invented "money" as the means by which we can legally acquire physical atoms (materialism). That is all "money' can do! It cannot purchase spiritual things; it can only purchase physical things. Thus, ALL sin stems from the "love of money"—which is a fervent desire to obtain dirt (God's creation). THAT is the very root of selfishness, pride, and sin. See, if nothing existed to be selfish or prideful about, there would be no selfishness or pride. Do you understand? How very sad that "greed for dirt" will be the root cause of the sin (evil) in everyone who loses (forfeits eternal life) in God's Game of Life. And Lucifer, the 1st sinner, is the prime example of this stunning truth!

To attain a "God-like (controlling)" status, Lucifer realized he would have to persuade Adam & Eve's spirits to disobey God and obey him. Consequently, Lucifer's pride and greed manifested itself in the sin (iniquity) of a lie, which led to the sin (iniquity) of murder. He cajoled Eve to disobey God's 1 simple Commandment and eat the fruit from the forbidden tree of the knowledge of good & evil. Satan's plan worked! He became the God of this world (age): *"In whom the **god of this world** hath blinded the minds of them which believe (love) not" (II Corinthians 4:4)*. Oh, but he will pay an awful price for his victory at the close of 7,000 years! But before I talk about the consequence of that sinful day for Lucifer, let us take a more detailed look at what transpired in the Garden of Eden on the day of original sin.

Lucifer demonstrated his crafty wisdom towards Eve by cleverly twisting the truth into a lie: *"Now the serpent (Lucifer) was more subtil than any beast of the field...And he said unto the woman (Eve), Yea, hath God said, Ye shall NOT eat of EVERY tree of the garden? (Genesis 3:1)*. Do you perceive the slyness of this lie? God did not tell Adam & Eve they could NOT eat from EVERY tree...He said only 1 tree! I can almost see Eve's pretty head turn sideways as she contemplated. It was the first time she ever heard a lying question!

At first, Eve did well in deciphering Lucifer's lying play on words, because she remembered God's words (law) of truth: *"And the woman said unto the serpent, We may eat of the fruit of the trees of the garden: But of the fruit of the tree which is in the midst of the garden, God hath said, Ye shall not eat of it, neither shall ye touch it, lest ye die*

(Genesis 3:2, 3). See, she KNEW God's Word (Law)! Oh, if only she would have trusted and obeyed it no matter what anyone else told her. But next, Lucifer went straight for the jugular with an outright lie: *"And the serpent (Lucifer) said unto the woman, **Ye shall NOT surely die**: For God doth know that in the day ye eat thereof, then your eyes shall be opened, and ye shall be as gods, knowing good and evil" (Genesis 3:4, 5)*. How pathetic! Lucifer always has some other reason to convince mankind that God is the one lying. **He is still doing this today**!!!

This time Eve bit: *"And when the woman saw that the tree was good for food, and that it was pleasant to the eyes, and a tree to be desired to make one wise, she took of the fruit thereof, and did eat, and gave also unto her husband with her; and he did eat" (Genesis 3:6)*. That was it! The deed was done! Mankind DISOBEYED God's 1 Law, sinning against Him, and death ensued instantly. I will explain EXACTLY what died very shortly. But before you scoff at this anecdote of a serpent talking to a woman, I want to give you something to ponder on how the scene may have gone down.

The Bible says angels were created to be "ministering spirits", right? Well, how do you suppose they do that? Do you think angels stroke our hair and rub our shoulders to attend to us? Maybe they do, but I sure do not feel it. No, my friend, angels TALK to us! Remember, angels are made of the same invisible "spirit material" that makes up our spirit. Therefore, having like material, they can communicate with us because "spirit material" contains thoughts, desires, & emotions. Do you understand? Make no mistake about it, angels were created to talk to us; thus, some of the thoughts in our spirit are from them! Most people are dreadfully naive of this significant truth, but I urge you to be aware of the voices (thoughts) in your head (spirit).

At times we even vocalize thoughts and ideas in our spirit that came from angels! Jesus recognized Lucifer's angelic voice speaking through his Disciple, Peter: *"And he (Jesus) began to teach them, that the Son of man must...be killed, and after three days rise again...And Peter took him, and began to rebuke him. But when he (Jesus) had turned about...he rebuked Peter, saying, **Get thee behind me, Satan**: for thou savourest not the things that be of God, but the things that be of men" (Mark 8:31-33)*. See, Jesus knew it was Satan who had put

55

these thoughts in Peter's head. I know it is hard to conceive, but good angels and fallen angels speak to every one of us from time to time. Sometimes they speak directly to us in our own mind (spirit) and other times they talk to us through other people's mouths (spirits)!

I will share a dramatic personal story with you proving our thoughts are not always our own. I moved from Pennsylvania to Tennessee in the fall of 1996. During the summer of 2005, I decided to drive home and visit my folks over the Thanksgiving holiday. (Remember my dad's profile appeared on May 6th of that year? Well, I was excited to let my mom and brother see it! In fact, that fall I spent $500 dollars making 2 beautifully framed copies for them and those 2 pictures traveled as cargo with me.) But the moment I made the decision to go home, an overwhelming feeling of dread hit my gut that something terrible would occur during the 735 mile drive. It was just thoughts in my spirit, but it was like they originated from somewhere else! Now I had made the journey many times over the course of 9 years, but NEVER once had I had a premonition like this. In fact, whenever I would think about the trip I would get the same sick feelings.

Finally, the morning of November 19 arrived and I awoke to a blaze of anxiety, but I had taken the vacation time off from work months earlier, so I was going regardless! The laborious trip is a monotonous, mostly highway drive that takes about 12 hours to complete. I started off and soon forgot my trepidation. Four hours later, while driving past Bristol on Interstate 81, I was delighted to encounter snow falling. (I do not get to see much snow living in Nashville.) Then, all of a sudden, a massive wave of fear hit me like a dagger to the heart, and I shrieked, "You can't stop me Devil!" My own bloodcurdling yell startled me, and I wondered why I had reacted like that. But I soon forgot the "event" as the snow subsided and I settled in for the boring 324 mile crossing through the state of Virginia. (I did not realize the "snowy-incident" was a warning of the imminent future!)

When I reached Pennsylvania it was nighttime. Drifting mentally, I missed my exit off the PA Turnpike and had to exit onto an unfamiliar country road. I did not care, though, because I was close to home and excited to see momma. (Thoughts of danger were now completely gone from my mind.) The road I was traveling on was very

56

dark and unimaginably curvy and hilly. Then a dense snow started falling, and I was amazed at how fast the conditions turned treacherous! As the thick snow quickly covered the road, I struggled to see the edge of it in the blackness, going up and down and this way and that. It was so dark I could make out nothing I was passing! It was like driving in complete blackness, except for my headlights illuminating the blinding white, falling snow. My senses jacked like the hair on a spooked alley cat, and I took a death grip on the steering wheel while slowing to around 40 miles an hour. (Thinking back now, I am astonished that in that bad situation NO thoughts arose in my spirit concerning the months of alarm I had had over the trip!)

What happened next, however, my soul will never forget, even though it played out in just a few, dramatic seconds. All of a sudden, out of seemingly nowhere, headlights appeared behind me, and it took only seconds to realize they were gaining fast! I thought, "In these conditions... they must be crazy!" Then, <u>instantly</u>, I heard a resounding voice in my spirit urge, "Just pull over, stop your car, and let the lights behind you go past!" (Now that is a notion I would NEVER have normally had, but the voice was so overbearing that I <u>immediately</u> obeyed.) I hit the brakes and stopped my car!!! (Reaffirming chapter 2, notice what actually took place...thoughts in my spirit moved the atoms in my foot to depress the brake pedal.) And there I sat, stopped and stunned at my decision to stop. Then my distracted eyes bloomed large as they left the lights in my rearview mirror to make out the moving shape of the shadowy object standing on the road in front of me. For about 20 feet ahead, camouflaged in the dense snow, was a massive buck lunging wildly at the open air. After about 5 great confused heaves, he turned and vanished into the blackness.

I burst into uncontrollable tears as the sudden realization of what just happened, hit me! The Bible says it best: *"God is our refuge and strength, <u>a very present help in trouble</u>" (Psalms 46:1).* And: *"For <u>**he (God) shall give his angels charge over thee, to keep thee in all thy ways**</u>. They shall bear thee up in their hands, lest thou dash thy foot against a stone" (Psalms 91:11, 12).* I finally realized an angel had been warning me about this day for months. I might have died if I had collided with that deer that night, because I was traveling, unbuckled, in a small, rusty, low-to-the-ground 1984 Honda Accord. Without a doubt, the huge buck would have rolled up over my hood and landed God knows where. I know God's angel(s) saved my life that night, and I look forward to the day I can hug his/her neck in thanks. Yes, truly, angelic spirits <u>minister</u> (talk) to us in our spirits!

But angelic <u>spirits</u> can do more than just communicate with us; they can <u>INHABIT</u> physical dirt bodies as well—human or animal! Jesus often confronted people with fallen angels (demons) inside them: *"And when he (Jesus) was come to the other side... there met him two* ***POSSESSED with devils****...And, behold, <u>they cried out, saying, What have we to do with thee, Jesus, thou Son of God? Art thou come hither to torment us BEFORE the TIME?</u>...So the devils besought him, saying, If thou cast us out, suffer us to go away into the herd of swine. And he said unto them, Go. **And when they were come out, they went INTO the herd of swine**: and, behold, the whole herd of swine ran <u>violently</u> down a steep place into the sea, and perished in the waters"* (Matthew 8:28-32). I have no idea how extra "spirit material" can fit inside of a body's physical pile of atoms, but it can! In fact, <u>multiple</u> fallen angels can take up residence inside a physical body, continuously influencing thoughts, desires, & emotions. (It is very possible a demon spirit(s) entered the erratic behaving deer in my encounter above, intending to kill me! If it/they would have been successful in AD 2005, you would not be reading this book.)

Equipped with an understanding of how angels "minister" to us, allow me to now present you with a plausible scenario for how the interaction between Lucifer and Eve may have developed in the Garden of Eden. I am NOT saying this is <u>definitely</u> how it happened, but just consider the possibility. Maybe Lucifer's angelic spirit inhabited a "snakelike" looking creature, guided it up into the tree of the knowledge of good & evil, and led it to begin eating some of its fruit. (God did not say the animals could not eat the fruit from the forbidden tree!) Then, Eve comes along, looks up into the tree, and beholds the creature eating the tree's fruit. Next, <u>thoughts</u> start to invade her mind (spirit) because of the situation she is beholding, but the thoughts are actually coming from Lucifer, who has created the entire "set-up"!

Listen to Eve's thoughts, "A creature is eating the fruit from the forbidden tree and is not dying. It even seems to be enjoying the fruit, so it must be good to eat. Did not God say this tree was for the <u>knowledge</u> of good & evil? Hmmm, I bet it would make us wise. I would probably be as smart as God! Well, I am convinced I will not die, because the creature is still moving, so I am going to eat some of the tree's fruit." Eve then grabs a piece of fruit and disobeys God by taking a bite.

Wow, did you comprehend that? The serpent-like creature (Satan) might have been just talking in Eve's mind (spirit) the same way angelic voices still talk to us today! Friend, nothing has changed; angels are just doing what they were created to do. So perhaps the serpent in the Garden of Eden was merely a creature Lucifer inhabited to use as the instrument he needed to do his "dirty" work, inundating Eve's spirit with deceiving thoughts that eventually led her to disobey God. I do not know for sure if this is how it all went down, but it is a possibility.

Alright, so <u>what</u> <u>DIED</u> the <u>DAY</u> Adam & Eve sinned? Remember, God said: *"But of <u>the tree of the knowledge of good and evil</u>, thou shalt NOT eat of it: for **<u>in the DAY that thou eatest therof thou shalt surely DIE</u>**" (Genesis 2:17)*. Well Adam & Eve both ate the forbidden fruit, but did they die <u>THAT</u> day? The Bible says Adam & Eve went on to have children, and Adam lived to be 930 years old: *"And all the days that Adam lived were <u>nine hundred and thirty years</u>: and he died" (Genesis 5:5)*. So what is up? Did God lie? Not a chance! The answer to this seeming contradiction lies in a <u>correct</u> understanding of what constitutes TRUE death: Friend, <u>the only real death is SPIRITUAL death</u>!!! What is that you ask? It is when a spirit (soul) is <u>separated</u> from God's Spirit of <u>Life</u>. THAT is the death Adam & Eve experienced the <u>MOMENT</u> they ate the fruit from the forbidden tree!

Remember what we learned in the last chapter? Physical death on this Earth is nothing but a release of our spirit to another location. It is merely a "shedding" of our physical dirt body. That is NOT true death!!! When Adam "died" physically 930 years later, his spirit (soul) simply went to another place. Oh, <u>but it was still SEPARATED from God's Spirit of Life</u>; thus, he REMAINED spiritually dead! See, Adam & Eve's souls were already dead while they were "living" on planet Earth: It was like unscrewing 2 light bulbs from a fixture with electricity flowing through it; the light went OUT! Oh sure, the light bulbs still exist, but they are separated from their "life-source" and therefore dead. In the analogy, the electricity is God's "life-giving Spirit" and the 2 light bulbs represent Adam & Eve's souls. Do you understand? Sin (disobedience) disconnected their souls from God's Spirit of Life and it was "lights-out" (or spiritual death). Sure, Adam & Eve's souls (spirits) still existed, but they were disconnected from God's eternal life-giving Spirit. Remember God is the source of all life; consequently, to be spiritually separated from Him is to be truly dead, and sin INSTANTLY separated Adam & Eve's spirits from God's Spirit!

This instantaneous spiritual separation (death) was conveyed dramatically in the Bible story by God immediately driving Adam & Eve out of the Garden of Eden, where the "tree of life" stood: *"So he (God) **DROVE out the man**; and he placed at the east of the garden of Eden Cherubims, and a flaming sword which turned every way, to keep the WAY of the tree of life"* (Genesis 3:24). See, the "tree of life" represents God's life-giving Spirit, and the WAY to Him was now barricaded!!! There could not have been a sadder day in the history of mankind. Sure, mankind still existed, but spiritually they were like walking dead people, with no way to repair the divide between them and God.

The spiritual death that took place TO Adam & Eve's souls was further confirmed by the language now used to describe Adam & Eve's new spiritual (thoughts, desires, & emotions) condition. God told Eve: *"I will greatly multiply thy **SORROW** and thy conception in **SORROW** thou shalt bring forth children; and thy desire shall be to thy husband, and he shall rule over thee"* (Genesis 3:16). Unto Adam he said: *"Because thou hast hearkened unto the voice of thy wife…CURSED is the ground for thy sake; in **SORROW** shalt thou eat of it all the days of thy life; THORNS also and thistles shall it bring forth to thee…In the SWEAT of thy face shalt thou eat bread"* (Genesis 3:17-19). The language oozes of an existence spiritually separated from God! The word "sorrow" is translated from the Hebrew words "*iṣṣābôn*" meaning: pain, hardship, distress; and "*eṣeb*" meaning: pain, toil, hard work. See, after transgressing, mankind's world became one of pain, sorrow, and hard work. Life on Earth became a restless struggle. These were/are the symptoms of spiritual death!

60

Notice, too, the ground was now cursed? Remember, it is the ground's atoms that become the food we eat that forms the physical body our soul resides in. Subsequently, all bodily sickness, disease, and abnormalities have their root cause in this cursed dirt! And what does dis-ease equal—e.g. arthritis, cancer, etc? PAIN!!! Friend, illnesses are a permanent reminder of Adam & Eve's sin and the subsequent spiritual separation (death) that took place. Notice, also, God created a physical, seeable reminder of sin's consequence for mankind. What was it? It was THORNS and THISTLES!!! Grab a thorn and what happens? You feel PAIN and agony. (Keep these God-given symbols of sin's resulting **SORROW** tucked away in your memory, for God will use them to communicate to mankind later in the Bible!)

The Bible hints at what it is like to be in perfect spiritual union with God: *"In thy (God's) presence is fullness of joy; at thy right hand there are pleasures for evermore" (Psalms 16:11).* Is this what we find for Adam & Eve now? No!!! That close divine presence of God's glorious Spirit was gone. After sinning, listen to what Adam's first emotion was when he heard God's voice calling him in the Garden: *"I was afraid" (Genesis 3:10).* Wow, it was fear!!! But we already learned God is LOVE, and the Bible says to be wholly, spiritually connected to "Love" is like the following: *"God is love...**There is NO fear in love; but perfect love casteth out fear**: because fear hath torment" (I John 4:16, 18).* Do you see? Thus, Adam's spiritual emotion of "fear" solidified the spiritual separation (death) that occurred.

God further explained the spiritual separation (or loss of closeness to God's Spirit of Life) by recording Adam & Eve found themselves NAKED: *"And the eyes of them both were opened, and they KNEW that they were naked" (Genesis 3:7).* While this, no doubt, was a physical, seeable "thing" (or reality), it actually symbolized the "spiritual nakedness" Adam & Eve's spirits were now experiencing. Do you see? It was as if God's presence (or glory) came off of them. (But stay tuned, for God will use this "nakedness-situation" to immediately do something for Adam & Eve that actually set up the "system" or "process" by which He would be able to SECRETLY prophesy about the coming Messiah's redemptive work! I will cover all this in detail in the *"Isaac"* chapter)

61

Even God's first Biblically recorded question to Adam, after his sin, substantiated the spiritual separation: *"And the LORD God called unto Adam, and said unto him, __Where art thou__?" (Genesis 3:9).* What a spot-on question authenticating the "loss of closeness" (or death) that had occurred between God's Spirit and Adam & Eve's spirits! I can almost hear God's concerned voice echoing throughout the Garden of Eden like a loving Shepard's steady voice hollering for the helpless lamb that has gone astray. Yes, truly, Adam & Eve spiritually DIED the instant they disobeyed God and ate the forbidden fruit!

But here now is the awful truth; the spiritual death Adam & Eve experienced was automatically passed on to every future born human being's soul, because sin (disobedience) had now become a part of mankind's spirit. This was/is known Biblically as the 1st DEATH. I do not claim to understand how a baby's spirit growing inside a mother's womb carries this spiritual separation (death), but the Bible confirms it does: *"Wherefore, __as by one man (Adam) sin entered into the world, and death (spiritual separation from God) by sin__; and __so death (spiritual separation from God) passed upon all men, for that ALL have sinned__" (Romans 5:12).* In other words, EVERY human soul born on Earth—except Jesus Christ's—has taken part in the 1st Death! (Incidentally, once something is dead, for it to have life again, it needs to be "__reborn__" or "*__born again__*"! Ah, that jolted your noggin, huh? I will disclose more about this in the "*Abraham*" chapter.)

Ok…in the first paragraph of this chapter, I said understanding precisely what happened TO Adam & Eve's spirits (souls) is the key to understanding the ancient Bible stories because it set up a particular "theme" God employed over and over again in them. Do you remember? Well, here is that spiritual theme: "**BONDAGE**"!!! Look, when someone is unwillingly separated from someone else, they are considered in bondage. It is like being kidnapped or imprisoned: The person kidnapped or imprisoned is forcefully separated from who and what they love. THAT is bondage! And what separated Adam & Eve's spirits—and thus, ALL mankind's spirits—from God's Spirit? It was SIN!!! **Thus, God now viewed mankind's souls as being in BONDAGE to sin and its resulting death**.

Another way the Bible describes this "bondage" is by declaring mankind's souls were now "UNDER the Law of sin & death". Remember God's 1 Law was to not eat the forbidden fruit or death would be the consequence? Well, Adam & Eve disobeyed the Law and death ensued; therefore, their souls—and ALL mankind's souls—were now deemed UNDER the death penalty of the Law of sin. Do you understand? It is no different than being convicted of 1st degree murder in a town with a Law in their books stating for that charge the death sentence will be enforced. While you are sitting on death row, you are UNDER the penalty of the Law. Or simply put; you are under the law!

Envision mankind's spiritually separated (dead) condition as being like their souls were now locked away inside a barred cell, apart from God. They were captured, bound up, imprisoned, and enslaved by Satan who persuaded them to sin against God. They were under God's Law! They were dead—spiritually separated from God—with no hope of ever getting out of the "bondage predicament" on their own because sin's death curse was continually passed on to every soul. What an impossible, helpless situation it was for mankind's souls! If God did not have a plan to intervene personally, mankind would be spiritually separated from God forever; thus, eternally DEAD.

Oh, but glory to God, He had conceived a plan which would unlock the cell door and free mankind's souls out from under the death penalty of the Law!!! In other words, God had devised a plan of deliverance, redemption, or salvation—use whichever word you like!— for mankind's souls, opening a WAY back to Him. And amazingly, God had concocted the plan even before the foundation of the world for He knew sin would arise in His spirit children. It was ALL part of the "setup" of His Game of Life! But the wonderful "salvation plan" was to remain a colossal secret for 4,000 years, even though God slowly— albeit, unknowingly to mankind—began unveiling the details of His plan by controlling the "events" in ancient Bible stories!!! (I will reveal more about this and why God did this in coming chapters.)

But for now, in the Garden of Eden God immediately hinted at the "plan of redemption" to Adam & Eve—and thus, to all mankind— garnering HOPE in them for a future day of reconciliation with Him! While talking to the serpent, God made an obscure promise: "*And I will put enmity between thee (serpent) and the woman (Eve), and between thy seed and her seed, IT shall BRUISE thy head, and thou shalt BRUISE His heel" (Genesis 3:15).* This ambiguous prophesy was promising a future <u>MAN</u> child—*"born of the seed of a woman"*—who would crush Lucifer's head, taking back the power of spiritual death he held over mankind's souls, effectively freeing them from their bondage. In other words, God was foretelling of a Messiah—a Savior, a Redeemer, or a Deliverer—that would one day bruise the serpent's head, while the Devil struck **his** heel. Though Adam & Eve did not know it, this was to be Jesus Christ!

The Apostle Paul later wrote about how God will ultimately fulfill the Garden of Eden promise through Christ: *"And the **God of peace shall BRUISE Satan** under your feet" (Romans 16:20).* Notice the same language? But before that happened, Satan would have to bruise Christ first: *"**he (Jesus) was BRUISED for our iniquities (sin)**" (Isaiah 53:5).* See the fulfillment? Confirming Jesus came to free mankind's souls out from under the Law of sin, Paul penned: *"But when the fullness of the time was come, God sent forth his Son, made of a woman...To REDEEM them that were UNDER the LAW" (Galatians 4:4, 5).*

Paul further wrote about the Messiah's work: *"For there is one God, and one mediator between God and men, the MAN Christ Jesus; Who gave himself a RANSOM for all" (I Timothy 2:5, 6).* Notice how this verse confirms the "<u>bondage</u> scenario" mankind's souls were in? The word "ransom" is from the Greek word "*antilytron*" meaning: <u>ransom, the purchase price to bring liberation from oppression; the means to redemption</u>. See, you cannot have a "ransom" unless someone or something is bound. And Christ's death was to be the ransom price!

Allow me to now briefly introduce you to God's plan of salvation (redemption or deliverance) for mankind's souls. Here is what it would require: <u>God</u> would <u>PERSONALLY</u> have to birth another man on Earth—"a 2nd Adam"—born of <u>His</u> (Holy Spirit) seed and a woman's seed, in order that this child's pure spirit would NOT carry sin's death curse. This child would then have to grow and live on Earth, being tempted in everyway by Satan to do evil (sin), yet NEVER SIN!!! Please understand the Biblical truth: <u>only SIN causes death (spiritual separation from God): "For the wages of sin is death"</u> (Romans 6:23).

64

Therefore, this sinless man's soul would have NEVER died, spiritually! Yet, he would CHOOSE to die—separate himself from God's Spirit—because God wanted him to for mankind's sake. In so doing, he would die in mankind's place, pay their death sentence, and free them from their bondage to the Law of sin & death, effectively opening a WAY for their souls to return to God! In other words, through this man's death mankind could escape the death consequence of their sins—which is to say mankind could be **FORGIVEN of SIN**!!! Do you understand? This man was to be Christ Jesus, and his sinless death was a worthy ransom price to pay for ALL mankind's sins: *"Yes, because of God's great kindness, **Jesus tasted death for EVERYONE in ALL the world**" (Hebrews 2:9, Living Bible).*

Therefore, God's Garden of Eden promise to Adam & Eve gave ALL mankind reason to hope for a coming day of Godly deliverance from their spiritually separated (dead) condition. And undoubtedly, the promise was passed down to ALL mankind. Think about it; Adam lived to be 930 years old, so for all those years mankind could just ask him about IT firsthand. (That is almost the entire 1ˢᵗ millennial day of God's complete 7 millennial day plan!) Subsequently, as Adam & Eve had children and there children had children and mankind populated Earth, they ALL knew the SORROW (suffering, pain, and work) would one day end. They knew someday they COULD receive spiritual LIFE again by being reunited with God's Spirit of Life! They did not know the details of God's plan of deliverance, but they knew they could trust His Word of Promise.

Which brings us now to the most important question any soul living on Earth at anytime could ever ask: **What** must **I DO** to be reunited with God's Spirit and obtain eternal LIFE? In other words, what must I myself **DO** to have the forgiveness Christ would/did provide applied to my sins? Is there anything? Or can/could mankind DO whatever they want/like during their time on Earth and still obtain eternal life? I think you know the answer to that question is NO!!! So what is it? Is there some magic words we need to utter? Is there some contract we need to sign? Is there something we need to learn? Do we need to frequent a certain building once a week? Please, please—I am as serious as a heart attack!—just tell me plainly and honestly what **I**

65

must **DO** to obtain eternal life. I do not care how hard or easy it might be, just do NOT lie to me about something as gravely important as my ETERNAL destiny!!! Friend, if that is your heart, you have come to the right place, for in this book I am about to turn on a 50 thousand megawatt light bulb, illuminating the TRUTH.

Remember, now, for the first 4,000 years of mankind they will know NOTHING about the MAN Jesus who will come to Earth and die on a cross! So learning or knowing that story must have NOTHING to do with what **WE** must DO to obtain eternal life!!! Do you see? For what kind of a loving God would secretly hide the very information His spirit children needed to hear, learn, and know to make it back to Him? That would be sick!!! That would make God a hideous monster! Friend, God would NEVER do that to His spirit children! So WHAT is the TRUTH! What did/does mankind have to DO to obtain eternal life? The answer lies in a most overlooked, under-preached, and miscomprehended portion of Scripture. And yet, it is glaringly obvious! The answer is contained in the story of Adam & Eve and the NAME of the forbidden tree. Do you remember what it was called? It was the tree of the **KNOWLEDGE** of GOOD & EVIL!!!

Listen to God's pronouncement concerning the change IN Adam & Eve's spirits after they ate the fruit from the forbidden tree: *"Behold, the man is become as one of us, to KNOW good and evil"* *(Genesis 3:22)*. What do you think that meant? What EXACTLY did Adam & Eve learn? In other words, what precisely was put INSIDE their spirits (thoughts, desires, & emotions) the moment they sinned? Well, what is the difference between good & evil? I know you know! Name something EVIL: How about lying, murder, stealing, idolatry, covetousness, blaspheming God's name, etc.? Yes, yes, yes!!! Name something GOOD: How about not lying and telling the truth, not murdering but forgiving those who wrong you, not blaspheming but glorifying God's name? And on and on I could go. But what are these things? **THEY ARE THE 10 COMMANDMENTS!!!**

That is right my friend; the moment Adam & Eve sinned (disobeyed God's 1 Law) by eating the fruit from the forbidden tree of the KNOWLEDGE of good & evil, they instantly knew God's 10 Commandment Law—for obeying or disobeying them is the difference

66

between good & evil, respectively. There are NO other "items" that distinguish good & evil! So to "DO evil" by disobeying any of the 10 Commandment Law was/is now mankind's definition of "sin": *"Whosoever committeth sin transgresseth also the law: for **SIN is the transgression of the law**" (I John 3:4)*. Do you see? Thus, EVERY soul that has EVER lived on planet Earth has had a choice to "DO good" or to "DO evil (sin)", meaning obey or disobey God's 10 Commandments!!!

The Bible absolutely proves ALL mankind has known the 10 Commandments by cleverly incorporating each of them into ancient Bible stories that occurred LONG before Moses—who received the written 10 Commandments during mankind's 2,638th year—was every born! As we traverse the ancient Bible stories in this book, I will point out many of these "sin encounters" to authenticate this TRUTH. Incidentally, we can confirm the 9th Commandment, *"Thou shalt not lie"*, right now! After listening to the serpent and eating the forbidden fruit and then experiencing horrendous spiritual death and banishment from the Garden of Eden, do you think Adam & Eve now understood what a lie was? Lucifer said they would not die, but they did!!! You are greatly deceived if you do not believe from this incident that ALL mankind knew exactly what a lie was and that it was EVIL!

Digressing slightly, for those of you still wrestling with the idea that maybe God does not exist and the Bible is just a silly book written by men…then who invented the **10** Commandments in it? Why did they not pick 5, or 8, or 11, or some other number? Friend, I will teach you something incredible God showed me. How many fingers do you have? And toes? 10 of each, right? Do you think mindless macroevolution over millions of years turned rock into a human being with 10 fingers and 10 toes? No, my friend THAT is a FAIRY tale! Rather, God created the physical, dirt bodies that would house the souls of His spirit children to contain **10** appendages on their extremities because He knew the difference between good & evil was completely divided into and encompassed by **10** Commandments!!!

Are you stunned? You should be! Look, God could have created our physical bodies to have any number of fingers and toes, but He chose 10 because He wanted mankind to have a PERMANENT bodily

67

reminder of the law of good & evil. In other words, the laws of good & evil are mimicked on our hands and feet. (Keep this amazing revelation in the back of your mind, because it will be the reason behind the method of physical death God allows mankind to invent to kill His Son, our blessed Savior Jesus Christ, in order to communicate a message to mankind. I will reveal this point in the *"Moses"* chapter.) And what does mankind use to physically DO the works of good or evil? Their HANDS & FEET!!! Maybe now you can fully appreciate the proverb: *"My son... lay up my (10) commandments with thee. Keep my commandments, and LIVE; and my law as the apple of thine eye. **Bind them upon thy (10) FINGERS**" (Proverbs 7:1-3).* If on Earth you have been blessed to have a Bible in your possession, it is an embarrassment if you cannot look at your fingers and list off God's 10 Commandments!

In the *"love"* chapter of this book I am going to positively, Biblically prove to you "OBEYING the 10 Commandments" is literally the WORKS (or deeds) of Love! Consequently, I have renamed the 10 Commandments the "**10 Love Commandments**". And to embed this truth into your spirit, throughout this book I will refer to them as such. Therefore, GOOD = LOVE and EVIL (sin) = NOT LOVE. This is the $E = mc^2$ equation of the Bible—i.e. it is the simple equation that ties all the Biblical concepts together, making the Bible extremely simple to understand. Always remember, God = love = good, and Satan = not love = evil. Consequently, to willingly choose to "DO good" by obeying the 10 Love Commandments is to know God, which is to know love. But to willingly choose to "DO evil (sin)" by disobeying the 10 Love Commandments is to serve Satan, which is to NOT know love (God).

Alright, so back to the question of what did Adam & Eve's souls—and subsequently all mankind's souls—have to DO to obtain eternal life? Friend, ALL they had to DO is willingly choose to live their lives by the way of good (love) over the way of evil (sin), as outlined by obedience to the 10 Love Commandments. Thus, every person born on planet Earth has had an equal chance at receiving forgiveness for their sins and obtaining eternal life, no matter how remote their location or if they ever heard about God, the Bible, or Jesus. See, the WAY back to God was/is written IN their hearts! If they chose love (good), they chose to serve God and will obtain eternal life. But if they chose sin

68

(evil), they chose to serve Satan and will utterly perish. Paul wrote: *"**He (God) will punish sin wherever it is found**. He will punish the heathen when they sin, even though they never had God's <u>written</u> laws (The Bible), **for down in their hearts they know right from wrong. God's laws are written WITHIN them**; their own conscience accuses them...And God will punish the Jews for sinning because they have his written laws (The Bible) but don't obey them. They know what is right but don't do it. **After all, salvation is NOT given to those who KNOW what to do, UNLESS THEY DO IT.** The day will surely come when at God's command Jesus Christ will judge the secret lives of EVERYONE, their inmost thoughts and motives; <u>this is all part of God's great PLAN which I proclaim</u>" (Romans 2:12-16, Living Bible).* Friend, make no mistake about it...the Apostle Paul knew the truth!!!

Here is truth: The <u>same</u> thing Adam & Eve had to <u>DO</u> to obtain eternal life is the <u>same</u> thing **YOU** & **I** need to <u>DO</u> to obtain eternal life! Did they know the story of Jesus? Nope!!! Do you need to know the story of Jesus to obtain eternal life? Nope, not at all! Is it ultimately going to be because of the man Jesus' redemptive work at the cross that allows ANY of us to make it back to God? Absolutely, 100% YES!!! That is the story of <u>HOW</u> God made "forgiveness for our sins" possible. <u>And we have ALL sinned at least once</u>; thus, we ALL need Christ's work of atonement applied to our sins to return to God. **But THAT is a TRUTH whether we know it or not**!!! Do you understand? What **WE** (as spirit children of God) MUST <u>DO</u> to receive that forgiveness is willingly choose to forsake evil and follow God's way of love, as outlined by obeying the 10 Love Commandments. THAT has <u>ALWAYS</u> been and still remains mankind's duty or part in obtaining eternal life! In other words, even from the very beginning <u>ALL</u> mankind has possessed the knowledge of what they "NEEDED TO DO" to obtain eternal life. How about praising God for his fairness to ALL mankind!

The Bible has a special word encapsulating "<u>what mankind must DO</u>" to obtain eternal life: **R-E-P-E-N-T**!!! Jesus preached: *"EXCEPT ye REPENT, ye shall ALL likewise perish" (Luke 13:3).* This is probably the most misunderstood word in the Bible. It is translated from the Greek word "*metanoeō*" meaning: <u>to repent, TO CHANGE any or all of the elements composing one's life: attitude, thoughts, and</u>

behaviors concerning the demands of God for right living. And what is "right living"? Friend, it is "obeying the 10 Love Commandments"!!! Do you see? "To repent" means to CHANGE from doing evil to doing good! "Repentance" is NOT just saying you are sorry for your past sins and it is NOT a 1 time decision. "Repentance" is PROOVING you are sorry for your past sins by stopping doing them and willingly choosing to follow God's WAY of love via obedience to the 10 Love Commandments—which is a continual, daily choice!!! That is the ONLY Biblical PATH that leads to eternal life! See, repentance takes place in our heart. The only chance we have of obtaining eternal life for our soul is to "**repent** of sin (evil)" while our soul still resides in our physical body down here on Earth and then continue living that way till the day we physically "die" or Christ returns.

Listen to what John the Baptist was preaching on the banks of the Jordan River: *"the word of God came unto John…And he came into all the country about Jordan, preaching **the baptism of repentance FOR the remission of sins**" (Luke 3:3)*. Do you see? "Willful cessation of sin" is what we MUST DO **FOR** forgiveness of our sins!!! The word "remission" is from the Greek word *"aphesis"* meaning: forgiveness, pardon, release, cancellation of a debt. See, John knew exactly what people needed to DO to receive the forgiveness Christ would soon provide. In fact, in Luke chapter 3, Luke records some of the specific things John the Baptist was telling people to DO to PROVE they had repented of sin. I encourage you to read the chapter right now. But I will deal with the "things" he was saying to DO later, proving they are all "10 Love Commandment things". I have much more to say about "REPENTANCE", and I will absolutely prove to you that IT is the path that leads to eternal life by explaining the hidden meaning and purpose behind God's creation of the Israelite "bondage-to-Promise Land" story. (This will ALL be carefully explained in the *"Moses"* and *"Wilderness"* chapters.)

Going back to chapter 1 *"God's Master Time Plan,"* can you NOW see the incredible fulfillment of God's 1ˢᵗ Creation day's prophetic words during mankind's 1st millennial day of history? Listen to it again: *"In the beginning God created the heaven and the earth…and darkness was upon the face of the deep…And God said, Let there be light…**And***

70

*God saw the light, that it was **GOOD**: and God **DIVIDED** the light from the darkness*. And *God called the light Day, and the darkness he called Night*. And the evening and the morning were the FIRST day" *(Genesis 1:1-5)*. Do you understand? Again, these words foretold during mankind's 1st millennial day (first 1,000 years) of history, light & dark would become divided or discernible in their hearts. In other words, mankind would KNOW the difference between good (light) & evil (dark). Is that not awesome?

As the Holy Spirit continued to write the Bible, over and over again it confirmed these comparisons: good = God = light = day; and evil = Satan = darkness = night. Listen to Paul writing to the believers: "But ye, brethren, are not in darkness, that that day should overtake you as a thief. *Ye are all the children of the LIGHT, and the children of the DAY: we are not of the NIGHT, nor of DARKNESS*" *(I Thessalonians 5:4, 5)*. John penned: "***God is light**, and in him is no darkness at all*" *(I John 1:5)*. Jesus declared: "And *this is the condemnation, that **light is come into the world, and men loved darkness rather than light, because their deeds were evil. For every one that DOETH evil hateth the light**, neither cometh to the light, lest his DEEDS should be reproved*" *(John 3:19, 20)*. Could it be any clearer?

When God's light blinded Saul (Paul) on the road to Damascus, do you remember what He commissioned Paul to go into the world and encourage people to DO? Jesus told him: "*To open their eyes, and **to TURN them from DARKNESS to LIGHT, and from the power of SATAN unto GOD, that they MAY receive forgiveness of sins**" (Acts 26:18)*. In other words, Jesus instructed Paul to persuade people to TURN from "doing evil (darkness)" to "doing good (light)"—meaning stop disobeying and start obeying God's 10 Love Commandments. God told Paul to tell the people if they would live this repentant lifestyle, He would forgive their sins and give them inheritance in the Kingdom of God, the place of eternal life. Now THAT is what Paul was traveling everywhere and teaching mankind to DO!

Let us now return to that fateful day of original sin in the Garden of Eden and look first at the Biblical passages confirming Lucifer's fall from grace occurred THAT day and then at God's judgment on him: "*And the LORD God said unto the SERPENT, Because thou hast*

71

done this, _thou art cursed_ above all cattle, and above every beast of the field; _upon thy belly shalt thou go_, and dust shalt thou eat all the days of thy life" (Genesis 3:14). We know that God is talking here to the angel Lucifer, because later John ties all the names of him together in the book of Revelation: "And the great _dragon_ was cast out, **_that old serpent, called the Devil, and Satan,_** which deceiveth the whole world: _he was cast out into the earth, and his angels were cast out with him_" (Revelation 12:9). Apparently a large number of angels were initially under Lucifer's control or else he persuaded a large group of them to join him in his act of rebellion against God. Either way, God cursed them all, and they became known as "fallen angels" or "demons".

Do you detect how God's cursing of the SERPENT to crawl on his belly in the dirt symbolically resembles how Lucifer was "_cast out into the Earth_"? Compare God's words to the serpent in Genesis with Isaiah's words regarding Satan's fall: "How art thou _fallen from heaven_, O LUCIFER, son of the morning! How art thou **_CUT DOWN TO THE GROUND_**" (Isaiah 14:12). Do you see the similar language? This is what propels me to believe the "fall" of Lucifer and his angels from heaven (lofty-to-low position) occurred the very day he lied to Eve in the Garden of Eden. And since Jesus has always existed, he watched Lucifer fall from grace that fateful day and talked about it during his Earthly ministry: "I beheld Satan as lightning fall from heaven" (Luke 10:18). Yes, it truly appears Lucifer's "spiritual fall" occurred in the Garden of Eden after he left greed goad him to lie!

Now, remember I told you God has given mankind certain physical, seeable "things" to represent invisible, spiritual "things"— like thorns representing the sorrow (pain) of sin's consequence or 10 fingers and 10 toes representing the 10 laws of good & evil—in order to communicate more easily with mankind about the invisible, spiritual world? Well, what was God's physical symbol for Lucifer (Satan)? It was a snake!!! So it appears God actually cursed a "serpent-like" looking creature that initially had legs—possibly for its involvement in the sin—to a life of crawling around on its belly! A snake slithering around in the dirt would be an everlasting visual reminder to mankind of their enemy, Satan, and how he slyly murdered them spiritually— separated their spirit from God's Spirit—in the Garden of Eden. Imagine

72

the humiliation of a creature losing its legs and having to get around on its stomach! What an awesome picture of "Satan's fall". He was truly "*cut down to the ground*" because of his insidious sin against God and mankind. (Note: Scientists have now discovered fossil evidence of snakes once having legs!)

Consider all the confrontations between mankind and snakes throughout history. Every time a human being crushed a serpent's head or a serpent struck a human's heel, it was a picture of what would happen between Christ and Lucifer at Calvary! Every frightful encounter visually displayed the ferocious, continuing war being fought between God and Satan in the spirit world over human souls! Picture a little girl with pigtails running from an old barn to the farmhouse at night screaming, "Daddy, there's a snake in the barn!" Then carefully, dad, mom, and the little girl go tip-toeing through the darkness out to the barn, where dad deftly takes a shovel off the wall. The night air is tense and no one dares make a sound as the little girl's terrified eyes point daddy in the right direction. Suddenly, the light from mom's flashlight illuminates the beady eyes and the hissing tongue—and wham!—dad's shovel crushes the serpents head! This time mankind got the better of the ongoing war, but next time it might be the serpent! But no matter how this scene has played out down through the corridor of time, every skirmish has been an awesome visual spectacle of the constant battle waging in the invisible spirit world!

And what will be the eternal, end result of God's judgment on Lucifer and his demons? Oh, it is horrific!!! For God created a place of <u>everlasting</u> fire during his 6 day Creation in preparation of Satan's sin! Jesus uttered a parable confirming <u>why</u> God created a lake of fire: *"Depart from me, ye cursed, into <u>everlasting fire, PREPARED for the devil and his angels</u>" (Matthew 25:41).* Thus, in the Garden of Eden, God officially convicted and sentenced Lucifer and his demons to that appalling place, and they now serve time like inmates on death row awaiting their day of punishment. That day will be after planet Earth completes 7,000 trips around the sun: *"And <u>the devil that deceived them was cast into the lake of fire and brimstone…and shall be TORMENTED day and night for ever and ever</u>" (Revelation 20:10).* What an awful price to pay for the ugly sin of greed!

But remember, in God's 7 day (7,000 year) plan, He will lock Satan up in the bottomless pit at year 6,000, during Jesus Christ's 2nd Coming to planet Earth: *"And he laid hold on the dragon, that old serpent, which is the Devil, and Satan, and **bound him a thousand years**, And cast him into the bottomless pit, and shut him up, and set a seal upon him, that he should deceive the nations no more, till the thousand years should be fulfilled: and after that he must be loosed a little season"* (Revelation 20:2, 3). The Devil and his demons know all too well their time is fixed. This is why the demons living in two Gergesene men asked Jesus: *"Art thou come hither to torment us **before the time**? (Matthew 8:29).* Do you see? John the revelator wrote: *"Woe to the inhabitants of the earth and of the sea! For the devil is come down unto you, having great wrath, because **he knoweth that he hath but a short time**"* (Revelation 12:12).

Interestingly, God banished Lucifer and his demons to serve out their remaining time on planet Earth. And do you know what they are doing with their limited time? They are trying to take as many of God's spirit children (mankind) with them as they can to the lake of fire!!! They roam over Earth possessing, deceiving, and influencing God's spirit children into doing evil—disobeying God's 10 Love Commandments: *"Be sober, be vigilant; because your adversary the devil, as a roaring lion, walketh about, seeking whom he may devour"* (I Peter 5:8). THAT is there gig! They know their future is dark and hopeless; therefore, they cannot stand God's spirit children because they know they still have a <u>chance</u> at being reunited with God again one day.

See, God's judgment on Lucifer and his demons was quick, brutal, and final. He gave them NO hope for redemption! I believe God had no tolerance for Lucifer's sin because <u>it originated in his OWN heart</u>. In other words, no one else coerced Lucifer into sinning; he turned evil all on his own! And that is why God's punishment was hopelessly severe. But God had mercy on mankind, giving them a second chance at life, because their sin was a result of Lucifer's enticement. Incidentally, God has not changed his stance toward those who coerce others to sin. Jesus warned: *"whosoever shall OFFEND one of these little ones that believe in me, it is better for him that a millstone were hanged about his neck, and he were cast into the sea"* (Mark 9:42). "Offend" is from the Greek word "*skandalizō*" meaning: to cause to sin, cause to fall (into sin), offend; to fall away (from the faith), go astray. Clearly, God's punishment will be harsh on those who "cause others to sin", just like it was on Lucifer and his angels.

Well, my dear friend THAT is how God set up the Game of Life. And it was all planned by Him from before Creation! After the momentous day of sin in the Garden, God's gameboard for His master plan on Earth was fully open and ready to be played. It was now, "Game on!" And God would receive pleasure watching His spirit children play. Every soul of mankind born on Earth was like a new game piece being divvied out and put in position to play. And as stated earlier in this chapter, the objective of the Game was/is for God's spirit children to obtain eternal life by returning to God: *"The wicked will finally lose; the righteous will finally win"* (Proverbs 21:18, Living Bible).

After 7,000 years, there will be a great Day of Judgment that every soul born on Earth will partake in standing before the throne of God: *"And I saw the dead, small and great, stand before God; and the books were opened…and the dead were judged out of those things which were written in the books, **ACCORDING TO THEIR WORKS**… And death and hell were cast into the lake of fire. This is the SECOND death. And whosoever was not found written in the book of life was cast into the lake of fire"* (Revelation 20:12-15). Do you understand, clearly, what we will **ALL** get judged on? It is our WORKS—what we have DONE!—during our time down here on planet Earth!!! Those souls who have willfully continued to DO evil (disobey the 10 Love Commandments) will perish in the lake of fire—which is known as the 2nd Death because it will be PERMANENT separation from God's Spirit of Life. But those who repent of evil (sin) by choosing to DO good (obey the 10 Love Commandments) will enter the Kingdom of God and receive eternal life, having right to the Tree of Life: *"Blessed are they that **DO his (10 Love) commandments**, that they may have right to the TREE OF LIFE, and may enter in through the gates into the city"* (Revelation 22:14).

Friend, the stakes in the Game of Life are extremely high: Your priceless soul's ETERNAL destiny is on the line! **And the Game is almost over!!!** Year 6,000 is fast approaching with the return of Jesus

Christ to planet Earth and the setting up of his 1,000 year Earthly, Sabbath reign. If the first 6,000 years of mankind's history were equated to a 60 minute football game, approximately 12 seconds would be left on the clock till Christ's return at the writing of this book in AD 2008. That is how late it is! There will be a bodily resurrection at year 6,000, but it will ONLY be for those souls, living during mankind's first 6,000 years, who DID good (obeyed the 10 Love Commandments): *"But the rest of the dead lived not again until the thousand years were finished. This is the first resurrection. Blessed and HOLY is he that hath part in the first resurrection: on such the second death hath no power, but they shall be priests of God and of Christ, and shall reign with him a thousand years" (Revelation 20:5, 6).*

Do you want to live in Jesus Christ's glorious Earthly Kingdom, or do you want to perish in his 2nd Coming fury? (I am about to tell you exactly what will take place on Earth during his 2nd Coming, through Noah's story!) The choice is yours. I wish you could see the angel's faces and hear their joyful singing over one sinner that repents—forsakes the way of evil. But inevitably, Jesus declared in the end our souls are going one of two places: *"Marvel not at this: for the hour is coming, in the which ALL that are in the graves shall hear his voice, And shall come forth; they that have DONE good, unto the resurrection of life; and they that have DONE evil, unto the resurrection of the damnation" (John 5:28, 29).* God have mercy on us all.

Chapter 4

Noah

"And the waters increased, and BARE UP the ark,
and it was LIFT UP above the earth"
(Genesis 7:17)

At first glance, the story of Noah appears to be little more than an anecdote about God's awful judgment on a world of ungodly people. And while this assessment is true, the tale is in fact <u>MUCH</u> more: <u>The story of Noah was/is actually a detailed, prophetic picture of Jesus Christ's 2<u>nd</u> Coming</u>!!! In other words, it is a prophetic story that is yet to be fulfilled! The account is bristling with prophetic revelation about the events that will transpire during mankind's 6,000th year. I know it is mind-boggling to contemplate that God would cause worldwide devastation to occur because He wanted to secretly foretell to mankind how this age would come to an end, but He did!

But before we investigate the revelation of the story of Noah, I want to first make known something God was clandestinely doing from the beginning of Creation; He was making sure a <u>record</u> of the names of every father in the lineage of the coming Messiah was kept [See Figure #3]. Subsequently, the complete genealogy of Jesus Christ is documented in the Bible, which spans the first 4,000 years of mankind! This is a remarkable achievement if you think about it, for no other complete genealogy of anyone else from the beginning of time has survived that length of history! God certainly did NOT need to give mankind an undying witness of his Son's bloodline from Adam, yet it is just another piece of evidence of the Bible's amazing nature.

But in addition to simply keeping track of the patriarchal genealogy of Jesus Christ, here is what else God was <u>doing</u> with THOSE fathers: He would <u>deliberately</u> pick certain ones to control specific events in their life, in which the specific details of the events <u>secretly</u> PROPHESIED about His future plans for His spirit children in the Game of Life. To be more exact, the prophetic details ALWAYS concerned the 2 comings of the Messiah (Jesus Christ) and the "<u>what</u> he would do" and the "<u>when</u>" of those 2 comings! But here is what is even more remarkable; <u>the NUMBER of the patriarch (God was using to prophesy through) in the enumerative genealogy of the Messiah (Jesus Christ) had prophetic significance with respect to what God was foretelling through their life</u>!!! I know this is all dizzying to comprehend, but this is where the Bible takes a detour from all other books and becomes noticeably, divinely inspired! To get the full effect of God's stunning prophetic wisdom, you must try and imagine living in the day of these ancient Biblical people with no knowledge of the future. Try and visualize where all God's spirit children were living on Earth at the time, internalizing their limited understanding of God's master plan. If you can do that, you will witness the incomparable foreknowledge of God.

For instance, the <u>7</u>th father on the direct genealogical descent to Jesus was a man named Enoch. He was born in the 622nd year after Creation—which would have been around <u>3350 BC</u> (3972 BC – 622 years). Can you envisage the time? There has been no Noah, no global flood, no Abraham, no Jacob, no nation of Israel, no Moses, No David, No Daniel, No Jesus, No book of Revelation, NO BIBLE! There has only been the dreadful day of sin in the Garden of Eden and Adam still walking Earth to talk with, firsthand, about it. In this setting and time period—probably in the area of Mesopotamia—do you know what God was prophesying through Enoch? Listen: *"And Enoch also, the <u>SEVENTH from Adam</u>, prophesied of <u>THESE</u>, saying, **Behold,***

78

Figure # 3
Genealogy of Jesus

1.	Adam	31.	Obed
2.	Seth	32.	Jesse
3.	Enos	33.	David
4.	Cainan	34.	Solomon
5.	Mahalaleel	35.	Roboam
6.	Jared	36.	Abia
7.	Enoch	37.	Asa
8.	Methuselah	38.	Josaphat
9.	Lamech	39.	Joram
10.	Noah	40.	Ozias
11.	Shem	41.	Joatham
12.	Arphaxad	42	Achaz
13.	Salah	43.	Ezekias
14.	Eber	44.	Manasses
15.	Peleg	45.	Amon
16.	Reu	46.	Josias
17.	Serug	47.	Jechoniah
18.	Nahor	48.	Salathiel
19.	Terah	49.	Zorobabel
20.	Abraham	50.	Abiud
21.	Isaac	51.	Eliakim
22.	Jacob	52.	Azor
23.	Judas	53.	Sadoc
24.	Phares	54.	Achim
25.	Esrom	55.	Eliud
26.	Aram	56.	Eleazar
27.	Aminadab	57.	Matthan
28.	Naasson	58.	Jacob
29.	Salmon	59.	Joseph
30.	Booz	60.	Jesus

the Lord COMETH with ten thousands of his saints, To execute judgment upon ALL, and to convince all that are UNGODLY among them of all their UNGODLY DEEDS which they have UNGODLY COMMITTED" (Jude 1:14, 15). Is that not amazing? God was already foretelling of the Messiah, Christ's 2nd Coming!!!

In other words, God was speaking through Enoch about the "event" that would kick off the 7th day (or year 6,000) of his 7,000 year plan! Do you know "what" is going to happen? God gave a secret, prophetic clue to the people of Enoch's day through a supernatural event He controlled in Enoch's life—namely, the way He "took him" from Earth: ***"Enoch was TRANSLATED that he should not see death; and was not found, because God had translated him: for before his translation he had this testimony, that HE PLEASED GOD" (Hebrews 11:5).*** Wow! The word "translated" is from the Greek word *"metatithēmi"* meaning: to change (from one place or position to another); to bring back; to take away. Do you see? God was foreshadowing, through Enoch's translation, the way in which He would "snatch away" all the godly people from off the surface of planet Earth at Christ's 2nd Coming! See, friend, there will be people living on Earth (around AD 2028) who will NEVER physically die; their spirit and body will just vanish (change) during the 2nd Advent. Now look, God could have translated the 3rd, 4th, 5th, 9th, or any other "numbered father" in the patriarchal lineage of the coming Messiah, but He chose the 7th! Why? Because through this "detail" He was again secretly revealing and confirming the TIMING of Christ's 2nd Coming to Earth to begin the millennial Sabbath day reign—i.e. at the start of the 7th millennial day. Therefore, this small, seemingly-insignificant detail actually reinforced God's 7 day (7,000 year) plan for mankind's time on Earth, which He had secretly foretold from Creation in the 7 day Creation event.

Digressing, how do you suppose Enoch—living 2,000 years before Moses received the 10 Love Commandments on Mount Sinai— knew what constituted *"ungodly deeds"*? What ARE *"un-godly deeds"*? Well, since God is love, then they must be "un-loving deeds". And what are these? They are the deeds (works) of **DISOBEYING** THE 10 LOVE COMMANMDENTS—i.e. murder, blasphemy, idolatry, thievery, lying, etc.!!! See, Enoch's words are proof again that ALL mankind has known the difference between good & evil—as outlined by obedience or disobedience to the 10 Love Commandments, respectively. And

80

Enoch was prophesying that God will *"execute judgment"* on these "ungodly people" living on Earth at Christ's 2nd Coming! If you want to know more about what these "ungodly people" are like—what they DO—read Jude's short Biblical letter, noting how Enoch knew ALL about them by *"prophesying of THESE"*!

Incidentally, did you notice WHY God translated Enoch? It was because while he lived on Earth his deeds (works) *"PLEASED God"*. How do you suppose a person pleases God? Friend, there is only 1 way and that is by living your Earthly life in obedience to His 10 Love Commandments: *"And whatsoever we ask, we receive of him, because we KEEP his commandments, and DO those things that are PLEASING in his sight"* (I John 3:22). In Hebrews: *"Now the God of peace…make you perfect in every GOOD WORK to DO his will, working in you that which is WELL PLEASING in his sight"* (Hebrews 13:20, 21). See, friend, Enoch knew Gods 10 Love Commandments, and he OBEYED them! THAT is why he *"pleased God"*, and that is why God translated him. And only those people who live like Enoch will be translated off Earth's surface the Day of Christ's 2nd Coming!!!

Continuing to support the fact that ALL mankind has known God's 10 Love Commandments, let us consider God's 6th Love Commandment *"Thou shalt not murder"*. You have most likely heard the Bible story about Adam & Eve's children, Cain & Abel (probably occurring within mankind's first 100 years) where Cain murdered Abel because of jealousy: *"Not as Cain, who was of that wicked one, and slew his brother. And wherefore slew he him? **Because his own WORKS were EVIL, and his brother's righteous**"* (I John 3:12). After God punished Cain severely for his murder—read about it in Genesis chapter 4—do you think mankind clearly understood "murder" was evil? OF COURSE!!! Friend, ALL mankind has known God's 6th Love Commandment *"Thou shalt not murder"*.

Alright, let us now investigate Noah's life and see what God was secretly prophesying through the DETAILS. First of all, Noah was the 10th generational father from Adam on the direct genealogical line to the Messiah. "10" is God's number for order, stemming from His perfect Law of Love—namely, the 10 Love Commandments. See, if ALL mankind obeyed God's 10 Love Commandments, Earth would be full of God (love) and perfectly ordered. In other words, the chaos resulting from sin would cease! THIS is precisely what will take place on Earth at Christ's 2nd Coming and during his 1,000 year reign. Thus, God picked the 10th generational father from Adam to "work with" in revealing the "events" which will lead to His restoring order to Earth— i.e. Christ's 2nd Coming at year 6,000! I could write 20 pages on God's implications behind the number "10" as it relates to Bible stories— e.g. our tithe is a 10th, the Antichrist will soon divide Earth into a 10 kingdom confederation, etc—but let it be known: God's PROPHETIC revelation through the story of Noah began with Him picking Noah as the 10th generational father on the direct genealogical descent to Jesus.

Simple math applied to Genesis chapter 5 reveals Noah was born 1,056 years after Creation—which would have been 2916 BC (3972 BC – 1,056 years) on our current Gregorian calendar. Thus, Noah was born 56 years into the 2nd millennial day of God's 7 millennial day, master plan. Remember the verbiage of Day 2 in the Creation story secretly prophesied of the great flood waters? Listen to it again: *"And God said, Let there be a firmament in the midst of the WATERS, and let it divide the WATERS from the WATERS. And **God made the firmament, and divided the WATERS which were under the firmament from the WATERS which were above the firmament**...And the evening and the morning were the SECOND day"* (Genesis 1:6-8). God planned for Noah to live 950 years on Earth: *"And all the days of Noah were nine hundred and fifty years: and he died"* (Genesis 9:29). Subsequently, Noah lived almost every year of the 2nd millennial day, and the great flood happened near the middle of it!

Continuing to use Noah's life for His prophetic purpose, God gave him his name! In ancient Biblical times names had significance, and the connotation behind the name *"Noah"* further divulged what God would reveal through his life. In ancient Hebrew, the name *"Noah"* meant: rest, comfort. Again, what is Jesus' 2nd Coming about? It is to set up the 7th millennial day of REST, the Sabbath day!!! It is when Christ will lock up the deceiver Satan and establish order, peace, and rest to planet Earth. The words in Genesis show God prophesying right through Noah's father Lamech's lips: *"And he (Lamech) called his name **Noah**, saying, This same shall comfort us concerning our work and toil of our* *hands, because of the ground which the LORD hath cursed" (Genesis 5:29).* Wow! Are you kidding me? THAT is EXACTLY what Jesus Christ is coming to do at year 6,000!!! Remember, we work and toil as a result of sin, for God cursed the ground after Adam & Eve's sin. Well, Jesus Christ is going to rectify that situation at his 2nd Coming!

Jesus often talked about the purpose of his 2nd Coming while on Earth. One time, he said, *"Come unto me, all ye that labour and are heavy laden, and I will give you rest" (Matthew 11:28).* Jesus knew he had come to Earth to die for mankind's sins, freeing them from their bondage to sin & death. Thus, Jesus was/is the ONLY one who can truly give us REST from sin's consequence (work, toil, suffering, and death) and he will do it, officially, during mankind's 6,000th year. In the book of Hebrews, the coming 7th millennial day Kingdom of God on Earth is described as a period of "rest" for the believers that enter it: *"There remaineth therefore a rest to the people of God. For he (Jesus) that is entered into his rest, he also hath ceased from his own works, as God did from his (on the seventh day of creation). **Let us labour therefore to enter into that rest**" (Hebrews 4:9-11).* Do you see we are to *"labor* TO *enter into that rest"*? What does that mean? It means exactly what it says: We must DO something to enter God's millennial, restful kingdom. What must we do? We must repent (stop sinning) and obey God's 10 Love Commandments!

Friend, I want you to fully understand Lamech's prophetic words about his son, Noah, were REALLY prophetic words about the Messiah! In other words, God was saying through Lamech, "The events I will control in Noah's life will be a futuristic glimpse of the things I will do through Christ." Do you see? Explicitly, the meaning behind Noah's name and 10th generational number pointed to the fact that the "events in his life" were going to foreshadow the events of Jesus Christ's 2nd Coming, for this is when Christ will set up the millennial day of rest, restoring order and peace to a sin-sick, confused Earth. To be blunt, the "work of Noah's life" was to be a prophetic picture of the "work of Christ's life"! Let us look at the stunningly details.

As Noah aged, God summed up the spiritual condition of people's hearts living in his day: *"And God saw that the wickedness of man was great in the earth, and that EVERY imagination of the thoughts of his heart (spirit) was only evil continually" (Genesis 6:5)*. Is that not an amazing statement? Remember, our spirit (soul) contains our thoughts, desires, & emotions. How can folk's "thoughts and desires" be evil, continually? Oh, they can!!! And today, just like in Noah's day, most folk's are. Listen, since we learned the "love of money (acquiring dirt)" is the root of ALL evil (disobedience to the 10 Commandments), then a world of people who only <u>mentally</u> strive to make more money to acquire more dirt (possessions) than the next guy is ALL it takes to have a world of people whose "thoughts" are evil continually! Do you understand? People who love money (dirt) <u>incessantly</u> steal, lie, murder, cheat, Sabbath break, blaspheme, etc. in their covetous, idolatrous pursuit of it. Does that sound like the motivation and drive in most people's hearts today? I certainly think so! Friend, the hearts (thoughts, desires, & emotions) of people living right before Jesus' 2nd Coming will be <u>persistently</u> evil, just like they were in Noah's day. And that time is NOW!!!

The Bible records Noah was a *"preacher of righteousness"*: *"And spared not the old world, <u>but saved Noah the eighth person, a</u>* **<u>preacher of righteousness</u>**, *bringing in the flood upon the world of the ungodly" (II Peter 2:5)*. What is a "preacher of <u>righteousness</u>"? Well, what is righteousness? The Bible has the answer: *"My tongue shall speak of thy WORD:* **<u>for ALL thy (10 Love) commandments ARE</u>** **<u>righteousness</u>**" *(Psalms 119:172)*. See, Noah was preaching "obedience to the 10 Love Commandments"!!! But how could that be when it was still well over a 1,000 years until God would write them on stone tables and give them to Moses around 1300 BC? Do I need to repeat it again? <u>Because ALL mankind's spirits knew them ever since Adam & Eve ate from the tree of the knowledge of good & evil!</u> Subsequently, here is where Noah's life began mimicking the life of the coming Messiah, for Jesus too would be a preacher of righteousness (obey the 10 Love Commandments). In fact, Jesus is preaching "righteousness" through the very words I am writing in this book, because his Spirit lives in me. He is warning people of the coming mayhem, just like Noah did in his day. And, friend, time is quickly running out!

Fed up with the wickedness, God told Noah He was going to destroy planet Earth and ALL the evil people: *"And God said unto*

84

*Noah, **The end of all flesh** is come before me; for the earth is filled with violence through them; and, behold, **I will destroy them WITH the earth**" (Genesis 6:13).* Sound like today? Mankind is committing violence everywhere! Did you notice <u>exactly</u> what God was going to DO to all the sinful people? He would destroy their physical (dirt) flesh! Do you understand? In other words, all God was really doing was terminating the time their souls had to live on planet Earth. The very moment the wicked people drowned in the deluge, their spirits went off to hell! THIS is <u>precisely</u> what God is about to do to ALL the ungodly people living on Earth at Christ's 2nd Coming! Their flesh will be annihilated, freeing their souls to go to the place of torment for the 1,000 year millennial reign of Jesus Christ. (By the way, do you <u>really</u> think a loving God would "cut-short" the time His spirit children had to live on Earth—i.e. destroy their flesh—if they did not KNOW they were doing wrong? OF COURSE NOT!!! Friend, the people of Noah's day <u>KNEW</u> they were doing evil.)

Did you notice planet Earth was to be destroyed, too? Now <u>why</u> would God want to do something like that? Why not just obliterate all the immoral people? You know, as well as me, God could have killed the evil people anyway He wanted. He could have sent a death angel around like He did years later in Egypt. He could have plagued them all with a deadly virus. He could have spoken the word, and they would have ALL vanished into thin air. So WHY would God desire to devastate <u>the entire surface of planet Earth</u> along with all the ungodly people? The answer is simple: I have already told you the <u>ONLY</u> reason this story is taking place is because God wanted to prophesy about the Messiah's 2nd Coming! Consequently, since God knew the entire surface of planet Earth would be wiped out at Christ's 2nd coming, He had to keep the story of Noah prophetically accurate!

Most folks today—even preachers—are dreadfully unaware of what is going to take place on planet Earth at the end of the 6th millennial day (6,000th year). But friend, without a doubt, <u>it will ALL go down like the story of Noah predicts</u>! Planet Earth will not vanish from our solar system, but its SURFACE will be totally destroyed like it was in Noah's day. Jesus referred to the Day of his 2nd Coming as like a *"thief in the night"*. Biblically, the Day is also known as the *"Day of the Lord's*

85

wrath"! Peter writes about it: *"But the day of the Lord will come as a thief in the night; in the which the heavens shall pass away with a great noise, and the elements shall melt with fervent heat,* **the earth also and the works that are therein shall be burned up**. *Seeing then that ALL these things shall be dissolved, what manner of persons ought ye to be in all holy conversations and GODLINESS"* (II Peter 3:10, 11). Do you see? Heed Peter's words and clean up your life because the great bonfire is about to happen! Stop wasting your life striving to obtain worthless dirt possessions! They are **ALL** going to burn! Rather, strive to be holy, righteous, and blameless—i.e. strive to be "GODLY" (obey the 10 Love Commandments).

So how will the righteous people living on Earth be spared at the time of Jesus' 2nd Coming? The story of Noah has the answer! God told Noah to make an Ark, giving him detailed instructions on how to build it: *"Make thee an ark of gopher wood; rooms shalt thou make in the ark, and shalt pitch it within and without with pitch…a window shalt thou make to the ark…and the door of the ark shalt thou set in the side thereof; with lower, second, and third stories shalt thou make it"* (Genesis 6:14-16). Expand your mind and think intelligently about this story. WHY would God ask Noah to build an Ark? I realize God told Noah the world would perish in a great flood, but why did God not tell Noah and his family to simply stand in a particular spot on Earth while He walled up the water around them during the flood, like He would do later for the Israelites at the Red Sea? See, God can do anything! There must be at least 100 other ways God could have saved Noah's family from the coming flood, so why an Ark? You already know the answer: This is God's prophetic story about Christ's 2nd Coming and it HAD to be accurate! God knew during mankind's 6,000th year (at Jesus' 2nd Coming) the godly people will rise up off of planet Earth to meet Jesus in the air. Subsequently, Noah's family HAD to rise up off of planet Earth's surface!!!

Now you TRULY know WHY God chose a "global flood" as His method of destruction. It was so He could have Noah build an Ark that would float on top of the water, "rising up" off of Earth's surface above the destruction taking place below! Try and wrap your head around that kind of forethought on God's part: This required God inventing and designing the water molecule as a part of Creation, knowing it would be able to lift things up. It is almost mind-numbing to conceive how God had everything thought out beforehand! I actually cannot think of another _natural_ way God could have precisely showed the coming "rapture" of the believers with the technology that existed in Noah's day. What else could have lifted human bodies up off of Earth's surface, hundreds of feet into the air? What kind of a God is this who foretells the future by _controlling_ the physical universe, causing detailed events to occur? Friend, He is _AWESOME_!!!

Thousands of years after Noah's day, God finally came right out and point-blankly revealed all the godly people who ever lived on Earth will receive new bodies, resurrecting and "rising up off of planet Earth" into the air during Christ's 2nd Coming. Paul wrote: _"For the Lord himself shall DESCEND from heaven with a shout...and **the dead in Christ shall rise first**: Then **we which are alive and remain shall be caught up together with them in the clouds to meet the Lord in the air**: and so shall we ever be with the Lord"_ (I Thessalonians 4:16, 17). Do you see? This is when ALL the righteous will enter God's Kingdom to forever be with the Lord—known as the 1st resurrection of the dead (only the saints). At that time, all the righteous spirits (souls) will receive amazing new bodies, like Jesus received when he _resurrected_ from the dead. If you remember, he was able to eat fish with the disciples, yet he could appear and disappear, passing through walls! How would you like a painless body like that?

Friend, you are only _beginning_ to understand the true prophetic power behind the story of Noah, for let us now look at what the "Ark" represents: It symbolizes the Kingdom of God! Watch how closely God precisely designed the "Ark" to portray the spiritual Kingdom of God—i.e. the place where God's Spirit dwells. God instructed Noah to build the Ark with a lower, second, & third story. Why not 2, 4, or 5 levels? Because thousands of years later, God would reveal to the Apostle Paul that the "Kingdom of God" has THREE levels!!! Paul recorded in the Bible: _"I knew a man in Christ...such an one caught up to the **third heaven**"_ (II Corinthians 12:2). This is the only place in the Bible making reference to a 3rd heaven, which implies the spiritual (heavenly) Kingdom of God has a first, second, & third level!

God gave Noah specific dimensions for building "windows" in the Ark. Many times the Bible describes the spiritual Kingdom of Heaven as having windows. (By the way, the "Kingdom of God" and the "Kingdom of Heaven" are the same entity.) God mentioned it in the story of Noah; *"...and the <u>windows of heaven</u> were opened" (Genesis 7:11)*. God told the prophet Malachi: *"Bring ye all the tithes into the storehouse...and prove me...saith the LORD...if I will not **<u>open you the windows of heaven</u>**, and pour you out a blessing, that there shall not be room enough to receive it" (Malachi 3:10)*. Do you see? God had Noah build windows in the Ark because God regards his spiritual Kingdom as having windows! In other words, God and His angels can see what is going on down here on Earth, which means the resurrected righteous at Christ's 2nd Coming will be able to witness the destruction of Earth from heaven just like Noah's family did from the Ark.

God commanded Noah to construct **1** door in the side of the Ark. Later on Earth, Jesus often talked about the <u>DOOR</u> that enters the Kingdom of God. Jesus said, *"**<u>I am the door</u>**: by me if any man enter in, he shall be saved" (John 10:9)*. Again, he said, *"Verily, verily, I say unto you, <u>He that entereth not by the DOOR into the sheepfold, but climbeth up some other way, the same is a thief and a robber</u>" (John 10:1)*. Are you starting to see how an "Ark" was the PERFECT way for God to symbolize the "Kingdom of God"—i.e. the only place of safety available for a soul on Earth to escape the soon coming Day of the Lord's wrath?

Oh, but the story just keeps getting better! For God told Noah to build <u>ROOMS</u> in the ark!!! This is an awesome picture, because 2,500 years later when Jesus walked the Earth, he told his disciples: *"In my Father's house (Kingdom of God) are many **<u>mansions</u>**: if it were not so, I would have told you. <u>I GO TO PREPARE A PLACE FOR YOU. And if I go and prepare a place for you, I will come again, and receive you unto myself; that where I am, there ye may be also</u>" (John 14:2, 3)*. The original Greek word in the ancient Biblical manuscripts translated "mansions" in our English Bible is *"monē"* and it actually meant: <u>ROOM(S); dwelling place, or abode</u>. Is that not incredible? In other words, the disciples would have understood Jesus as saying, *"I go to prepare <u>rooms</u> for you in the Kingdom of God,"* <u>exactly</u> like God had

88

instructed Noah to prepare IN the Ark!!!

Conjure up an image of Noah (1,500 years into the history of mankind) working diligently building an Ark. He has no Bible to read, for it does not exist. He knows nothing about the man Jesus who will come to Earth and die on a cross, because God has not even begun to reveal His plan of redemption. He knows the story of Adam & Eve and their Garden of Eden incident, but other than that he is merely going on faith (belief) that he has heard from the invisible Creator God to build an Ark. So day in and day out he keeps cutting and hewing gopher wood and preparing pitch, while preaching destruction is coming to planet Earth! Each bucket of pitch he spread, each log he carefully cut, and each room he completed in the Ark visually depicted the coming Messiah's work of preparing rooms in the Kingdom of Heaven to rescue (save) his believers. What an awesome, prophetic scene!

Noah was, almost certainly, clueless that one day the story of the events of his life would be included in a book (written by God for mankind) called the Bible. He probably had no idea the Ark he was building represented the Kingdom of God, and the flood he was about to live through would be his biggest sermon of all: For his story stood/ stands as a prophetic witness and warning to all future generations of the coming day of God's wrath at Christ's 2nd Coming! And Noah surely did not see me, Gabriel, in these last days, receiving from God and revealing to His spirit children the true meaning behind his story! But I say again, as the people of Noah's day watched Noah erect an Ark, they were REALLY seeing futuristically into the invisible spirit world at Jesus Christ preparing rooms in the Kingdom of God (the spiritual place of safety and rest) to rescue all the righteous from the coming day of God's destruction on Earth.

See, the story of Noah is a prophetic PARABLE! Do you understand? A "parable" is a brief story with symbolic meaning. When the Messiah, Jesus, finally arrived on planet Earth, he often spoke in parables. That is because the words he spoke came FROM God the Father: *"For I have not spoken of myself; but the Father which sent me…whatsoever I speak therefore, even as the Father said unto me, SO I SPEAK" (John 12:49, 50)*. Friend, God has NEVER changed; He has ALWAYS spoken to mankind in parables for the Old Testament stories are all parables! And in this parable "Noah" represented the Messiah and the "Ark" symbolized the Kingdom of God. Let us now carefully observe the soon coming fulfillment of the parable.

When Noah finished the ark, God commanded him to enter it: *"And the LORD said unto Noah, **Come thou and ALL thy HOUSE into the ark; for thee have I seen righteous before me** in this generation" (Genesis 7:1)*. See, once again, only righteous people will enter the Kingdom of God! And who is a righteous person from God's perspective? Do you need to hear it again? It is someone who lives their life always striving to obey God's 10 Love Commandments. Therefore, God basically told Noah (and I am paraphrasing), "I have been watching you and your family's words and deeds, and you are the only ones I have found worthy to enter the Ark (Kingdom of God)!"

Observe how perfect God is with his Biblical choice of words in this prophetic parable. The key word here is *"house"*. God told Noah only "HIS *house"* could enter the Ark! Read it again, above. Thus, 8 people—comprised of Noah & his wife and his three sons & their wives (Noah's daughters in law)—climbed in the Ark. The Bible would later say: *"By faith Noah, being warned of God of things not seen as yet, moved with fear, prepared an ark to the **saving of his HOUSE"** (Hebrews 11:6)*. Alright, so WHO is getting to enter the Ark (Kingdom of God) at Jesus' 2nd Coming? Friend, it is ONLY the "HOUSE of Christ"!!!

The Bible later declared: *"But **Christ as a son over HIS OWN HOUSE: whose HOUSE are we**, if we hold fast the confidence and the rejoicing of the hope firm unto the end" (Hebrews 3:6)*. Do you see? The Bible literally interprets itself by calling ALL the righteous people who ever lived on Earth "the *house* of Jesus Christ"!!! Is that not incredible? See, it is a spiritual term: When the Spirit of Christ (Holy Spirit) lives inside your physical body—manifested by your spirit's willful desire to be Holy (obey the 10 Love Commandments)—then you are "housing Christ". In that state, you are 100% part of the *"spiritual house of Christ"*, for Christ (love) lives in you! Listen to Peter: *"Ye also, as lively stones, are built up a SPIRITUAL HOUSE…acceptable to God by Jesus Christ" (I Peter 2:5)*. Yes, the parable of Noah was perfect right down to the very words used! And now you know why

90

God could NOT have allowed a stranger of Noah's family (house) to enter the Ark, because then the story would NOT have been an accurate PROPHETIC parable. See, there HAD to be just 1 house of people in the Ark, because only 1 house of people will rise up off of Earth's surface during Jesus' 2ⁿᵈ Coming surviving the ruin. And THAT house will be "Christ's house"!

To clarify further, when we repent of sin by turning to the way of righteousness (obey the 10 Love Commandments) the Bible says at that point we officially become a SPIRITUAL son or daughter of God (love). We are literally Christ's spiritual sons & daughters! And these are the sons and daughters that will enter the Kingdom of God, just like Noah's sons and daughters entered the Ark! Paul sagaciously wrote: *"For if ye live after the flesh, ye shall die: but if ye through the Spirit do mortify the DEEDS of the body, ye shall live. For as many as are led by the Spirit of God, they are the Sons of God...ye have received the Spirit of adoption, whereby we cry, Abba, Father" (Romans 8:13-15).* See, when we willingly purge our life of sin we are adopted as true spiritual sons and daughters of God (love). It is only then that you are truly a part of Christ's House!

Understand the transformation takes place in your spirit (thoughts, desires, & emotions). You will have a totally new mindset driving you to obey God's 10 Love Commandments, for the Spirit of Christ is the Spirit of love! Paul wrote: *"That the righteousness of the law might be fulfilled in us, who walk not after the flesh, but after the Spirit...For to be carnally minded is death; but to be spiritually minded is life and peace. Because the carnal mind is enmity against God: for it is NOT subject to the law of God, neither indeed can be. So then they that are in the flesh CANNOT PLEASE GOD. But ye are not in the flesh, but in the Spirit, if so be that the Spirit of God dwell in you. Now if any man have NOT the SPIRIT OF CHRIST, he is NONE of his. And if Christ be in you, the body is dead because of sin; but the Spirit is life because of RIGHTEOUSNESS. But if the Spirit of him (God) that raised up Jesus from the dead dwell in you, he that raised up Christ from the dead shall also quicken your mortal bodies by his Spirit that dwelleth in you" (Romans 8:4-11).* Do you see? If you have truly repented of sin—i.e. if you willfully desire to obey God's righteous 10

Love Commandment Law—then your lifestyle (thoughts & deeds) will prove your soul has repented and Christ's Spirit of Love lives in your heart, which confirms you ARE a spiritual son or daughter of Christ's House. THESE are the godly people who possess God's powerful, life-giving Spirit inside them, which will bodily raise them to life at Christ's 2nd Coming!

Returning to the parable of Noah, let me acknowledge 2 other ways in which Noah was like the coming Messiah. The Bible says Noah feared and obeyed God: *"By faith Noah, being warned of God of things not seen as yet, moved with FEAR, prepared an ark to the SAVING of his house"* (Hebrews 11:6). The Bible also reports: *"And Noah DID according unto ALL that the Lord commanded him"* (Genesis 7:5). Do you see? Noah feared and obeyed God's every word. And what does the Bible record about Jesus' human Earthly ministry: *"Who in the days of his flesh, when he had offered up prayers and supplications with strong crying and tears unto him (God) that was able to save him from death, and was heard in that he FEARED; Though he were a Son, yet learned he obedience by the things which he suffered; And being made perfect, **he became the author of eternal SALVATION unto all them that OBEY him**"* (Hebrews 5:7-9). See, Jesus also feared and obeyed God, and it was his obedience to the cross that will one day save his spiritual House! Friend, Noah & Jesus were both motivated by fear to obey God no matter what they had to suffer in their physical, fleshly bodies. AND WE SHOULD BE NO DIFFERENT!!!

Next, we read God commanded Noah to take animals into the Ark. Consequently, we can rest assured animals will be in the Kingdom of Heaven! And sure enough, 2,000 years later, the prophet Isaiah described Christ's Earthly millennial Kingdom: *"The wolf also shall dwell with the lamb, and the leopard shall lie down with the kid; and the calf and the young lion and the fatling together; and a little child shall lead them"* (Isaiah 11:6). Friend, God passionately loves His created animals. They are all part of His good pleasure, and they too will be delivered from the bondage of sin's curse at Christ's 2nd Coming! Remember the Earth's ground (soil) was/is cursed from Adam & Eve's sin? This means every atom on planet Earth was/is cursed! And since animal's physical bodies are made from the food they eat—the atoms

92

of which come from the ground and the air—their bodies are cursed, too. Friend, literally "ALL of Earth" is under the curse: *"The creature (animals) itself also shall be delivered from the **bondage of corruption** into the glorious liberty of the children of God. For we know that the whole creation groaneth and travaileth in pain together"* (Romans 8:21, 22). What a marvelous time of regeneration for Earth the millennial 7th day will be!

Oh, but there is even MORE prophetic information to be gleaned from the story (parable) of Noah concerning Jesus' 2nd Coming! But since this next subject is very hotly debated today, I want to preface it with a solemn warning: Stop arguing and bickering with your supposed-to-be Christian brothers about it!!! We are commanded to love each other, not fight over a moot point. The issue I speak of concerns the TIMING of the saint's translation (rapture). There is a Biblical theory claiming the great tribulation (spoken about by Christ and described in the book of Revelation) will be contained in a final 7 year period on Earth, leading up to Christ's 2nd Coming at year 6,000 and the setup of his Earthly millennial Kingdom. But here is the controversial issue; some feel the saint's rapture will take place BEFORE the 7 year great tribulation period (known as pre-tribulationists), some feel the saint's rapture will take place in the MIDDLE of the great tribulation period (known as mid-tribulationists), and some feel the saint's rapture will take place at the END of the great tribulation period (known as post-tribulationists).

I have NO issue with respect to whatever you want to believe concerning this topic, because you are NOT required to be right about it to obtain eternal life! Do you understand? Therefore, stop fighting—borderline hating!—your brother over it. You are NOT leading an ungodly world towards God (love) with your pathetic squabbling!!! This is just another unimportant (with respect to obtaining eternal life) matter Satan uses to make you look like an unloving fool. Rather, live and preach obedience to the 10 Love Commandments! With that said, I will give you my humble, Biblical opinion on the matter.

To be a PRETRIBULATIONIST is to believe Christ will make 3 Comings to Earth. But, friend, Christ NEVER said that; when he vanished in the clouds, two men in white said he will come back in *"like manner"*—which clearly meant <u>only</u> once! This stance raises a whole conundrum of problems: If Christ comes in the clouds to rapture his saints 7 years before he comes back again to setup his Earthly millennial Kingdom, what happens to ALL the ungodly people on Earth at his 3rd Coming? Do they just get to enter into his millennial, peaceful Kingdom, receiving beautiful new translated bodies? Wow, that must be nice! Or do they ALL die? If so, how? Are there converted saints living during the 7 year tribulation? If so, what happens to them at Christ's 3rd Coming? Do they NEVER have to rise to meet Christ in the air? Do they just translate on Earth? For that matter, what is going to happen TO Earth during these 2 Comings? Ah, the puzzling questions are almost limitless towards this position.

I have all the same perplexing questions for a MIDTRIBULATIONIST as I do for a pretribulationist. Friend, I am about to Biblically show you (through the details in Noah's parable) that Christ is NOT coming back during mankind's 5,993rd year, nor during mankind's 5,996½th year! He is coming back to Earth ONLY 1 more time and it <u>WILL</u> <u>BE</u> during mankind's 6,000th year! (Later in this book, in the *"Joshua"* chapter, I will absolutely prove to you that Christ's 2nd Coming, and subsequent rapture of the saints, will happen at the very END of the great tribulation period!) Subsequently, I wholeheartedly <u>know</u> POSTRIBULATIONISTS will be correct in the end. But, for now, let us take a better look at the issue through Noah's story.

Listen to the following detail; Noah's house entered the Ark <u>7 days</u> BEFORE the flood began: *"And Noah went in, and his sons, and his wife, and his son's wives with him, into the ark...**And it came to pass AFTER seven days**, that the waters of the flood were upon the earth" (Genesis 7:7, 10).* At first glance, this fact would appear to substantiate pre-tribulationism theory. However, notice the Ark does not "lift up off planet Earth (rapture)" <u>UNTIL</u> the deluge (destruction) begins; thus, Noah's house was NOT raptured 7 days earlier. Rather, this detail seems to indicate that <u>ALL</u> the righteous people who will enter the Kingdom of God will make their "repentance-decision" some period of time (possibly 7 years) BEFORE Christ's return to Earth. Do you understand? In other words, this small detail in the story of Noah seems to be revealing there will be a cut-off time on Earth, after which NO ONE else will repent of sin—i.e. be saved by entering the Kingdom of God!

Listen, once the "Spirit of Christ (love)" lives inside your heart (thoughts, desires, & emotions), technically you are already <u>IN</u> the <u>spiritual</u> Kingdom of God. In other words, you are already in the Ark! Jesus said, *"Behold, <u>the kingdom of God is within you</u>" (Luke 17:21).* See, it is a "spiritual event". I know it is hard to grasp, but look, thousands of years later in the book of Revelation God talked about a "sealing of the saints" BEFORE the tribulation mayhem begins: *"And I saw another angel ascending from the east, <u>having the SEAL of the living God</u>: and he cried with a loud voice to the four angels, to whom it was given to hurt the earth and the sea, Saying, <u>Hurt not the earth, neither the sea, nor the trees,</u> **<u>till we have SEALED the servants of our God in their foreheads</u>**" (Revelation 7:2, 3).* This verse proves saints are still going to be here during the coming tribulation, but God will give them unwavering spiritual strength—sealing them in their mind!—to be able to endure anything the antichrist unleashes!

Look, at some point the antichrist will offer ALL Earth's people, including God's saints, his mark—which only with it will you be able to buy and sell! When is that? Could THAT be the deciding factor or the "last chance" for people to enter the Kingdom of God? Could that happen 7 years before Christ's rapturous return? Maybe! If you receive the Antichrist's mark, you will perish: *"<u>If any man worship the beast and his image, and receive his mark in his forehead, or in his hand, The same shall drink of the wine of the wrath of God</u>...and he shall <u>be tormented with fire and brimstone</u>...and they have no rest day nor night, who worship the beast and his image, and whosoever receiveth the mark of his name" (Revelation 14:9-11).* The time of the mark's issuance (for commerce reasons) could be the point when the door to the Ark closes for ALL the people on planet Earth!

Several times the book of Revelation confirms people enduring God's wrath during the great tribulation will NOT REPENT of their wickedness: *"<u>And the rest of the men which were not killed by these plagues yet REPENTED NOT of the works of their hands</u>, that they should not worship devils, and idols of gold, and silver, and brass, and* stone, and of wood...*Neither REPENTED they of their murders, nor of their sorceries, nor of their fornication, nor of their thefts"* (Revelation: 9:20, 21). Do you see? It is like these people's hearts are divinely hardened!!! Probably, they have already received the antichrist's mark to be able to buy and sell; thus, no matter what their going through their hearts will NOT "turn to God (love)" by willingly choosing to obey His 10 Love Commandments. This is so sad, I could cry! So, again, the details in the story of Noah seem to be saying there will be a point near the end of the 6,000 years—probably 7 years—when everyone that is going to enter the kingdom of God (repent of their wickedness) will have done so, being sealed in their forehead (spirit). After that time, it appears no one else on Earth will repent of their wickedness until Jesus Christ's appearance in the clouds.

But no matter what it means exactly, allow me to say for the record; the detail of Noah's house ENTERING the Ark 7 days BEFORE the deluge began most certainly has prophetic meaning!!! And in the book of Daniel's prophecies: 1 day = 1 year. Thus, let me forewarn you to be on the lookout for something VERY spiritually important to occur around AD 2021!

Alright, after Noah's house and the animals were safe inside the Ark, the Bible says GOD shut the door: *"and the **LORD shut him in**"* (Genesis 7:16). The language here is again prophetically perfect!!! Speaking in a parable through Christ 2,500 years later, God made it crystal clear HE will shut the door to the Kingdom of God. Once that happens, it will be too late; NO ONE will enter in after that time!!! Jesus uttered, *"**When once the master of the house is risen up, and hath shut to the door**, and ye begin to stand without, and to knock at the door, saying, Lord, Lord, open unto us; and he shall answer and say unto you, I know you not whence ye are: Then shall ye begin to say, We have eaten and drunk in thy presence, and thou hast taught in our streets. But he shall say, I tell you, I know you not whence ye are; **depart from me, ALL YE WORKERS OF INIQUITY**. There shall be weeping and gnashing of teeth, when ye shall see Abraham, and Isaac, and Jacob, and all the prophets, in the kingdom of God, and you yourselves thrust out"* (Luke 13:25-28). See, in this parable, God is the "master of the house", and GOD WILL SHUT THE DOOR to the

96

kingdom of God in the end, JUST like the words in Noah's parable had precisely foretold!

Did you notice WHY God will not allow the unrighteous to enter? It is because when they had a chance—i.e. the door to the Ark was fully open—to repent of their sins, they DID NOT!!! They just kept on willfully sinning (working iniquity)—disobeying the 10 Love Commandments—and entertaining every voice in their head that made them believe they will be ok with God. I am begging you to not make this mistake!!! God is not bluffing. He is dead serious about you choosing to stop sinning! Jesus' prophetic parable above was most likely, also, a historic glimpse back-in-time at what occurred during Noah's day after God shut "Noah's house" in the Ark: The ungodly people outside, getting pelted by the falling raindrops, were most likely pounding on the Ark's wooden door, screaming and crying, "Let us in! Let us in! You preached in our streets; we heard your righteous words! We just did not want to change then, for we enjoyed our sins. But we want to change NOW!!! Please, please let us in!" Oh, friend, do NOT make the dreaded mistake of continuing to willfully sin! **TODAY** is the day of salvation; NOW is the time to repent!!!

Well, everything was in place for the wrath of God (devastation) to commence: Noah's house and all the animals were in the Ark, and God had safely shut the door. I want you to now realize an important fact about God's chosen "instrument of destruction": It was something mankind had NEVER seen before! Say, what? Oh, mankind had seen water before, but not pouring down from the sky in sheets! For it had NEVER rained on planet Earth: *"For the LORD God had not caused it to rain upon the earth...But there went up a mist from the earth, and watered the whole face of the ground" (Genesis 2:5, 6).* See, since Creation Earth had been watered by a mist springing up from the ground. God confirmed mankind had never before seen rain in the book of Hebrews: *"By faith Noah, being warned of God of things not seen as yet" (Hebrews 11:7).* Can you imagine? Subsequently, in this respect, Noah's story (parable) was again precisely accurate in foreshadowing the future, because no one living today has ever witnessed fire burning Earth's ENTIRE surface! It is an almost unimaginable, unthinkable event—exactly like "rain" was to the people of Noah's day! (By the way, can you see the precise, prophetic picture of God's coming day of wrath with "fire & brimstone <u>raining</u> down from the sky" during Christ's return to Earth as demonstrated by "rain pouring down from the sky" in Noah's story?)

But then the unthinkable happened! Water burst violently out of the Earth's crust—probably resulting in today's global oceanic fault lines!—and came pounding down on planet Earth. The Bible testifies: *"the same day were <u>all the fountains of the great deep broken up</u>" (Genesis 7:11)*. And it rained for 40 days! Now watch the parable of Noah unfold in perfect revelatory fashion…as the flood waters began to rise and demolish planet Earth and all the ungodly, Noah's house (family) was "rising up off Earth's surface" safely in the ark: *"and the waters increased, and <u>bare up the ark</u>, and <u>**it was lift up above the earth**</u>" (Genesis 7:17)*. This could not have been a more perfect vision of Christ's 2nd Coming! As the Ark rose-up off of planet Earth into the air, it perfectly depicted how this age of mankind's history will come to an end—namely, by God's 1 house of righteous sons and daughters being lifted up off of planet Earth to meet the Lord in the air!

The Bible records <u>ALL</u> flesh died: *"And <u>**ALL flesh died that moved upon the earth**</u>, both of fowl, and of cattle, and of beast, and of every creeping thing that creepeth upon the earth, <u>and every man</u>: All in whose nostrils was the breath of life, of all that was in the dry land, died…and <u>Noah only remained alive, and they that were with him in the ark</u>" (Genesis 7:21-23)*. So it SHALL BE at Jesus Christ's 2nd Coming! All flesh will perish, except for one righteous house of people (the house of Christ) whose flesh will be instantly transformed into glorified bodies, while rising up off of planet Earth's surface, safely, into the air above the ensuing carnage below. Oh what a Day that will be!!!

It would be thousands of years later until God would begin to give visions of Christ's 2nd Coming to His Israeli prophets. And it was then that He clearly revealed the "instrument of Earth's destruction" at Christ's 2nd Coming will be <u>FIRE</u>!!! The 8th century BC prophet Joel wrote a horrifying, graphic description of the great day of the Lord's wrath: *"For <u>the day of the LORD cometh</u>…A day of darkness and of gloominess, a day of clouds and of thick darkness…<u>**A fire devoureth before them; and behind them a flame burneth: the land is as the**</u>*

*garden of Eden before them, and behind them a desolate wilderness; yea, and NOTHING shall escape them...Before their face the people shall be much pained: all faces shall gather blackness...They shall run to and fro in the city; they shall run upon the wall, they shall climb up upon the houses...The earth shall quake before them; the heavens shall tremble: the sun and the moon shall be dark, and the stars shall withdraw their shining...And the Lord shall utter his voice before his army...for he is strong that executeth his word; for **the day of the LORD is great and very terrible**; and who can abide it? (Joel 2:1-11).* Wow, do you see? The panicked chaos described here almost certainly describes what was happening to the ungodly people of Noah's day as they were running from the flood waters. But of course...because "Noah's flood event" was a prophetic vision of Jesus' 2nd Coming!!!

Without question, ALL the ungodly people's flesh on planet Earth will be consumed by fire on the terrifying day of the Lord's Coming. Around 400 BC, the prophet Malachi prophesied: *"For, behold, **the day cometh, that shall BURN as an oven**; and ALL the proud, yea, and ALL that DO wickedly, shall be stubble: and **the day that cometh shall BURN them up**...But unto you that fear my name shall the Sun of righteousness arise with healing in his wings; and ye shall go forth, and grow as calves of the stall. And ye shall tread down the wicked; for they shall be ashes under the soles of your feet in the day that I shall do this, saith the LORD of hosts"* (Malachi 4:1-3). Do you understand this Scripture? On the terrible day of the Lord's wrath the wicked people's physical flesh will be burned up and turn to ashes on Earth. Then, once God regenerates planet Earth into a paradise—which He can do in a split second (remember the feeding of the 5,000?)—He will replant the righteous people back down on a new Earth, where they will walk all over the ashes (atoms) of the wicked people's flesh during the 7th millennial day: *"The righteous shall inherit the land, and dwell therein for ever"* (Psalms 37:29).

And now it is time for God's "home-run detail" in the story of Noah, absolutely authenticating His Creation of planet Earth was/is a 7 day (7,000 year) plan, with the 7th millennial day's restful Sabbath being kicked off during year 6,000 at Christ's 2nd Coming! Are you ready for this? Are you sitting down? It is a seemingly insignificant and

99

yet stunningly amazing little detail. In fact, the detail further verifies the story of Noah is exactly what I am telling you…a prophetic picture of Christ's 2nd Coming! The divinely orchestrated detail is the "AGE of Noah" when the flood occurred. Do you know how old he was? He was 600 years old!!! The Bible records: *"And Noah was **six hundred years old** when the flood of waters was upon the earth" (Genesis 7:6).* Are you kidding me? Think of all the possible ages Noah COULD have been when the flood hit: He could have been anything…186, 387, 480, 500, 622 or whatever! So WHY would God have wanted him to be 600 years old? **Because the story of Noah is EXACTLY what I am telling you**: It is a prophetic parable from God to mankind concerning Christ's 2nd Coming. **And through this "little" detail God was confirming the "EVENT" WILL absolutely, positively take place during mankind's 6,000th year!!!**

All these years, one seemingly insignificant little Bible fact in the story of Noah actually loomed large with powerful, prophetic importance; a Biblical secret concealed by God down through over 4,000 years of time! Can you imagine how stunned I was when God revealed the true meaning behind the story of Noah to me? This prophet was dumbfounded!!! In the 14th Century BC, speaking to the Israelites, Moses KNEW God had secrets: *"There are secrets the LORD your God has NOT revealed to us" (Deuteronomy 29:29, Living Bible).* See, Moses and the Israelites knew the details of the story of Noah, but they did NOT know the secrets contained in them, because God did not want them revealed at that time. Friend, the things I am telling you came from God!!! They are not my wisdom! I could have read the story of Noah a thousand times over and never understood what it truly signified.

I can honestly say to you what Daniel told Nebuchadnezzar when God revealed the secret of the king's dream to him: *"There is a God in heaven that revealeth secrets…**But as for me**, this secret is not revealed to me for any wisdom that I have more than any (other person) living" (Daniel 2:28, 30).* Friend, I am no smarter than any other person and I am not worthy to kiss Jesus' feet! But what I do have inside of me is an unshakeable faith in a Living God and a holy, righteous, fear of Him that courses through my veins. And God said: *"**The SECRET of the LORD is with them that fear him**; and he will shew them his*

100

covenant" (Psalms 25:14). The word "secret" comes from the Hebrew word _"sôd"_ meaning: confidential talk, conspiracy; council, confidant. Friend, God has ordered me to write this book to let the world know the secrets He has revealed to me. So I am doing what He asked!!!

Consequently, in the story (parable) of Noah, Noah's age of 600 years represented 6,000 years of mankind's history, after which Jesus' 2nd Coming will play out EXACTLY like the devastating worldwide flood (and Ark) scenario. Now, since Noah was born during mankind's 1,056th year, the global flood let loose on planet Earth during mankind's 1,656th year—which was during the 2nd millennial Day of God's 7 millennial day (7,000 year) master plan—just like Day 2 of the Creation narrative had foretold! Using today's Gregorian calendar and prediction of AD 2028 as the 6,000th year, I calculated the flood took place during 2316 BC (3972 BC - 1,656 years). But, unquestionably, Jesus Christ will set up his 1,000 year (7th day Sabbath) Earthly reign during Earth's 6,000th year! No demon in hell can stop God's plan, for God's prophetic WORD will ALWAYS be fulfilled. In other words, the Bible will NEVER be found a lie. Therefore, it WILL happen!!!

Hopefully, after reading this chapter, you can now fully understand the true weight of Jesus' words: _**"But as the DAYS of Noah were, SO shall ALSO the COMING of the Son of man (Jesus) BE**. For as in the days that were before the flood they were eating and drinking, marrying and giving in marriage, until the day that Noah entered into the ark, And knew NOT until the flood came, and took them all away; so shall also the coming of the Son of man be"_ (Matthew 24:37-39). See, even Jesus himself confirmed the "story of Noah" was actually a depiction of his 2nd Coming! What more proof do you need? Truly, ALL the DAYS of Noah (including his first 600 years) were perfectly depicting the future events AND timing of Christ's 2nd Coming!

Knowing now the divine, hidden significance behind Noah's story, I do not see how it is possible for anyone—even a scientist!—to doubt the account actually happened. Wake up to truth, my friend, for the secrets contained in Noah's story (parable) prove planet Earth is not quiet 6,000 years old. Scientist's lies need to stop!!! They universally— except for a few—do NOT accept the validity of the worldwide flood of Noah. Yet, God had their evil, dim-witted minds pegged 2,000 years ago: *"For this **they willingly are ignorant** of, that by the word of God the heavens were of old, and the earth standing out of the water and in the water: **Whereby the world that then was, being overflowed with water, perished"** (II Peter 3:5, 6)*. Frankly, I am stunned at such voluntary stupidity from a group of people who are <u>supposed</u> to be in search of truth! Friend, chew on it, digest it, and accept it—<u>A DEVASTATING GLOBAL FLOOD HAPPENED!!!</u>

And the Earth that existed BEFORE the worldwide flood of Noah's day transpired was <u>completely</u> different from the world we know today. First of all, everything lived for a very long time—humans lived for almost 1,000 years! There is scientific evidence of a higher atmospheric oxygen content and greater magnetic field, probably contributing to the longer lifespan. Huge dinosaurs and many other strange creatures roamed a mostly land (probably close to 80% land) planet. And the ground received its moisture from a mist coming up from the Earth.

Meanwhile, mankind began as just Adam & Eve in a gorgeous garden probably in the area of Israel today. Archeological digs prove the first signs of ancient mankind on Earth are in the area of the Middle East, for that is the only location on planet Earth with extremely <u>ancient</u> stone foundations and pottery buried in the dirt. You cannot dig anywhere else on Earth and find 5,000 year old stone foundations, clay pots, and man-made "things". Furthermore, mathematical human population studies suggest mankind's population could only have been around "a few people" somewhere around 2000 BC. In other words, there is much evidence supporting the global flood and a 6,000 year old Earth!

After the catastrophic inundation abated, planet Earth was transformed from a mostly land covered planet to a mostly water (about 70% water) covered planet! Undoubtedly, today's massive oceans covering Earth were formed from the global flood water, as the water that was <u>IN</u> the Earth came bursting <u>OUT</u>. If you want solid evidence of Noah's flood, just go to the beach and stare at the ocean; there is a lot of water out there!!! I know the geographical changes to planet Earth resulting from the worldwide flood are hard to imagine, but the evidence is all around us: Earth is covered with layered sedimentary (water debris-sorted) rock, while fossilized trees exist throughout these layers buried in prostrate, oblique, and upright positions, and some fossilized trees (polystrate fossils) pass right through rock layers scientists maintain are millions of years apart! Now come on!!! Furthermore, huge dinosaurs could not escape the massive flood's power and depth, thus they are found fossilized, too—along with many other animals and creatures—in asphyxiated positions in the flood's churned up mud (now rock). Yes, the scientific evidence for a global flood is colossal, but the spiritual significance and meaning behind the details of Noah's story is the greatest evidence of all!

As I close this chapter, I want to leave you with 1 final stimulating thought: When the ravaging, global flood of Noah's day was over, planet Earth obtained a <u>NEW</u> way of being watered…moisture evaporating from the now massive oceans condensed into clouds which were driven inland by wind and dumped on the ground in the form of rain. <u>This was all totally new to mankind</u>! After the horrifying experience of the 1st Great rainstorm, can you imagine the fear Noah and his family (and their soon born children who would repopulate Earth) would have felt the next time they saw rain? They would have panicked in terror!!! <u>THAT</u> is why God declared a rainbow—a now 1st time possible natural phenomena formed by sunlight passing through rain!—as a visual reminder to mankind He would NEVER again destroy Earth with water: "*<u>I do set my bow in the cloud, and it shall be for a token of a covenant between me and the earth…and the waters shall NO more become a flood to destroy ALL flesh</u>*" *(Genesis 9:13, 15).* Wow, so out of love, God made mankind a "rainbow promise" to slowly ease their fear of rain.

One day while I was writing this chapter it began raining like cats and dogs. Stepping into my garage, I raised the overhead garage door and stood staring at a torrential rain cutting through a black, ominously rumbling sky. I watched the pounding raindrops bounce crazily off the blacktop, then quickly gather into puddles which filled up and let loose in tiny streams that raced downhill into the grass. Suddenly, it hit me like a ton of bricks; <u>I was witnessing evidence of Noah's global flood!!!</u> Friend, <u>EVERY TIME it rains it is PROOF of the 1st great rainstorm and a perpetual reminder of God's coming wrath</u>! Then a cold chill ran down my spine as the wind blew some of the rain in on me, and I got a quick mental flash of the wicked people's pandemonium as they tried to escape death in the rising water! Their hopeless frantic running, ghastly contorted faces, and gnarled fingers zipped across my mind like flickering images from a horror movie.

So the next time the sky cracks and the lightning flashes in a rainstorm, think about how much God abhors sin (disobedience to the 10 Love Commandments) and bear in mind there is ANOTHER global disaster coming soon! This time God will annihilate planet Earth's surface and all the ungodly people's flesh with a ravaging fire: "**For our God is a consuming fire**" (Hebrews 12:29). Truly, Jesus Christ's 2nd Coming will commence with a burning, global inferno, playing out in perfect prophetic fulfillment of the global devastation of Noah's day: *"But as the days of Noah were, SO shall ALSO the coming of the Son of man be." (Matthew 24:37)*. I pray you find the courage, will, and fear to forsake the way of evil (sin) before that terrible Day of the Lord arrives!

Chapter 5

Abraham

"And there was a FAMINE in the land;
and Abram went DOWN into Egypt to sojourn there"
(Genesis 12:10)

After the devastation of the worldwide flood in 2316 BC was over and the massive quantity of water had receded into its new, low-lying, oceanic dwelling places, much less land area now existed above water. Throughout the humungous oceans, this pristine ground now dotted planet Earth in the basic 7 continental shapes we know on the map today. Noah's house of 8 people and all the animals stepped off the Ark—which had come to rest on Mount Ararat (located in modern day Turkey)—onto a new and different planet Earth. Children were soon born, as mankind set out repopulating Earth. Archeological digs prove mankind first settled in and created city-states all around the Middle Eastern area known today as the "Fertile Crescent"—stretching up the Tigris & Euphrates Rivers of Mesopotamia, across to the Jordan River & Mediterranean Sea of Canaan, and back down to the Red Sea & Nile River in Upper Egypt. It was a time long before the Medes & Persians, Greeks, and Romans (who would rise to power during the 1ˢᵗ millennium BC) dominated the area.

In this setting, <u>292</u> years after Noah's Flood, Abram (Abraham) was born [See Figure #1, page 12]. Abraham was another 10 patriarchal generations removed from Noah. And one day during his life God indirectly told him the Messiah would someday come from his lineage! Thus, Abraham became the 20th generational father (from Adam) on the direct genealogical descent to the coming Messiah. Oh, and God had BIG plans for the events in this man's life!!! For this would be the man through whom God would begin revealing to mankind—albeit, clandestinely!—His great plan of redemption (salvation or deliverance) for their souls. In other words, by controlling certain events in Abraham's life, God was going to secretly PROPHESY about the work Jesus would do during his 1st Coming—specifically, year 4,000! And just like Enoch & Noah's generational numbers had spiritual meaning with respect to what God was revealing through the events in their life, so too did Abraham's number of 20.

"20" was/is God's number for "redemption". Imagine that!!! To confirm this (once the nation of Israel was established) God commanded all the males, age 20 and up, to pay a yearly "20 gerahs" ransom-offering for their souls: *"Then shall they give every man a RANSOM for his soul unto the LORD...This they shall give...half a shekel after the shekel of the sanctuary: (**a shekel is twenty gerahs**:) an half shekel shall be the offering of the LORD...**from twenty years old and above**, shall give an offering unto the LORD...to make an ATONEMENT for your souls" (Exodus 30: 12-16).* Do you see? In God's eyes the number "20" stood/stands for atonement (or redemption) and ransom: This is precisely what Jesus Christ was coming to DO and PAY for mankind's souls! Therefore, I will tell you again; by choosing Abraham as the 20th patriarch on the direct genealogical descent to the Messiah, God was saying, "I am going to control and manipulate certain events in Abraham's life to prophetically start revealing my plan of deliverance for mankind's souls." Realize though, at the time, mankind did NOT know God was doing this!!! Shoot...most folks today—even preachers!—still do not know God DID this, for they do not know what the Old Testament stories are about! (In the "*Moses*" chapter, I am going to surprise you with something else God DID with the redemption-number "20" solidifying Christ died during mankind's 4,000th year!)

Digressing a little, observe God's mesmerizing omniscience

106

on display in this little-known, amazing fact in Abraham's life: <u>God planned for Abraham to be born during mankind's **1,948**<u>th</u> year (1,656 (flood) + 292)</u>! Do you recognize the number? It is the number of the year on our <u>current</u> Gregorian calendar that Israel—the fig tree—was reborn as a nation (**<u>AD 1948</u>**)! Jumping ahead briefly…Abraham was to be the grandfather of Jacob, whose name God would change to <u>Israel</u>; thus, <u>Abraham was the grandfather of the nation of Israel</u>! Do you think the "year-number" exactness of "Abraham's birth" and "Israel's rebirth" is a coincidence? Friend, not a chance!!! God foresaw "last-days" mankind creating a yearly calendar based on Jesus' birth—He even knew they would be wrong on that fact by a few years!—and He planned for Israel to be reborn on the <u>same</u> numbered year as Abraham's birth from Creation. This is just God, again, cleverly demonstrating His "ability to know the future", <u>proving</u> to us (or giving us evidence) that He exists and that He had the entire Game of Life mapped out before He even founded planet Earth. So, for the record, Abraham was born around 2024 BC (3972 BC – 1,948).

Interestingly, Noah was still living during the first 58 years of Abraham's life! The Bible documents Noah lived 350 years after the flood: *"And <u>Noah lived after the flood three hundred and fifty years. And all the days of Noah were nine hundred and fifty years: and he died"</u> (Genesis 9:28, 29).* (Remember, Abraham was born 292 years after the flood.) So here is food for stimulating thought: Abraham might have heard a firsthand account from Noah of the horrendous, global flood! Picture little Abraham sitting at old Noah's feet listening to how he built an Ark to the saving of his family (house). Consider Abraham's reaction to the righteous "fear of God" flashing in Noah's eyes as he recounted the moment it first began to rain! I can see young Abraham's eyes grow wide with horror as Noah told him about the people screaming and banging on the door of the Ark wanting in, but God had already shut the door! No doubt, Noah's unwavering, raw belief in the invisible Creator God, entrenched in his cracking voice, would have made a lasting impression on Abraham.

In any case, history confirms the "global flood story" passed along orally to mankind during the centuries following the flood. As people spread out across planet Earth, obviously the horrifying flood tale went with them: There are nearly 100 similar flood accounts known among native people across the globe. Almost every indigenous tribe still recounts some form of the diluvian tale. One of the earliest forms of writing archeologists have unearthed is "cuneiform", and it exists on thousands of clay tablets excavated from Middle Eastern soil. What do you suppose was the underlying, prevailing theme in those writings? Almost universally, they express anxiety, concern, and dread of a flood! Friend, it took a long time for the fear of the "flood incident" to leave the hearts of mankind. Nowadays, it is completely gone!

For whatever reason, Abraham clearly <u>believed</u> in the invisible Creator God (love) because the Bible says: ***"<u>Abraham obeyed my (God's) voice, and KEPT my charge, my commandments, my statutes, and my laws</u>"*** *(Genesis 26:5)*. Say what? Friend, here is the <u>DEFINITIVE</u> proof of what I have been telling you: <u>ALL mankind's hearts have known God's 10 Love Commandments</u>! For how could Abraham have <u>KEPT</u> all of God's <u>laws</u>, <u>commandments</u>, and <u>statutes</u> if he did not know them? (Moses would not receive the 10 Love Commandments on Mount Sinai until over 600 years later!) Friend, I rest my case: The moment Adam & Eve ate the forbidden fruit from the tree of the knowledge of good and evil, ALL of God's future-born spirit children on Earth were born <u>knowing</u> the difference between good & evil in their heart—which is obedience or disobedience to the 10 Love Commandments, respectively. And what made Abraham special in God's eyes was that he followed after the WAY of good, obeying God's 10 Love Commandments!

But if you still do not believe me, let us keep Biblically proving mankind's knowledge of EACH of the 10 Love Commandments long before Moses' time. In the 9th chapter of Genesis, you will find a story proving mankind knew God's 5th Love Commandment, *"Honour thy father and mother"*. For after the flood, Noah's son Ham saw his dad drunken and uncovered in his tent. But instead of humbly covering his father's nakedness and shutting his mouth about it, Ham went and jokingly told his 2 brothers, Shem & Japheth, about it! When Noah found out what Ham had done, he CURSED his descendants. Read about it! Then ask yourself, "After being cursed, do you think Ham knew he had done evil (wrong)?" Friend, HE KNEW BEFORE THAT!!! ALL

108

mankind knows they are to <u>respect</u> their parents.

Here is another story, in the 20th chapter of Genesis, proving mankind knew God's 7th Love Commandment, "Thou shalt not commit adultery". The king of Gerar, Abimelech, took Abraham's wife Sarah into his courts for he did not know she was married. But God came to Abimelech in a dream, saying: "*Behold, thou art but a DEAD man, for the woman (Sarah) which thou hast taken; for she is a man's wife*" *(Genesis 20:3)*. Do you think Abimelech did NOT know adultery was a sin? Shoot, he feared for his life!!! But God kept him from SINNING: "*I (God) also withheld thee from SINNING against me: therefore suffered I thee NOT to touch her*" *(Genesis 20:6)*. Please read the full story and then ask yourself, "<u>WHEN</u> did mankind learn "adultery" was a <u>sin</u>?" The answer is blatantly obvious…when Adam & Eve sinned! (Incidentally, more proof mankind knew "lying" was a sin is contained in the same story.)

Alright, let us now delve into God's prognostications through the adventures in Abraham's life. Abraham lived with his wife Sarai (Sarah) in his father's clan in Haran. But when Abraham was 75 years old, God told him: "***Get thee out of thy country, and from thy kindred, and from thy father's house***, *unto a land that I will show thee: And I will make of thee a great nation, and I will bless thee…and **in thee shall all the families of the earth be blessed**" (Genesis 12:1-3)*. Now why would God tell Abraham to leave his father? Why could not Abraham's ENTIRE clan go? Because, friend, God has just begun another parable and it has to be accurate in every way!!! Oh sure, Abraham is going to live these events, but they are speaking symbolically and spiritually about the Messiah! In other words, through His words to Abraham, God was already revealing hidden details about His plan of deliverance for mankind's bound souls. (Remember, mankind's souls are helplessly separated from God's Spirit of life.)

See, "<u>*ALL*</u> *the families of the Earth*" would be blessed through what the Messiah would do for them on the cross. But for THAT to take place, <u>the Messiah would have to leave his Father's house and kindred (angels) in Heaven and come to planet Earth</u>! Do you understand? God's instructions to Abraham were actually a prophetic, behind-the-scenes glimpse at His conversation with Jesus before Earth's establishment:

"Son, one day you will need to 'get thee out of Heaven', away from Me (your Father) and go to planet Earth. And through what you will do there on a cross, all My spirit children will be blessed. And, eventually, I will make of thee (and your 'house' of people) a great nation there." See, God was <u>prophesying</u> about the Christ! NOW you know why God told Abraham to leave his father. And now you know in this story (parable) Abraham represents Jesus.

Note: it is now mankind's 2,023rd year (1656 + 292 + 75) or roughly 1949 BC (3972 BC – 2,023). What does that mean? It means the 3rd millennial day in God's 7 day (7,000 year) master plan has begun! THIS would be the millennium God had penciled in to covertly make known the coming redemptive work of His son, the Messiah Jesus! God will secretly deal with the revelation 3 times—in Abraham's life, Jacob's life, and in the nation of Israel's life. All of these stories are REALLY parables, and they will <u>all</u> occur during the 3rd millennial day! Thus, the 3rd millennial day in God's 7 day (7,000 year) master plan for mankind was for furtively foretelling how He would deliver mankind's souls from their bondage to sin and death.

Abraham obeyed God and departed from his father's house with a few people and his wife Sarah. So in this story (parable), Abraham represents Jesus leaving his Father's house. Truly, the Bible affirms Jesus left all the treasures of glory in heaven—his Father, the angels, etc—to come to Earth and <u>bless ALL the souls of mankind</u> by freeing them from bondage: *"But we see Jesus, <u>who was made a little lower than the angels for the suffering of death</u>, crowned with glory and honour; that he by the grace of God should taste death for every man... <u>**in bringing many sons unto glory**</u>"* (Hebrews 1:9, 10). Paul wrote: *"For ye know the grace of our Lord Jesus Christ, that, <u>though he was rich, yet for your sakes he became poor</u>"* (II Corinthians 8:9). Do you see? Jesus left the splendor of Heaven to become a man, in the flesh, on this sin-sick Earth. And he did it for us!!!

When Abraham arrived in Canaan—present day land of Israel—God told him: *"<u>Unto thy SEED will I give this land</u>"* (Genesis 12:7). This, too, is about Jesus! Paul understood it: *"<u>Now to Abraham and his SEED were the promises made.</u> He saith not, And to seeds, as of many; but as of one, And <u>**to thy seed, WHICH IS CHRIST**</u>"*

(Galatians 3:16). Do you understand? See, the "seed promise" God made to Abraham was NOT about the Jews or the Earthly nation of Israel: It was a prophecy about the coming Messiah, Jesus Christ!!! Jesus was going to be the "spiritual seed" that would BIRTH a spiritual harvest of ALL the righteous spirit children counted worthy to enter the kingdom of God: And it is Jesus who will be given the land of Israel to rule Earth from in the coming Kingdom of God and forever! So, in actuality, God's covenantal "seed promise" to Abraham was merely a promise that the Messiah, Jesus, would one day come through his loins: *"For verily he (Jesus) took not on him the nature of angels; but **he took on him the seed of Abraham**" (Hebrews 2:16)*.

Allow me to further clarify the true meaning of God's covenantal "seed promise", because it can be an esoteric concept. Look, for something to be born or birthed it ALWAYS requires a seed—like an azalea seed produces azaleas or an acorn seed produces an oak tree. In other words, where there is a "seed" there is potential for life, because once a seed is planted something can be born. Do you understand? Well, do you remember from chapter 3 that after Adam & Eve sinned in the Garden of Eden, mankind's souls were DEAD, for sin had separated their spirits from God's Spirit of Life? Alright, then it would take a SEED to birth them back to life!!! And, in God's plan of redemption, Jesus would be that "spiritual seed".

But here is the key; for a seed to produce (or birth) a harvest, it must be planted in the Earth! See, only after burying an acorn seed in the ground (symbolizing death) does it crack open and burst forth with life, popping a green stem into existence! Look, the moment the Messiah was conceived by the Holy Spirit in Mary's womb, the "sinless spiritual seed" able to birth life into mankind's dead souls was in existence. But for that to occur, the seed would have to be buried (die)!!! Thus, Jesus died spiritually and physically on a cross and was planted in the heart of the Earth. But 3 days later, He burst forth with resurrection life! And now he stands alone as the ONLY ONE—the "spiritual seed"—possessing the life-giving power whereby mankind's souls can obtain eternal life.

Jesus understood all of this; listen to his words as he wrestled with the emotional pain of his imminent death: *"The hour is come, that* the Son of man should be glorified. Verily, verily, I say unto you, *Except a corn (seed, kernel of grain) of wheat fall into the ground and die, it abideth alone:* **but if it die, it bringeth forth much fruit**" *(John 12:23, 24).* Do you see? Jesus knew he had to die to bring forth a spiritual harvest of souls! He knew he was the fulfillment of the covenantal "seed promise" given to Abraham, Isaac, & Jacob in the Old Testament Scriptures, and that after his death and resurrection, he would have the power to birth mankind's dead spirits (souls) back to life!

Incidentally, this is what Jesus meant when he informed Nicodemus, *"**Except a man be born again**, he cannot see the kingdom of God" (John 3:3).* See, mankind's souls need to be spiritually "reborn" to return to God. Jesus noticed Nicodemus' confusion and said, *"You, a respected Jewish teacher, and yet you don't understand these things?" (John 3:10, Living Bible).* Look, Nicodemus and the Jewish priests taught from the Law (Old Testament Scriptures) and prided themselves to be from Abraham's physical seed. They thought God's covenantal "seed promise" to Abraham was about them—the Jewish people and the nation of Israel—but it was not! It was about the Messiah, the very ONE talking to Nicodemus!!! Consequently, after scolding Nicodemus on his ignorance, Jesus immediately shifted the conversation to his imminent death: *"And as Moses lifted up the serpent in the wilderness, even so must the Son of man (Jesus) be lifted up" (John 3:14).* In other words, Jesus was revealing to Nicodemus that he would have to die to become the "spiritual seed" whereby mankind's souls could be "born again". Nicodemus probably still did not understand Jesus' train of thought, but make no mistake about it; Jesus was/is the fulfillment of God's covenantal "seed promise" to the Patriarchs.

And since Jesus is the "spiritual seed", then those people who repent of sin—willingly choose to live righteously by obeying the 10 Love Commandments—will one day become his "spiritual harvest". This is why Jesus often told parables relating his 2nd Coming to a "harvest" or "reaping" event: *"The harvest is the end of the world (age); and the reapers are the angels" (Matthew 13:39).* He told his Disciples: *"The harvest truly is plenteous, but the labourers are few; Pray ye therefore the Lord of the harvest, that he will send forth labourers into his harvest" (Matthew 9:37, 38).* Do you understand? Everyone

112

who ever lived on planet Earth, who chose to live righteously, will be "harvested" at Jesus' 2nd Coming, for Jesus is the "spiritual seed" that grew (or made possible) that harvest! Listen to God prophesying through Isaiah, around 800 BC, about the coming Messiah: *"when his SOUL has been made an offering for sin, then he (Jesus) shall have a multitude of children, many heirs" (Isaiah 53:10, Living Bible).*

One day soon, God will make Jesus ruler of planet Earth, and it is his righteous spiritual children birthed by his "spiritual seed" that will become THE great nation, inhabiting Earth: *"The kingdoms of this world are become the kingdoms of our Lord, and of his Christ; and **HE shall reign for ever and ever**" (Revelation 11:15).* In other words, the great nation God promised Abraham was REALLY prophecy about the coming, 7th millennial day, great nation made up of all the harvested "spiritual" children of Abraham"—those who obey the 10 Love Commandments. God confirmed a "child of Abraham" in His eyes is NOT an Israelite per se, but rather ANY spirit child on Earth exhibiting faith (love): *"Even as Abraham believed God, and it was accounted to him for righteousness. **Know ye therefore that they which are of faith, THE SAME ARE THE CHILDREN OF ABRAHAM**. And the scripture, foreseeing that God would justify the heathen through faith, preached before the gospel unto Abraham, saying, In thee shall all nations be blessed. **So then they which be of faith are blessed with faithful Abraham**" (Galatians 3:6-9).* Do you see? I will discuss clearly what it truly means to have FAITH in God (love) in the *"Faith"* chapter. You will discover the Biblical term "faith" actually means "to have faith in love (God)", which is ONLY proved (shown) by obeying the 10 Love Commandments. This is why the Bible says, *"Faith without works (the works of love) is dead"*, meaning it is nonexistent. Remember Abraham obeyed all of God's Commandments...THAT is what proved his faith (belief) in God (love).

It is vital that you understand God's "chosen people" are ALL the righteous souls who have ever lived! God's "chosen spirit children" cannot be identified by some meaningless, Earthly title like an Israelite, Russian, Egyptian, Babylonian, or American. These are merely nationality-tag names given to physical groups of people. Friend, the name of the country you lived under while on planet Earth will NOT make a hill of beans of difference on Judgment Day. Paul recognized this and wrote: "*There is neither Jew nor Greek, there is neither bond nor free, there is neither male nor female:* for ye are ALL one in Christ Jesus. And *if ye be Christ's, then are ye Abraham's seed, and heir according to the promise*" *(Galatians 3:28, 29)*. Do you understand? God's "chosen people" are those with Christ's Spirit of love living inside their hearts. THESE are the people who will be heirs of the coming, promised Great nation, ruled by Jesus Christ.

See, friend, in God's eyes we are ALL His spirit children. He loves us ALL equally for He is no respecter of persons: "*For there is NO respect of persons with God*" *(Romans 2:11)*. In other words, He does NOT favor one person over another! Whomever you are reading this book, you mean as much to God as Abraham did. No Israelite or Jew is any more valuable to God then you are! God's "chosen people" will come from all nationalities! Think about it logically; there will be thousands and thousands of Israelites in hell, just as any other nationality. Were any of them God's "chosen people"? No!!! God's "chosen souls" will ALL receive eternal life because they will have REPENTED—chose the WAY of good (love) over the Way of evil (sin) by obeying the 10 Love Commandments.

Returning to the story (parable) of Abraham, do you know who his WIFE Sarah represents? She represents the "bride of Christ"! See, this is just another way the Bible spiritually characterizes those people who make the decision to live their lives in obedience to the 10 Love Commandments. Not only are they the spiritual "sons & daughters of Christ", part of the "house of Christ", "born again" of his "spiritual seed", and spiritual "children of Abraham; but they are also considered "married to Christ": "*Wherefore, my brethren, ye also are become dead to the law by the body of Christ; that ye should be married to another, even to him (Jesus) who is raised from the dead, that we should bring forth fruit unto God*" *(Romans 7:4)*. Do you see? People that live righteously (bear fruit)—you will learn what "bearing fruit" truly means in the "*Bearing Fruit*" chapter—are deemed "*married to Christ*". Jesus often spoke in parables about a coming spiritual wedding, when ALL the righteous people are reconnected with God: "*And Jesus answered and spake unto them again by parables, and said, The kingdom of heaven is like unto a certain king (God), which made a marriage for his son (Jesus)" (Matthew 22:1, 2)*. Consequently, this is just another way the Bible expresses the ending of our present age...the righteous will be allowed into a wedding and the unrighteous will not. Subsequently, in this story (parable), Sarah epitomizes the "bride of Christ"!

Let us examine what happens next in the narrative (parable): *"And **there was a famine in the land**; and Abram went DOWN into Egypt to sojourn there; for the famine was grievous in the land" (Genesis 12:10)*. The "famine theme"—which we will find more of in other ancient Bible stories—symbolizes what happened to planet Earth after Adam & Eve sinned. Mankind's spiritual separation from God (source of life) was/is indicative of a spiritual starvation or a great famine. In other words, in this part of the story (parable) Abraham futuristically represents the Messiah coming down to this sin-filled, spiritually-famished Earth! Notice God's impeccably correct (physical to spiritual) detail in the story...for which direction did Abraham travel? He went DOWN into Egypt! Friend, this is symbolic of Jesus having to leave Heaven and come down to Earth to rescue "fallen" mankind. (Remember, also, sin caused a great "spiritual fall" to Satan and his angles and they were cast down to Earth.) Try and fathom the fact that God planned from Creation to have a great ancient nation, Egypt, rise up south of the promise land—where Abraham was sojourning in Canaan—to precisely fit this prophetic parable!

In this parable, the "physical nation of Egypt" represents "all of fallen Earth" where Lucifer and his angels have set up their kingdom of darkness. And the Egyptian Pharaoh represents Lucifer! (Remember, Lucifer wanted what was God's in the Garden of Eden—namely, ruler-ship over all of planet Earth & God's spirit children—and, subsequently, he became the *"God of this world"* by coercing Adam & Eve to sin.) God symbolized ALL of this in the story (parable) by having "Pharaoh capture Sarah": *"And it came to pass, that, when Abram was come into Egypt, the Egyptians beheld the woman that she was very fair. The princes also of Pharaoh saw her, and commended her before Pharaoh: and **the woman was TAKEN into Pharaoh's house**" (Genesis 12:14, 15)*. Do you see? Through this story (parable), God is secretly recreating an accurate picture of the "bondage situation" plaguing mankind's

115

souls! Thus, Sarah was enslaved by Pharaoh in Egypt, just like Adam & Eve and ALL of mankind's souls were enslaved by Lucifer in the Earth. In other words, Sarah (representing the one day "bride of Christ") was now in bondage to Pharaoh (Satan). Once God had this "bondage scenario" set up, He could now disclose how HE would free mankind's souls (or Sarah in this parable)! Of course, keep in mind it was ALL one big prophetic secret.

So, how was Sarah delivered (saved)? **GOD** **personally did it!!!** Genesis records: *"And the **Lord plagued Pharaoh** and his house with great plagues because of Sarai Abram's wife...And Pharaoh commanded his men concerning him (Abram): and they sent him away, and his wife, and all that he had"* (Genesis 12:17, 20). Ah, do you see? It was a supernatural deliverance! God delivered Sarah by plaguing Pharaoh! See, Abraham's men did not go into Pharaoh's house with swords and fight for his wife's freedom because that would not have fit what God was revealing through the parable. No, her salvation was COMPLETELY by God's hand alone! Do you recognize God's plan of deliverance for the souls of mankind taking shape? Mankind's salvation (freedom) would be a supernatural GIFT from God. Paul would write: *"Therefore as by the offence of one (Adam) judgment came upon all men to condemnation; even so by the righteousness of one (Jesus) **the FREE GIFT** came upon all men unto justification of life"* (Romans 5:18). Friend, mankind could not deliver himself because all mankind had sinned. Thus, God would personally have to deliver mankind's souls. Paul later confirmed: *"To wit, that **God was in Christ, reconciling the world unto himself,** not imputing their trespasses unto them"* (II Corinthians 5:19). Yes, God freed mankind's souls from bondage to sin through Jesus (repairing the breech between mankind's spirit and His) exactly like God personally freed Sarah in this parable!

Ah, but God had one more detail to control to make the story (parable) perfect. The Bible says Abraham left Egypt rich: *"And Abram went up out of Egypt, he, and his wife, and all that he had...And Abram was very rich in cattle, in silver, and in gold"* (Genesis 13:1, 2). Where did Abram get these riches? *"And he (Pharaoh) entreated Abram well for her (Sarai) sake; and he had sheep, and oxen, and he asses, and menservants, and maidservants, and she asses, and camels"*

116

(Genesis 12:16). In other words, Abraham & Sarah left Egypt with Pharaoh's riches after God supernaturally delivered them. What does this represent? This is precisely what happened to mankind's souls after God delivered them out of bondage to sin & death through Jesus. See, mankind was spiritually poor (separated from God's spirit!), but after Christ's work of redemption at the cross we became spiritually rich (able to be reunited with God's spirit, again)!

Paul stated: *"For ye know the grace of our Lord Jesus Christ, that, though he was rich, yet for your sakes he became poor, **that ye through his poverty might be rich**" (II Corinthians 8:9)*. Ah, do you now see the truth? Jesus left his Father in Heaven and came to Earth in human form to die; thus, he became spiritually poor (spiritually separated from his Father on the cross). But his work (death) delivered our souls from spiritual death (separation from God's Spirit) and afforded us the opportunity to someday exist in oneness with God; thus, he made us spiritually rich! NOW you know why Abraham & Sarah left Egypt rich.

Today, "preachers" lacking in spiritual discernment will devilishly claim Abraham's wealth implies God wants everyone to be materialistically wealthy now on Earth. Do you recognize the idiocy of that notion? The story of Abraham being rich had <u>NOTHING</u> to do with God desiring mankind to have materialistic (dirt) wealth: It is a parable!!! Thinking God wants mankind to be materialistically wealthy because Abraham left Egypt with its riches is like thinking Jesus' parable of the seed-sower means God wants us all to be farmers. What absolute absurdity!!! Folks, as I have already stated, the ancient Old Testament stories are <u>all</u> parables—i.e. they are meant to explain important spiritual "concepts" concerning mankind's souls.

Therefore, the story (parable) of Abraham was an extremely accurate, prophetic portrayal of what God would do for mankind's souls through Christ's work on the cross. God would take back the power Satan had over our soul's death by freeing us from our bondage to sin, making us spiritually rich again. The Bible proclaims: *"Forasmuch then as the children are partakers of flesh and blood, he (Jesus) also himself likewise took part of the same; **that through death he might destroy him (Satan) that had the power of death, that is, the devil; And**</u>

117

deliver them who through fear of death were all their lifetime subject to bondage" (Hebrews 2:14, 15). In other words, just like Abraham left with Pharaoh's riches, so too Jesus would leave the cross with Satan's riches—namely, the power OVER mankind's spiritual death!

Now, like I said earlier in this chapter; God will secretly deal with this subject matter (His "plan of deliverance" for mankind's souls) 2 more times by orchestrating the events in other ancient Bible stories, and we will investigate these parables soon. Each successive time, God added a few more details, clandestinely revealing a little more about exactly how and when the Messiah would come and deliver our souls. Thus, this parable of Abraham & Sarah was just an initial, abbreviated look at God's plan of redemption—i.e. the basic "framework" of the plan (plot) was there. And always remember it was ALL a secret mystery: Even the Jewish priests did not understand what God had done and said through the ancient Bible stories!

But rest assured, around 1950 BC—for the 1st time ever!—God had secretly revealed His plan for delivering mankind's souls from their bondage to sin & death through the story (parable) of Abraham & Sarah in Egypt. Stay alert, for God does not wait long until He delves into the topic again! The next time God picks up the "prophetic redemption story" is through Abraham's grandson, Jacob, and his dealings with Laban. Then, finally, God pulls out all the stops and secretly reveals ALL the details of His plan of salvation through 1 final, massive story (parable) involving Jacob's (Israel) children in Egypt.

Those of you possessing some spiritual discernment should recognize (by Abraham & Sarah's experience in Egypt) God was actually giving Abraham a taste of what his future children (the Israelites) would go through in Egypt—specifically, bondage and God's supernatural deliverance! In fact, one dark night God just came right out and told Abraham what would befall his descendants: *"And he (God) said unto Abram, Know of a surety that thy seed shall be a stranger in a land that is not theirs, and shall serve them; and they shall afflict them four hundred years; And also that nation, whom they shall serve, will I judge: and afterward shall they come out with great substance"* (Genesis 15:13, 14). Those that have ears, do you hear?

Chapter 6

Isaac

*"Take now thy son, THINE ONLY SON Isaac, whom thou lovest…
and offer him there for a burnt OFFERING"*
(Genesis 22:2)

Abraham's wife Sarah was barren. But 25 years after God had told Abraham to leave his father's house, Sarah—age 90!—conceived a miracle baby named Isaac. The account of Isaac is a prophetic parable, too! Every detail of the story was arranged and controlled by God to secretly prophesy about the coming Messiah. For the first time ever, God would disclose to mankind: A SUPERNATURALLY-BORN, HUMAN BEING'S DEATH (as a blood sacrifice) would be necessary to atone for mankind's sins! THAT is what the prophetic story (parable) of Abraham, Sarah, & Isaac was/is all about!

Now it is debatable whether or not Abraham, Sarah, or Isaac understood this was the purpose of what God put them through, but certainly no one else got it! The Jewish people of Jesus' day had NO CLUE a sinless human being had to be sacrificed for mankind's sins. And this is exactly as God planned it, for had they known His plan they would NEVER have killed Jesus Christ. Paul even said such: *"But we speak the wisdom of God in a mystery, even the HIDDEN wisdom, which God ordained before the world unto our glory: **Which none of***

119

the princes of this world knew: for had they known it, they would NOT have crucified the Lord of glory" (I Corinthians 2:7, 8). Wow!

Is it not amazing to realize the Jewish Priests and religious leaders of Jesus' day had no inkling of God's plan of salvation? They knew every facet of Abraham & Sarah's story concerning Isaac; they probably read the account from their scrolls often in the synagogues on Sabbath days. Yet, they had NO idea what it signified! Consequently, they had no reservations about killing a sinless, miracle worker like Jesus when he arrived, and God's redemption plan unfolded without a hitch. Friend, the story (parable) of Abraham, Sarah, & Isaac is a truly remarkable account, for God manipulated the events like a top-notched director who knows the value of foreshadowing, revealing stunning detail into the Messiah's future birth and precise method of execution he would suffer paying the ransom for mankind's sins.

But before we analyze the narrative of Abraham, Sarah, & Isaac, let us turn back the game clock to the period RIGHT AFTER Adam & Eve's sin in the Garden of Eden; for there is overlooked Biblical evidence God <u>immediately</u> broached the idea of "a sacrifice for sin" with mankind. Here is the simple but eye-opening verse: "***And the Lord God*** *clothed Adam and his wife with garments made from SKINS OF ANIMALS" (Genesis 3:21, Living Bible).* Wow, remember Adam & Eve's "discovery of their nakedness" was a result of their sin, symbolizing their spiritual separation from God? So what did God do to "COVER their SIN"? He sacrificed (killed) an animal!!! Friend, although this scene was literal, it had a much more important spiritual connotation: This was God's way of <u>secretly</u> saying a "blood sacrifice" would be necessary to atone for (or cover) mankind's sins. Later, King David spoke in similar terms about what happens to a righteous (repentant) person's soul when Christ's completed work of atonement (forgiveness) is applied to their sins: "<u>Blessed are they whose iniquities are forgiven, and whose SINS ARE COVERED</u>" (Romans 4:7). Do you see? Friend, undoubtedly, God <u>introduced</u> the Messianic concept of "a sacrifice for sin" with mankind IN the Garden of Eden.

Then, after Adam & Eve's expulsion from the Garden, we read in the Bible that Eve conceived 2 sons, Cain & Abel, who were "making <u>sacrifices</u>" to God! Did you ever wonder <u>WHY</u> they were doing that?

120

The Bible is silent on the reason, but this story again seems to confirm God instituted the concept of "a sacrifice for sin" with Adam & Eve (and all mankind) after their sin. Think about it; without sin (disobedience to God) having entered mankind's spirits, I can see NO logical reason why God would have desired mankind to "sacrifice things" to Him. Do you understand? In a perfect, sinless world...why would God have wanted mankind to slaughter His beautifully created animals?

Yet, archaeology confirms earliest mankind WAS building sacrificial altars! For example, where there are ancient cave paintings there are stones piled into obvious altars! Therefore I ask you, if ancient mankind never had an encounter with a God, what possessed them to start killing animals in a sacrificial manner? Seriously, think about that!!! If the concept of "God" is some dreamed-up fairytale, how did mankind conjure up the idea of "killing animals" for Him or Her? I just cannot make the connection! Do you understand? Ah, but it appears very logical when considering the Biblical account of mankind's SIN in the Garden of Eden. Yes, surely, God introduced the "sacrifice for sin" concept of His redemption plan to mankind from the beginning—i.e. "offer up" or "sacrifice" something to atone for sin. And every ancient culture did it!

Moreover, in the Biblical Cain & Abel account, God went a step further in secretly foretelling His Messianic salvation plan for mankind's souls by accepting Abel's "lamb offering" and rejecting Cain's "fruit of the ground offering". The Bible records: *"Abel was a keeper of sheep, but Cain was a tiller of the ground" (Genesis 4:2)*. Do you see? This was God's surreptitious way of saying only BLOOD would be an acceptable "sacrifice for sin". See, there is NO blood in vegetables or grain! Imagine, even from the beginning of time, God put His prophetic stamp of approval on the notion of a "sacrificial lamb". But now in the story (parable) of Abraham, Sarah, & Isaac—a little over 2,000 years into the history of mankind—God is going to ratchet up His "sacrificial lamb concept" by unveiling it would take a HUMAN sacrifice! A Messiah!!! And sure enough (even though mankind did not know it) Jesus was to become the truly accepted "sacrificial Lamb of God": *"In whom we have redemption through his (Jesus) blood, the forgiveness of sins, according to the riches of his grace" (Ephesians*

1:7). Let us take a look at the account.

Try and put yourself in Abraham' sandals, viewing the situation from his perspective. Imagine not knowing anything you know today about the man Jesus. In other words, you are totally in the dark (as well as the rest of the world) about God's plan of redemption. Then, one day when Abraham is 99 years old, the invisible, creator God comes and reconfirms the covenantal "seed promise" He made with you when you were younger: *"I am the Almighty God; walk before me, and be thou perfect...I will establish my covenant between me and thee and thy seed after thee in their generations for an everlasting covenant, to be a God unto thee, and to thy seed after thee. And **I will give unto thee, and to thy seed after thee, the land wherein thou art a stranger, all the land of Canaan, for an EVERLASTING possession; and I will be their God**" (Genesis 17:1, 7, 8)*. Friend, once again, God's promise here is talking about the "spiritual seed", Jesus Christ! For only those *"born again"* of the "spiritual seed' of Christ (love) will live eternally. (Note: God's land promise is an everlasting one, signifying eternal life in the Kingdom of God.)

In the 1ˢᵗ century AD, God prophesied through John the Revelator about the time after His 7 day (7,000 year) plan is over: *"I saw a new heaven and a new earth: for the first heaven and the first earth were passed away; and there was no more sea...And I heard a great voice out of heaven saying, Behold, the tabernacle of God is with men, and he will dwell with them, and **they shall be his people, and God himself shall be with them, and be their God**" (Revelation 21:1, 3)*. Do you see the same futuristic *"I will be their God"* language in John the Revelator's writing and God's covenantal "seed promise" to Abraham? That is because they are the same topic! Again, everyone who chooses to live righteously (obeys the 10 Love Commandments) is a "spiritual child of Abraham" no matter what nationality name they live under while on planet Earth. THESE are the "spirit children" to whom the covenantal "seed promise" God made with Abraham will apply, for God will be their God, forever and ever!!!

Honestly, again, ALL the covenantal "seed promise" meant for Abraham was that the Messiah (Savior), Jesus, would one day come from his lineage and that he could be a part of the Messiah's great earthly Kingdom if he continued to walk perfectly before God by obeying His 10 Love Commandments. Do you understand? Listen closely to God's covenantal words to Abraham: *"I will establish my covenant **between me and thee** and **thy seed after thee in their generations** for an everlasting covenant, to be a God unto thee, and to thy seed after thee"* (Genesis 17:7). God is REALLY saying (and I am paraphrasing), "Abraham, the 'spiritual seed of the Messiah' is going to come from your lineage, and I will continue to make that declaration (covenant) to each of your descendants in their generations." In other words, God was going to mark the patriarchal path to the Messiah by continually affirming it with whoever was next on the list! Is that not incredible? And if you know the Bible, you know God did just that!!! For the complete patriarchal genealogy of Jesus Christ is recorded there [See Figure #3, page 79]. There were 40 patriarchs after Abraham until the Messiah! How and why do you think this lineage was known throughout all those centuries? Think about it!

After reaffirming the covenantal "seed promise" with Abraham (while still talking) God then informed him his barren wife, Sarah, would bear him a son! Do you understand what God was doing? God just transitioned from the covenantal "seed promise"—which was/is ALL about the Messiah!—to now talking about Isaac. And what was Isaac going to represent? The MESSIAH, the "spiritual seed"—miracle birth & human sacrifice!!! In other words, God had not switched subjects at all: His entire conversation with Abraham was about the Messiah, Jesus—the "spiritual seed". So in its entirety, here is what God was really saying to Abraham (and I am paraphrasing), "Abraham, I promise you the Messiah—the "spiritual seed" whereby all righteous souls will obtain eternal life—will one day come from your lineage, and I will continue to confirm this covenantal "seed promise" with each of your descendants in their specific generation, continually tracing the patriarchal path to the Messiah. But for now, allow Me to secretly show you things concerning the coming Messiah ("the spiritual seed") by controlling the circumstances in your life, for your barren wife is about to have a miracle baby—patriarch #21 on the direct genealogical descent to the Messiah—and I am going to ask you to sacrifice him!"

Wow, my gut tells me Abraham did not understand ANY of this!

But let us investigate how God used Isaac's life to prophesy of the coming Messiah. It began with his strange birth, for Sarah had been barren her entire life: *"Sarai was barren; she had no child" (Genesis 11:30)*. But now at 90 years old and WELL past her childbearing years, God told Abraham she will bear him a son! Abraham just laughed: *"Then Abraham fell upon his face, and laughed, and said in his heart, Shall a child be born unto him that is an hundred years old? And shall Sarah, that is ninety years old, bear?" (Genesis 17:17)*. Do you understand what is taking place here? A barren woman is past her ovulation days: *"Now Abraham and Sarah were old and well stricken in age; and it ceased to be with Sarah after the manner of women" (Genesis 18:11)*. Yet, God declares she will have a son!!! Friend, God is revealing the way in which the Messiah will be born—namely, SUPERNATURALLY! Isaac's birth will be a supernatural birth!!! Over 1,500 years later, God forthrightly authenticated the Messiah's birth would be a supernatural birth by prophesying through Isaiah's lips: *"Therefore the Lord himself shall give you a sign; Behold, **a virgin shall conceive**, and bear a son, and shall call his name Immanuel (God with us)" (Isaiah 7:14)*.

God rebuked Abraham; *"Is any thing too hard for the LORD? At the time appointed I will return unto thee, according to the time of life, and Sarah shall have a **son**" (Genesis 18:14)*. Like I said before, I doubt Abraham realized his circumstances were God's way of revealing things to him about the coming Messiah. But in this announcement to Abraham God was foretelling the Messiah would be a MAN, because Sarah would bear a SON. Also, take into account that God had a set time for the birth! Look at God's words again. Do you notice God had an exact time appointed? This is exactly the way it would be with the Messiah! After Christ's death, resurrection, & ascension, Paul wrote: *"But when the FULLNESS of the TIME was COME, God sent forth his Son, made of a woman" (Galatians 4:4)*. Do you see? You will soon learn, unequivocally, everything had to occur on time concerning Jesus, because he HAD to be ready to die on Earth during mankind's 4,000th year! Friend, it was all God's plan from the beginning: He had an EXACT time appointed!!!

Then, the Bible records: *"And the **LORD visited Sarah** as he* had said, and the **LORD DID UNTO SARAH** as he had spoken. *For Sarah conceived, and bare Abraham a son in his old age, at the set time of which God had spoken to him" (Genesis 21:1, 2).* The manner in which the Bible records *"the Lord visited Sarah"* and *"the Lord did unto Sarah"* sounds uncannily similar to the way the angel Gabriel described Mary would conceive: *"The Holy Ghost shall **come upon thee**, and the power of the Highest shall **overshadow thee**: therefore also that holy thing which shall be born of thee shall be called the Son of God" (Luke 1:35).* Do you see? Sarah's divinely born child, Isaac, was a prophetic picture of the divinely born Messiah child, Jesus!

Abraham was 100 years old when Isaac was born. Let us orient ourselves to where we are at this time in God's 7 day (7,000 year) master plan. Abraham being 100 years old would place Isaac's birth during mankind's 2,048th year (1948 + 100 years) or approximately 1924 BC (3972 BC – 2,048): *"And Abraham was an hundred years old, when his son Isaac was born to him. And Sarah said, God hath made me to laugh, so that **ALL that hear will laugh with me**" (Genesis 21:5, 6).* Even this verse was spiritually prophetic, because the Messiah's birth was truly a joyous occasion for all mankind! The very night Jesus was born, an angel of the Lord heralded to shepherds in a field; *"Fear not: for, behold, I bring you good tidings of GREAT JOY, which shall be to all people. For unto you is born this day in the city of David a Saviour, which is Christ the Lord" (Luke 2:10, 11).* Truly, mankind can be forever joyful of the Savior's birth.

Furthermore, Abraham named the supernaturally born child "Isaac" meaning "laughter". This was/is a very portentously fitting name for the Lord Jesus, because he will surely have the last laugh on all those who live wickedly: *"The wicked plotteth against the just, and gnasheth upon him with his teeth. The Lord shall LAUGH at him: for he seeth that his day is coming...**FOR THE LORD LOVETH JUDGMENT**, and forsaketh not his saints; they are preserved for ever: but the seed of the wicked shall be cut off" (Psalms 37:12, 13, 28).* Jesus told the righteous: *"Blessed are ye that hunger now: for ye shall be filled. Blessed are ye that weep now: **for ye shall laugh**" (Luke 6:21).* Yes, "laughter" was a very appropriate name to represent the coming Messiah, for someday the righteous will ALL laugh—along

125

with Sarah!—because of the miraculously born Messiah.

Years passed, and then one day when Isaac was a young boy God asked Abraham to do an appalling thing: <u>He commanded him to sacrifice his son</u>! Listen to the account: *"And he (God) said, Take now thy son, **thine only son** Isaac, **whom thou lovest**, and get thee into the land of Moriah; **and offer him there for a burnt offering** upon one of the mountains which I will tell thee of" (Genesis 22:2)*. Can you imagine Abraham's reaction? He must have thought God went crazy!!! Is that not a stunning request from God? Yes, in that time period it surely was, but not now when we know what God was doing! God was prophesying almost 2,000 years ahead of time—by controlling the circumstances in Abraham's life—that the Messiah would have to be offered up as a <u>HUMAN SACRIFICE</u>! Even the exact words God spoke to Abraham were prophesying of what <u>HE</u> would have to do someday with his son: *"**For God so loved the world**, **that he gave his ONLY begotten Son**, that whosoever believeth in him should not perish, but have everlasting life" (John 3:16)*. What poetic beauty!

Did you notice God had a SPECIFIC mountain he wanted Abraham to offer Isaac upon in the land of Moriah? Why? Well the land of Moriah is where the city of Jerusalem would later reside. Thus, it is believed God actually led Abraham to the exact location where Jesus would be crucified almost 2,000 years later! Knowing how precise God is with things, I would not doubt this was the case. Picture Abraham standing on the very ground where the Son of God would be crucified almost 2,000 years later, playing out the part by willingly choosing to offer up his only son!!! It is truly mind-boggling to grasp God's stealthy prophetic precision in divulging His plan of redemption. Every detail was unveiling Jesus' future work at the cross—even the location!

If you have not already figured it out, in this story (parable) Abraham represents God, Sarah represents Mary, and Isaac represents Jesus. Watch the prophetic parable unfold with stunning exactness! Abraham prepared the wood for the burnt offering, like God would prepare (grow) the wood (tree) Jesus would be hung on: *"And Abraham rose up early in the morning, and saddled his ass, and took <u>TWO of his young men with him</u>, and Isaac his son, and <u>clave (split) the wood</u> for the burnt offering, and rose up, and went unto the place of which God* had told him" *(Genesis 22:3)*. When they came near to the sacrifice site, Abraham told the 2 men to wait with the ass, while he and Isaac went and made the sacrifice. (The "two men" Abraham took with him pictured the 2 men who would die alongside Jesus!)

Next, Abraham gave the wood to Isaac to carry!!! Yes, Isaac carried the wood he would be sacrificed upon up a hill—probably the same hill!!!—Jesus would carry the wood he would be sacrificed upon: *"And **Abraham took the wood of the burnt offering, and LAID IT UPON Isaac his son**; and he took the fire in his hand, and a knife" (Genesis 22:6).* How do you like God's perfectionism in the details so far? It would not surprise me one bit if Abraham had bundled the wood in such a way that Isaac was able to carry it on his shoulders, just like Jesus would carry a wooden beam on his shoulders nearly 2,000 years later! What meticulous prophetic accuracy!

As they walked up the hill, a brief Biblically-recorded dialogue transpired between Abraham & Isaac that is the zenith of prophetic utterances. Isaac asked the infamous question: *"Behold the fire and the wood: but **where is the lamb** for a burnt offering?" (Genesis 22:7).* To which Abraham replied, *"My son, **God will provide HIMSELF a lamb** for a burnt offering" (Genesis 22:8).* Wow, these prophetic lines of dialogue are far better then the most famed "one-liners" in movies today—e.g. "I'll be back" or "Make my day"—for truly God would provide the Lamb, and it would be His very own Son—which was Him! Therefore, in this terse exchange, God solidified the Messiah would be known as the "Lamb of God". And sure enough, John the Baptist recognized Jesus some 2,000 years later: *"The next day John seeth Jesus coming unto him, and saith, **Behold the Lamb of God**, which taketh away the sin of the world" (John 1:29).*

Next, the Bible documents: *"And they came to the place which God had told him of; and Abraham built an altar there, and laid the wood in order, and **bound Isaac his son, and laid him on the altar upon the wood**" (Genesis 22:9).* I told you...details, details, details! Can you visualize this amazing prophetic scene? Isaac is tied up and laid upon wood, just like Jesus would be bound upon a wooden cross. What is even more remarkable about this prophetic story (parable) is "death by crucifixion" would not be invented till around 500 BC! So

127

God was giving Abraham & Isaac a visual image of the future suffering of the Messiah's crucifixion at a time when they could not have possibly dreamed of the brutality of that cruel death. Friend, indubitably, God knows everything, including the future!!!

Well, you know the rest of the story; God stops Abraham right before he slays his son! Then, Abraham turned and saw a ram caught by his horns in some underbrush: *"And Abraham lifted up his eyes, and looked, and behold behind him **a RAM caught in a thicket by his horns**: and Abraham went and took the ram, and offered him up for a burnt offering in the stead of his son" (Genesis 22:13)*. Hmmm....I wonder how a lamb just happened to arrive at the perfect time? Do you know what a "ram" is? A ram is a <u>male</u> sheep! Friend, even the ram God provided symbolized the <u>man</u> Jesus. The original Hebrew word translated *"ram"* was *"ayil"*, meaning: <u>ram, a male sheep generally more aggressive and protective of the flock</u>. Did you catch that? When Jesus came to planet Earth, he often referred to himself as the shepherd of the flock. So he was the Lamb of God, but <u>he was also the leader of the flock</u>, just like the RAM caught in the thicket!

Eventually, God made the covenantal "seed promise" with Isaac, assuring the Messiah would come through his lineage: *"And the LORD appeared unto him (Isaac), and said, <u>Go not down into Egypt</u>; dwell in the land which I shall tell thee of: Sojourn in this land, and I will be with thee, and will bless thee; for unto thee, and <u>unto thy seed, I will give all these countries</u>, and I will perform the oath which I sware unto Abraham thy father; And I will make <u>thy seed</u> to multiply as the stars of heaven, and will give unto thy seed all these countries; and **<u>in thy seed shall all the nations of the earth be blessed</u>" (Genesis 26:2-4)*. In other words, Isaac became the 21st father on the direct genealogical descent to the Messiah.

Chapter 7

LOT

"Then the LORD rained upon Sodom and upon Gomorrah
BRIMSTONE and FIRE from the LORD out of heaven;
And he overthrew those cities"
(Genesis 19:24, 25)

During Abraham's lifetime, God also prophetically revisited the subject of Jesus' 2nd Coming. This will be God's second time of revealing information concerning mankind's future 6,000th year on Earth. It was accomplished through the story (parable) of Abraham's nephew, Lot, who lived in a city called Sodom. Without a doubt, God caused the story (parable) to happen, and included it in the Bible, so He could secretly foretell more information concerning Jesus' 2nd Coming!

In the story of Noah, we learned Christ's 2nd Coming will occur during year 6,000, proceeding with 1 house of righteous people—the spiritual "house of Christ"—being lifted up into the air, while planet Earth's ENTIRE surface is destroyed. You are about to learn the story of Sodom & Gomorrah has a strikingly similar set of circumstances, because as I have said it is about the SAME subject: Jesus' 2nd Coming. But this time around God will disclose precisely HOW the righteous people will be lifted up into the air, and by exactly WHAT means He will destroy Earth and all the ungodly people's flesh.

129

What is absolutely remarkable about the story (parable) of Sodom & Gomorrah is God caused it to happen while Abraham's wife Sarah was pregnant with Isaac!!! In other words, while God was clandestinely prophesying information concerning the Messiah's 1st Coming through Isaac's supernatural birth, He was also secretly revealing things concerning his 2nd Coming through the destruction of Sodom & Gomorrah. Is that not incredible? God was controlling the events in 2 separate situations, AT THE SAME TIME, all to reveal future events concerning the Messiah's 1st & 2nd Comings! Friend, God was working prophetic double-time during mankind's 2,048th year.

Allow me to set the 1924 BC scene. It has been 392 years since the worldwide flood, and Noah has been dead for only 42 years. By now people have dotted the Fertile Crescent with little city states, and certainly a few people have ventured off a lot farther towards Earthly ground that would later become known as Europe, Africa, & Asia. In this setting and time period, nestled next to the Dead Sea in Canaan, existed the cities of Sodom & Gomorrah. Note: Geographically, the ground surrounding the Dead Sea is the lowest land above water on Earth's surface—approximately 1,378 feet below Sea Level! (By comparison, the Grand Canyon is only 278 feet below sea level.) No rivers flow out of the Dead Sea; it is only a catch basin for rain water and the Jordon River. Thus, since it only loses water by evaporation, salt minerals stay behind and today the water is over 8 times saltier than the ocean! White salt deposits encrust its shores and cliffs, and nothing lives in the harsh water. In the language of Abraham's day, the sea was simply known as the "Sea of Salt".

Lot was a good man who feared God and lived righteously (obeyed the 10 Love Commandments) but he had moved his family to the rich city of Sodom, where the people lived wickedly. The Bible records: *"And the LORD said, Because **the cry of Sodom and Gomorrah is great, and because their sin is very grievous**; I will go down now, and see whether they have done altogether according to the cry of it, which is come unto me" (Genesis 18:20, 21)*. Around 1,400 years later, God told the prophet Ezekiel about the sins of Sodom: *"Behold, this was the iniquity of thy sister Sodom, pride, fullness of bread, and abundance of idleness was in her and in her daughters, neither did she strengthen*

130

*the hand of the poor and needy. And they were haughty, and committed abomination before me: **therefore I took them away as I saw good"** (Ezekiel 16:49, 50).* Sodom's citizenry sounds eerily similar to the populace living in Noah's day! Do you remember? Wicked people are only out for themselves and their own sinful gratification; the thoughts in their head (spirit) are continually selfish. They care nothing at all about helping the poor on Earth who desperately need their help. God will annihilate the flesh of these type people during his 2nd Coming, sending their souls to a hellish torment!

After reflecting on their sins, God decided to wipe out the inhabitants of Sodom & Gomorrah. (But remember, it is really all part of His secret plan to foretell more about Christ's 2nd Coming!) So what did God choose to use as a "vehicle" to destroy Sodom & Gomorrah? Fire & brimstone!!! How about that? It would be more than a thousand years later until God would prophesy plainly through the Israeli prophets about the coming fiery day of the Lord's wrath at Christ's 2nd Coming. Zephaniah foretold: *"The great day of the LORD is near...That day is a day of wrath, a day of trouble and distress, a day of wasteness and desolation...A day of the TRUMPET...And I will bring distress upon men, that they shall walk like blind men, because they have sinned against the LORD: and **their blood shall be poured out as dust, and their flesh as the dung**. Neither their silver nor their gold shall be able to deliver them in the day of the LORD'S wrath; but the **WHOLE LAND shall be devoured by the FIRE of his jealousy"** (Zephaniah 1:14-18).* The word "land" here is translated from the original Hebrew word "*eres*" meaning: world, earth, all inhabited lands. The word "whole" is from the Hebrew word "kōl" meaning: all, everyone, everything, totality of a mass or collective. What a shocking day it will be for planet Earth!!! But back in 1924 BC, God was giving mankind a glimpse into how this age would come to an end by obliterating everything in the cities of Sodom & Gomorrah—houses, animals, people, & land—with a raging fire!

Watch the incredible detail of the story (parable) of Lot play out in perfect, parallel prophetic format to the story of Noah—i.e. 1 righteous house of people rescued UPWARD while everything else is destroyed beneath! So who was saved from the destruction? It was ONLY Lot's house: Lot, Lot's wife, and Lot's 2 daughters. Do you recognize God's precision in controlling and telling a prophetic story? In this parable, Lot's family symbolized the spiritual "house of Christ"—i.e. all the righteous souls who ever lived—for they are the only one's who will be saved from God's wrath on the great day of Jesus Christ's 2nd Coming!

But how exactly was Lot's family rescued out of the wicked city? It was by ANGELS!!! The Bible proclaims: *"And **there came two angels to Sodom at even**...And while he (Lot) lingered, the men (two angels) laid hold upon his hand, and upon the hand of his wife, and upon the hand of his two daughters; the LORD being merciful unto him: and they brought him forth, and set him without the city"* (Genesis 19:16). 2,000 years later, Jesus confirmed it would be angels who would gather up all the righteous people and whisk them out of here right before God burns planet Earth: *"And then shall appear the sign of the Son of man (Jesus) in heaven: and then shall all the tribes of the earth mourn, and they shall see the Son of man coming in the clouds of heaven with power and great glory. And **he shall send his ANGELS with a great sound of a TRUMPET, and THEY shall gather together his ELECT from the four winds, from one end of heaven to the other**"* (Matthew 24:30, 31). See, through the angelic rescue in the story (parable) of Lot, God was secretly prophesying that it will be angels who will save (rapture) the righteous at Jesus' 2nd Coming!

Incidentally, it is blatantly obvious Jesus' words I cited in the verse above ARE the "rapture event" because the angels are gathering up the "elect" at the sound of a TRUMPET: *"For the Lord himself shall descend from heaven with a shout, with the voice of the archangel, and **with the TRUMP of God**: and the dead in Christ shall rise first: Then we which are alive and remain shall be caught up together with them in the clouds to meet the Lord in the air"* (I Thessalonians 4:16, 17). Do you see? So when does the "rapture event" take place? The answer is in Jesus words right before the verse I sighted in the paragraph above: *"Immediately **AFTER** the tribulation of those days shall the sun be darkened...the powers of the heavens shall be shaken: AND THEN... they shall see the Son of man coming in the clouds..."* (Matthew 24:29, 30). Friend, there will be NO "rapture event" 7 years before Christ returns!!! He is coming back ONCE, and it will be at the sound of a trumpet during year 6,000, immediately <u>AFTER</u> the great tribulation of the Antichrist's reign is finished.

Furthermore, the "elect" the angels are gathering up are not just Jewish people as some falsely proclaim: <u>They are EVERYONE who has ever lived righteously on Earth—in the grave or out</u>!!! Listen to Paul's words constituting who the "elect" are in God's eyes: "<u>Where there is neither Greek or Jew, circumcision nor uncircumcision, Barbarian, Scythian, bond nor free</u>: but CHRIST IS ALL, AND IN ALL. <u>Put on therefore,</u> **AS THE ELECT OF GOD,** <u>holy and beloved, bowels of mercies, kindness, humbleness of mind, meekness, longsuffering; Forbearing one another, and forgiving one another…And above all these things put on charity (LOVE), which is the bond of PERFECTNESS…</u> (for with God) <u>there is NO respect of persons</u>" (Colossians 3:11-14, 25). See, the "elect" are not the Jewish people, per se; they are EVERYONE who has ever decided to repent of sin and live righteously on Earth—obey the 10 <u>Love</u> Commandments—until the moment they physically die or Christ returns! THESE are the "elect souls" the angels will gather up at Christ's 2nd Coming.

Returning to the parable, which <u>direction</u> did Lot's family go? Well, I already told you the cities of Sodom & Gomorrah were located alongside the Dead Sea—the lowest land spot above water on planet earth!—therefore, they went <u>UP</u> to escape Sodom! The angels told Lot's house to flee to the mountain: *"<u>Escape for thy life</u>; look not behind thee, neither stay thou in all the plain; **<u>escape to the mountain</u>**, lest thou be consumed" (Genesis 19:17).* So Lot and his family ascended: *"**<u>Lot went UP</u>** out of Zoar, and dwelt in the mountain, and his two daughters with him" (Genesis 19:30).* Friend, God's parables are always accurate! (Do you recognize the incredible wisdom of God to carry out this story on the lowest land above water on planet Earth, ensuring the prophetic accuracy of the "rapture event"?)

And what happened to Sodom & Gomorrah? <u>EVERYTHING was burnt to ashes</u>: *"Then **<u>the LORD rained upon Sodom and upon Gomorrah brimstone and fire from the LORD out of heaven</u>**; And he <u>overthrew those cities, and ALL the plain, and ALL the inhabitants of the cities, and that which grew upon the ground" (Genesis 19:24, 25).* Do you see? <u>Everything</u> was destroyed by the <u>FIRE</u>, just like everything was destroyed in Noah's day. Friend, make no mistake about it, the entire surface of planet Earth will be destroyed by fire during Jesus' 2nd Coming and only 1 house of righteous souls will be saved from the annihilation! Immediately afterwards, God will <u>regenerate</u> planet Earth back to its original Garden-of-Eden-like conditions with beautiful new foliage and new land mass; then, He will return all the righteous people who ever lived back to Earth to live and reign with Jesus Christ a thousand years! Jesus said, *"ye which have followed me, in the REGENERATION when the Son of man shall sit in the throne of his glory..." (Matthew 19:28)*. Do you see? Earth will be physically re-born!

Now we all know the tale of how Lot's wife looked back on the ensuing, fiery carnage of Sodom & Gomorrah, and the Bible records she turned into a pillar of salt: *"But his (Lot's) wife looked back from behind him, and she BECAME a pillar of salt" (Genesis 19:26)*. The angels had warned Lot's family to NOT look back as they fled to safety! Knowing Sodom & Gomorrah were located alongside the "Sea of <u>Salt</u>", can you now imagine what happened to Lot's wife? Lot's family was most likely fleeing alongside the edge of the Dead Sea, and when she looked back God smote her—possibly with a heart attack—and she fell dead. It would not have taken long for the waves of the Dead Sea to encrust her body with white salt deposits. But in the terror of the moment, I am sure Lot and his 2 daughters just kept running for fear they would perish, too! But days or week's later, Lot probably returned to see/get his wife's stiff, rigor-mortised body, and she would have looked as if she BECAME a pillar of salt! Friend, Bible stories are not silly fables; they are TRUTH!

But the crucial lesson to be learned from Lot's wife is God does not want us to be attached (to love) <u>any</u> materialistic items on Earth. We should always be ready and looking forward to leaving this sin-sick Earth at any moment. If that is not your outlook, then something is wrong in your heart! Jesus said, *"<u>In that day (Day of the Lord)</u>, he which shall be upon the housetop, and his STUFF in the house, <u>let him not come down to take it away:</u> and he that is in the field, <u>let him likewise not return back</u>. **Remember Lot's wife**. <u>Whosoever shall seek to save his life shall lose it; and whosoever shall lose his life shall preserve it</u>" (Luke 17:31-33)*. Friend, God is DEAD serious about this;

134

if you are emotionally involved with your dirt possessions, you have a heap of trouble ahead of you. (I will show you later in this book that a person who loves possessions is really an IDOL WORSHIPPER! And you <u>cannot</u> willfully disobey the 2nd Love Commandments and enter God's Kingdom.) So I am begging you to kill your desire for this depraved world and prepare to meet God! (By the way, did you notice Jesus' words in the verse above tacitly confirmed the story of Sodom & Gomorrah—even what happened to Lot's wife!—was a parable about the "day of the Lord", which is Christ's 2nd Coming?)

Lot possessed the correct spiritual attitude: The Bible records the sin in folks around him literally <u>vexed</u> his righteous soul! Peter wrote: *"For if God...<u>turning the cities of Sodom and Gomorrah into ashes</u> condemned them with an overthrow, <u>making them an ENSAMPLE unto those that after should live ungodly</u>; And <u>delivered just Lot, vexed with the filthy conversation of the wicked</u>: **(For that righteous man dwelling among them, in seeing and hearing, vexed—tortured, tormented—his righteous soul from day to day with their UNLAWFUL deeds)**; The Lord knoweth how to deliver the godly out of temptations, and <u>to reserve the unjust unto the day of judgment to be punished</u>"* (II Peter 2:4-9). See, God made the inhabitants of Sodom & Gomorrah an <u>example</u> of what will happen in the future to ALL ungodly people at Christ's 2nd Coming! Notice Peter called their deeds "unlawful"? How could that be in 1924 BC—600 years before Moses received the 10 Love Commandments? Friend, this is just more Biblical evidence EVERYONE who has ever lived on Earth has known the <u>10 Love Commandments</u>, for they are written in our hearts. And Lot was tortured daily from the <u>unlawfulness</u> (disobedience to the 10 Love Commandments) going on around him!

Eventually, through direct words, Jesus straightforwardly authenticated the story of Sodom & Gomorrah was actually a futuristic look at his 2nd Coming: *"<u>Likewise also as it was in the days of Lot; they did eat, they drank, they bought, they sold, they planted, they builded; But the SAME DAY that Lot went out of Sodom it rained fire and brimstone from heaven, and destroyed them ALL. Even THUS shall it be in the day when the Son of man (Jesus) is revealed</u>"* (Luke 17:28-30). Pay close attention to Jesus' words *"the <u>SAME DAY</u>"* lot escaped, fire destroyed <u>ALL</u> the ungodly. Friend, the "rapture of the saints" and the "destruction of the wicked" will take place on the <u>SAME</u> <u>DAY</u>! It will happen <u>exactly</u> like the stories of Lot & Noah prophetically reveal! It is the great day of Lord's wrath at Christ's 2nd Coming, and nothing will survive on planet Earth! Amazingly, the ungodly people will have NO clue their destruction is imminent. Life will be proceeding just like it always does; people all caught up in their pursuit of worthless dirt, caring nothing about God (love).

But then like "a thief in the night" Jesus will arrive! Paul wrote: *"For yourselves know perfectly that **the day of the Lord so cometh as a thief in the night**. For when they shall say, Peace and safety; <u>then sudden destruction cometh upon them</u>, as travail upon a woman with child; and **THEY SHALL NOT ESCAPE**. But ye, brethren, are not in darkness, that that day should overtake you as a thief. Ye are all the children of the light, and the children of the day: we are not of the night, nor of darkness. <u>Therefore let us not sleep, as do others; but let us watch and be sober</u>" (I Thessalonians 5:2-6).* See, the righteous should ALWAYS be ready for Jesus Christ's return—which means we should always be living our lives in obedience to God's 10 Love Commandments! The word "sober" is translated from the Greek word "*nēphō*" meaning: <u>to be self-controlled, clear-headed</u>. Are you "watching soberly" for his 2nd Coming? Do you have an eye on the sky, or do you not care? Are you bursting with excitement to meet Jesus, or are your thoughts consumed with your present, materialistic dealings on Earth? Have you purged your spirit of sin, or are you still willfully living wickedly? Friend, your eternal destiny is at stake, so I am warning you to REPENT!

Chapter 8

Jacob

"Jacob hath TAKEN AWAY all that was our father's;
and of that which was our father's
hath he gotten ALL this GLORY"
(Genesis 31:1)

Abraham's son, Isaac, eventually married a young woman named Rebekah when he was 40 years old. And Rebekah conceived twins, Jacob & Esau, when Isaac was 60 years old: *"And when her (Rebekah) days to be delivered were fulfilled, behold, there were twins in her womb...and Isaac was threescore years old when she bare them" (Genesis 25:24, 26)*. Therefore, Jacob & Esau were born during mankind's 2,108[th] year or <u>1864 BC</u> (3972 BC – 2,108) on the Gregorian calendar: They were born 452 years after the global flood of Noah's day. God will secretly manage events in Jacob's life to farther reveal details about His plan of redemption for mankind's souls—i.e. how mankind's spirits will be delivered from their <u>bondage</u> to sin & death!

One day God confirmed the covenantal "seed promise" with Jacob, solidifying the torch had been passed to him to be the 22nd patriarch since Adam on the direct genealogical descent to the birth of the Messiah [See Figure #1, page 12]. Jacob was traveling northward, through the land of present day Israel, on a journey to the city of Haran, where his mother's brother Laban lived. On this trek, Jacob lay down to sleep one night and dreamt of a ladder rising up to heaven. During the dream, God verified the covenantal "seed promise" was with him: *"And he (Jacob) dreamed, and <u>behold a ladder set up on the earth, and the top of it reached to heaven</u>: and behold the angles of God ascending and descending on it. And, behold, the LORD stood above it, and said, I am the LORD God of Abraham thy father, and the God of Isaac: the land whereon thou liest, to thee will I give it, and to thy seed...**<u>and in thy seed shall all the families of the earth be blessed</u>**" (Genesis 28:12-15).* Thus, the path to the Messiah—the "spiritual seed"—would now run through Jacob's linage!

Eventually, Jacob arrived in Haran, and it was there that God's 2nd prophetic story (parable) began concerning <u>how</u> He would free mankind's souls from bondage. Allow me to briefly refresh your memory of what we learned so far about the subject through the story (parable) of Abraham & Sarah in Egypt: Sarah (bride of Christ) was imprisoned by Pharaoh (Satan) in Egypt (Kingdom of Darkness on Earth); GOD <u>supernaturally</u> plagued Pharaoh, forcing him to free Sarah; then, Abraham (Jesus) and Sarah left with Egypt's riches. The key point to comprehend from the parable: <u>GOD delivered Sarah out of bondage</u>! God was saying to mankind, "I will <u>personally</u> deliver your souls from your bondage to sin & death, for you are all powerless to free yourselves because you have ALL sinned." And we know in time, God worked through <u>sinless</u> Jesus to pay our death sentence and free our souls. With these points in mind, let us investigate the story (parable) of Jacob & Laban, for it will contain all the same elements and more! And as always, keep in mind no one understood what these stories represented back then. But now that we have the completed Word of God (Bible), there is no excuse for us to not understand the true meaning behind these Old Testament stories.

In Jacob's bondage parable, God will reaffirm the overall length of time for completion of His Game of Life is a factor of 7. (Remember the <u>7</u> day Creation week was God's TIMING secret to His master plan for mankind on Earth, and remember Moses would be the first man to prophetically receive God's time key of 1 day = 1,000 years, but he would not be born until the 14th century BC.) Consequently, in Jacob's day mankind was still pretty much in the dark about knowing exactly how long it would be until God would restore all things, closing out this age of sin. Let us take a look at Jacob's account.

In Haran, Jacob immediately fell in love with Laban's beautiful daughter Rachel and decided to work 7 years for her hand in marriage. Let me tell you upfront who the players represent in this prophetic parable. Jacob represents Jesus, Rachel represents the "bride of Christ"—all the righteous souls who ever lived on Earth, and Laban represents Satan. Thus, from Jacob's (Jesus) perspective, Rachel (bride of Christ) was in bondage to Laban (Satan) and the 7 years he would work for her represented God's 7 day (7,000 year) master time plan for mankind on Earth! See, truth be told, when the 7th millennial day is over Satan will be given a short time to deceive the spirit children born during Christ's millennial reign: *"And when the thousand years are expired, Satan shall be loosed out of his prison, And shall go out to deceive the nations which are in the four quarters of the earth" (Revelation 20:7, 8)*. Consequently, Jesus' completed bride will not be finished until the 7,000 years are over and done and God brings the New Jerusalem city down onto a new Earth. Until that time, Jesus will never stop working for his "bride" during the 7,000 years!

Envision Jacob sweating and laboring day in and day out for 7 years to obtain the bride he dearly loves! What an awesome picture of Jesus' love for his "bride" and what he has been doing for almost 6,000 years now. For remember, he never sleeps: *"He that keepeth thee will not slumber" (Psalms 121:3)*. Friend, God is deeply in love with His spirit children, and He wants us to be with Him forever! So day and night He pleads with us in our hearts to stop sinning by choosing the way of good (love) over the way of evil (sin)—i.e. obey the 10 Love Commandments. Yes, certainly, Jesus is working indefatigably for his bride!

When the 7 years were over, Laban tricked Jacob on his wedding night and in the darkness sent his oldest daughter Leah into Jacob's tent to consummate the marriage. Thus, Leah became Jacob's wife. Jacob was initially furious, but he decided to work another 7 years for Laban to obtain Rachel, also, as his wife. This he did and received her hand in marriage as well. The reason God allowed the "7 year scenario" to play out twice was to place His iron clad guarantee on His 7 day (7,000 year) plan! In short, when God prophesies something <u>twice</u> it means it is SURE. In other words, it cannot and will not be changed or altered. Do you understand? Friend, you can rest assured God's 7 day (7,000 year) plan for mankind's time on Earth WILL happen!

I will provide 2 Biblical examples of God prophesying the same thing twice, representing the event was SURE. In time, Jacob & Rachel had a son Joseph, whom God gave 2 similar dreams: *"And <u>Joseph dreamed a dream</u>...For, behold, we were binding sheaves in the field, and, lo, <u>my sheaf arose, and also stood upright; and, behold, your sheaves stood round about, and made obeisance to my sheaf</u>... And <u>he dreamed yet ANOTHER dream</u>...and, behold, <u>the sun and the moon and the eleven stars made obeisance to me"</u> (Genesis 37:5-9).* Do you see? These were 2 <u>prophetic</u> dreams dealing with the <u>same</u> issue, ENSURING its future occurrence. And sure enough, around 30 years later Joseph's 11 brothers bowed down to him in Egypt!

In Egypt, Joseph also interpreted 2 prophetic dreams God gave Pharaoh: *"And Pharaoh said unto Joseph, In my dream...**<u>seven KINE (cows), fatfleshed and well favoured...And, behold, seven other kine came up after them, poor and very ill favoured and leanfleshed...And I saw in my dream, and, behold, seven EARS</u>** <u>came up in one stalk, full and good: And, behold, seven ears, withered, thin, and blasted with the east wind, sprung up after them"</u> (Genesis 41:17-23).* Joseph's interpretation: *"**<u>THE DREAM IS ONE</u>**: <u>God hath shewed Pharaoh what HE IS ABOUT TO DO</u>. The seven good kine are seven years; and the seven good ears are seven years: **THE DREAM IS ONE**. And the seven thin and ill favoured kine that came up after them are seven years; and the seven empty ears blasted with the east wind shall be seven years of famine...<u>Behold, there come seven years of great plenty throughout all the land of Egypt: And there shall arise after them seven years of famine"</u> (Genesis 41:25-30).* Friend, listen; when God prophesies something <u>twice,</u> the event <u>ALWAYS</u> happens. And, as you know, Joseph did not seek to avert God's prophecy, rather he diligently prepared for its consequences!!!

NOW you know why God manipulated the circumstances in Jacob's service to Laban, having him work a 7 year cycle TWICE for a bride: It prophetically indicated His 7 day (7,000 year) master TIME plan for mankind on Earth is SURE. Jesus WILL receive his COMPLETED bride when 7,000 years are passed! Nothing can or will stop it!!! Incidentally, this is why when I soon prove to you in the "*Moses*" chapter that Jesus' death absolutely occurred during mankind's 4,000th year, you can get excited about witnessing Jesus' 2nd Coming around AD 2028!

After Jacob worked 14 years and married Laban's two daughters, Leah & Rachel, he worked another 6 years for Laban gaining flocks for himself, until he "escaped" during the 20th year. Is that not interesting? Now we see the number "20" again!!! Do you remember its meaning? It is God's number for redemption, deliverance, freedom, or salvation!!! In other words, in this story (parable) God is verifying (by incorporating the number "20") He truly is prophesying about the Messiah's future work of redemption as HE delivers Jacob's wives, children, and flocks from Laban's bondage! Do you understand? God simply wanted to put his numerical seal on the parable.

It is crucial you get the picture Jacob and his family were treated like slaves by Laban during the 20 years. Listen to Jacob's words to Laban about the situation: *"This TWENTY years have I been with thee; thy ewes and thy she goats have not cast their young, and the rams of thy flock have I not eaten. That which was torn of beasts I brought not unto thee; I bare the loss of it; of my hand didst thou require it, whether stolen by day, or stolen by night. **Thus I was; in the day the drought consumed me, and the frost by night; and my sleep departed from mine eyes**" (Genesis 31:38-40).* Do you see? Jacob was not treated well! Laban lorded over him, his wives, and his children. THAT is the depiction of bondage! Furthermore, Laban did NOT want Jacob and his family to leave because he was exploiting them for his own good and power. Sound like Satan's power over mankind's spiritual death after Adam & Eve sinned in the Garden of Eden?

Laban continued deceiving Jacob to keep his family in bondage. The Bible even records how many times Laban defrauded Jacob! Jacob lamented to Laban, *"Thus have I been TWENTY years in thy house; I served thee fourteen years for thy two daughters, and six years for thy cattle: and **thou hast changed my wages TEN times**" (Genesis*

31:41). Remember I told you every little detail in God's ancient Old Testament stories had spiritual implication? Well, stunningly, in this small "10 detail" God was representing "<u>ALL</u> of sin" because ALL sin falls under disobedience to the **10** Love Commandments! Remember, Laban symbolizes Satan, the one who <u>tricked</u> mankind into sinning against God. Thus, God is embodying ALL OF SIN through Laban's 10 deceits. But God is about to <u>supernaturally</u> deliver Jacob's family from Laban! Thus, through this "10 detail" God was foretelling to mankind, "One day I will COMPLETELY free your souls from your bondage to <u>ALL</u> OF SIN!" (Do you comprehend how God was developing the "problem and <u>solution</u>" of mankind's spiritual plight through these Old Testament anecdotes? I sure hope so!!!)

In this parable, God opened the spiritual door a little farther and allowed mankind a look into His heart concerning their helpless spiritual condition caused by Satan, for God told Jacob; *"I have seen <u>ALL</u> that Laban doeth unto thee" (Genesis 31:12).* Is that not awesome? God was REALLY saying He saw <u>everything</u> Satan had done and was doing to His spirit children! In other words, through this divine statement, God lovingly declared He had NOT forgotten about mankind's dilemma on planet Earth.

Fed up with it, God told Jacob to take his wives and children and leave Laban: *"I am the God of Beth-el...now arise, <u>GET THEE OUT FROM THIS LAND, and return unto the land of thy kindred" (Genesis 31:13).* Do you understand what God is spiritually expressing? God is saying He wants His spirit children to be freed from their bondage and to come back home to live with Him in the Kingdom of God. Thus, God told Jacob to return to his <u>Father's</u> land: *"And the Lord said unto Jacob, <u>Return unto the land of thy fathers</u>, and to thy kindred" (Genesis 31:5).* This is like the Father God telling Jesus to bring his "bride" back home to His land, the Kingdom of God!

Look, let me explain something; in these "redemption parables" the <u>actual</u> Earthly land of Canaan (where the nation of Israel would exist) represents the spiritual Kingdom of God, the place of eternal life where God dwells! Do you understand? In other words, in the story (parable) of Abraham & Sarah in Egypt, after they escaped Egyptian bondage by God's hand it was then <u>POSSIBLE</u> for them to travel

142

back to Canaan—i.e. the spiritual "Promise Land" of God's eternal, covenantal "seed promise" to all righteous souls. NOW do you truly see what God is saying through these parables? God's supernatural deliverance of mankind's souls, from their bondage to sin & death, would make it POSSIBLE for them to return to the Kingdom of God, meaning to obtain eternal life! I left all this out, initially, because I did not want to confuse you, but I believe you can handle it now. I do not want to get into a geography lesson in this book, but trust me the actual Earthly land God promised Abraham, Isaac, & Jacob spiritually represents the Kingdom of God! So in these "redemption parables" you will always find the people in bondage in an actual location on Earth apart (separated) from Canaan (the Promise Land)—like Abraham & Sarah in Egypt or Jacob in Haran, which was in the land of modern day Turkey!

Now you know for the "deliverance story (parable)" to be spiritually accurate, we need the "exchange-of-riches" part to occur. Therefore, the Bible chronicles a lengthy report on how Jacob ended up with Laban's riches! Incidentally, from God's perspective the "becoming rich part" in these "salvation parables" represents Him taking back the SOULS of His spirit children from Satan's death grasp. So after Jacob acquired Laban's wealth, listen to how spiritually prophetic the words of Laban's sons were in the Bible: *"And he (Jacob) heard the words of Laban's sons, saying, **Jacob hath taken away all that was our father's (Laban); and of that which was our father's hath he gotten ALL this glory**" (Genesis 31:1).* Wow! Do you see? This is like hearing demons—Laban's (Satan) sons—foretelling JESUS would one day take back ALL of Satan's glory and power! And he DID, at the cross: *"Worthy is the Lamb that was slain to receive power, and **RICHES**, and wisdom, and strength, and honour, and **GLORY**, and blessing" (Revelation 5:12).* Hallelujah! Yes, truly, Jesus and his bride were made spiritual rich at the Cross of Calvary.

Moreover, to further portray in this parable the "riches" Jesus would take back from Satan were mankind's souls, the "riches" Jacob stripped from Laban were his flocks! The Bible refers to ALL of us as God's sheep: *"**All we like sheep** have gone astray; we have turned every one to his own way" (Isaiah 53:6).* Thus, spiritually, God was showing how He would work through Jesus to reclaim His flocks (spirit children). It is a powerful representation! But pay particular close attention to the fact that it was <u>GOD</u> who was doing the work! <u>GOD</u> made us spiritually rich through Jesus—i.e. enabled us sheep the possibility of going home to live with Him one day in His Kingdom. Thus, in the story, Jacob realized <u>it was God who prospered him</u>, and he told his wives: ***"GOD hath taken away the cattle (flock) of your father, and given them to me"*** *(Genesis 31:9)*. Again, almost 2,000 years later Paul would write: *"And <u>all things are of God</u>, who hath reconciled us to himself by Jesus Christ...To wit, that **<u>GOD was in Christ, reconciling the world unto himself</u>**, not imputing their trespasses unto them" (II Corinthians 5:18, 19)*. Do you see? <u>GOD performed the work of reconciliation—i.e. He repaired the divide between His Spirit and mankind's spirit!</u>

Listen to the spiritually profound response of Jacob's wives (bride of Christ) after Jacob (Jesus) informed them God wanted them to leave Laban's (Satan) bondage: *"That's fine with us! <u>There's nothing for us here—none of our father's wealth will come to us anyway! He has reduced our rights </u>to those of foreign women; <u>HE SOLD US</u>, and what he received for us has disappeared. **<u>The riches God has given you from our father were legally ours and our children's to begin with</u>**! So go ahead and do whatever God has told you to" (Genesis 31:14-16, Living Bible)*. Wow, this is spiritually deep!!! Long story short, planet Earth was given to mankind by God at Creation: Adam & Eve were told to take dominion (a "kingdom term") over planet Earth. But mankind lost the title deed to Earth when Satan stole it from them during the "day of sin" in the Garden of Eden. But God won it back for us through Jesus, and the ruler-ship of planet Earth now legally belongs to Jesus Christ. And one day soon the resurrected righteous will share in this inheritance, reigning as kings with Christ: *"Unto him (Jesus) that loved us, and washed us from our sins in his own blood, <u>And hath made us kings and priests unto God</u>" (Revelation 1:5, 6)*. Now slowly and carefully read Jacob's wives words, again! Could you have dreamed the Old Testament stories were gushing with that amount of spiritual implication?

Next, in the story flow, comes the deliverance scene—i.e. Jacob's family leaves (or becomes free of) Laban. Since we understand

144

the prophetic spiritual significance behind the story (parable), we know GOD will have to be the reason Jacob's family is delivered. Thus, in the parable God supernaturally SAVES Jacob's family! But first, I want you to appreciate the Bible's portrayal of the utter hopelessness of Jacob's family being able to leave Laban on their own accord; Laban sneered at Jacob, *"It is in the power of my hand to do you hurt" (Genesis 31:29)*. Do you see? To put it plainly; Laban possessed the manpower to keep Jacob's house under his control or to kill them. THIS perfectly represented Satan's FULL power over mankind: Since we ALL sinned, our souls could never have escaped his evil clutch.

Consequently, because of the dangerous situation Jacob's family fled secretly from Laban: *"And Jacob stole away unawares to Laban the Syrian, in that he told him not that he fled. So he fled with all that he had; and he rose up, and **passed over** the river" (Genesis 31:20, 21)*. If you have not already figured it out, this prophetic "redemption parable" of Jacob & Laban is foreshadowing God's coming "grand prophetic redemption parable" of the Israelites—Jacob's children!—escaping the Pharoah of Egypt! In other words, God is allowing Jacob to "live a glimpse" of the "bondage & deliverance scenario" his children will soon endure by putting him through his current circumstances! Jacob, most likely, did not realize it…but you should!!! In the above "escape scene" Jacob is experiencing a foretaste of the future Exodus of the Israelites out of Egypt and the Red Sea crossing. Subsequently, God first introduced the term "PASS-OVER" right here in this story in the Bible! Look at the verse above, again: *"and passed over the river"*. Friend, GOD coined the Bible's arguably most important phrase *"Passover"*, and it spiritually represents mankind's souls "passing-over" from death (separation from God's Spirit) to life (reunion with God's Spirit). That is what the "deliverance scene" symbolizes in these "redemption stories (parables)"!

A chase scene ensued. Laban was livid when he found out Jacob's house deserted him, and he tracked him down: *"And it was told Laban on the third day that Jacob was fled. And he took his brethren with him, and PURSUED after him seven days' journey; and they overtook him in the mount Gilead" (Genesis 31:22, 23)*. Can you foresee the Pharaoh and Egyptian chariots chasing after the fleeing Israelites in this event? Jacob's family was undergoing the same terrifying experience!!! Appreciating God's prophetic <u>precision</u> in telling a story (parable), probably even the 3 & 7 day time markers occurring here were the same periods of time it took Pharaoh to <u>decide</u> & <u>track down</u> the escaping Israelites—there is Biblical evidence suggesting this is true! <u>Unquestionably, though, in both cases it would take God's supernatural intervention to SAVE (or deliver) the runaways</u>. In other words, GOD would be the reason they would be set free!

So how did <u>God</u> SAVE Jacob's family when Laban had the military might over them? During his pursuit of Jacob, God appeared to Laban in a dream and warned him, pointblank, to NOT hurt Jacob! When Laban overtook Jacob's company, he told him, ***"It is in the power of my hand to do you hurt****: but the God of your father spake unto me yester-night, saying, Take thou heed that thou speak not to Jacob either good or bad" (Genesis 31:29)*. Do you see? Jacob's family was as good as goners (or at least would have been returned to bondage) but GOD stepped in and delivered them by supernaturally communicating with Laban to not hurt them and let them go! And the deliverance of mankind's bound souls would be a gift from God someday as well!

God's prophetic "redemption story (parable)" of Jacob & Laban concluded with Jacob's clan making a JOURNEY to Canaan: *"Jacob journeyed to Succoth, and built him an house...And Jacob came to Shalem, a city of Shechem, which is in the land of Canaan" (Genesis 33:17, 18)*. See, since God had set Jacob's family free from Laban, they were now <u>ABLE</u> to journey back to Canaan (the "Promise Land"). The parable prophetically meant ALL mankind would be <u>ABLE</u> to journey back to the "Promise Land"—i.e. the place of eternal life where God dwells—because God planned from the beginning of time to free their souls from Satan's bondage or power of death. **It does NOT mean they ALL WOULD, it only means they ALL COULD!!!** God will divulge <u>EXACTLY</u> what is involved (from mankind's side) in the "spiritual journey" that will take a soul to the Promise Land (Kingdom of God) in His "grand redemption parable" involving the Israelites. (I will reveal this information in the *"Wilderness"* chapter.)

Allow me to now briefly discuss with you how God was already working to "setup" His massive, all-revealing, secret, prophetic,

146

redemption, Israelite story (parable) during Jacob's lifetime—which, as you probably know, would consist of Jacob's descendants winding up in bondage in Egypt and then being supernaturally delivered by God. The "setup" began during the 20 years Jacob spent working for Laban! During those years, Jacob fathered 11 of the 12 sons that would later become known as the 12 tribes of Israel. After Jacob's clan was free from Laban, God renewed the covenantal "seed promise" with him and changed his name to Israel: *"And God said unto him, Thy name is Jacob: **thy name shall not be called any more Jacob, but Israel shall be thy name**: and he called his name Israel" (Genesis 35:10).* That was when the name "Israel" was birthed! Then, after God changed Jacob's name to Israel, his wife Rachel died giving birth to his final son, Benjamin. These 12 sons were the initial children of the future nation of Israel.

So WHAT was God's reason for creating an Earthly nation called Israel? Did you ever think about it logically? Look, God created ALL His spirit children from one man, Adam, and He has NO favorites for He loves them all!!! He also created ALL the nations under which His spirit children would reside during their time on Earth, determining their boundaries and times to exist before Creation: *"He (God) created ALL the people of the world from one man, Adam, and scattered the nations across the face of the earth. He decided beforehand which should rise and fall, and when. He determined their boundaries" (Acts 17:26, Living Bible).* See, the various nations are all part of God's 7,000 year gameboard, and the people living under those nations ALL have Adam & Eve's physical blood coursing through their veins. Furthermore, we know and understand God placed inside the heart of ALL His spirit children, since the dawn of time, a consciousness knowing right from wrong; thus, everyone has KNOWN what they needed to DO to obtain eternal life—choose good over evil (obey the 10 Love Commandments). So I ask again; what on Earth was God's purpose for creating the nation of Israel after 1/3 (over 2,000 years) of His 7 millennial day plan was over?

The primary reason: God wanted to secretly prophesy in greater detail the future events affecting mankind's souls via the Messiah's (Jesus) 1st & 2nd Comings, and by prophesying of these spiritual things through controlling the circumstances (events) of a large group (nation) of people, He knew it would be impossible for mankind to hide what

He had done! See, historians cannot deny the reality of an ancient Israel nation and their "Passover observance" existing long before Jesus was born. Do you understand? Thus, when you learn how Jesus perfectly fulfilled every detail of the Israelites "Passover incident" you will absolutely **KNOW** there is a "being" out there who knows the future! That "being" is God!!! <u>So God "performed" ALL the Biblical prophetic stories (parables) just so mankind would have further cause to believe He exists. THAT is why God wrote the Bible for mankind! It is strictly so we might have greater faith in Him (love)</u>.

Consequently, God initially birthed a nation of Israeli people simply to lead them through a "bondage circumstance" that secretly told the story of what happened to mankind's souls after Adam & Eve's sin in the Garden of Eden, and then to clandestinely prophesy of what the coming Messiah would do for their souls—namely, deliver them out of bondage to sin & death—by perfectly manipulating a deliverance scenario! Afterward, God would make sure a written record of the story would be composed in a book for mankind to read called the Bible. Comprehension of the striking, prophetic, spiritual implications behind the details of the Israelite's story (parable) is the tangible proof God exists, because the account undeniably proves "someone" knew/knows the future. And mankind knows this is NOT possible in the natural world!!! Thus, anyone who honestly studies what God has revealed to me in this book will KNOW God exists, because the Bible's complexity, conformity and farsightedness are an impossible hoax! Consequently, we have <u>NO</u> excuse today to not believe in God (love)—by choosing the WAY of good (love) over the WAY of evil (sin)—and receive eternal life.

God will lead Jacob's descendants through an amazing, 440 year long, prophetic situation (parable). In totality, the sequence of events will secretly foretell dazzling spiritual revelation into the Messiah's 1st & 2nd Comings!!! In other words, the grand story (parable) dealt with <u>how</u> God would provide freedom for mankind's spiritual bondage during year 4,000 and then <u>how</u> He would whisk the righteous few into His heavenly Kingdom during year 6,000 when Christ establishes his 1,000 year Earthly reign. Yes, friend, this is the GRANDADDY of all prophetic stories (parables) in the Bible!!! For it even provides <u>undeniable</u> proof into **EXACTLY** what mankind had/has to <u>DO</u> to

148

obtain eternal life! Full understanding of the parable will elucidate all of Paul's confusing New Testament writings concerning salvation.

After the Israelite's story (parable) was completed during mankind's 2,678th year with Joshua's conquest of Jericho, God then established the nation of Israel in the land of Canaan. It was from that time until roughly 400 BC that God rose up prophets among the Israeli people who wrote direct prophetic Scripture passages concerning Jesus' 1st & 2nd Comings. These passages are contained in the books of the prophets of the Old Testament. A study of the fulfillment of these passages during Jesus' 1st Coming is staggering, and hundreds are yet to be fulfilled preceding and during Jesus' 2nd Coming! Many of these "end time" prophetic verses center around the "re-born" nation of Israel, which leads me to the secondary purpose for God creating the nation of Israel: to be a prophetic "*clock-on-the-wall*" for mankind to watch to know what time it is in God's 7 day (7,000 year) master plan!

Friend, the rebirth of the physical nation of Israel in AD 1948, after millennia of non-existence, was like an alarm clock going off for mankind that we are now in the final days of God's 6th millennial day! (God clearly prophesied through the Israeli prophets of the reemergence of Israel on the map right before the culmination of 6,000 years.) But, for the most part, mankind has hit the snooze button on this alarm buzzer, and most people are drifting back to sleep at a time when the alarm is about to sound again with the TRUMPET of God at Jesus' 2nd Coming!!! Do you understand without having created a physical, visible nation of people called Israel God would not have had an "entity" to prophecy about to give mankind signs pointing to Christ's imminent return? Thus, a secondary reason God created the nation of Israel was to give mankind an observable "thing" (a prophetic clock!) to watch closely near the end of the 6th millennial day.

Never forget God is no respecter of any person. This is because we are ALL His spirit children and His love is a universal constant for HE IS LOVE! In other words, God does not have favorites because His love is naturally perfect and true towards everyone. God's great love was shown towards ALL mankind by sending His only Son, Jesus, to die for everyone: Salvation was/is for ALL people equally the same! Many times the Bible declares God is NO respecter of persons: "***Neither doth***

149

God respect any person" *(II Samuel 14:14).* Paul wrote: *"knowing that your Master (God) also in heaven; **neither is there respect of persons with him**" (Ephesians 6:9).* Peter realized God viewed all mankind the same when he witnessed a Roman officer (a non Jew) receiving the Holy Spirit: *"Then Peter opened his mouth, and said, **Of a truth I perceive that God is no respecter of persons**: But in EVERY NATION he that feareth him, and worketh righteousness, is accepted with him" (Acts 10:34, 35).* The Greek word translated "respect" is *"prosōpolēptēs"* meaning: one who shows favoritism, partiality. Do you understand? God has never and NEVER WILL show favoritism toward any person! All people are viewed alike in His eyes; He is NOT willing that ANY should perish, but that all should repent.

I said all that to say this; what God FAVORS about "Israel" is not the physical Jewish people but the NATION!!! Do you understand? A "nation" is a living entity by and of itself. It is a dynamic organism that can exist for hundreds of years—or forever if God so desires!—as its inhabitants constantly change. It can conquer people and claim them under its nationality, but then another nation can immediately invade and conquer them and those SAME people will be now under that nationality! Do you see? Therefore, try and understand what God loves about "Israel" is the nation. It is the apple of His eye! Zechariah penned: *"For thus saith the LORD of hosts; After the glory hath he sent me unto the nations which spoiled you: for he that toucheth you (Israel) toucheth the apple of his (God's) eye" (Zechariah 2:8).* And friend, as I have clearly stated earlier in this book, one day the populace of the ETERNAL nation of Israel will be ALL the righteous souls who ever lived on Earth—the TRUE spiritual, Jewish children of Abraham!—and Jesus Christ will be their Lord and King: *"For he is not a Jew, which is one outwardly (physically)...But he is a Jew, which is one inwardly; and circumcision is that of the heart, in the spirit" (Romans 2:28, 29).*

One morning God furnished me with an incredibly revealing parable clarifying the correct view we should have of the nation of Israel and God's motive for creating it. It proceeds as follows: A guest speaker was slated to deliver an important message to the children of a certain high school. The day he arrived all the kids in the school—9th, 10th, 11th, & 12th grades—gathered in the auditorium to hear his talk. About 1/3rd of the way into his speech he asked for volunteers from the audience to come up front and enact out a skit to demonstrate and elucidate the central theme of his discourse. By the time the guest speaker was done talking, everyone had received his message.

Do you comprehend the parable of the guest speaker? Here is the interpretation: The guest speaker is God and the High School is planet Earth, the school's 4 grades of children represent ALL of God's spirit children from the 4 corners of Earth, the message God is communicating is EVERYTHING INVOLVED in His plan for the reunion of mankind's souls with His Spirit, and the volunteers are the people of the nation of Israel. Do you see? God's message was/is for ALL His spirit children! The volunteers (the Israeli or Jewish people) were the "chosen ones" only with respect to being picked by God to help communicate His message to ALL mankind by enacting out a skit (parable). See, the guest speaker did not favor the volunteers; His message and love was for everyone in the high school. Likewise, God does not favor Israelites; His message and love is for ALL mankind!

Let us now plunge into the action of God's prophetic play performed by Jacob's descendants. The opening scene involves Jacob (Israel) and his children ending up in Egypt. (Remember Abraham & Sarah's parable?) Here is how it happened: Jacob's son Joseph was sold as a slave by his jealous brothers to traveling merchantmen heading to Egypt. But after 30 years in Egypt, Joseph ascended from a slave to governor under Pharaoh—who do you think was responsible for that fortunate turn of events? Of course…God is controlling EVERYTHING! At that time God's story (parable) really kicked into gear, for the Bible says a famine covered the Earth: *"the famine was over ALL the face of the earth" (Genesis 41:56).* (Do you remember it was a famine that caused Abraham & Sarah to end up in Egypt in their story?) Well, here it is again! Do you remember the spiritual implication? Adam & Eve's sin in the Garden of Eden left ALL mankind's souls spiritually starved (separated from God)—which was classified by God as "in bondage to sin & death".

Hearing of food in Egypt, Israel (Jacob) sent his remaining sons down there to acquire some. Not recognizing Joseph, the sons ended up bowing down low to their brother. They were astonished and elated to

151

learn he was still alive and had risen to such a lofty position in Egypt. Long story short, Joseph reconciled with his brothers and invited his father's (Israel) clan to come and live in Egypt with him, where there was plenty of food. (Incidentally, there is a clear example of mankind knowing God's 8th Love Commandment *"Thou shalt not steal,"* long before Moses received the 10 Love Commandments on Mount Sinai, in the tale of Joseph hiding his silver cup in Benjamin's sack and then accusing his unsuspecting brothers of thievery in Genesis chapter 44!) After a little Biblical investigative work, one learns Israel and his entire family of 70 souls entered Egypt during mankind's 2,238th year or around 1734 BC (3972 BC – 2,238)! The informative verse: *"Jacob (Israel) lived seventeen years after his arrival (in Egypt), so that he was 147 years old at the time of his death"* (Genesis 47:28, Living Bible). Therefore, Jacob (Israel) entered Egypt when he was 130 years old. Remember, he was born during mankind's 2,108th year [See Figure # 4].

Friend, God now has everything setup perfectly in this story to secretly reveal the deliverance work of the coming Messiah, Jesus. For Israel and his descendants are living in "bondage"—technically meaning separated from Canaan (the Promise Land). And God will milk this story (parable) for every bit of prophetic value He can get out of it by intimately controlling EVERY detail. Yet, no one understood what God was doing or saying through the adventures of Israel's descendants! In the New Testament, Biblical passages hint at the true purpose and meaning behind the Israelites miraculous escapade, but only the Holy Spirit can clearly reveal the meaning of these verses to someone! (I will point them out in later chapters in this book.) But, certainly, the Jewish people of Jesus' day had NO idea what the birth of their nation "out of bondage" represented, for they did not understand mankind's spirits (souls) were in bondage to sin & death!

Listen, one day Jesus told a crowd of Jews, *"If ye continue in my word, then are ye my disciples indeed; And ye shall know the truth, and **the TRUTH shall MAKE you FREE**"* (John 8:31, 33). This confused the Jews greatly, and they looked at Jesus and barked: *"We be Abraham's seed, and were never in bondage to any man: how sayest thou, Ye shall be made free?"* (John 8:33). Do you see? They were spiritually clueless! They could ONLY think in physical, natural terms.

152

Figure # 4
The Life of Jacob (Israel)

Year	Event	Verse(s)
2,108	Jacob & Esau born (Isaac 60 yrs old)	Gen 25:26
	Esau sells his birthright to Jacob	Gen 25:29-34
	Possibly Jacob & Esau 20 to 30 yrs old?	
2,148	Esau, 40 yrs old, marries Judith (Isaac 100 yrs old)	Gen 26:34
2,168	Jacob deceives Isaac for Esau's birthright	Gen 27:1-40
	Isaac (120 yrs old) was old and eyes dim	Gen 27:1
	Jacob flees immediately, Esau wants him dead	Gen 27:41, 42
	Jacob flees to Haran, where Laban lives	Gen 27:43-45
	Jacob's ladder dream (covenantal "seed promise")	Gen 28:10-14
2,188	Jacob completes 20 yr service for Laban	Gen 31:41
	Rachel births Joseph	Gen 30:25
	Jacob wrestles Angel, named changed to "Israel"	Gen 32:24-28
2,208	Joseph enters Egypt as slave (20 yrs old?)	Gen 37:1-36
2,228	Isaac dies (180 yrs old), Jacob & Esau bury him	Gen 35:28,29
2,238	Jacob's clan moves to Egypt because of famine	Gen 46:1-7
2,255	Jacob dies (147 yrs old), lived 17 yrs in Egypt	Gen 47:28
2,558	Moses born	Acts 7:20-36
2,638	Moses (80 yrs old) leads exodus out of Egypt	Exo 12:29-39
	430 yrs in Egypt includes Joseph's 30 yrs	Exo 12:40,41
	400 yrs in Egypt starts with Jacob (Israel)	Acts 7:6

They did not understand that SIN had positioned ALL mankind's souls in bondage—i.e. separated from God's Spirit. Jesus tried to clear up their puzzlement by saying: *"Verily, verily, I say unto you, **Whosoever committeth sin is the servant (slave) of sin**. And the servant abideth not in the <u>house</u> forever: but the Son abideth ever. If the Son therefore* *shall make you free, ye shall be free indeed" (John 8:34-36).* Do you understand? Christ was saying he had come as God's sinless Lamb to set the souls of ALL mankind free from their bondage to sin & death by spiritually dying in their place, paying the death penalty, but if someone willfully continues to sin (disobey the 10 Love Commandments) then they are STILL in bondage to the Law of sin & death and their soul will ultimately perish on Judgment Day! THAT is why we **MUST** *"continue in his word"* to KNOW the truth. (I will reveal what "truth" is in the *"truth"* chapter.)

In the grand story (parable) of the Israelites, God will work through a man named Moses to free them out of their Egyptian bondage. As you will soon see, God's use of the man Moses was to prophetically reveal how He would work through the man Jesus to deliver mankind's souls out of bondage. In other words, the Israelites "exodus scene" from Egypt was strictly for the purpose of furtively disclosing the work of the coming Messiah. To be blunt: Moses represents Jesus in the parable!

Hang on to your hats, for it is going to be a mind-blowing ride!!! It is positively staggering to comprehend how God caused and controlled every circumstance surrounding the Israelites escape from Egypt, journey through the wilderness, and victorious entrance into Canaan (the Promise Land) just for the purpose of foretelling the future to mankind—all so we might have further reason and cause to believe in Him!!! So sit back, visualize, and enjoy God's impeccable use of the Israelites, Egyptians, Pharaoh, and Moses as His chosen volunteers from the audience of mankind to play out a "skit" secretly revealing His "redemption plan" to free mankind's souls out of bondage to sin & death.

154

Chapter 9

Moses

"And the LORD brought us forth out of Egypt...
WITH AN OUTSTRETCHED ARM...
and with signs, and with wonders"
(Deuteronomy 26:8)

After a few hundred years in Egypt, the children of Israel had flourished, multiplying to a great number. Then, a new Pharaoh arose, bitterly enslaving them: *"Therefore they did set over them <u>taskmasters</u> <u>to afflict them with their burdens</u>...And **<u>they made their lives bitter with</u> <u>hard BONDAGE</u>**, in mortar, and in brick, and in all manner of service in the field" (Exodus 1:11, 14)*. This Israelite "bondage scene" perfectly portrayed what existed in the spirit world: Lucifer and his demons (Pharaoh and his Egyptian taskmasters) held and kept God's spirit children (Israelites) in harsh bondage to sin & death—i.e. separated from God. (Remember, <u>sorrow</u>, <u>pain</u>, and <u>work</u> was/is the consequence of sin!) Do you see how God had created a spiritually-accurate, physical scenario ripe for (secretly and prophetically) revealing the supernatural (divine) deliverance work of the coming Messiah? Alright then, enter stage front...Moses!

Moses would be 80 years old when he went in front of Pharaoh to free the Israelites: *"And <u>Moses was fourscore years old</u>, and Aaron* *fourscore and three years old, <u>when they spake unto Pharaoh</u>" (Genesis 7:7)*. Thus, I have calculated his birth during mankind's 2,558ᵗʰ year, since Jacob (Israel) entered Egypt in the 2,238ᵗʰ year and 400 years later God freed them through Moses. (Do the simple addition and subtraction.) Subsequently, on the Gregorian calendar Moses was born around 1414 BC (3972 BC – 2,558). In other words, Moses arrived on God's gameboard around the middle of the 3ʳᵈ millennial day in His 7 day (7,000 year) master plan for mankind on Earth. Watch carefully as God controls the events in Moses' life to secretly paint a precise picture of the coming Messiah Jesus' life—specifically, what he will endure and do on Earth! Try and picture God, behind the scenes, directing every secret prophetic circumstance.

Moses was born during a time when Pharaoh had made an edict to have all Israelite, newborn, male children killed: *"And he (Pharaoh) said, When ye do the office of a midwife to the Hebrew women, and see them upon the stools; <u>**if it be a son, then ye shall kill him**</u>" (Exodus 1:16)*. This event prophesied of what it would be like when the Messiah was born, for Jesus would be born under the same conditions: King (Herod) declared death to the children in the town where Jesus was born: *"Then Herod...sent forth, and <u>**slew all the children**</u> that were in Beth-lehem, and in the coasts thereof, from two years old and under" (Matthew 2:16)*. Around 600 BC, the prophet Jeremiah had foretold of these things concerning the coming Messiah: *"Then was fulfilled that which was spoken by Jeremy the prophet, saying, In Rama was there a voice heard, <u>lamentation, and weeping, and great mourning, Rachel weeping for her children, and would not be comforted, because they are not</u>" (Matthew 2:17, 18)*. This prophecy was/is contained in Jeremiah 31:15. See, Moses' birth foreshadowed the situation surrounding Jesus' birth: women weeping for their dead children!

Fearing for baby Moses' life, what did his mom do? She built an ARK to hide him in!!! The Bible records: *"And the woman conceived, and bare a <u>son</u>: and when she saw him that he was a <u>goodly</u> child, she hid him three months. And when she could not longer hide him, <u>**she took for him an ARK of bulrushes, and daubed it with slime and with pitch, and put the child therein**</u>" (Exodus 2:1-3)*. Are you kidding me? I could think of a hundred other things she could have done to hide the baby, but she built an ARK, like Noah! Who do you think placed this remedy in her mind? That is right…God did, because this is HIS prophetic story about the coming Messiah, and an "ark" ALWAYS represents the spiritual Kingdom of God! Remember in Noah's story? In that account the Ark (Kingdom of God) was rising up off of Earth's surface holding 1 house of righteous people in its possession. But now in this story the ark (Kingdom of God) is holding a baby! See, by incorporating an "ark" into the events of baby Moses' life, God was clandestinely revealing the Messiah would come to Earth as a baby! When Jesus grew up and began his ministry, he forcefully proclaimed; *"The TIME is fulfilled, and the **kingdom of God is at hand**: REPENT ye, and believe the gospel" (Mark 1:15).* Yes, the "kingdom of God" had arrived just like the story of Moses had predicted it would…in the form of a baby!

The Hebrew word for "ark" is *"tēbâ"* and it simply means: box-shaped thing: chest, ark, basket. Astonishingly, the night Jesus was born he was placed in a "box-shaped thing" (manger) because Mary & Joseph could not find any available rooms in Bethlehem. Who do you think was controlling the events of that night? Right, again!!! Friend, God is a masterful storyteller and the harmony between the events in Moses' & Jesus' life is breathtaking. Look, Noah & Moses' mother both built wooden "box-shaped things" (representing the Kingdom of God) that drifted on top of water; then, God authoritatively connected the Messiah back to those stories by having him lie in a wooden "box-shaped thing" the night of his birth! Truly, the "ark" symbolizes the Kingdom of God. (You will soon learn in the *"wilderness"* chapter that God had plans for ANOTHER "ark" to be built! And it too will symbolize the spiritual "Kingdom of God".)

Floating in the reeds along a river's edge, the ark was found by Pharaoh's daughter and she kept the baby! Now what are the chances of that? Remember, Pharaoh's house represents Satan's Kingdom, and Satan became the "god of this world" when he coerced mankind to sin. So, in this detail God was revealing the Messiah would have to come to Satan's world (planet Earth) to be tempted by him. Listen to what was written in the New Testament about Moses: *"By faith Moses, when he was come to years, REFUSED to be called the son of Pharaoh's*

157

daughter; ***Choosing rather to SUFFER AFFLICATION with the people of God, than to enjoy the pleasures of sin for a season"*** *(Hebrews 11:24, 25)*. Does this sound like Jesus? Of course! Christ <u>refused</u> ALL of Satan's sinful, self-pleasuring temptations, and decided rather to SUFFER the AFFLICTION of the cross!

Pharaoh's daughter named the baby from the way she found him. She called him "Moses", meaning "drawn out", because she drew him out of the water: *"And the child grew, and she brought him unto Pharaoh's daughter, and he became her son. And <u>she called his name Moses</u>: and she said, Because <u>I drew him out of the water"</u> (Exodus 2:10)*. Friend, <u>GOD</u> led her to give the baby that name! She was, unknowingly, prophesying that God would work through Moses to "draw out" or deliver His people (children of Israel) from Egyptian bondage! And of course this represents the Messiah's work for Jesus would "draw out" mankind's souls from Satan's oppressive grasp.

Further solidifying the prophetic connection between Moses & Jesus, God also planned for Jesus to spend a little time in Egypt as a child! An angel advised Mary and Joseph to flee to Egypt with baby Jesus to escape king Herod's child killing spree: *"behold, the <u>angel of the Lord appeareth to Joseph in a dream</u>, saying, Arise, and take the young child (Jesus) and his mother, and <u>flee into Egypt</u>, and be thou there until I bring thee word: for Herod will seek the young child to destroy him.* ***<u>When he arose, he took the young child and his mother by night, and departed into Egypt</u>"*** *(Matthew 2:13, 14)*. Matthew notes in his Gospel that the prophet Hosea had prophesied this about Jesus; *"And (Joseph, Mary, and Jesus) was there (in Egypt) until the death of Herod: that it might be fulfilled which was spoken of the Lord by the prophet, saying, <u>Out of Egypt have I called my son</u>" (Matthew 2:15)*. This prophecy is contained in Hosea 11:1. Why is God doing all of this? Why go to such great lengths to parallel the details between Moses & Jesus' life? Because God wanted/wants mankind to **KNOW** the deliverance He worked through Moses was, truly, a <u>prophetic</u> picture of the deliverance He would work through Jesus!

Returning to the story flow, one day at the age of <u>40</u> Moses saw an Egyptian taskmaster beating an Israelite slave. Out of anger, Moses struck the taskmaster and killed him! Do you understand what this

158

incident is about, spiritually? Friend, God allowed this event to happen as a powerful VISUAL representation of what the Messiah was coming to planet Earth to do—namely, beat down Satan!!! See, Moses destroyed the Egyptian taskmaster like Jesus would destroy Satan's kingdom. And since it would be an invisible, spiritual war, God drummed up this little incident in Moses' life to SHOW mankind the Messiah's work! Later, Jesus said, *"And from the days of John the Baptist until now the **kingdom of heaven suffereth violence**, and the violent take it by force" (Matthew 11:12).* Friend, Jesus came to conquer the Devil and take back his power over our sin & death, freeing mankind's spirits from bondage. Jesus won that spiritual war!!! John the Revelator later confirmed the victory: *"I (Jesus) am he that liveth, and was dead; and, behold, I am alive for evermore, Amen; and have the keys of hell and of death" (Revelation 1:18).* Yes, undoubtedly, Jesus defeated Lucifer and his cohorts (in the spiritual realm) just like Moses defeated the Egyptian taskmaster (in the physical realm)! NOW you know the spiritual significance behind the confrontation of Moses killing the Egyptian. Oh, but there is more revelation behind the incident's details!

After Christ's ascension, a man named Stephen became the first martyr for spreading the Good News about how Jesus Christ was the Messiah and how he had fulfilled the Old Testament Scriptures. Stephen had perfect understanding of the true spiritual implications behind the ancient Bible stories (parables) in the Jewish scrolls because he was full of the Holy Ghost, and he gave an impressive Biblical summary in front of the council of the high priest—which I encourage you to read in Acts chapter 7—before they killed him. He began with the story of Abraham and ended with Solomon's story, but in between he brought up the incident of Moses killing the Egyptian taskmaster because he KNEW its true, prophetic, spiritual meaning!

Listen to his amazing summarization: *"And Moses was learned in all the wisdom of the Egyptians, and was mighty in words and in deeds. And when he was FULL forty years old, it came into his heart to visit his brethren the children of Israel. And seeing one of them suffer wrong, he defended him, and **AVENGED him that was oppressed**, and smote the Egyptian: **For he supposed his brethren would have understood how that GOD by his hand would deliver them: but they understood*** *not" (Acts 7:22-25)*. Wow, do you understand what Stephen is saying? The Holy Spirit speaking through his lips KNEW the story of Moses was prophetically ALL about the Messiah, Jesus. Thus, by recalling this incident of Moses' Stephen was declaring Jesus had come to Earth to avenge the oppressed souls of mankind, and that even though he supposed the Jews would recognize him as their Savior and that God's hand was working through him to deliver them and ALL mankind from sin's bondage: THEY DID NOT!!!

See, the Jewish religious leaders of Jesus' day had NO idea the tale of Moses' skirmish in their scrolls was actually prophesy about THEM that THEY would NOT recognize Jesus as their Savior! Is that not absolutely stunning? Having just killed Jesus, the Jews—slowly catching Stephen's drift—listened, hotly, as he rolled on with his monologue: *"And the next day he (Moses) shewed himself unto them (Israelites) as they strove, and would have set them at one again, saying, Sirs, ye are brethren; why do ye wrong one to another? But he that did his neighbor wrong thrust him away, saying, **Who made thee a ruler and a judge over us?**" (Acts 7:26, 27).* Oh, my!!! Friend, Jesus came to set mankind's souls at ONE again with God's Spirit by paying the death penalty for our sins of "wronging God and our neighbor" (which is disobeying the 10 Love Commandments). But the Israelite's comment *"Who made thee a ruler and a judge over us"* again, unwittingly, prophesied the Jews would reject Jesus as their Savior and King! Yet, without question, Jesus IS the "Ruler and Judge" over ALL mankind. (Another prophetic revelation behind a detail of this "beat-down incident" in Moses' life is coming near the end of this chapter and it will AMAZE you; then, I will finish Stephen's dramatic story in the *"Holy Spirit"* chapter!)

Let us return to Moses' account in the 14th Century BC. After the Pharaoh learned of his killing an Egyptian, Moses fled from Egypt, and the next 40 years he spent watching sheep for a man named Jethro in the land of Midian: *"Now Moses kept the flock of Jethro...and he led the flock to the backside of the desert, and came to the mountain of God, even to Horeb" (Exodus 3:1).* This part of Moses' story (parable) reveals the coming Messiah, Jesus, would be a shepherd! Oh, but not of physical sheep, but of mankind (spiritual sheep)! Jesus emphatically

160

pronounced: *"**I am the good shepherd: the good shepherd giveth his life for the sheep***...I am the good shepherd, and know my sheep, and am known of mine" (John 10:11, 14).* See, a GOOD shepherd will put his life on the line to protect and defend his sheep, and Jesus was on Earth to do EXACTLY that! In fact, Jesus would give his life for his sheep during mankind's 4,000[th] year, just like Moses watched over his sheep for 40 years. Again, God is painting a picture-perfect portrait of Jesus' life through Moses' life.

Guiding sheep through a desert and now 80 years old, one day Moses was accosted by God from a burning bush: *"I am the God of thy father, the God of Abraham, the God of Isaac, and the God of Jacob...I have surely **seen the affliction of my people** which are in Egypt, and have **heard their cry** by reason of their taskmasters; for **I know their SORROWS**; And I am come down to DELIVER them out of the hand of the Egyptians, and to bring them up out of that land unto a good land and a large, unto a land flowing with milk and honey...Come now therefore, and I will send thee unto Pharaoh, that thou mayest bring forth my people the children of Israel out of Egypt" (Exodus 3:6-10).* Wow, by now you should understand EXACTLY what God is saying here, spiritually! What perfect language to describe mankind's spiritual condition after Adam & Eve's sin, for God saw it all!!! He knew well the pain, sorrow, and tears. But He was going to send the Messiah to Earth to deliver us and bring all righteous souls back home to the Kingdom of God (Promise Land).

It is here at the "burning bush scene" that God first describes the "Promise Land" as *"a land flowing with milk and honey"*. Remember, the "Promise Land" also symbolizes the "Kingdom of God (or Heaven)"—i.e. the spiritual place where God dwells, the Tree of Life stands, and all the righteous souls will live eternally! Knowing this, you should now recognize God has the Israelite's story (parable) set up perfectly to clearly EXPOSE the TRUTH concerning **EVERYTHING** involved in mankind's spiritual journey back to union with Him—i.e. mankind's freedom (salvation) from bondage to sin & death and what (if anything) mankind needs to DO to make it to and enter the Promise Land and receive eternal life! In other words, avidly studying every detail of God's parable concerning what it took for the Israelites to enter

161

the Promise Land uncovers PRECISELY what it takes for a human soul to obtain eternal life by entering the Kingdom of God (The Land flowing with milk and honey)!!!

THIS was the amazing spiritual revelation God gave me on the Sabbath morning of Saturday December 8th, 2007, right after I woke up, while still lying in my bed!!! It was like a super-bright light bulb clicked on, illuminating the TRUTH of the Bible's entire purpose and meaning! I have attended thousands of church services and NEVER heard this truth. Friend, the only reason God created the Israelite's bondage, freedom, and journey to the Promise Land story was to plainly explain everything involved with mankind's spiritual journey back to God. Allow me to briefly introduce you to the parable's 5 step Truth:

1. **Physical**: While the Israelite children were in bondage to the Egyptians, they had NO possible way to get to the Promise Land in Canaan because the Egyptians held the power of death over them—i.e. the Egyptians would kill them if they tried to leave.

   Spiritual: While God's spirit children were in bondage to sin, they had NO possible way to get to the Kingdom of God (the place of eternal life where God's life-giving Spirit dwells) because they had ALL sinned. Therefore, Satan held the power of death over them—i.e. sin had mankind's souls hopelessly, spiritually separated from God's Spirit of Life.

2. **Physical**: God personally, supernaturally delivered the Israelite children out of Egyptian bondage by working through Moses to plague Pharaoh 10 times.

   Spiritual: God personally, supernaturally delivered His spirit children out of bondage to sin by working through Jesus to atone for ALL their sins—i.e. disobedience to the 10 Love Commandments).

3. **Physical**: God's salvation placed the Israelite children in

a wilderness, but at least a WAY to the Promise Land was now open—i.e. Canaan land was attainable.

Spiritual: God's <u>salvation</u> placed His spirit children in a wilderness, but at least a WAY to the Kingdom of God was now open—i.e. eternal life was attainable.

4. **Physical**: IF the Israelite children would obey God's 10 Love Commandments (written by God's finger on stone), He would lead them through the wilderness on a <u>journey</u> to enter the Promise Land.

   Spiritual: IF God's spirit children will obey His 10 Love Commandments (written on their hearts by God), He will lead them through the wilderness on a <u>journey</u> to enter the Kingdom of God and obtain eternal life!

5. **Physical**: IF the Israelite children willingly disobeyed God's 10 Love Commandments, they would DIE in the wilderness and <u>never</u> enter the Promise Land.

   Spiritual: IF God's spirit children willingly disobey His 10 Love Commandments, they WIll DIE in Earth's wilderness and <u>never</u> enter the Kingdom of God—i.e. they will NOT inherit eternal life!

Are you stunned? How simple! How beautiful! How pure! This revelation is PRICELESS. It would easily be worth 1 million dollars for this revelation!!! What would you pay to absolutely <u>KNOW</u> how to obtain eternal life for your soul? What would you pay to have all your Biblical confusion cleared up? Friend, the spiritual message delivered by the guest speaker God through the skit enacted by the "chosen" Israelite's story (parable) explains EVERYTHING involved in mankind's spiritual journey back to God, for it brings to light "obtaining eternal life" is a "2-part process" or "2-part equation": (Christ's sinless death) + (your repentance) = eternal life!!! Look, "God's salvation (or deliverance) part" was 100% His doings ("*not of any man's works*"), but "mankind's part" is to REPENT of sin (stop disobeying and start obeying God's 10 Love Commandments). See, IF these 2 conditions (parts) are met, that soul will obtain eternal life! And you know as well as me "God's part" was/is already done, met, & finished through Jesus Christ at the Cross of Calvary, effective for EVERY man or woman who has EVER lived on Earth. So how are you doing with your part?

Let me show you how valuable comprehension of this Israelite story (parable) is at clearing up satanically inspired, Scripture-twisted confusion (regarding what a soul MUST DO to obtain eternal life) by giving you some food-for-thought questions. For instance, while the Israelites were in bondage in Egypt could they have freed themselves and entered Canaan (the Promise Land) simply by making the decision to start obeying God's 10 Love Commandments? ABSOLUTELY NOT!!! That was NOT going to free them from the Egyptians! Do you see? Likewise, a soul's decision to start obeying God's 10 Love Commandments would never ALONE have allowed them to return to God and obtain eternal life in His Kingdom, for ALL mankind was already in bondage to sin because "*WE ALL have SINNED*".

Consequently, the Israelites NEEDED God's GIFT of supernatural deliverance (salvation) through Moses to free them from their Egyptian bondage, which THEN made their decision to obey God's 10 Love Commandments in the wilderness the deciding factor in their obtaining entrance into the Promise Land. Likewise, mankind's souls NEEDED God's gift of supernatural deliverance (salvation) through Christ's sinless death on the cross to free them from their bondage to sin, which THEN makes our decision to obey God's 10 Love Commandments (repentance) the deciding factor in our obtaining eternal life by entering the Kingdom of God. Do you understand? In other words, MANKIND CAN NEVER BRAG THAT THEY WILL OBTAIN ETERNAL LIFE BECAUSE OF THEIR WORKS ALONE!!! That is just plain silliness. Thus, Paul accurately wrote: "*Not of works, lest any man should BOAST*" *(Ephesians 2:9)*. But be forewarned, Paul is in NO WISE implying here that our works (obeying the 10 Love Commandments) do not matter! To believe that is to ignore the rest of his writings. I will discuss more of this, later.

164

Here is another question that can be fully elucidated through careful thought (or consideration of) the Israelite's story (parable), and I will give a for-instance scenario: After let us say some 30 years in the wilderness, do you think a young 20 year old Israelite's <u>KNOWLEDGE</u> and <u>BELIEF</u> in the <u>STORY</u> of HOW God delivered the Israelites out of Egyptian bondage through Moses would <u>ALONE</u> allow him/her to obtain entrance into Canaan (the Promise Land)? In other words, this child was born in the wilderness sometime after God's miraculous deliverance event had happened through Moses and has only been told the story! The correct answer to the question is...ABSOLUTELY NOT!!! Friend, Israel's freedom (salvation) gift through God's hand was a FACT regardless of what any Israelite thought about it. Do you understand? Likewise, whether or not you have heard, know, or believe in Christ's freedom (salvation) story—i.e. dying on a cross, rising from the dead, etc.—is <u>BY ITSELF</u> useless in obtaining your soul eternal life!!! Friend, mankind's salvation (freedom from sin) is a FACT whether you believe it or not. Wrestle with this revelation until you understand it completely!

Consequently, **ALL** a new Israelite child needed to <u>DO</u> to obtain entrance into the Promise Land was "OBEY God's 10 Love Commandments" as you will soon clearly see in the *"Wilderness"* chapter. (Note: The child's parents told them the amazing story of God's deliverance through Moses ONLY to bolster their belief in the invisible, Almighty, Creator God so the child would have further reason to WANT to OBEY God's 10 Love Commandments!) Likewise, **ALL** God's spirit children need to <u>DO</u> to obtain eternal life (enter the Kingdom of God) is to "OBEY God's 10 Love Commandments"! (Note: We, too, should tell all mankind the amazing story of God's deliverance through Jesus—especially, how he fulfilled all the secret, prophetic stories in the Old Testament Scriptures!—ONLY to bolster their <u>belief</u> in the invisible, Almighty, Creator God so they will have further reason to WANT to OBEY God's 10 Love Commandments.) See how clear the "Truth" becomes by understanding the Israelite's account? You can answer all of your questions concerning "how to obtain eternal life" by addressing them through the Israelite's story (parable)! I will discuss many New Testament Bible verses throughout the rest of this book, and

165

if you keep this Israelite parable in mind, you will understand every passage perfectly!

Alright, let us return to the amazing story of Moses at the "burning bush event". After God instructed him to go before Pharaoh and demand he let the Israelite children go, Moses was fearful Pharaoh would not believe he had heard from the Creator God, so God gave him a convincing sign: *"And the LORD said unto him, What is that in thine hand? And he said, A rod. And he said, Cast it on the ground. And he cast it on the ground, and **it became a serpent**; and Moses fled from before it" (Exodus 4:2, 3).* How about that? God could have turned Moses' rod into anything, but He turned it into a snake!!! Why? Think about it friend, mankind knew the story of Adam & Eve in the Garden of Eden, and they knew what a <u>serpent</u> represented. It embodied Satan: It was God's physical symbol of the "evil one" who had tricked mankind into their pitiful, sorrowful, sinful condition. Moses shrieked back in horror at the sight of a serpent! But then God commanded Moses to take the serpent by the tail, which turned the snake back into a lifeless rod. Do you see what God was doing? This was a <u>perfect</u> sign to convince Moses he was conversing with the one, true, powerful God that had created heaven and Earth. Through this miraculous sign involving the supernatural appearance and disappearance of a serpent, God was actually declaring to Moses, "I AM the one who has power over Lucifer and sin; thus, I AM the one who can and will deliver mankind's souls!"

Moses obeyed God and stood before Pharaoh demanding he free the Israelites. But God hardened Pharaoh's heart 10 times so He could send <u>10</u> supernatural plagues on him through Moses' hand to symbolically prophesy the Messiah Jesus would FULLY free mankind's souls from <u>ALL</u> of sin, for ALL moral sin is wrapped up in the 10 Love Commandments! Therefore, this part of the story (parable) supports the previous story (parable) of Jacob & Laban, where Laban deceived Jacob 10 times. Friend, make no mistake about it, God displayed <u>10</u> acts of DIVINE power to prove his victory (freedom) over sin would be complete! Later, the Bible validated: *"the <u>blood of Jesus Christ his Son cleanseth us from **ALL** sin"</u> (I John 1:7).* See, God could have sent 3, 5, 6, 7, 12, 18, or any number of plagues on Pharaoh, but only 10 perfectly

166

articulated what He was expressing, spiritually!

Now you know why God kept hardening Pharaoh's heart after each plague: *"And Moses and Aaron did all these wonders before Pharaoh: and the LORD hardened Pharaoh's heart, so that he would not let the children of Israel go out of his land" (Exodus 11:10)*. Friend, God was telling the story of our salvation and every detail had to be perfect! There <u>HAD</u> to be 10 supernatural plagues to represent God's total triumph over sin. Shoot, God was not only controlling the Pharaoh's heart; He was controlling <u>EVERYTHING</u> that was happening!

After 9 supernatural plagues of frogs, flies, locusts, etc. it was time for the 10th and final plague. And what would it be? The plague of <u>DEATH</u>! Now how perfect is that? For from WHAT was Jesus coming to Earth to free mankind's souls? <u>Spiritual</u> DEATH—spiritual separation from God!!! In other words, God chose the perfect final divine (supernatural) plague to correctly represent the Messiah's future work of deliverance. Not knowing what God was doing and infuriated at Pharaohs continual hardened heart, Moses fumed to Pharaoh: *"Thus saith the LORD, About midnight will I go out into the midst of Egypt: And **<u>all the firstborn in the land of Egypt shall DIE</u>**, from the firstborn of Pharaoh that sitteth upon his throne, even unto the firstborn of the maidservant that is behind the mill; and all the firstborn of beasts...And he went out from Pharaoh in a great anger" (Exodus 11:4-8)*. See, God has set up a spiritually flawless liberation scene, because the Israelite children are going to escape bondage as they, simultaneously, are being saved from death. It was/is an impeccable picture of what Jesus did for mankind, spiritually, at the cross of Calvary!

Furthermore, thrown into the mix of this "deliverance-from-death scene" will be God's FULL development of His "sacrificial lamb" concept. (Remember, He had intermittently hinted at the concept throughout history by clothing Adam & Eve's "nakedness" with animal skins He slaughtered in the Garden of Eden, accepting Abel's lamb offering, and providing a ram for Abraham's sacrifice after stopping him from slaughtering his son, Isaac.) But now my friend, the <u>prophetic</u> detail God reveals, yet conceals, concerning the coming Messiah's life in His <u>exact</u> instructions for the Israelite's "sacrificial lamb" flaunts ridiculously crazy wisdom. I pray I can express it clearly so that you

167

can truly grasp it all! Then, as always, cogitate the remarkable fact that the Jewish people of Jesus' day did not understand their (and ALL mankind's) Messiah had to first be God's "Sacrificial Lamb" and that he was perfectly fulfilling everything God had asked their fathers (the Israelites) to do with their lamb the week they escaped Egyptian bondage over 1,300 years earlier!

Here was God's deal with the Israelites in Egypt: To be safe from the 10th and final death plague, they were to "kill a lamb" and smear its <u>blood</u> on the doorposts of their houses; then when the death angel saw the blood he would PASS-OVER them and not kill anyone in that <u>house</u>! (Eventually, the lamb became known as the "Passover Lamb".) Now where did God get a crazy idea like that? Just think of the almost limitless number of "things" God could have asked the Israelites to do to escape the death plague! I could think of a thousand different things God could have had them do, but to "kill a lamb" would not have been one of them. Do you see? But God wanted to further develop the concept of a "sacrificial lamb" because it secretly prophesied that it would take a MAN'S sinless blood—as the true sacrificial Passover Lamb!—to atone for mankind's sins, freeing their souls from spiritual death. Let us investigate God's amazing, PROPHETIC instructions concerning Israel's Passover lamb.

Incidentally, as God furnished Moses with each specific, detailed instruction concerning the Passover lamb, one wonders if the Israelite children were thinking, "Moses, what is the purpose of ALL this? Your instructions sound psychotically crazy!" Friend, God got right down to the nitty-gritty and even told them <u>exactly</u> what day of the month to pick their lamb and what day of the month to kill it! Come on! Who cares, right? WHAT on planet Earth was God up to with all this exactness? Oh, my friend, it is absolutely, positively, prophetically stunning!

Allow me to set the stage: It was now mankind's 2,638th year (1334 BC) after Creation; thus, it is approximately the middle of God's 3rd millennial day in His 7 day (7,000 year) plan for mankind on Earth. It is early springtime in Egypt—probably only days before the spring equinox!—and God instructs Moses: *"<u>This month shall be unto you the beginning of months: it shall be the first month of the year to you</u>. Speak ye unto all the congregation of Israel, saying, <u>In the **TENTH DAY of**</u>*

168

this month *they shall take to them every man a LAMB, according to the* *house of their fathers, a LAMB for an house… And ye shall keep it up until* *the* **FOURTEENTH day** *of the same month: and the whole assembly of* *the congregation of Israel shall* *kill it in the evening" (Exodus 12:2, 3,* *6).* Note: The Israelites used a lunar calendar, alternating 29 & 30 day months based on the moon's apparent 29½ day cycle. Consequently, their months began when the first sliver of the new moon was seen. So, from the above verse we know a new lunar month must have just begun when God talked to Moses about the details of the sacrificial lamb, because He said, *"This month…"* Therefore, the night they were to "choose a lamb" was less then 10 days away because God said pick the lamb on the 10th day of that month and kill it on the 14th day! WHY did God single out the 10th & 14th days of a lunar month? The answer to this is mind-boggling, and I will tell you soon! But for now just know this 1st month on the Jewish calendar later became named the month of "*Nissan*".

God continued to speak to Moses: *"Your lamb shall be…a* *MALE of the first year" (Exodus 12:5).* Here, God was resolutely revealing the Messiah, Jesus, would positively be a man! Sure enough, the angel of the Lord told Joseph: *"Joseph, thou son of David, fear not* *to take unto thee Mary thy wife; for that which is conceived in her is of* *the Holy Ghost. And* *she shall bring forth a SON, and thou shalt call his* *name JESUS: for* *HE shall save his people from their sins" (Matthew* *1:20, 21).* Without a doubt, Jesus was a man, and THAT is why God demanded the Israelite's Passover lamb be male.

God charged Moses: *"Your lamb shall be WITHOUT BLEMISH"* *(Exodus 12:5).* With this command God foreshadowed the Messiah would live a sinless life! Later, Peter wrote about Jesus: *"…because* *Christ also suffered for us,* **WHO DID NO SIN***, neither was guile found* *in his mouth" (I Peter 2:21, 22).* Yes, only a 100% sinless human being could pay the awful "death penalty" for mankind's sins by offering themselves up as a sacrifice. And THAT is exactly what Jesus did!!! Peter exclaimed: *"But with the* *precious blood of Christ, as of a* *LAMB* *WITHOUT BLEMISH and without spot" (I Peter 1:19).* Therefore, as the children of Israel were intently inspecting their flocks for a male lamb without defect, spot, or wrinkle, they were unsuspectingly and unknowingly foreshadowing the purity of the true, sacrificial, Passover Lamb of God, who was Jesus Christ!

God then instructed Moses to caution the Israelites to not break a bone of their chosen lamb: *"And the LORD said unto Moses and Aaron, This is the ordinance of the Passover...NEITHER SHALL YE BREAK A BONE thereof"* (Exodus 12:43, 46). Friend, this amazingly foretold that Jesus would not have a bone broke in his body!!! Centuries later, around 1000 BC, God prophesied directly through King David the same thing about the coming Messiah: *"He keepeth all his bones: not one of them is broken"* (Psalms 34:20). Astonishingly, the day Jesus hung on the cross not one bone in his body was broken, even though the two thieves who were crucified alongside of him both had their legs broken to hasten their death: *"Then came the soldiers, and brake the legs of the first, and of the other which was crucified with him. But when they came to Jesus, and saw that he was dead already, they BRAKE NOT HIS LEGS...For these things were done, that the scripture should be fulfilled, A bone of him shall not be broken"* (John 19:32-36). Do you see? God knew everything the "Lamb of God (Jesus)" would go through, and He was perfectly, prophetically representing it through the Israelite's Passover lamb in Egypt!

God commanded the Israelites to kill their lamb on the 14th of Nissan and to eat its flesh that night: *"And they shall EAT THE FLESH in that night, roast with fire, and unleavened bread; and with bitter herbs they shall eat it"* (Exodus 12:8). See, when you eat something IT becomes a part of you—i.e. atoms in the food lodge in the cells of your physical body and are carried around with you for years! Subsequently, the spiritual implication behind *"eating the flesh of the lamb"* is very deep and powerful. Jesus would say, *"Verily, verily, I say unto you, Except ye EAT THE FLESH of the Son of man, and drink his blood, ye have no life in you. **Whoso eateth my flesh, and drinketh my blood, hath eternal life**; and I will raise him up at the last day"* (John 6:5). The Jewish people who were listening to Jesus speak did not understand he was the true Passover Lamb and that he was talking spiritually, so they grumbled; *"How can this man give us his flesh to eat?"* (John 6:52). But do you know what Jesus meant? Do you know what it means to *"eat Christ's flesh"*?

Friend, Jesus is the "Word of God"! John wrote: *"And the Word was made flesh, and dwelt among us" (John 1:14)*. You will learn in the *"Word of God"* chapter that the "WORD OF GOD" to mankind is for them to love Him and to love their neighbor as themselves, which simply means to obey the 10 LOVE Commandments! Look, do you remember God IS love? Well, since Jesus came FROM God, then he was a walking "fleshly" embodiment of Love. In other words, Jesus was Love (the Word of God) in the flesh—obviously, because he never disobeyed any of the 10 Love Commandments, for he never sinned. So here is the meaning of Jesus' words: If you want to obtain eternal life, you will have to eat Love, which is Jesus' spiritual flesh or his words. "Love" will then lodge in your spirit, propelling you to WANT to obey God's 10 Love Commandments. Yes, friend, Jesus' alarming words to *"eat my flesh"* were really nothing more than a fancy way of again commanding people to REPENT of sin (by obeying the 10 Love Commandments) to obtain eternal life!

Listen, to *"eat Christ's flesh"* is a spiritual thing. Jesus confirmed: *"It is written, Man shall NOT live by bread alone, but by every WORD that proceedeth out of the mouth of God" (Matthew 4:4)*. See, eating fleshly food (atoms) can only sustain your physical body, but to eat God's WORDS (DO the 10 Love Commandments) will sustain your soul eternally!!! Therefore, I pray you masticate a healthy serving of Jesus' flesh daily, until His Love metabolizes into your heart, oozes out of you mouth, and turns your soul into love. Jesus said, *"He that EATETH MY FLESH, and drinketh my blood, dwelleth in me, and I in him" (John 6:56)*. Now you know why God commanded the Israelites to *"eat the flesh"* of their Passover lamb. Everyone who receives eternal life will have eaten the Words (flesh) of the true Passover Lamb of God (Christ)!

Returning to God's instructions to Moses concerning the Israelite's Passover lamb, He commanded the Israelites to spread the blood of their sacrificed lambs on the 3 doorposts of their houses: *"And they shall take of the blood, and strike it on the two side posts and on the upper door post of the houses, wherein they shall eat it...And the blood shall be to you for a token upon the HOUSES where ye are: and when I see the blood, I will PASS OVER you, and the plague shall not*

be upon you to destroy you, when I smite the land of Egypt" (Exodus
12:7, 13). Therefore, that fateful night in Egypt when the death angel
was riding, only people inside houses with the "BLOOD of the LAMB"
on them were saved from death. (Remember, if God's "Spirit of Love"
dwells inside your heart, then you are part of the "HOUSE of Christ".)
Can you visualize the precise, prophetic, spiritual picture God was
painting through the Israelite's story (concerning the coming Messiah)
with the saving "blood of a lamb" running down the wooden doorposts
of their houses? The bloody sight foreshadowed Jesus' death: blood
running down the center wooden beam (upper door post) where Jesus
head hung and two ends of the wooden cross beam (two side posts)
where Jesus hands were nailed! And Jesus did it all to save mankind's
souls from spiritual DEATH, just like God saved the Israelites from the
plague of death!!!

See, the REAL death Jesus experienced on the cross was spiritual
separation from his Father (the source of all life). That is why Jesus
vociferated, *"My God, my God, why hast thou forsaken me?" (Mark
15:34).* Look, Jesus' death on the cross was an invisible, spiritual event.
In other words, the real battle was being waged in the spirit world! Jesus
was winning victory over true death (spiritual separation from God) for
mankind's souls by separating his soul from God's Spirit: *"when thou
(God) shalt make his (Jesus) SOUL an offering for sin" (Isaiah 53:10).*
But for our sakes, God made the imperceptible event openly visible
and knowable to mankind by creating the whole prophetic "sacrificial
Passover Lamb" scenario. THAT is how God confirmed to mankind
the "spiritual event" actually took place and that our soul's freedom has
been won!!! Do you understand? Thus, from our perspective, when we
speak of our spiritual deliverance we talk about the BLOOD of Jesus
Christ. Why is that? It is because the soul resides in the blood, and
Christ's soul is what God "offered up" as a ransom for our sins! Paul
wrote: *"Giving thanks unto the Father...Who hath DELIVERED us
from the power of darkness, and hath translated us into the kingdom of
his dear Son: **In whom we have redemption through his blood, even
the forgiveness of sins"** (Colossians 1:12-14).* Truly, we have been
delivered from sin's death curse by the holy, righteous blood of the
Lamb, which now has POWER to save our souls—i.e. provide us with

172

forgiveness for our sins—from eternal, spiritual death!

Notice, of all God's created, physical animals He chose a white lamb to symbolize the Messiah's spiritual purity. See, a sweet, humble, innocent lamb harms nothing and cannot speak or defend itself. Around 800 BC, Isaiah prophesied about the coming Messiah: *"He (Jesus) was oppressed, and he was afflicted, yet he opened not his mouth: **he is brought as a LAMB to the slaughter**, and as a sheep before her shearers is dumb, so he openeth not his mouth"* (Isaiah 53:7). See, Jesus was THAT Lamb!!! The Bible records: *"And when he (Jesus) was accused of the chief priests and elders, he answered nothing. Then said Pilate unto him, Hearest thou not how many things they witness against thee? And he answered him to never a word; insomuch that the governor marvelled greatly"* (Matthew 27:12-14). Friend, Jesus was/is the innocent, loving, Passover Lamb of God!

Alright…back in Egypt, 1334 BC, sundown finally occurred bringing in nighttime and the beginning of Nissan 14th. And God's secret, prophetic, "salvation" story (parable) played out according to His plan like a well-conducted symphony: The Israelites killed their 10th-of-Nissan chosen, unblemished, male lamb; collected its blood and applied it to the 3 doorposts of their house; roasted its unbroken-boned flesh with fire and consumed it; then cowered in fear, waiting inside their houses as God's death angel PASSED OVER killing all the Egyptian firstborn. As you can imagine, the cry in Egypt was terrible that night for <u>every</u> "house" without blood on its doorposts had something dead in it! In a panic, Pharaoh rose up in the middle of the night and demanded the Israelites leave Egypt, immediately. See, **GOD** was <u>supernaturally DELIVERING</u> the Israelites from their bondage!!!

Of course the parable would NOT be spiritually accurate without the Israelites leaving with Egypt's riches! So like Abraham & Sarah escaped with Pharaoh's riches and Jacob ran away with Laban's riches, the Israelites fled with Egypt's riches: *"And the children of Israel did according to the word of Moses; and they borrowed of the Egyptians jewels of silver, and jewels of gold, and raiment: And the LORD gave the people favour in the sight of the Egyptians, so that they lent unto them such things as they required. **And they SPOILED the Egyptians**"* (Exodus 12:35, 36). (Notice again how God was <u>controlling</u> everything:

for "*the LORD gave the Israelites favor*!") Friend, God's prophetic parable HAD to be spiritually accurate. Stunningly, the Holy Spirit moved Paul to use the EXACT same language (as Moses above) in describing Jesus' invisible, spirit-world victory over Satan as he died on the cross for mankind's sins, making us spiritually rich: "*And **having SPOILED principalities and powers**" (Colossians 2:15)*. Do you see? God used the word "*spoiled*" in both cases to further confirm the Israelite story was/is precisely what I am telling you: A secret, prophetic parable about mankind's Messiah.

Next, came the chase scene. (Remember Laban pursuing Jacob?) God hardened the Pharaoh's heart one last time, and in front of the Red Sea God played out the final scene of the Israelite's deliverance from their Egyptian bondage, visually showing and foretelling what would "happen" in the invisible, spirit world as the Messiah delivered mankind's souls out of bondage while dying on a cross! In other words, the scene was "set up" PERFECTLY by God to display the freedom the Messiah would one day win for His spirit children: The RED Sea represented a physical obstacle **impossible** for the Israelites to cross or PASS OVER on their own accord, just like sin in the hearts of ALL mankind had our souls permanently separated from God's Spirit of Life and made spiritually reuniting with Him **impossible**. Watch now as God works through Moses (representing Jesus) in a "specific manner" to PART the Red Sea and supernaturally free the Israelites, all to visually demonstrate how He would one day work through the Messiah to supernaturally free mankind's souls and open up a way for them to PASSOVER to (or reunite with) Him!

Trapped in front of the impassable Red Sea, God told Moses to stretch out his hands: "*And the LORD said unto Moses…lift thou up thy rod, and stretch out thine hand over the sea, and divide it: and the children of Israel shall go on dry ground through the midst of the sea*" (Exodus 14:15, 16). Moses obeyed, God parted the Red Sea, and the Israelites scurried across to freedom on dry ground. Later, Moses would write about God's salvation: "*And the LORD brought us forth out of Egypt with a mighty hand, and **with an outstretched arm**, and with great terribleness, and with signs, and with wonders*" (Deuteronomy 26:8). Do you see? The scene foreshadowed the way in which Jesus

174

would deliver mankind's souls out of bondage: With <u>outstretched arms</u> on a cross, <u>dividing</u> the temple veil in two which led into the Holy of Holies (the place where God's Spirit dwelled!), symbolizing the <u>WAY</u> back to God was now open to mankind's souls: *"And Jesus cried with a loud voice, and gave up the ghost. <u>And the vail of the temple was rent in twain from the top to the bottom</u>" (Mark 13:37, 38).* See, God could have told Moses to "strike" the water to part it, but that would not have been an accurate portrayal of the "manner" in which the Messiah would free (deliver) us.

Then, God finished off his spiritually accurate parable by making an "OPEN SHOW" of His victory over the Egyptians (Satan's kingdom) by destroying <u>ALL of them</u> in the Red Sea. THIS was to <u>precisely</u> represent how God would destroy <u>ALL of Satan's power of death</u> over mankind's souls through Jesus! How did it happen? God caused the Egyptians to pursue the Israelites into the parted red sea: *"And <u>the Egyptians pursued, and went in after them to the midst of the sea</u>, even all Pharaoh's horses, his chariots, and his horsemen" (Exodus 14:23).* Then, God told Moses to raise his arms once again: *"And the LORD said unto Moses, <u>Stretch out thine hand</u> over the sea, that the waters may come again upon the Egyptians, upon their chariots, and upon their horsemen" (Exodus 14:26).* This time when Moses (Jesus) *"stretched out his hands"* God destroyed the Egyptian army in the sea: *"And the waters returned, and covered the chariots, and the horsemen, and <u>ALL</u> the host of Pharaoh that came into the sea after them; **there remained not so much as one of them**" (Exodus 14:28).* What an awesome, <u>FUTURISTIC</u>, visual display of God's total annihilation of Satan's spiritual kingdom of darkness through the Messiah on the cross over 1,300 years later. Paul wrote about what <u>Jesus' death DID in the invisible, spirit world</u>: *"And <u>having spoiled principalities and powers</u>, he (God working through Jesus) made **a SHEW of them OPENLY, triumphing over them in it**" (Colossians 2:15).* Do you see? Paul's Messianic description is <u>EXACTLY</u> what God DID to the Egyptians at the Red Sea!

Listen to the Psalmist's words recounting God's deliverance of the Israelites and victory over the Egyptians: *"He (God) rebuked the Red Sea also, and it was dried up: so he led them through the depths…*

*And **he (God) SAVED them from the hand of him that hated them, and REDEEMED them from the hand of the enemy**. And the waters covered their enemies: there was not one of them left" (Psalms 106:9-11)*. Wow, is that not a perfect summation of what God did for us though Jesus' death on the cross? God <u>SAVED</u> us and <u>REDEEMED</u> us from the hand of our enemy, Satan, who hated us: "<u>Who *(Jesus) gave himself for us, that he might REDEEM us from ALL iniquity (sin)* " (Titus 2:14)</u>!!! Yes, truly, God's deliverance (salvation) of the Israelites at the Red Sea was a secret, prophetic story (parable) representing how God would deliver (save) mankind's souls from bondage to sin & death (spiritual separation from His Spirit) through the Messiah, making reunion with Him (eternal life) possible.

Jesus summed up his Earthly mission for mankind's souls when he said, *"The thief (Satan) cometh not, but for to steal, and to kill, and to destroy: **I am come that they might have life**, and that **they might have it more abundantly" (John 10:10)**.* See, Satan came/comes to kill and destroy mankind's souls—to permanently separate them from God's Spirit in hell—but Jesus came to Earth to give mankind's souls life—to make REUNION with God's Spirit of Life possible! Jesus accomplished this "<u>*MIGHT* have life</u>" part on the cross when he paid mankind's death sentence for sin, giving ALL of our souls a CHANCE at "spiritual life" again by opening up a WAY back to God! The word "abundantly" comes from the Greek word "*perissos*" meaning: <u>exceeding, going beyond</u>. In saying "*that they might have life more <u>ABUNDANTLY</u>*", Christ was referring to the <u>ETERNAL LIFE</u> only the righteous souls (those who repent of sin!) will obtain one day when they receive their glorified bodies and enter into the glorious, spectacular Kingdom of God —i.e. the place where the lion will lie down with the Lamb, where there will be no more pain or tears, etc! Now <u>THAT</u> is why Jesus came to Earth!!!

Did you notice Jesus' words above had/have absolutely <u>NOTHING</u> to do with gaining or obtaining materialistic possessions down here on planet Earth right now? Yet, today, spiritually deceived, devil-inspired, self-indulgent, prideful, prosperity-gospel "preachers" falsely flaunt this Bible verse like a neon sign to continually promote their own greed! Can you hear them? "I am living the ABUNDANT life!" Ugghhhhhh…I want to vomit every time I hear one of these

176

vipers twist my Savior's powerful spiritual words of Truth above only to promote their own covetousness!!! Millions will be led to hell by internalizing these "preacher's" (agents of Satan) message, for "greed for dirt" is the <u>root</u> of ALL evil (sin)! (I will tell you the unadulterated Biblical truth about money in the "*Love of Money*" chapter later in this book.) But for now please realize and understand NO ONE on Earth today is living the "*abundant life*" Jesus referred to, for it will only occur when the righteous receive their new bodies in his Kingdom! Mankind has not even dreamed of that kind of <u>ABUNDANT</u> life. That is why Paul wrote: "*<u>Eye hath not seen, nor ear heard, neither have entered into the heart of man, the THINGS which God hath prepared for them that love him</u>*" (I Corinthians 2:9).

Let us return to God's Israelite "salvation story (parable)" and see what else we can learn from it about our soul's salvation. God recorded 2 reasons in the Bible for saving (or delivering) the Israelites out of Egyptian bondage. You will learn they are the <u>exact</u> same 2 reasons God saved (or delivered) mankind's souls out of sin's bondage! Listen to God's motives for saving the Israelites: "*The LORD did not set his love upon you (Israelites), nor choose you, because ye were more in number than any people; for ye were the fewest of all people: **But because <u>the Lord LOVED you</u>, and because <u>he would keep the OATH which he had sworn unto your fathers</u>**, hath the LORD brought you out with a mighty hand, and <u>redeemed</u> you out of the house of bondmen, from the hand of Pharaoh king of Egypt*" (Deuteronomy 7:7, 8). See, God's 2 reasons for redeeming (saving or delivering) the Israelites out of Egyptian bondage were "love & a promise". Let us now take a look at what the Bible says were the 2 reasons God delivered mankind's souls out of bondage to sin.

Remember God's <u>promise</u> to Adam & Eve in the Garden of Eden? The Bible records: "*And I will put enmity between thee (Satan) and the woman, and between thy seed and her seed; <u>it shall bruise thy head, and thou shalt bruise his heel</u>*" (Genesis 3:15). See, God had PROMISED mankind a savior from a woman's seed from the beginning, which was Mary's child, Jesus! And, of course, God LOVES His spirit children: "*For <u>God so LOVED the world, that he gave his only begotten Son</u>, that whosoever believeth in him should not perish, but have everlasting life.*

177

For God sent not his Son into the world to condemn the world; but that the world through HIM might be SAVED" (John 3:16, 17). Paul wrote: *"But God commendeth his LOVE toward us, in that, while we were yet sinners, Christ died for us" (Romans 5:8)*. There you have it...the 2 reasons are the same!!! God saved (delivered) mankind's souls from bondage to sin & death because He loved us and promised He would. Thus, even God's 2 reasons for freeing the Israelites from Egyptian bondage (love & a promise) perfectly foretold WHY He would free mankind's souls. Seriously, could the "salvation story (parable)" of the Israelites have been any more prophetically, spiritually accurate?

Oh, but there is even more God clandestinely prophesied about mankind's salvation through the details He controlled in the Israelite's story! And these details, staggeringly, dealt with the TIMING of the fulfillment of His plans by the Messiah!!! I know it is mind-boggling to believe God did this, but He did. In fact, God not only prophesied the year the Messiah would deliver mankind's souls out of bondage, but He had also foretold the very day during THAT year! Incidentally, God has done the very same thing concerning the Messiah's 2nd Coming!!! I know, I know: *"But of that DAY and HOUR knoweth no man" (Matthew 24:36)*. Yet Jesus commanded: *"when ye shall see all these things, KNOW that it is near, EVEN AT THE DOORS" (Matthew 24:33)*. You are going to learn in this book that even though God clearly prophesied the YEAR (and DAY during THAT year!) of Christ's 2nd Coming, it is still IMPOSSIBLE to pinpoint when that VERY day is! And it is preposterous for someone to think they know the hour! Therefore, listen to me plainly; Jesus words *"of that day and hour knoweth no man"* were/are true—of course!—for I CANNOT give you an ABSOLUTE date or hour for Christ's return, but I will eventually tell you what God has clearly prophesied about "it" through the circumstances He controlled in the Israelite's story, but this will not be complete until the last chapter, *"Joshua"*.

By the way, keep in mind the parable God so graciously gave me of the Guest Speaker: The Israelites are God's chosen volunteers enacting out a "skit" to help God communicate His message—which at the time was mostly prophetic!—to ALL mankind. This means to turn your head away from the "things" God asked the Israelites to do

178

(because you do not want to hear or learn about that "boring stuff") is like sticking your fingers in your ears and covering your eyes with the palms of your hands the moment the Guest Speaker called the volunteers upfront during his speech at the High School. Please do NOT be that dumb! With that said, let us return to the Israelite's story (parable) and investigate the secret meaning behind God's 3 "timing details"—which foretold exactly <u>WHEN</u> Jesus would <u>PROVIDE</u> <u>SALVATION</u> for mankind's souls during His 1st Coming.

Let us begin by investigating God's seemingly psychotic 2 requirements (details) that the Israelites <u>choose</u> their Passover lamb on the 10th of Nissan and <u>kill</u> it on the 14th of Nissan. Come on!!! What is up with God? Why so specific, and why THOSE particular days of a lunar month? You should clearly know by now God has a reason and purpose for EVERYTHING He does! And since Jesus fulfilled <u>every</u> "condition" God gave the Israelites concerning their Passover Lamb— i.e. male, unblemished, no bone broke, etc.—it should be of NO surprise to you that the true Passover Lamb, Jesus, fulfilled these prophetic conditions (dates), too. And he most certainly did!!! But I must tell you the WHOLE story of what God did concerning this "subject" to do it justice, so bare with me on this moderately complex matter.

Back in 1334 BC, the Israelites were now in a wilderness on the Saudi Arabia side of the Red Sea, having just watched the Egyptian army drown. It is here, during the next several months that God gave Moses many more specific instructions for the fledgling nation of Israeli people to carry out—e.g. detailed dimensions for building a moveable, tent-like tabernacle; detailed designs for crafting specific items to go inside the tabernacle, like the Table of Showbread and the brazen ALTAR for making daily sacrifices, etc. Later, under King Solomon's rule in the 10th century BC, the tabernacle was built as a building known as the Temple. A study of the Tabernacle (Temple) and its "items" reveal a shadow of the Messiah's work! But I want to look at something else God instituted with the Israelites—namely, 7 Holy Convocations or Feasts (festivals) to be observed annually. (Do not forget, all of these "things" God is asking the Israelites to do are still part of the skit He is directing them to play out to communicate a message (or information) to ALL mankind!)

The 7 yearly Feasts, also, prophetically spoke about the Messiah (Jesus) and the "things" he would accomplish for mankind's souls. But what is positively stunning is the "time (day) of year" God established for the Feasts to be observed annually was actually the EXACT time "during the year" when Christ would fulfill the "meaning" behind that particular Feast! In other words, the 7 Feasts were/are prophetic, yearly DATES (based on the Israelite's lunar calendar) and "subjects" the Messiah would/will satisfy!!! Of course the Israelites did not know this either at the time, but in hindsight Jesus fulfilled the "topics" of the first 3 Feasts on their EXACT day(s) during his 1st Coming (during year 4,000), and he fulfilled the 4th Feast's "topic" on its exact day that same year, which happened to be 10 days after his ascension into heaven. And we would be naïve to not realize he **WILL** fulfill the "topics" of the last 3 Feasts on their exact (yearly celebrated) day(s) during his 2nd Coming [See Figure #5 page 182].

The 7 Holy Feasts encompass a total of 18 days throughout the year, and 7 of those days are High Sabbaths. (Please understand since the Feast days are specific NUMBERED days based on a lunar month, which is 29 or 30 days—not an even multiple of 7—they can and do fall on any given day of the week—Sun, Mon, Tues, Wed, Thu, Fri, or Sat—depending on the year in question. Think about it!) Therefore, the 7 Holy SABBATH Feast days—"*thou shalt do no work*" days—are called "High Sabbaths", because they are Sabbaths IN ADDITION to the weekly 7th day Sabbath. The Apostle Paul was referring to these "High Sabbath" days when he wrote: "*Let no man therefore judge you in meat, or in drink, or in respect of an HOLYDAY, or of the new moon, or of the SABBATH days: **Which are a shadow of things to come**" (Colossians 2:16, 17)*. Do you see? The 7 Holy Feast day(s) are holydays (of which 7 of the 18 are High Sabbaths!) and God instituted them with the Israelite people to be a prophetic "*shadow of things*" the Messiah would fulfill for mankind's souls!

Allow me to briefly reveal the Messiah's fulfillment of the first 3 Feasts right now. These are the Feast of Passover, the Feast of Unleavened Bread, and the Feast of First Fruits—which all occurred/ occur over a consecutive 8 day period in the Jewish 1st month of Nissan [See, again, Figure #5 page 182]. It is essential you understand HOW the

180

Messiah precisely fulfilled these 3 Holy Feasts during the single YEAR of his death, burial, and resurrection (which like I said was mankind's 4,000th year) and especially what "day of the week" the Feast day(s) fell on THAT year! Then, I can explain to you the mind-boggling revelation of WHY God told the Israelites in Egypt to choose their lamb on the 10th of Nissan and sacrifice it on the 14th of Nissan.

The 1st Holy Feast God established with the Israelites in the wilderness—actually, God instituted the observance of this yearly Feast with the Israelites while they were still in Egypt, just days before their Exodus—was the **Feast of Passover**, to be observed on the 14th of Nissan. This yearly Feast commemorated the VERY night the Israelites escaped from Egypt, which is the night they killed their Passover lamb and the death angel PASSED OVER the blood-drenched doorposts of their houses: *"These are the feasts of the LORD, even holy convocations, which ye shall proclaim in their SEASONS. In the __fourteenth day of the first month (Nissan) at even (evening) is the LORD'S Passover__ (Leviticus 23:4, 5).* "Passover" celebrates mankind's spiritual passing-over from death (separation from God) to life (reunion with God). But here is the staggering fact: The Messiah (Jesus) ACTUALLY died on the 14th of Nissan! In other words, the true "Passover Lamb of God" was slaughtered the very same day the Israelites killed their Passover lambs back in Egypt over 1,300 years earlier. Friend, Jesus literally became Israel's (and ALL mankind's) Passover Lamb! Paul later wrote: *"For even CHRIST OUR PASSOVER is sacrificed for us" (I Corinthians 5:7).* Talk about being totally in the dark; the Jewish people had NO CLUE what the story of the Israelite's Passover lamb in their scrolls represented, or they certainly would NEVER have killed Jesus on the VERY SAME DAY of the year! Is what they did not stupefying? (I will confirm to you Christ died on the "Feast of Passover" shortly.)

The 2nd Holy Feast God established with the Israelites in the wilderness—God also instituted the observance of this yearly Feast with the Israelites while they were still in Egypt, just days before their Exodus—was the **Feast of Unleavened Bread**, to be observed from the 15th to 21st of Nissan. In other words, the Feast of Unleavened Bread was celebrated on the NEXT 7 days directly following the Feast of Passover on the 14th of Nissan. Do you see? This yearly 7

181

Figure # 5
Israel's Feasts

Feast (Holy Days)	Month (#)	Day (s)	High Sabbath(s)
Passover	Nissan (1st)	14	no
Unleavened Bread	Nissan (1st)	15-21	15 & 21
First Fruits	Nissan (1st)	*	no
Pentecost		**	yes
Trumpets	Tishri (7th)	1	yes
Atonement	Tishri (7th)	10	yes
Tabernacles	Tishri (7th)	15-21	15 & 22

*   The day after the weekly 7th day Sabbath occurs during the Feast of Unleavened Bread.

**   50 days after the day of First fruits.

Note:

God designed 7 Feasts with 7 High Sabbath days.
The 7 High Sabbath days occur on any given day of the week.
Jesus fulfilled the first 3 Feasts during his 1st Coming.
Jesus fulfilled the 4th Feast 10 days after his ascension
Jesus will fulfill the last 3 Feasts during his 2nd Coming!

day Feast commemorated the Israelites remarkable, hasty 7 day escape from the Egyptians (during which they had no time to leaven bread) concluding at the Red Sea fiasco: "_Seven days shall ye eat unleavened bread...And in the first day there shall be an holy convocation, and in the seventh day there shall be an holy convocation to you; no_ *manner of work shall be done in them...And ye shall observe the feast of unleavened bread...by an ordinance for ever.* ***In the first month (Nissan), on the fourteenth day of the month at even (evening), ye shall eat unleavened bread, until the one and twentieth day of the month at even***" *(Exodus 12:15-18).* (Notice, the 15th and 21st days of Nissan were/are High <u>Sabbath</u> days, which fell/fall yearly on any given day of the week, just like the Feast of Passover's 14th of Nissan!) In the Bible "leaven" is pictured as "sin": *"Beware ye of the leaven (sin) of the Pharisees, which is hypocrisy" (Luke 12:1).* Therefore, Christ's <u>SINLESS</u> (without leaven) life lived was the reason God did not allow his body (flesh made of bread) to decay in the tomb: THIS was the fulfillment of the Feast of Unleavened Bread! Eventually, by the time of Christ, the Jewish people referred to all 8 of these days (14th through 21st of Nissan) as the "Passover season". However, the start of the Feast of Unleavened Bread (15th of Nissan) was REALLY when the Passover celebration kicked off.

The 3rd Holy Feast God established with the Israelites in the wilderness was the **Feast of First Fruits**, to be observed on the <u>day AFTER the weekly 7th day Sabbath occurs during the 7 day Feast of Unleavened Bread</u>. This yearly Feast day commemorated the BEGINNING of the winter grain harvest: *"When ye...shall reap the harvest thereof, then <u>ye shall bring a sheaf of the FIRSTFRUITS of your harvest unto the priest</u>: And he shall wave the sheaf before the LORD, to be accepted for you:* ***on the morrow after the Sabbath*** *the priest shall wave it" (Leviticus 23:9-11).* A sheaf of barley would be harvested and brought to the tabernacle (temple) as a thanksgiving offering to God for the harvest. Only <u>after</u> the Feast of First Fruits was over could the Israelites use the winter harvest for their daily use. Friend, Jesus <u>resurrected</u> from the grave at the VERY start of the day of Feast of First Fruits (sundown Saturday) the year of his death, burial, & resurrection. In other words, he <u>literally</u> became the "First Fruit resurrection of the dead" of the harvest of saints to occur at Jesus' 2nd Coming! Paul wrote: *"But now is <u>Christ risen from the dead, and BECOME the FIRSTFRUITS of them that slept</u>...But every man in his own order: <u>Christ the FIRSTFRUITS; afterward they that are Christ's at his coming</u>" (I Corinthians 15:20, 23).* Is that not amazing? Still,

183

the Jews were unaware that the Messiah (Jesus Christ) was precisely fulfilling these prophetic Feast days on the VERY day(s)!

Let us take an accurate look now at what took place the ACTUAL 7 day week the "Lamb of God" died for the sins of mankind—which is, without question, the most momentous week in mankind's history! Bear in mind, God's day begins at sundown and ends the following day's sundown. God established this fact from the 1st day of Creation: *"And God called the light Day, and the darkness he called Night. And the evening and the morning were the first day" (Genesis 1:5).* See, a day starts with the dark period (evening) and ends with the light period (morning). Think about it logically; Adam & Eve had no clock in which to tell time, so they distinguished one day from the next simply by observing when the sun slipped out of sight over the horizon. At that point, a new day had begun!

Furthermore, you must understand the "7 day weekly cycle" has NEVER been broken since Creation! In other words, mankind has been counting the same 7 days, over and over again, since the dawn of time! (If you will give it some thought, you will realize the 7 day weekly cycle is independent of ANY monthly or yearly calendar mankind has invented.) Time scholars admit they can trace the unbroken 7 day week (in the written record) back to around 1500 BC! And before that time they have no reason or cause to believe it was ever broken either. In the Bible, you will detect Noah was keeping track of the 7 day week—and God's lunar-based monthly calendar!—while on the Ark, and certainly mankind has done so since Adam. As stated earlier in this book, the 7 day week was invented by God as a perpetual reminder of His master Time plan for mankind on Earth! Consequently, every time a 7 day week passes, mankind—cognizant or not—pays homage to God's 7 day (7,000) year master plan! (Incidentally, God's weekly 7th day Sabbath—His blessed day of rest from work, signifying Christ's coming millennial day Earthly Kingdom!—always begins sundown Friday and ends sundown Saturday. IT has NEVER changed since the dawn of time!!! Therefore, the 1st day of the work week always commences at sundown Saturday.

Ok…probing the Bible's 4 New Testament Gospels messianic account (record), it is EASY to determine what "numbered" day of the

184

week Jesus "died on" and "resurrected on" the YEAR of his death. Let us take a look. The Jewish religious leaders asked Jesus one day to show them a sign or miracle from heaven, proving he was the Messiah. Jesus barked, *"An evil and adulterous generation seeketh after a sign; and <u>there shall NO sign be given to it</u>, BUT the <u>SIGN of the prophet Jonah</u>: For **<u>as Jonah was three days and three nights in the whale's belly; so shall the Son of man be three days and three nights in the heart of the earth</u>**" (Matthew 12:39, 40).* Wow, so the ONLY <u>proof</u> Jesus claimed—all miracles aside—would prove he <u>WAS</u> the Messiah was if he spent <u>exactly</u> 72 hours in the ground! See, Christ knew <u>exactly</u> how long the Jewish people considered a "day" or "night" to be: *"Jesus answered, Are there not <u>twelve hours in the day</u>?" (John 11:9).* (Note: No matter where on Earth, if over a year's time you total up all its "day" & "night" hours, they will EQUAL each other. And the spring and fall equinoxes are the 2 days during the year that EVERY spot on Earth experiences 12 hours of day and 12 hours of night, and Passover occurs around the spring equinox!) Thus, from all this information, we <u>know</u> Jesus intended to be in the grave for 36 hours of day and 36 hours of night, or 72 complete hours—not a minute more or less! In fact, if Jesus was <u>not</u> in the Earth (grave) for 72 hours, then Jesus Christ is a phony and <u>NOT</u> the Messiah, according to his own words.

Knowing Christ spent 72 hours in the grave (3 full days & 3 full nights) proves he resurrected the same "time of day" he was buried. Do you understand? Think about it! So, does the Bible reveal what "time of day" Christ was buried? Yes, it does!!! The Bible is clear he was buried near sundown: *"The Jews therefore, because <u>it was the preparation</u>, that the bodies should not remain upon the cross on the Sabbath day, (**<u>for that Sabbath day was an HIGH day</u>,**) besought Pilate that their legs might be broken, and that they might be taken away" (John 19:31).* See, Jesus was dying on the cross on the 14th of Nissan (Passover), or the "preparation day" for the High Sabbath (start of Feast of Unleavened Bread) on the 15th of Nissan. And it was a Jewish defilement for dead bodies to hang on a tree during a High Sabbath; therefore, in the late afternoon Joseph of Arimathaea traveled to Pilate, begged for Jesus' body, removed it from the cross, wrapped it in linen, transported it to a new tomb, and rolled a stone across the entrance. Since the Bible records Jesus died sometime after 3pm and sunset was near 6pm (spring equinox time), I believe the stone was being rolled across the entrance to the tomb at the same time as the sun was slipping out of sight over the horizon! (But then I have a keen appreciation for God's precision with "things".) Thus, <u>Jesus resurrected at SUNDOWN</u>, 3 days later!

Now, if we knew what "day of the week" the tomb was <u>found</u> empty, we could simply backtrack to the previous sundown and know what "day of the week" Christ resurrected and backtrack 3 more days to know what "day of the week" he died and was buried. Well, the Bible plainly reports: *"The <u>FIRST day of the week</u> cometh Mary Magdalene early, <u>when it was yet dark</u>, unto the sepulcher, and seeth the stone taken away from the sepulcher" (John 20:1).* Friend, Mary arrived sometime after sundown Saturday (which begins the <u>dark period of the 1ˢᵗ day of the week</u>) but the stone was already rolled away and Jesus' body was gone!!! An angel exclaimed to her, *"Be not affrighted: Ye seek Jesus of Nazareth, which was crucified: <u>HE **IS** RISEN; he is not here:</u> behold the place where they laid him" (Mark 16:6).* So, unmistakably, Jesus resurrected at <u>sundown</u> <u>Saturday</u>, the close of the weekly 7ᵗʰ day Sabbath! Imagine, the SAME day God blessed and set apart as <u>HOLY</u> from Creation was the <u>VERY</u> day God planned for the <u>Holy</u> Messiah to bless ALL Mankind's souls by rising from the dead and winning victory over death: *"<u>God blessed the seventh day, and sanctified it</u>" (Genesis 2:3).* Truly, the 7ᵗʰ day was/is a blessed day for mankind! Subsequently, back tracking 3 days, we clearly compute Jesus' burial was at sundown Wednesday, which was <u>the END of the 4ᵗʰ day of a week</u>!!!

Alright, I want to pause here—as you keep the above truth in the back of your mind (for I will get back to it!)—and switch gears to investigate another <u>prophetic</u> detail in the Israelite's story (parable) that CLEARLY—yet, no one understood it!—revealed the <u>YEAR</u> the Messiah would deliver mankind's souls out of bondage. It is this fact: <u>God delivered the Israelites out of bondage through Moses after being in bondage for exactly 400 years, which secretly foretold God would DELIVER mankind's souls out of bondage through Jesus after 4,000 years</u>!!! Do you see? Friend, God had Jesus Christ penciled in to absolutely, positively, 100% DIE on Earth during mankind's 4,000ᵗʰ year! Remember, God had told Abraham His plans: *"And when the sun* *was going down, a deep sleep fell upon Abraham; and, lo, a <u>horror</u> <u>of great darkness</u> fell upon him. And he (God) said unto Abraham,* ***<u>Know of a surety that THY seed shall be a stranger in a land that is</u>*** ***<u>not theirs, and shall serve them; and they shall afflict them FOUR</u>*** ***<u>HUNDRED years</u>****...<u>and afterward shall they come out with great</u> <u>substance</u>" (Genesis 15:12, 13).* Do you think God just picked this "400" year number out of a hat, devoid of any purpose or reason? Come on!!! Look, God could have chosen ANY number of years to leave the Israelites in bondage—87, 123, 160, 245, 300, or whatever! But He chose 400 because it too was a secret piece of <u>prophetically</u> accurate information in the Israelites "salvation" story (parable) concerning the "time" of mankind's salvation.

Now in the Bible you will discover two "number of years' after which God freed the Israelites—namely, 400 & 430. This apparent contradiction is NOT a contradiction at all! The 430 year time frame <u>INCLUDES</u> the 30 years Jacob's son Joseph spent in Egypt by himself before Jacob's (Israel) clan entered Egypt due to the famine. Listen, clearly, to the verse: *"<u>Now the sojourning of the CHILDREN OF</u>* *<u>ISRAEL, who dwelt in Egypt, was four hundred and thirty years</u>. And* *it came to pass at the end of the four hundred and thirty years...that* *ALL the hosts of the LORD went OUT from the land of Egypt" (Exodus* *12:40, 41).* See, the phrase *"children of Israel"* has to include Joseph's time, for he WAS <u>one</u> of Israel's children! But God's "prophetic <u>Israel</u> clock" only started when Abraham's grandson Israel (Jacob) himself and his 11 sons entered Egypt—which was 30 years after Joseph's arrival.

Consequently, the martyr Stephen understood God's prophetic timetable when he spoke in front of the high priest: *"And God spake on* *this wise, <u>That his (Abraham's) SEED should sojourn in a STRANGE</u>* *<u>land; and that they should bring them into bondage, and entreat them</u>* *<u>evil FOUR HUNDRED YEARS...after that shall they come forth" (Acts</u>* *7:6, 7).* See, the time starting with "<u>Abraham's</u> SEED" could only start when <u>HIS</u> seed, Jacob, entered Egypt. I had to clear this up for those of you who will Biblically investigate—which I encourage you to do!— the "things" God has revealed to me.

Hopefully, you now appreciate why the number "40" was so significant to God and prevalent in the Bible: rain of Noah's flood lasted 40 days and 40 nights, Israel in bondage 400 years, Moses on Mount Sinai 40 days receiving the 10 Commandments, Israel wandered 40 years in the wilderness, King Saul reigned 40 years, King David reigned 40 years, King Solomon reigned 40 years, Jesus tempted 40 days in the wilderness and ascended 40 days after his resurrection, etc. Do you see? Friend, the Bible is satiated with the number 40!!! THAT is because God KNEW from the Creation of the World the 4,000th year would be the "special year" He would show His incredible love for ALL mankind's souls by giving His beloved, sinless son as a sacrifice for their sins, freeing them from bondage: *"For God so loved the world, that he gave his only begotten Son...that the world THROUGH HIM might be SAVED" (John 3:16, 17).* Therefore, the root reason God continually used the number "40" in the Bible was because the Messiah was slated to die during mankind's 4,000th year! Throughout history, God was like an excited "fellow" who knew a VERY GOOD secret about something VERY IMPORTANT and was "busting at the seams" wanting to tell the people he LOVED (His spirit children) about it. Subsequently, He kept dropping prophetic hints—through use of the number 40!—about WHEN the "secret" would happen. Finally, the night Jesus was born He could stand it no longer and sent an angel heralding to shepherds: *"Fear not: for, behold, **I bring you GOOD tidings of GREAT JOY**, which shall be to all people. For unto you is born this day in the city of David a Saviour, which is Christ the Lord" (Luke 2:10, 11).*

Incidentally, there are MANY more prophetic clues God gave in the Bible confirming the Messiah, Jesus Christ, would and did DIE on mankind's 4,000th year. I'll point several out now. Earlier in this chapter I told you the spiritual significance behind the story of Moses slaying an Egyptian taskmaster. But did you notice how old Moses was when he killed the Egyptian—a symbol of Jesus winning victory over Satan? That is right...40!!! Listen to Stephen, again: *"And when he (Moses) was FULL FORTY years old, it came into his heart to VISIT his brethren...And seeing one of them suffer wrong, he defended him, and AVENGED him that was OPPRESSED, and SMOTE the Egyptian" (Acts 7:23, 24).* Friend, Moses could have been 28, 32, 45, or "any number" of years old when he killed the Egyptian, but only "40" was the correct "age" to prophetically convey, accurately, what God was

188

revealing behind the incident! Now you know the "rest of that story"!

Another Biblical prophetic story with details secretly screaming Jesus came to Earth to give "spiritual life" to mankind's dead souls (by dying for their sins during year 4,000) is the "account" of Jesus raising Lazarus from the dead. Do you remember how many days Lazarus was dead? Listen to Martha's reply to Jesus after he commanded the stone be rolled away: "*Lord, by this TIME he stinketh: for **he hath been dead FOUR DAYS**" (John 11:39)*. Wow, do you see? It was about one month before Christ was to be crucified—in other words, it WAS mankind's 4,000 year!—and Jesus stood in front of a tomb about to "raise to life" a man who had been dead 4 days! Friend, listen to me; this incident of "Christ giving Lazarus life" was all planned by God to be a beautiful, visual (observable) display of what Christ was about to do for mankind's invisible souls—namely, give them "spiritual life" after 4 full days (4,000 years) of death!!! Jesus (knowing he was about to go to the cross) spoke the most wonderful, spiritual words to Martha right before granting Lazarus life, solidifying what the whole scene represented: "*I AM the resurrection, and the LIFE: he that believeth in me, THOUGH HE WERE DEAD, YET SHALL HE LIVE*" *(John 11:25)*.

Ah, but the prophetic revelations just keep coming! Do you need more Biblical evidence Jesus was sacrificed for mankind's sins during year 4,000? Alright, then investigate God's "required dimensions" for the Brazen Altar—the place where Israel's daily sacrifices were carried out, which was a daily prophetic picture of what the sacrifical Lamb of God, Jesus, was coming to Earth to do for mankind!—Solomon built for the Temple in the 10th century BC: "***Moreover he made an ALTAR of brass, TWENTY CUBITS the length thereof, and TWENTY CUBITS the breadth thereof, and TEN CUBITS the height thereof***" *(II Chronicles 4:1)*. (Notice God's redemption number "20" is used twice in sizing the Altar.) BUT what was the VOLUME of the Brazen ALTAR, multiplying length x breadth x height? 4,000 cubic cubits!!! Yes, friend, even the FULLNESS of the Altar—where countless lambs were offered up for centuries, unknowingly, as a prophetic picture of Christ!—was secretly foretelling the **YEAR** of Christ's sacrificial death (mankind's 4,000th year). Paul wrote: "*But **when the FULNESS***

189

of the TIME was come, God sent forth his Son, made of a woman" *(Galatians 4:4).*

I wrestled with God on revealing the next two Biblical stories to you—which again contain details proving Christ delivered mankind out of bondage during mankind's 4,000[th] year—for I am ready to move on. Do you remember in the "*Introduction*" I told you God commanded me to fast 40 days for Him? Well, this was the reason…I had NO idea, but God wanted to reveal to me the approximate "timing" of Jesus Christ's return by making known to me the TRUE meaning behind the Bible's number "40"!!! And now He has ordered me to share it with you. In other words, what I suffered for (to receive) is now being handed to YOU on a silver platter! And you know the old adage; what someone gets for free, they do not cherish! Consequently, if you have been blessed to come across this book in your life, you should get on your knees tonight and thank the living creator God that He wanted YOU to know His secrets.

You probably remember learning the following two stories as a child, for they are classics. Yet, they are SO MUCH MORE than what you thought. They are SO MUCH MORE than just a "neat tale"! Friend, they are again prophetic stories (parables) God controlled to tell mankind about the coming Messiah. And I am going to be brief with them because I want YOU to desire God's Word! I want YOU to lust after the creator God's message to all mankind. I want YOU to pant for His thoughts. To put it plainly: I WANT YOU TO READ THE BIBLE!!! If you do not have a desire for the Creator's Words—the very One who gave you breath!—something is wrong in your spirit (heart).

Around 1100 BC, God devised another Israelite "bondage scenario" and this time He rose up a man named Samson to be the deliverer. Samson was born to a barren woman who had been told by an angel she would conceive (understand?): "*Behold now, thou art barren… but thou shalt conceive, and bear a SON" (Judges 13:3)*. To make an incredible, spiritually-enlightening story short…In his DEATH, with "arms stretched out" between two pillars, Samson avenged (saved) the Israelites from the enemy (Philistines)! But here is the prophetic "timing detail": "*So the LORD let them (the Israelites) be conquered by the Philistines, who kept them in subjection for FORTY years*" (Judges

190

13:1, Living Bible). See, God raised up Sampson, as the deliver, after Israel was in bondage for 40 years!

Around 1000 BC the Israelites and Philistines were at war again, and God felt like controlling another story to prophesy about the Messiah, Jesus! The Philistines had a warrior champion—a giant of a man—named Goliath who was teasing, tormenting, and placing fear into the Israelite's hearts (understand?). So God raised up a MAN to <u>deliver</u> them! He was born in <u>Bethlehem</u> and anointed as a <u>King</u>, and he was the 33rd patriarch in the direct lineage to the Messiah! Do you know his name? That is right, the "sheep-keeper" David. And you know the story…David killed the beast Goliath by hitting him in the forehead with a stone and then chopping off his head. Whereby, David <u>avenged</u> the Israelites from the enemy. But how long had Goliath kept the Israelites in fear: "*And <u>the Philistine (Goliath) drew near morning and evening, **and presented himself FORTY days**</u>*" *(I Samuel 17:16)*. Wow! Friend, I am telling you the truth: <u>Jesus Christ DELIVERED mankind out of bondage during mankind's 4,000th year</u>!!!

Additionally, it is Biblically obvious God had a <u>SET</u> <u>TIME</u> for the Messiah to be crucified because Jesus Christ's words proved he knew it! During his 3½ year ministry he would say things like: "*<u>My TIME is not yet come</u>*" *(John 7:6)*. Do you see? Why do you think Christ said "things" like this? Friend, he <u>knew</u> there was a specific time for him to die!!! He <u>knew</u> he HAD to fulfill every PROPHETIC "thing" God had written about him, for God will NEVER be found a liar! Incidentally, this is why angry crowds always failed in killing him at earlier times during his 3½ year ministry; he would simply pass right through them. Friend, it is <u>impossible</u> to change God's written, prophetic words about the Messiah! Oh, but when the TIME arrived for Christ's death, listen to his change of tune: "*<u>My TIME is at hand</u>*" *(Matthew 26:18)*. Luke reports: "*And it came to pass, **<u>WHEN THE TIME WAS COME</u>**…he STEDFASTLY set his face to go to Jerusalem*" *(Luke 9:51)*. See, once Jesus knew the TIME was at hand, he took on a FIXED demeanor! I believe he <u>knew</u> it was mankind's 4,000th year and he HAD to fulfill <u>ALL</u> that was written about him in the Old Testament Scriptures—which was all the <u>prophetic</u> stories I have just revealed to you!!!

191

So friend, what makes you think God has NOT foretold the "time" of Christ's 2nd Coming in the Old Testament stories (parables)? **HE HAS!!!** It was/is just secretly concealed in the details! And like Israel's deliverance from Egyptian bondage occurred after <u>400</u> years, signifying Christ would deliver mankind's souls from sin's bondage during mankind's 4,000th year; so Noah's house rising up off Earth's surface at his age of <u>600</u> years, signifies Christ's 2nd Coming (rapture) will occur during mankind's 6,000th year!!! <u>Now you **KNOW** why Christ will return right around AD 2028</u>. The time cannot be hastened nor delayed. It is a SET PROPHETIC TIME!!! God's Biblical prophetic word will <u>never</u> be found a lie; <u>Jesus Christ WILL return to planet Earth exactly 2,000 years from the year of his death</u>.

Alright, let us now return to our story of Jesus' crucifixion week—which was likely 28 AD (3972 BC – 4,000) on our current Gregorian calendar. Do you <u>now</u> see the significance of Jesus being killed and buried at the END of the 4th day of a week? Friend, through this happenstance, God was <u>punctuating</u> the reality of His 7 day (7,000 year) master Time plan which He had secretly foretold from the beginning in the 7 day Creation narrative! Do you remember the greater & lesser lights (Jesus & John the Baptist) being created during the 4th day? God had planned for John and Jesus to live and die during mankind's 4th millennial day, but Jesus was specifically to die during year 4,000—<u>the END of the 4th day!</u> Therefore, the <u>ACTUAL 7 day week</u> Jesus died for mankind's sins (occurring during mankind's 4,000th year) God secretly and accurately played out His Messianic 7 day (7,000 year) master Time plan for mankind on Earth, for Jesus was buried at the close of the 4th day (4,000th year) of the week.

Oh, but there is more! For you see not only was Jesus killed and buried on the 4th day of a week, but THAT day was the Israelites 1<u>4</u>th of Nissan (or Passover)—NOTICE the "<u>4</u>"? Yes, stunningly, even the <u>last</u> digits of the "numbered" days of the lunar month of Nissan were simultaneously playing (counting) out God's 7 day (7,000 year) master Time plan the WEEK of Jesus' death, burial, & resurrection! In other words, the 1st day of THAT week (sundown Saturday till sundown Sunday) was the 1<u>1</u>th of Nissan, the 2nd day of that week was the 1<u>2</u>th of Nissan, etc. You say, "Gabriel, this is too much to believe!" Oh, really?

192

Well, remember back in Egypt, in 1334 BC, God told the Israelites to CHOOSE their lamb on the 10th of Nissan? Well, here is God's secret: The "0" in the 10th represents "day 0" or "time period before Creation". In other words, the "0" symbolized the "time" before God's 7 day (7,000 year) master plan on Earth was ever set in motion. THAT was WHEN the Messiah (The Lamb of God) was truly chosen!!! Later, the Holy Spirit exposed this fact through Peter's pen: *"Forasmuch as ye know that ye were not redeemed with corruptible things...but with the precious blood of Christ, as of a lamb without blemish and without spot: **Who verily (truly) was FOREORDAINED BEFORE THE FOUNDATION OF THE WORLD**" (I Peter 1:18-20).* Wow!!! Do you see? Jesus was "chosen" as mankind's Savior (Messiah) before God even created the world! In other words, back in Egypt God was secretly disclosing (by ordering the Israelites to choose their lamb on the 10th of Nissan) the "Lamb of God" had ALREADY been chosen. Your head ought to be spinning by now! But if you love God, you also ought to be shouting in worship of His limitless wisdom!

Amazingly, God revealed the secret behind the "10th of Nissan" to me the moment I laid down to go to sleep around 12 midnight on May 14, 2008! ("May 14, 1948" was the day Israel came back on the map as a nation; thus, it was the very day of Israel's 60th anniversary.) I was in instant shock! My jaw must have dropped a foot, for my mind was nowhere near the subject. A voice from seemingly some other place (though inside my spirit) just plopped the revelation into my mind! To learn the numbered days of Nissan simultaneously aligned with the 7 day week that occurred during the week of Jesus' crucifixion (death) to once again confirm God's 7 day (7,000 year) master Time plan for mankind on Earth (with respect to the Messiah) was dumbfounding. Friend, Christ was picked as our Savior during millennial day "0" (10th of Nissan), was crucified and buried at the close of millennial day "4" (14th of Nissan), and WILL resurrect EVERYONE—the 2nd resurrection of the dead!—at the end of millennial day "7" (17th of Nissan). Jesus perfectly fulfilled every part of what the "numbered days of Nissan" prophesied the week of his death, burial, and resurrection. I jumped out of bed and hit my knees, bowing low in reverence to God for what He had showed me. And it was a goodly while later until I was able to fall asleep!

Allow me to NOW take you on a Biblical journey of Jesus' crucifixion week playing out, for I want you to possess a "behind-the-scenes" look at what God was TRULY saying through the circumstances (He arranged!) surrounding the way it all went down. The Apostle John writes: *"Then Jesus six days before the Passover came to Bethany, where Lazarus was which had been dead, whom he raised from the dead"* *(John 12:1)*. Listen, by Jesus' day the term "Passover" had become associated with the 7 day Feast of Unleavened Bread (or Passover Season): *"Now the feast of unleavened bread drew nigh, which is called the Passover"* *(Luke 22:1)*. Thus, John is recording Jesus came to Lazarus' house 6 days before the 15th of Nissan (the 1st day of the Feast of Unleavened Bread). The 14th of Nissan (the true ancient Israelite's "Feast of Passover" day) was now deemed "Preparation day" for everyone <u>prepared</u> during that day for the High Sabbath which occurred on the 15th of Nissan. And since the week Jesus died the 1<u>5</u>th of Nissan transpired on the 5th day of a week (sundown Wednesday till sundown Thursday) Jesus arrived in Bethany—a small town about 2 miles from Jerusalem—on the 9th of Nissan, which was sometime between sundown Thursday and sundown Friday, the day before the weekly 7th day Sabbath!

John testifies: *"**On the NEXT day** much people that were come to the feast, when they heard that Jesus was coming to Jerusalem, <u>Took branches of palm trees, and went forth to meet him, and cried, Hosanna: Blessed is the KING of Israel that cometh in the name of the Lord"</u>* *(John 12:12, 13)*. Friend, it was now the 10<u>th</u> of Nissan— *"the next day"*!!! Yes, it was a blessed, Holy, 7th day weekly Sabbath (sundown Friday to sundown Saturday)—not Sunday!—when Jesus rode humbly into Jerusalem on a donkey during the day, while crowds of people lay palm branches before him, unsuspectingly acknowledging (<u>choosing</u>) the true Lamb of God! Therefore, <u>Jesus perfectly fulfilled the 10th of Nissan</u>—the day God had commanded the Israelites choose their lamb back in Egypt over 1,300 years earlier!—through the "palm branch incident". In fact, the event (day) was so momentous on God's schedule that He foretold of it around 500 BC though the prophet Zechariah: *"<u>Rejoice greatly</u>, O daughter of Zion; shout, <u>O daughter of Jerusalem</u>; behold, <u>thy KING cometh unto thee: he is just, **and having salvation</u>**; lowly, and riding upon an ass, and upon a colt the foal of an* _ass" (Zechariah 9:9)._ Wow! (By the way, a "Sabbath day" perfectly represented what "time 0" was like in God's 7 day (7,000 year) plan for mankind—namely, before the world and Earth were created, it was a time of peace and rest because sin (evil) had not yet taken place. It was during a "time like this" the true "Lamb of God" was chosen as Savior of mankind!)

Four days later, Nissan 14th arrived at sundown Tuesday (God's official "Passover" day)! That night Jesus ate the Passover meal with his Disciples—which was the VERY same night the Israelite's had ate the Passover lamb that terrifying night in Egypt over 1,300 years earlier! It is mind-boggling to imagine the disciples eating the Passover meal with Jesus that highly-regarded Jewish night (fully knowing the "meal" commemorated the Israelite's night in Egypt when the lamb's flesh was eaten and its blood flowed down their wooden doorposts as a sign for the death angel to pass over them) yet, they did not know Jesus WAS (about to become) the true "Passover Lamb", even as: _"Jesus took bread, and blessed, and brake it, and gave to them, and said, Take, eat: this is MY body. And...took the cup, and...gave it to them...and ...said unto them, This is MY blood...which is shed for many" (Mark 14:22-24)._ Is that not stunning? They were clueless he was about to DIE later THAT very day, perfectly fulfilling the "killing of the lamb" on the 14th of Nissan!

After the meal that night, Jesus led his disciples out to the Garden of Gethsemane. Friend, now listen to me; God is about to oversee, control, and direct an incredible 14th of Nissan "seeable" physical show utilizing the Messiah's (Jesus) physical body to communicate EXACTLY what the Messiah was DOING for mankind—yet, no one at the time grasped the spiritual significance behind the details of what was happening to him! But in hindsight, this revelation greatly validates a Messiah (Jesus Christ) REALLY did DIE for the sins of mankind. Here is the first scene: God wanted Christ to be bound (captured) IN a GARDEN because Adam & Eve's souls had been bound (enslaved) by sin IN a GARDEN! Do you remember? Adam & Eve's sin in the Garden of Eden had separated mankind's souls from God's Spirit of Life and SORROW, pain, & work were the effects of that spiritual death! So listen to what was happening to Jesus' SOUL in the Garden of Gethsemane as he cried: "My SOUL is exceeding SORROWFUL, EVEN UNTO DEATH" (Matthew 26:38). Do you see? Jesus knew for the first time in his existence he was about to be separated from his Father: AND THE THOUGHT OF "THAT" WAS KILLING HIS SOUL! To be blunt, Jesus was already experiencing (feeling) the awful consequence of sin!!!

In agony, realizing his imminent abysmal fate, he prayed (talked to his Father) intensely, sweating what "looked like" great drops of blood: *"And being in an agony he prayed more earnestly: and his sweat was as it were great drops of blood falling down to the ground" (Luke 22:44)*. Ok, hold up a minute! Watch this! Do you know what phase the moon is in during the 14th day of a lunar month when counting day 1 on the first visible sliver of the new moon (which occurs 1 day after new moon)? It is full!!! And what can ONLY happen during a full moon? A lunar eclipse—i.e. Earth passes directly between the moon and sun. And what color is the moon during a lunar eclipse? Eerie Red! The ancients called the terrible omen a "blood moon"! Friend, a lunar eclipse can be at "totality" for over an hour, so it is VERY likely Jesus' sweat "looked like blood" because of the red-shift light emitted from the moon during a dark lunar eclipse!

While Jesus was still praying, a mob arrived to arrest (bind) him, and he stated to them: *"When I was daily with you in the temple, ye stretched forth no hands against me: but **THIS is your HOUR, and the power of darkness**" (Luke 22:53)*. Could it be these spiritual words of Jesus were being physically punctuated by the Father God in heaven, as a sin-filled Earth blocked out (eclipsed) the sun's light from reaching the moon for an hour—*"the hour of darkness"*? And what was the result of this "darkness"? The clue was written on the moon!!! Its uncanny, deep red glow silently screamed, "The Messiah's blood is going to flow!" Yes, friend, I believe the invisible, Almighty God was talking to His spirit children (mankind) on that all-important night through His created celestial bodies.

Peter seems to make mention of "this" happening on the day of Pentecost (occurring 50 days after Christ's resurrection and 10 days after his ascension) when the Holy Ghost descended and he stood up and addressed the people by quoting the prophet Joel: *"The sun shall be*

*turned into darkness, and the MOON INTO BLOOD...Ye men of Israel,
hear these words; **Jesus of Nazareth, a man approved of God among
you by miracles and WONDERS and SIGNS,** which God did by him
in the midst of you, as ye yourselves also know: Him, being delivered
by the determinate counsel and foreknowledge of God , ye have taken,
and by wicked hands have crucified and slain: Whom God hath raised
up, having loosed the pains of death" (Acts 2:20-24).* Do you see?
Remember, God *"turned the sun into darkness"* for 3 hours while Christ
was on the cross! So it is VERY likely He turned the *"moon into blood"*
the night of Jesus' arrest in the Garden of Gethsemane.

Try and wrap your brain around the idea that God purposely
created the moon to orbit planet Earth VISIBLY every 29½ days just
so a full moon would occur on the 14th of Nissan—the night He picked
for the Israelites "killing of the lamb" day back in Egypt—ensuring a
full moon would be in the sky (and more specifically a lunar eclipse!)
on the night and "time" of Christ's arrest! Then consider the year God
determined for Jesus to die for mankind's sins He planned for the 14th
of Nissan to occur on the "4th day of a week", which was concurrently
Earth's 4,000th year! Are you kidding me? What kind of a God is this
who possesses the wisdom, forethought, and power to intermesh the
"timing of His plans" into the orbits of His created celestial bodies?
Only THE One, True, Almighty, Father God!!!

Therefore, back in Egypt, 1334 BC, we now know God picked
the 14th day of a lunar month to lead the Israelites out of bondage for
many reasons: One of which was simply for the light of a full moon!
Yes, the night God's death angel rode through Egypt mercilessly killing
its firstborn (while the Israelites fled in haste) it was a full moon night.
It was "Pass-over"! It was Independence Day! And God showed His
infinite love by providing the Israelites with natural moonlight to
light their way because it would have been "rough-going" during the
darkness of a new moon! Picture the full moon's bright light glistening
off the desert sand and excited Israelite faces as they quickly escaped
there captors! It must have been an AWESOME sight.

Now fast-forward over 1,300 years, and Jesus was going though
hell that same (yearly commemorated) full moon night, becoming
mankind's Passover Lamb! Here is the next scene: God wanted Christ

197

to be captured (bound) for the <u>SAME REASON</u> mankind's souls had been captured (bound). Do you remember from chapter 3 what <u>motivated</u> Satan to lie to Eve to get her to sin against God, thus enslaving mankind? It was "greed for dirt". Remember Satan's heart was "lifted up" because of the *"abundance of his merchandise"* and he wanted control of MORE!!! In other words, if "money" would have been in existence while Adam & Eve lived in the Garden of Eden, Lucifer would have lustfully desired it because money equates to dirt (for that is all it buys). Consequently, God drummed up the whole "Judas Iscariot, 30-pieces-of-silver scenario" to accurately portray all this!

Look, if God had not planned for Christ's "night of capture" to transpire EXACTLY like He arranged it, the chief priests would have captured Jesus <u>anytime</u> they wanted, probably while he spoke to them in the temple—exactly like he told them when they came for him! But NO…this night was God's night!!! And God was accurately retelling mankind's "bondage-to-sin story" through the Messiah Christ. Thus, God scheduled Judas to betray the Messiah into the enemy's hand for 30 lousy coins: *"Then one of the twelve, called <u>Judas Iscariot</u>, went unto the chief priests, And said unto them, <u>What will ye give me, and I will deliver him unto you</u>? And they covenanted with him for* ***THIRTY pieces of silver***. *And from that time he sought opportunity to betray him"* (Matthew 26:14-16). Amazingly, the Bible even records: *"<u>Then entered Satan into Judas</u>" (Luke 22:3)*. See, Judas—with Satan in him!—betrayed Christ because of "greed for money (dirt)", exactly like the serpent—with Satan in him!—betrayed mankind because of "greed for money (dirt)". Both cases led to the capture or bondage of the one betrayed! This "development" was so important to God that He also prophesied of it directly through the prophet Zechariah around 500 BC: *"If ye think good, give me my price; and if not, forbear. <u>So they weighed for my price</u>* ***THIRTY pieces of silver***" *(Zechariah 11:12)*. How about that?

You ask, "Gabriel, what are you trying to tell me?" I am informing you God went to <u>GREAT</u> lengths to show (and absolutely confirm) to mankind the Messiah, Jesus, died spiritually—separated himself from God's Spirit—which means HE BECAME SIN!!! Paul wrote: ***"For he (God) hath made him (Jesus) TO BE SIN for us***,

198

WHO KNEW NO SIN; that we might be made the righteousness of God in him" (II Corinthians 5:21). THAT is why God was precisely controlling EVERY detail (location, time, and circumstances) of Christ's "day of death" to emulate Adam & Eve's (mankinds) "day of death" in the Garden of Eden. It was ALL so mankind's souls would KNOW (possess undeniable proof!) Jesus won their salvation!

As nighttime faded into morning on the 14th of Nissan, Christ's captors beat him, mocked him, spit on him, and flogged him! But here is the next scene: God wanted Christ to wear a "crown of thorns" so He put it into the mind of his captors to make one and press it into his skull! Do you remember what God's physical (seeable) symbol of sin's consequence was to mankind? It was THORNS & THISTLES! Recall sin brought forth pain; thus, God desired Christ to carry thorns on his head as a visual representation he was bearing sin's painful curse. God also prophesied "this" about the Messiah through the prophet Isaiah around 800 BC: *"Surely __he hath borne our griefs, and CARRIED our SORROWS__: yet we did esteem him stricken, smitten of God, and afflicted. But he was wounded for our transgressions, he was bruised for our iniquities" (Isaiah 53:4, 5).* Truly, Jesus suffered and endured the full weight of ALL mankind's sins.

In the early morning hours—around 9am—came the next scene: God wanted a prisoner (sinner) released while Jesus was simultaneously sentenced to death!!! Friend, this powerful scene was thought up by God years earlier for He had put it into the minds of the Jewish people to invent a custom whereby they REALESED (set free) A PRISONER on Passover Day! Pilate said: *"But ye have a custom, that I should RELEASE unto you one at the Passover: will ye therefore that I release unto you the King of the Jews?" (John 18:39).* Do you see? Mankind's souls had been prisoners—bound by sin (separated from God)—for 4,000 years! Thus, in this scene, God was visually playing out what would soon happen in the spirit world—namely, mankind's sinfully-bound, spiritually-dead souls would be SET FREE because faultless (sinless) Jesus would DIE in their (our) place!!! It was/is an incredibly moving scene as the people feverishly chanted: *"Away with this man (Jesus), and RELEASE unto us Barabbas: (Who for a certain sedition made in the city, and for murder, was cast into prison.)...Crucify him, crucify him" (Luke 23:18-21)*. Wow! Peter said it best, later: *"For Christ also hath once suffered for sins, **the JUST for the UNJUST**, that he might bring us to God, being put to death in the flesh, but quickened by the Spirit" (I Peter 3:18)*.

So Christ was led away, carrying a cross up Golgotha's hill—very likely the <u>same</u> hill Isaac ascended almost 2,000 years earlier with his father Abraham! At the top came the next scene: God wanted Christ to die in a manner where he was nailed to a tree through both hands and feet. Why? Do you remember I told you in chapter 3 that God created mankind's physical body to contain 10 appendages on its hands and 10 appendages on its feet to represent the 10 Love Commandments, encompassing <u>ALL</u> of the Law of sin? Subsequently, through this "method of physical death" God was symbolizing and affirming Jesus Christ was paying for <u>ALL</u> of the works of sin!!! Yes, GOD invented "death by crucifixion" hundreds of years earlier for this very purpose. This detail, again, was so important to God that He also prophesied of it through Zechariah: *"and they shall look upon me **whom they have PIERCED**, and they shall mourn for him, as one mourneth for his only son" (Zechariah 12:10)*. (Incidentally, the 10 fingers and 10 toes equal God's number of redemption, "20"!)

Some people inquire, "But why did Christ have to hang (die) on a tree?" Friend, it all goes back to the way sin originated in the Garden of Eden. Do you remember? Sin was represented as "fruit hanging on a tree"—namely, the <u>Tree</u> of the Knowledge of Good & Evil. Consequently, God wanted Christ's physical body to "hang on a tree" as, again, a visual picture of SIN. Christ BECAME sin even though he was sinless!!! Thus, he was a worthy sacrifice unto God to "<u>taste of death</u>"—which translates "<u>became sin</u>"—and in so doing he <u>removed</u> the curse of the Law (or the spiritual death sentence) ALL mankind was under! It was an act of PURE, UNSELFISH LOVE!!! Over 1,300 years earlier, God had informed the Israelites through Moses: *"<u>IF a man have committed a sin worthy of death, and he be to be put to death, and thou hang him on a tree</u>: His body shall not remain all night upon the tree, but thou shalt in any wise bury him that day; **(for he that is hanged (on a tree) is ACCURSED of God**)" (Deuteronomy 21:22, 23)*. See, the Jews understood clearly that a man hung from a tree was CURSED!

Thus, again, God wanted Christ to die in a "fashion" that mankind would <u>know</u> and <u>understand</u> he had BECOME the curse. Thus, Paul wrote: "*Christ hath redeemed us from the curse of the law, **BEING MADE A CURSE FOR US**: for it is written, Cursed is every one that hangeth on a tree" (Galatians 3:13)*.

God also prophesied of the Messiah's "manner of death" through an incident He controlled that happened while the Israelites wandered for 40 years with Moses in the wilderness. After grumbling and complaining to Moses that they did not have enough bread and water, God sent fiery serpents to bite and KILL many of the Israelites. Realizing they had sinned, the Israelites begged Moses to ask God to remove the snakes! What was God's solution? It must have seemed ridiculous to the people at the time, but to us now it is obvious it was <u>prophecy</u> about the Messiah: "*Make thee a fiery serpent, and SET IT UPON A POLE: and it shall come to pass, that every one that is bitten, when he looketh upon it, SHALL LIVE" (Numbers 21:8)*. Do you see? God was foretelling that when SIN (symbolized by a serpent) is crucified on a tree (pole), mankind's souls will receive life! That is why Jesus informed Nicodemus: "*As Moses lifted up the serpent in the wilderness, EVEN SO must the Son of man be lifted up" (John 3:14)*.

Hanging on the cross in distress, Christ uttered the sweetest words mankind has ever known, putting voice to EXACTLY why he was hanging there! Oh, sure, the terse sentence was directed toward the soldiers who had just crucified him, but it was meant for ALL mankind: "***Father, forgive them*** *" (Luke 23:34)*. Hands down, these are the greatest words in the Bible! If you love Jesus, they ought to move you to tears, for he did not have to do it! Christ could have summoned legions of angels to his rescue, and they would have squashed the Romans soldiers like little bugs. But then mankind's souls would have been lost forever, separated from God for all eternity: Friend, there was just too much <u>love</u> beating in the chest of that man struggling for his every breath on that old wretched cross to ever let that happen!

While suffering on the cross for 6 hours—approximately 9am till 3pm—Christ fulfilled many direct Old Testament prophecies about himself [See Figure #6]. But always remember (as stated earlier in this chapter) the REAL death Jesus was going through on the cross was "spiritual separation from his Father", acknowledged by him vociferating: *"My God, my God, why hast thou forsaken me?"* *(Mark 15:34)*. When the 6 hours—number of man—of torment were complete: *"Jesus knowing that ALL things were now accomplished (fulfilled)...said, **It is finished**: and he bowed his head, and gave up the ghost" (John 19:28, 30)*. Friend that was it, at that moment mankind's "spiritual redemption" was complete!!! Forgiveness for sin was now available to mankind through Christ's atoning work, meaning a WAY to return to God was now available (open)—and it was THROUGH CHRIST'S SINLESS DEATH. Thus, Jesus Christ rightly said: *"I am the WAY, the truth, and the life: **NO man cometh unto the Father, BUT BY ME**" (John 14:6)*. Oh, what a glorious day it was for mankind on Nissan 14th, year 4,000!

But God was not done talking to mankind through utilizing the Messiah's physical body. Look, if He had just let Christ die and be buried in the ground, mankind would not have understood God had provided their souls with resurrection LIFE through him! Thus, Jesus was taken down off the cross and buried in a tomb (*"the heart of the Earth"*) by sundown Wednesday, but 3 days & 3 nights later at sundown Saturday God bodily resurrected him to life at the very start of the Feast of First Fruits—the day after the weekly 7th day Sabbath occurs during the Feast of Unleavened Bread week—which was Nissan 18th that year. Friend, everything was perfect! It was like poetry in motion: Jesus fulfilled the Feasts of Passover, Unleavened Bread, and First Fruits precisely on their VERY days the year of his death!

After his resurrection, Jesus spent 40 more days on Earth (all during mankind's 4,000th year!) before ascending back up in the clouds to his Father. Oh, and he had a VERY important message for the disciples (and all mankind) to hear, learn, and share with others! Do you know what it was? Do you know what Jesus went around "telling people about" during those 40 days? Here is a hint: his "message" absolutely confirmed the Old Testament Scriptures were of Divine origin! In other words, his "message" proved the Creator God of the Bible was/is real—which means his "message" greatly increased mankind's faith (belief) in the reality of God! So, do you know what Jesus was revealing? HE WAS SHOWING AND TEACHING PEOPLE HOW HE HAD PRECISELY

202

Figure # 6
Prophecies fulfilled by Christ on Cross

Prophecy	Subject	Fulfillment
Isaiah 53:12	Crucified with transgressors	Mark 15:27, 28
Zech. 12:10	Hands & feet pierced	John 20:27
Psalm 22:7, 8	Scorned & mocked	Luke 23:35
Psalm 22:15	Thirst on cross	John 19:28
Psalm 69:21	Given vinegar & gall	Matt. 27:34
Psalm 109:4	Prayed for his enemies	Luke 23:34
Psalm 22:18	Soldiers cast lots for his clothes	Matt. 27:35
Psalm 34:20	No bones broke	John 19:32-36
Zech. 12:10	Side pierced	John 19:34
Isaiah 53:5	Vicarious sacrifice	Romans 5:6, 8
Isaiah 53:7, 8	Death of Christ	Acts 8:32-35
Deut. 21:23	Redeemed us from the curse	Gal. 3:13

FULFILLED PROPHECY AFTER PROPHECY WRITTEN ABOUT HIM BY GOD IN THE OLD TESTAMENT SCRIPTURES!!! Friend, his "message" was/is exactly what I am sharing with you in this book he has commanded me to write!

The VERY day of his resurrection on First Fruits, Jesus popped up beside two travelers who were walking towards a village called Emmaus and talking about the crucifixion that had just happened to him days earlier. They did not know it was Jesus, but listen to what the Bible records he began sharing with them: *"And beginning at MOSES and ALL the PROPHETS, **he (Jesus) expounded unto them in ALL the SCRIPTURES the THINGS CONCERNING HIMSELF"** (Luke 24:27)*. Wow!!! Are you kidding me…starting with Moses? Friend, Moses wrote the first 5 books of the Bible (Genesis, Exodus, Number, Leviticus, & Deuteronomy)! WHAT could have possible been written in them about the Messiah? Oh, come on, reader…have you read what I have written in this book so far?

Allow me to reiterate: Christ had just <u>fulfilled</u> the prophetic 7 day creation story's narrative in Genesis of God bringing into existence the sun and the moon on the 4th day; the prophetic story (parable) in Genesis of God accepting Abel's lamb offering; the prophetic story (parable) in Genesis of God delivering Abraham's wife Sarah from Pharaoh; the prophetic story (parable) in Genesis of God providing a lamb when Abraham almost sacrificed his son, Isaac; the prophetic story (parable) in Genesis of God delivering Jacob's family from Laban; the prophetic story (parable) in Exodus of God delivering the Israelites from Egyptian bondage through Moses, etc. And yes, friend, Christ most certainly shared with them how he was the fulfillment of the Israelite's Passover lamb, and that <u>Moses was a prophetic picture of him</u>! But Christ did not stop with Moses' writings (called the Torah); he went on to discuss the many <u>direct</u> prophecies penned about him by the traditional prophets in the Old Testament Scriptures [See Figure #7]. When Jesus was finished talking, do you think the two traveler's faith (belief) in "God, the Messiah (Jesus Christ), & mankind's salvation" was cemented? OF COURSE IT WAS!!! And you can rest assured they spread Christ's "prophecy-fulfilled revelation" to others, as did the Disciples, Paul, and many others.

In conclusion of this chapter, let us return to Moses' story and see how he was further a prophetic type of the Messiah, for even after the amazing "Red Sea deliverance incident" God continued to control the circumstances in his life to develop a picture of the coming Messiah. For example, Moses' spirit left Earth exactly <u>40</u> years after the year God had worked through him to deliver the Israelites out of Egyptian bondage: *"Moses was an <u>hundred and twenty years old</u> when he died"*

204

Figure # 7
Partial List Of Old Testament Messianic Prophecies

Prophecy	Subject	Fulfillment
Gen. 3:15	Born of woman's seed	Gal. 4:4
Gen. 12:2, 3	Born of Abraham's seed	Matt. 1:1
Gen. 17:19	Born of Isaac's seed	Matt. 1:2
Num. 24:17	Born of Jacob's seed	Matt. 1:2
Gen. 49:10	Descended from tribe of Judah	Luke 3:33
Isaiah 9:7	Heir to David's throne	Luke 1:32, 33
Isaiah 7:14	Born of a Virgin	Luke 1:26-31
Micah 5:2	Born in Bethlehem	Luke 2:4-7
Jer. 31:15	Slaughter of children by Herod	Matt. 2:16-18
Hosea 11:1	Flight to Egypt	Matt. 2:14, 15
Isaiah 40:3-5	John the Baptist as forerunner	Luke 7:24, 27
Psalm 2:7	Declared Son of God	Matt. 3:16, 17
Isaiah 9:1-2	Galilean ministry	Matt. 4:13-17
Deut. 18:15	Prophet to come	Acts 3:20-22
Isaiah 61:1, 2	Heal brokenhearted	Luke 4:18, 19
Isaiah 53:3	Rejected by his own (Jews)	John 1:11
Psalm 110:4	Priest after order of Melchizedek	Heb. 5:5, 6
Psalm 78:2	Spoke in parables	Matt. 13:35
Zech. 9:9	Triumphal entry	Mark 11:7-11
Psalm 41:9	Betrayed by friend (Judas)	Luke 22:47, 48
Zech. 11:12	Sold for 30 pieces of silver	Matt. 26:15
Zech. 11:13	End of Judas	Matt. 27:5-10
Isaiah 53:9	Buried with rich	Matt. 27:57-60
Psalm 16:10	Rose from dead	Mark 16:6, 7
Psalm 110:1	Ascend to God's right hand	Mark 16:19

(Deuteronomy 34:7). This happenstance paralleled the Messiah's life, because Jesus left Earth <u>40</u> days after God worked through him to deliver mankind's souls out of bondage to sin! Do you see? And on and on it went...Moses became God's lawgiver, as did Jesus; Moses spent 40 days fasting, as did Jesus; both their faces glowed

after dismounting a mountain; both were magnificent teachers; both were leaders of men; Moses sent out 12 spies, and Jesus sent out 12 disciples; both died on a hill. I think you get the point!

Thankfully—solidifying everything I have written in this chapter about Moses' life being "a prophetic picture of the Messiah" is absolutely true—at some point during the 40 years in the wilderness, God clearly disclosed to Moses the coming Messiah WOULD be "*like him*"!!! Listen to Moses' prophetic declaration to the Israelites: *"The LORD thy God will raise up unto thee a Prophet from the midst of thee, of thy brethren, **LIKE UNTO ME**; unto him ye shall hearken"* *(Deuteronomy 18:15)*. And yes, friend, without a doubt, Jesus was THAT prophet, for his life (like none others) was *"like unto Moses"*!

The Apostle Peter understood Jesus was THE prophet Moses had spoken of in the Old Testament Scriptures (scrolls)—obviously, since Jesus had just opened the Disciple's eyes to that truth!—and he preached it to the crowds 10 days after Jesus' ascension on the day of Pentecost : *"**The God of Abraham…hath glorified HIS Son Jesus**; whom ye delivered up…And killed the Prince of Life, whom God hath raised from the dead…REPENT (turn from your sinful ways) YE THEREFORE, and be converted, that your sins may be blotted out, when the times of refreshing shall come…And he shall send Jesus Christ… Whom the heaven must receive until the times of RESTITUTION of ALL THINGS…For **Moses truly said…A prophet shall the Lord your God raise up unto you of your brethren, like unto me**…And it shall come to pass, that every soul, which will not hear that prophet, shall be destroyed" (Acts 3:13-23)*. Do you see? No doubt about it, Jesus was THE PROPHET Moses had prophesied about to be *"like unto him"*!

Incidentally, did you notice in Peter's address above (coming only 50 days after Christ's redemptive work!) he unambiguously KNEW and DECLARED exactly what mankind MUST **DO** to obtain the "forgiveness for sins" Christ's blood had just provided? Do you see it? YE MUST REPENT OF YOUR SINFUL WAYS, meaning you MUST willingly choose to STOP sinning!!! And, friend, I am about to show you unmistakably in the next chapter entitled *"Wilderness"* the sins that will damn your soul (spirit) to the lake of fire for all eternity are totally and completely encompassed in the 10 Love Commandments,

206

for God is not yet done revealing "EVERYTHING involved in a soul's journey back to God" utilizing the Israelite's story (parable)! Realize, just because the Israelites are <u>free</u> from Egypt's bondage does NOT mean they are automatically guaranteed entrance into Canaan (Promise Land). <u>THEY still have a DECISIVE journey to make</u>!

I pray by now you have acquired a FULL appreciation and understanding of why God created a people called Israel and directed them through a story (parable) containing 400 years of bondage and divine deliverance via a man named Moses. <u>Every</u> detail was conceived by God to secretly prophecy about the true deliverer of mankind's souls, Jesus Christ!

Chapter 10

Wilderness

*"ALL the (10 Love) commandments which I command thee
this day shall ye observe to DO, THAT YE MAY LIVE…
and GO IN and POSSESS the LAND"*
(Deuteronomy 8:1)

Continue to bear in mind the big picture of what God is doing and saying through the Israelite's story (parable). Remember, they are God's volunteers playing out a skit for mankind to learn <u>EVERYTHING</u> involved (or EVERYTHING it will take) for a soul to be reunited with the source of all Life (God). Now as stated earlier, in the Israelite's story (parable) the physical land of Canaan was called the "Promised Land", but it represented the "Kingdom of God"—i.e. the place a soul must enter to "obtain eternal life". Thus, in the Israelite's skit God has done <u>His</u> <u>part</u> in helping the Israelites reach the land of Canaan (Promise Land) by doing for them what was impossible for them to do themselves—namely, He supernaturally delivered them out of bondage to Egypt. Likewise, God did <u>His</u> <u>part</u> in helping mankind's souls BE ABLE to enter the Kingdom of God (to obtain eternal life) by doing for us what we could NOT do for ourselves—namely, He supernaturally delivered us out of bondage to sin & death.

But you will soon learn in the story (parable) that God has now tossed the reigns over to the Israelites! In other words, reaching the land of Canaan (Promise Land) is now in their hands, meaning it is THEIR responsibility for it is within their ability. And the WAY to the Promise Land (Canaan) required a JOURNEY. Likewise, Jesus' death placed the spiritual reigns into mankind's hands. In other words, reaching the Kingdom of God (obtaining eternal life) is now in our hands, meaning it is OUR responsibility for it is within our abilities. ALL it requires is a "unique" journey through a wilderness. Friend, the next 40 years of the Israelite's skit (parable) are the most important from mankind's (our) standpoint, because in them God officially makes known (or writes down) the **EXACT requirements** of what the Israelites HAD to <u>DO</u> to reach and enter Canaan (Promise Land)—which are the EXACT same requirements a soul must follow (<u>DO</u>) to enter into the Kingdom of God and receive eternal life!!!

But before we learn about what the Israelites had to DO to enter the Promise Land, allow me first to say a few pertinent words about <u>why</u> God chose the physical location of a "wilderness" to play out this part of the story (parable). Friend, it is quite simple; a "wilderness" perfectly characterized Earth's spiritual condition after Adam & Eve's (mankind's) sin. The original Hebrew word translated *"wilderness"* is *"midbār"* meaning: <u>desert, wasteland, barren wilderness, desolate land that supports little life</u>. See, after mankind's original sin, Lucifer became the *"God of this world"* and sin ran <u>wild</u> infesting everything. And remember SIN is a "spirit killer" which separates the souls it infects from God's Spirit of Life. Hence, Earth became a <u>spiritual wilderness</u>—a desolate, barren place supporting NO life!

The Bible contains a futuristic passage describing folk's disdain when they will one day behold Lucifer: *"<u>They that see thee (Satan) shall narrowly look upon thee</u>, and consider thee, saying, **Is this the man that made the earth to tremble...That made the world as a WILDERNESS**...that opened not the house of his prisoners?" (Isaiah 14:16, 17)*. Do you see? The lie Lucifer told to persuade Adam & Eve into sinning against God turned planet Earth into a <u>barren</u>, <u>desolate</u>, <u>spiritual wilderness</u>. And it will stay that way until Christ's 2nd Coming and as Peter said: *"the times of refreshing shall come...the times of restitution of all things"* (Acts 3:19, 21). Thus, mankind was determined by God

210

(from the beginning) to live on an Earth that is a spiritual <u>wilderness</u>. IT was a crucial part of the setup of His Game of Life! Subsequently, a "physical wilderness" was the ideal symbolic place for God to convey His <u>requirements</u> for the Israelites (or mankind's souls) to reach the Promised Land (the Kingdom of God).

The story (parable) immediately reveals a flagrant truth... <u>OBTAINING ETERNAL LIFE IS A JOURNEY</u>! In other words, it is NOT a <u>ONE</u> time decision! You <u>cannot</u> saunter up the isle of a church to an altar and tearfully mumble some words that <u>permanently</u> guarantee your entrance into the Promise Land. Do you understand? "Obtaining eternal life" is a continual, daily, spiritual trek made everyday of your life! Paul understood this and wrote: ***"WORK OUT your own salvation with fear and trembling"*** *(Philippians 2:12)*. See, it is something you MUST "*work out*"! Other times Paul likened it to "running a race" or "fighting a battle". The Bible asserts: *"let us lay aside every weight, and <u>the SIN which doth so easily beset us</u>, and **<u>let us run with patience the RACE that is set before us</u>**" (Hebrews 12:1)*. Jesus knew it as a "WAY": *"Enter ye in at the strait gate: for wide is the gate, and **<u>BROAD is the WAY</u>** <u>that leadeth to DESTRUCTION</u>, and <u>MANY there be which go in thereat</u>: Because strait is the gate, and **<u>NARROW is the WAY</u>**, <u>which leadeth unto LIFE</u>, and <u>FEW there be that find it</u>" (Matthew 7:13, 14)*. Obviously, "entering the Promise Land" requires a spiritual expedition!

And although you might not want to hear it or believe it, you might as well receive Jesus' <u>sobering</u> words of TRUTH (in the verse above) into your spirit right now: **MOST** PEOPLE'S SOULS WILL NEVER ENTER THE PROMISE LAND (KINGDOM OF GOD): IN OTHER WORDS, THEY WILL **NOT** INHERIT ETERNAL LIFE BUT WILL PERISH IN THE WILDERNESS!!! Does that offend you? If so, then Christ's words of truth offend you! For Jesus declared *"FEW"* will obtain eternal life but *"MANY"* will perish in the lake of fire. Why is that? What is SO DIFFICULT for people to <u>DO</u> that they just will <u>not</u> do it to obtain eternal life? The answer to that question is <u>unmistakably</u> revealed in God's message He conveyed through the Israelite's story (parable), and I will share it with you shortly. But I must ask you...are YOU going to beat the odds? Are YOU going to be one of the righteous <u>few</u> who "obtains eternal life" by entering into God's glorious Kingdom? If you do not make it, you will be BEGGING for another chance in hell, but it will be TOO LATE!!! Therefore, do NOT mock the truth contained in the rest of this chapter, and <u>DO</u> what God is asking you to <u>DO</u> to obtain eternal life.

Alright, since we know "obtaining eternal life" is a journey, a battle, a race, a way, or a path, it becomes readily noticeable we can "get off course"! And yes, the Bible clearly teaches someone can be on the "*narrow path*" leading to eternal life for awhile and then "lose their way" and be on the "*broad path*" leading to destruction! Peter wrote: "*And <u>**when a person has escaped from the wicked ways of the world…**</u> <u>**and then gets tangled up with SIN and becomes its slave again, he is**</u> <u>**worse off than he was before**</u>…There is an old saying that "A dog comes back to what he has vomited, and a pig is washed only to come back and wallow in the mud again." <u>THAT is the WAY it is with those who TURN AGAIN TO THEIR SIN</u>*" (II Peter 2:20-22, Living Bible). Ah, come on reader…this verse just gave it away! Did you notice what "way" a person must walk to obtain eternal life? It is the SIN-LESS way!!! What is that? It is a <u>REPENTANT</u> <u>LIFESTYLE</u> lived by willingly choosing to "forsake the WAY of evil (sin) and follow after the WAY of good (love)" daily. In other words, the spiritual reigns God placed into mankind's hands—and He did it for <u>ALL</u> mankind from the very beginning!—leading to eternal life in the Kingdom of God is to <u>continually Obey His 10 Love Commandments</u>!!! See, the "*way*" that leads to eternal life is inside your heart (spirit)!!! It is a daily decision you make hour by hour and minute by minute: You MUST make a conscious effort to refuse to sin and then <u>never</u> go back to a life of sin. THAT is the "*NARROW WAY*" you MUST trod to obtain eternal life!

But never forget who gave us that opportunity (or power to control our own eternal destiny): **God did**!!! See, He could have left us in bondage to sin & death (spiritually separated from Him forever) with no chance of returning to Him. Do you understand? But NO…<u>GOD</u> <u>freed us from the clutches of sin's spiritual DEATH grasp via Jesus'</u> <u>sinless spiritual death on the cross</u>. That simply means through Christ's death we can be "forgiven of sins". And what can THAT do for us? It means the spiritual death we should ALL pay (throughout all eternity) for the sins we have committed—and we have ALL committed sin at one time or another!—can be paid for with Christ's <u>spiritual</u> <u>death</u>. And what does that ultimately mean for us? It means we can OBTAIN ETERNAL <u>SPIRITUAL</u> LIFE by being reunited with the source of all life (God the Father) in His Kingdom. But what MUST you <u>DO</u> to receive this "forgiveness for sins? **YOU MUST REPENT** (turn from your sins)—which means to show God RESPECT for the salvation He provided by continuously living a life of love (obey the 10 Love Commandments). So remember to <u>ALWAYS</u> give full credit and thanks to <u>GOD</u> for your salvation!

Well let us return to the Israelite's story (parable) in the wilderness and find out WHAT sin God wanted them to squelch to enter the Promise Land! In the third month after exiting Egypt, Moses and the Israelites arrived at Mount Sinai. Here, God gathered the Israelites at the base of the mountain, while He descended in a thick cloud of fire with thundering and lightning, and boomingly spoke the 10 Love Commandments to them: *"The <u>LORD talked with you (Israelites) face to face</u> in the mount out of the midst of the fire" (Deuteronomy 5:4)*. God spoke <u>ONLY</u> the 10 Love Commandments: *"<u>THESE words the LORD spake unto all your assembly in the mount out of the midst of the fire</u>, of the cloud, and of the thick darkness, with a great voice: and **<u>he added no more</u>**" (Deuteronomy 5:22)*. Friend, the 10 Love Commandments are the COMPLETE heart of the Law of Love!

Soon thereafter, Moses ascended to the top of Mount Sinai for 40 days and received the 10 Love Commandments (written by God's own finger) on stone tables: *"And the LORD delivered unto me two tables of stone **<u>written with the finger of God</u>**....And it came to pass at the end of forty days and forty nights, that the LORD gave me the <u>two tables of stone, even the tables of the COVENANT</u>" (Deuteronomy 9:10, 11)*. Notice, God called the stone tables containing the 10 Love Commandments the "Tables of the <u>Covenant</u>": *"And he (God) declared unto you <u>his covenant</u>, which **<u>he commanded you to perform</u>**, even **<u>TEN COMMANDMENTS</u>**; and <u>he wrote them upon two tables of stone</u>" (Deuteronomy 4:13)*. Friend, stone represents permanency! The 10 Love Commandments will never pass away because they are the very definition or deeds (works) of Love. And when someone disobeys

213

any of the 10 Love Commandments it is sin (which is rebellion against God, which is rebellion against LOVE)!

Now look, I have alluded to this fact over and over again in this book: God's 10 Love Commandments given to the Israelites at Mount Sinai were NOT something new to them AND NEITHER WAS THE COVENANT! Ever since Adam & Eve ate from the tree of the knowledge of good & evil, ALL mankind's hearts knew the 10 Love Commandments—for "obedience to them" or "disobedience to them" is the definition of good and evil, respectively. Remember, long before Moses was ever born Noah preached about them, Abraham obeyed them, and Enoch loved them. Long before Moses was born, Joseph accused Benjamin of stealing his silver cup, Abimelech accused Abraham of lying to him about his wife Sarah for he feared God's punishment if he would have committed adultery with her, Ham dishonored his father Noah by looking on his nakedness, and Cain coveted Abel's righteousness and murdered him. And there are many more examples in Genesis proving mankind has always known the 10 Love Commandments. Furthermore, there is now much historical evidence proving the same thing; long before Moses was ever born mankind (Sumerians, Babylonians, Egyptians, etc.) were worshiping idols, dishonoring the 7th day Sabbath, and no longer putting the Creator God first in their lives!

Friend, God had an oral COVENANT with mankind—spoken into their hearts (spirits)—about what was good and evil from the moment Adam & Eve sinned. The covenant declared IF a man/woman would follow the Way of Good (love) their soul would live eternally, but IF they followed the Way of Evil (sin) it would die one day after the Great Judgment! Long before Moses was born the inhabitants of Sodom & Gomorrah knew the covenant in their hearts and that they were living evilly and so did the people living in Noah's day! Subsequently, in the Israelite's story (parable), God was merely taking an already existing 2,638 year old (3972 BC till 1334 BC) oral agreement and officially writing it down, like drawing up a written contract with someone after having a verbal agreement with them for years. Do you see?

And WHY did God do this? Because the Israelite's story is a PARABLE (or a message) for ALL mankind!!! God was controlling,

214

directing, and writing the story (for His book the Bible) that would contain EVERYTHING involved with a soul's journey back to Him! Do you understand? Consequently, the story (parable) HAD to include a written copy of what mankind needed to DO (obey) to enter the Kingdom of God (Promise Land). Thus, God engraved the 10 Love Commandments on stone tables: *"And he (God) wrote them in two tables of stone, and delivered them unto me (Moses)" (Deuteronomy 5:22)*. See, on one hand the Bible is the amazing story of how God freed the souls of mankind from sin's death curse through the Messiah's work—secretly and prophetically written in the Old Testament Scriptures to prove it happened!—and on the other hand it is God's written instruction book for exactly what mankind must DO to obtain eternal life! So, without a doubt my friend, the Israelite's story (parable) of bondage, deliverance, and journey to the Promise Land is God's lead (central) story in His book the Bible.

God then declared to the Israelites, point blank: *"**ALL the (10 Love) commandments** which I command thee this day shall ye observe to DO, **THAT YE MAY LIVE**...and **GO IN and POSSESS the land which the LORD sware unto your fathers**" (Deuteronomy 8:1)*. Wow, it does not get any plainer than that! God was saying the Israelites (mankind) WILL possess the Promise Land (Kingdom of God) IF they obey the 10 Love Commandments!!! Listen to God's wish for the Israelites (mankind): *"O that there were such an HEART in them, that they would FEAR me, and **keep ALL my commandments ALWAYS**, that **it might be well with them**, and with their children for ever!" (Deuteronomy 5:29)*. Friend, this has always been the heartbeat of God towards ALL His spirit children since the dawn of time! Deep down inside they ALL knew right from wrong (good from evil), and IF they would have continually FEARED God and followed His way of love— obeyed the 10 Love Commandments—they would ALL have obtained eternal life by entering His Kingdom one day. But (like MOST people will do!) they turned their back on God (love) by willingly choosing to disobey His 10 Holy Love Commandments!

So, when the Messiah (Jesus) arrived on Earth did he confirm the "WAY" leading to eternal life in the Kingdom of God was/is by "obeying the 10 Love Commandments", proving the "wilderness part" of the Israelite's story (parable) was to express this truth? Yes, yes, yes!!! The Gospels record: *"And, behold, one came and said unto him (Jesus), Good Master, WHAT good thing SHALL I DO, that I may have eternal life? And he said unto him…IF thou wilt ENTER INTO LIFE, keep the (10 Love) commandments…Thou shalt do no murder, Thou shalt not commit adultery, Thou shalt not steal, Thou shalt not bear false witness, Honour thy father and thy mother"* (Matthew 19:16-19). See, Jesus was listing the 10 Love Commandments! Friend, it does not get any clearer or simpler than this; this is kindergartner material!!! If you want to receive eternal life, you MUST willfully choose to live your life in obedience to God's 10 Holy Love Commandments. But if you choose to live your life in willful disobedience to them, your soul will perish!

Back in the wilderness, in 1334 BC, God did something with the two tables containing the covenantal 10 Love Commandments that absolutely, positively proves "obeying them" IS the "WAY" to obtain eternal life in the Kingdom of God. Do you know what He did? He gave Moses detailed instructions for building an ARK to house them in!!! Listen: *"And they shall make an ARK of shittim wood: two cubits and a half shall be the length thereof, and a cubit and a half the breadth thereof, and a cubit and a half the height thereof"* (Exodus 25:10). Are you kidding me? Now WHAT on Earth could God have wanted with another ARK? Friend, He needed ANOTHER physical ark built—to AGAIN symbolize the "Kingdom of God" (the place of eternal life)— so this time He could place the 10 Love Commandments in it. In doing this, God was definitively affirming those souls who live their Earthly life by the Law of Love (obey the 10 Love Commandments) will one day reside IN the Kingdom of God and obtain eternal life!!! Do you remember what God called the 10 Love Commandments? He called them His COVENANT with mankind. So what was the Ark named? The Ark of the Covenant!

Friend, I am telling you God's placement of the 10 Love Commandments INSIDE the "Ark of the Covenant" unquestionably declares the souls who will obtain eternal life (by entering the Kingdom of God one day) will do so because of their decision at some point in their Earthly life to follow after and continue following after the WAY of love—which is the EXACT definition of "repentance"; to turn from one's sin by obeying the 10 Love Commandments! The Bible's message on "what a soul MUST DO to obtain eternal life" is crystal clear once the "Ark concept" is understood in God's Israelite story (parable). And "obedience to the 10 Love Commandments" is simply how someone "shows love towards God and their fellow man" as you will soon see in the "*love*" chapter. In other words, those souls that choose "to love" on Earth—which is how you choose God's WAY, because He IS Love—are the ones God will accept into His Kingdom. And now you know WHY God had the Israelites build an Ark to house the 10 Love Commandments in.

Hear Moses' Biblical witness of WHERE the two stone tables (etched with the 10 Love Commandments by God's own finger) were placed:*"And he (God) wrote on the tables...the TEN COMMANDMENTS, which the LORD spake unto you in the mount out of the midst of the fire in the day of the assembly: and the LORD gave them unto me. And I turned myself and came down from the mount, and **put the tables IN the ark which I had made; and THERE THEY BE**, as the LORD commanded me"* *(Deuteronomy 10:1-5).* Do you see? So WHO will get INTO the Kingdom of God? Indisputably, those individuals (souls) who willingly choose to obey God's 10 Love Commandments!

By the 10th century BC King Solomon was ruling over the nation of Israel, and he built the 1st Temple and moved the "Ark of the Covenant" within. And what was still INSIDE the Ark almost 400 years later? The Bible records: *"**There was NOTHING in the ark save the TWO TABLES which Moses put therein at Horeb**, when the LORD made a covenant with the children of Israel, when they came out of Egypt"* *(II Chronicles 5:10).* Friend, wherever the "Ark of the Covenant" is today, it no doubt holds two stone tables engraved by God's own finger with the 10 Love Commandments! And one day the Kingdom of God will FOREVER hold ALL the spirit children who preferred to live a "life of love" over a "life of sin" on planet Earth.

Now Moses received many other secondary laws from God that he (Moses) wrote down in a book with his OWN hands: *"And Moses wrote all the words of the LORD...and he took the book of the covenant, and read in the audience of the people: and they said,*

217

All that the LORD hath said will we do, and be obedient" (Exodus 24:4, 7). It is crucial to understand that this "book of the law" was kept in a pouch on the outside of the Ark of the Covenant! The Bible records: *"When Moses had finished writing down all the laws that are recorded in this BOOK, he instructed the Levites who carried the Ark containing the Ten Commandments to put this book of the law BESIDE the Ark, as a solemn warning to the people of Israel" (Deuteronomy 31:24-26, Living Bible).* Therefore, the 613 laws contained in the Torah "book of the law"—e.g. dietary laws, agricultural laws, clothing laws, circumcision laws, prayer laws, holyday laws, business laws, property laws, judicial laws, criminal laws, tax laws, sacrificial laws, war laws, etc.—are NOT required of mankind to enter INTO the Kingdom of God and obtain eternal life because they were NOT placed inside the Ark. Do you understand? Out of love, God gave the "book of the law" to the nation of Israel to help them govern their nation—and of course the "sacrificial laws and holyday laws" were for a "prophetic shadow" of the coming Messiah, Jesus Christ!

In addition to the book of the Law, by the time Christ arrived on Earth various Jewish sects had arisen in Israel (like the Pharisees & Sadducees) who had made up hundreds of additional laws. And although they tried to act and preach like those laws came from God, THEY DID NOT! Those laws were man-made legalism, and Jesus rebuked the Jewish religious leaders for them. Take for instance God's 4th Love Commandment *"Keep the Sabbath Day Holy"*—which was intended by God to be a joyful, weekly day in which mankind could rest from his/her work (one of sin's consequences) in anticipation, celebration, and reverence of God's coming 7th millennial day of rest on Earth—the Pharisees had invented many burdensome, hairsplitting restrictions to be observed on THAT day, like if someone "spit on the ground" they had sinned for "irrigating (working) the soil"! Are you kidding me? That is how ridiculous it had become!!!

The Pharisees completely misunderstood the momentous symbolic importance of the 10 Love Commandments being placed INSIDE the "Ark of the Covenant". Consequently, to their own peril, they would (at times) literally disobey the vital 10 Love Commandments in order to keep their man-made traditions—e.g. they would hate their

218

neighbor (which is murder in the heart!) because they did not wash their hands before eating! Many Biblical altercations arose between Jesus and the "religious leaders" over these man-made laws. But in Scripture— now listen to me clearly—you will <u>always</u> find Jesus endorsing (preaching) "obedience to the 10 Love Commandments" is the WAY to eternal life and "obeying man-made laws (or church traditions)" as having NO importance with respect to one's eternal destiny!

One day, some scribes and Pharisees asked Jesus, *"Why do thy disciples transgress the tradition of the elders? for they wash not their hands when they eat bread. But he answered...Why do ye also transgress the COMMANDMENT of GOD by your tradition? For **God commanded, saying, Honour thy father and mother...**" (Matthew 15:2-4).* Do you see? Jesus is <u>rightly</u> defending "obedience to the 10 Love Commandments" while simultaneously reducing the importance of man-made traditions. THAT is because Jesus <u>KNEW</u> (beyond a shadow of a doubt) "obedience to the 10 Love Commandments" was/ is crucial to mankind obtaining eternal life! He then went on to baffle and anger the Pharisees legalistic minds by showing them the utter worthlessness of their man-made, religious traditions.

The Pharisees were also hung up on dietary laws. One day in frustration, Jesus blurted, *"Don't you understand...Don't you see that anything you eat passes through the digestive tract and out again? But evil words come from an evil heart, and DEFILE the man who says them. **For from the HEART (spirit) come evil thoughts, murder, adultery, fornication, theft, false witness and blasphemy. THESE ARE WHAT DEFILE**; but there is NO SPIRITUAL (SOUL) defilement from eating" (Matthew 15:16-20, Living Bible).* Do you recognize the things Jesus listed as "defilers of the soul" are "disobedience to the 10 Love Commandments" things? Thus, once again, Jesus is verifying "disobeying the 10 Love Commandments" DEFILES a soul and will ultimately send it to its destruction in hell! Friend, if you want to sustain your physical body by consuming tarantulas or eating pig, go ahead: That will <u>NEVER</u> be the reason your soul ends up in the lake of fire! But if your spirit (thoughts, desires, & emotions) willfully choose to disobey the 10 Love Commandments, you will be in a heap of trouble on Judgment Day.

219

Paul penned: "*Know ye not that ye ARE the temple of God, and that the Spirit of God dwelleth in you?* ***If any man DEFILE the temple of God, him shall God destroy***" *(I Corinthians 3:16, 17)*. Do you see? This verse goes back to what I taught you in chapter 2 of this book: THE SPIRIT (SOUL) MATERIAL INSIDE YOUR PHYSICAL BODY CAME FROM GOD! In other words, God lives inside your body. See, God does not live in man-made church buildings: He lives in YOU!!! That structure (building) folks hold church services in is NOT the temple of God: YOU ARE!!! So Paul & Christ taught if you use your spirit (thoughts, desires, & emotions) to disobey the 10 Love Commandments (think thoughts of & do deeds of adultery, lying, murder, blasphemy, idolatry, thievery, covetousness, etc.) God will ultimately destroy your soul and body one day in the lake of fire.

Look, Paul dealt with the same religious ideology as Christ did, and you will find in his letters that he preached IDENTICAL to Jesus…"obeying religious (church) traditions" like circumcision, hand-washing, holidays, certain food abstentions, etc. is useless with respect to obtaining eternal life but "obeying the 10 Love Commandments" is crucial. In fact, Paul was SO sure "obeying the 10 Love Commandments" was/is the actions (works) that prove a soul's faith (belief) in God (love)—thus being mankind's part in the salvation equation—that he wrote in his letters several times "ALL who willfully disobey them will NEVER enter the Kingdom of God"! And I will prove this forthrightly. Friend, "obeying the 10 Love Commandments" is so vital to our eternal destiny that it behooves us to study them in depth, even though technically they are ALREADY written in our heart! So, indubitably, the next 20 or so pages in this book are BY FAR the most important, for if you will willfully make the decision to obey (DO) God's 10 Love Commandments—notice they are COMMANDS not suggestions!— your soul will obtain eternal life.

For your benefit I have created a two-sided (negative & positive) chart of the 10 Love Commandments—i.e. what "NOT TO DO" & what "TO DO" [See Figure #8]. After careful examination, you will find everything Jesus taught "not to do" and "to do" was/is based on the 10 Love Commandments. Consequently, the chart I made is the most important chart in the entire world, because it contains the

Figure # 8
The 10 Love Commandments
(The Golden Rule)

LOVE GOD

	DON'T	**DO**
1.	**Have gods before Creator God** love your life, save your life be selfish, be prideful, boast,	**Make creator God #1 in your life** hate your life, lose your life be humble, be unselfish,
2.	**Worship idols** love money, be greedy, love sinful pleasures	**Worship only Creator God** love God, fear God, seek after righteousness
3.	**Blaspheme God's name** profane, curse, damn, swear, talk filthy	**Glorify God's name** control tongue, speak pure sing hymns and praises
4.	**Forget To Keep Sabbath Holy** do business (work), talk idly, do your own pleasure	**Keep Sabbath Holy** delight in the Lord, honor the Lord

LOVE NEIGHBOR

5.	**Dishonor father & mother** disobey, be ungrateful, be unthankful	**Honor your father & mother** obey, thank, respect, be appreciative
6.	**Murder** fight, hate, despise, judge complain , be impatient	**Forgive** pray for enemies, do good to those hurt you
7.	**Commit Adultery** fornicate, lust sexually, be homosexual, be immoral	**Honor the marriage bed** be sexually pure, virtuous undefiled, innocent, clean
8.	**Steal** thieve, rob, gamble smuggle, take advantage of	**Give** charity, alms, tithe feed hungry, clothe naked
9.	**Lie** falsify, deceive, gossip, trick, cheat, trap, mock	**Tell Truth** be honest, share Gospel witness, preach, testify
10.	**Covet neighbor's things** desire, long for, crave envy, be jealous	**Love neighbor as yourself** pray for, help, serve, be kind, be longsuffering

information—if followed!—that will allow a soul to enter the Kingdom of God (Promise Land) and obtain eternal life. So please scrutinize the chart in depth. Copy it, enlarge it, miniaturize it, love it, memorize it, and imbed it in your heart. But most importantly…OBEY (DO) IT!!!

Now, as we analyze each of the 10 Love Commandments, I am going to first purposely point out in the Israelite's story (parable) how God declared "disobedience to EACH of them" was punishable by death! This "wilderness pronouncement" was enacted by God to again confirm and declare to ALL mankind: Willful disobedience to the 10 Love Commandments will bring forth spiritual death—i.e. the 2nd Death at the White Throne Judgment. I will then back this TRUTH up with Scriptures from Paul's New Testament letters reaffirming the fact. Ultimately, I want YOU to realize the "*narrow way*" leading to eternal life exists in your mind, and you turn onto (or get onto) that path (way) the moment your heart (spirit)—thoughts, desires, & emotions—decide to live in accordance to God's 10 Holy Love Commandments!

The **1st Love Commandment** is *"**Thou shalt have NO other gods before me**" (Exodus 20:3).* God knew the Israelites had been exposed to many false Egyptian gods while in Egypt, and He hated His spirit children's (mankind's) worship of these false gods. So God told Moses the punishment for the sin of "disobeying the 1st Love Commandment" was to be death! An example of one of these false gods was the god "Molech". The Bible records: *"And the LORD spake unto Moses, saying, Again, thou shalt say to the children of Israel, Whosoever he be of the children of Israel, or of the strangers that sojourn in Israel, **that giveth any of his seed (children) unto Molech: he shall surely be put to death**: the people of the land shall stone him with stones" (Leviticus 20:1, 2).* Obviously, God had NO tolerance for other gods coming before Him in His spirit children's lives!

Today people put anything and everything BEFORE God in their heart and lives—e.g. family, business, house, car, hobby, sports, movies, etc.—and this "forget-about-God" lifestyle will spell T.R.O.U.B.L.E. on Judgment Day! Today, most people's god is themselves: They are selfish, proud, boasters (usually overfed and oversexed) who love only themselves, and God declares their end will be certain destruction. Listen to Paul's alarming words about these type people: *"Being filled with all unrighteousness...haters of God (love)...proud, boasters...who knowing the judgment of God, that they which commit such things are worthy of death, not only do the same, but have pleasure in them that do them" (Romans 1:29-32).* Again, Paul writes: *"This know also, that in the last days perilous times shall come. For men shall be lovers of their own selves...boasters, proud...heady, high-minded,* **lovers of pleasures MORE than lovers of God***; Having a form of godliness...from such turn away...Ever learning, and never able to come to the knowledge of the truth" (II Timothy 3:1-7).* Yes, friend, the Apostle Paul fully believed people possessing this type of spirit (soul)—thoughts, desires, & emotions—will perish having NOT inherited the Kingdom of God (eternal life)!

Jesus clearly informed us of exactly what place God is to hold in our life: *"If any man come to me, and hate not his father, and mother, and wife, and children, and brethren, and sisters, yea, and HIS OWN LIFE also, he cannot be my disciple. And whosoever doth not bear his cross, and come after me, cannot be my disciple" (Luke 14:26, 27).* This ambiguous statement by Christ meant anyone who wants to follow (serve) God MUST love Him MORE than their own parents, siblings, children, or even their own life; otherwise, they will NOT be accepted by Him on Judgment Day! See, Jesus continually taught a message of "self-sacrificial love towards God and your fellow man" is the way to eternal life. He would say things like we need to "lose our life" or "hate our life" to obtain eternal life! But, today, Satan is literally preaching from the pulpits a 180 degree opposite, selfish message of "how to love your life on this Earth", and it is an ear-tickling sermon in which internalized will lead a soul to HELL!!! Yes, certainly, the 1st Love Commandment "Have NO other gods before me" is still in affect today with the same resulting consequence of death for its disobedience. Surely the God who gave us breath deserves the #1 place in our heart because if it was not for Him we would not even exist!

The **2nd Love Commandment** is *"**Thou shalt NOT make unto thee any graven image, or any likeness of any thing that is in heaven above, or that is in the earth beneath, or that is in the water under the earth: Thou shalt not bow down thyself to them, nor serve them: for I the LORD thy God am a jealous God" (Exodus 20:4, 5).*** In a few

223

short months after leaving Egypt the Israelites had already disobeyed this Commandment by melting down their gold jewelry and shaping it into the form of a calf and worshipping it. God informed Moses the punishment for the <u>sin</u> of "disobeying the 2nd Love Commandment" was to be death! He told Moses to ask the Israelites: *"Who is on the LORD'S side? Let him come unto me" (Exodus 32:26).* Then He told them who stood by Moses to slaughter all those who wanted to continue worshiping the golden calf: *"And he (Moses) said unto them, Thus saith the LORD God of Israel, Put every man his sword by his side, and go in and out from gate to gate throughout the camp, and **slay every man his brother, and every man his companion, and every man his neighbor**...and there fell of the people that day about three thousand men" (Exodus 32:27, 28).* It was a tragic loss for the fledgling nation of Israel, but God made His point abundantly clear that day…He despises idol worship!

Today, sadly, most people's idol is <u>money</u>—which is what the "<u>gold</u>-en calf" incident represented! People worship materialistic (dirt) possessions. See, a heart—thoughts, desires, & emotions—that constantly longs to acquire (thinks about making) money is a heart that LOVES money because whatever "dominates one's thought process" is what that spirit worships (loves). Paul made this point crystal clear in his letters: *"You can be sure of this: <u>The Kingdom of Christ and of God will NEVER belong to anyone who is impure or greedy, **for a greedy person is really an IDOL worshipper—he loves and worships the good things of this life more than God**" (Ephesians 5:5, Living Bible).* Do you see? The result on Judgment Day for "idolatry" will be the dreaded 2nd Death! Friend, folks that <u>live</u> to make money and acquire possessions have failed to grasp all they are striving to obtain is just dirt—in other words, it is useless in obtaining eternal life. But for their pleasure-seeking, greedy, dirt-idolatry they will forfeit their soul's chance at eternal life! Paul wrote: *"Now the <u>works of the flesh are manifest</u>, which are these; **Idolatry**, witchcraft...of the which I tell you before, as I have also told you in time past, **<u>that they which DO such things shall NOT inherit the kingdom of God</u>**" (Galatians 5:19-21).* Can it be any clearer? Paul firmly believed an idolater will NOT inherit the Kingdom of God!

John the Revelator prophesied about what the desires of people's hearts will be like during the great tribulation, right before Jesus' 2nd Coming: *"And the rest of the men which were not killed by these plagues yet REPENTED NOT of the works of their hands, that they should not worship devils, and idols of gold, and silver, and brass, and stone, and of wood: which neither can see, nor hear, nor walk"* (Revelation 9:20). Do you see? People's idols will continue to be money and materialistic (dirt) possessions made of gold, silver, brass, stone, and wood—e.g. houses, cars, furniture, etc! But these "things" have NO value because they are not spirit; they cannot see, hear, walk, or talk. Only "spirit material" has value, and THAT is what YOU should love! Certainly, the 2nd Love Commandment "Thou shall NOT worship idols" is still in affect today with the same resulting consequence of death for its disobedience. Friend, worship ONLY God, think about Him, talk (pray) to Him, respect Him, fear him, love Him, and make Him your reason for getting up every morning.

The **3rd Love Commandment** is ***"Thou shalt NOT take the name of the LORD thy God in vain; for the LORD will not hold him guiltless that taketh his name in vain"*** *(Exodus 20:7)*. In the new Israeli camp, God told Moses the punishment for the sin of "disobeying the 3rd Love Commandment" was to be death. There was a young man who cursed the name of the Lord, and the Israelite people brought him before Moses: *"And the Israelitish woman's son blasphemed the name of the LORD, and cursed...And they brought him unto Moses...And the LORD spake unto Moses, saying, Bring forth him that hath cursed without the camp; and let all that heard him lay their hands upon his head, and let all the congregation stone him" (Leviticus 24:11-14)*. Furthermore, God said: *"Whosoever curseth his God shall bear his sin. And he that blasphemeth the name of the LORD, he shall surely be put to death, and all the congregation shall certainly stone him: as well the stranger, as he that is born in the land, when he blasphemeth the name of the LORD, shall be put to death" (Exodus 24:15, 16)*. That is straightforward, huh? God is not joking around with people who abuse His Holy name!

So how does God feel today about the sin of people using His name in vain? Has he changed? Not one bit!!! The apostle Paul spoke about two men who cursed God: *"Holding faith, and a good conscience; which some having put away concerning faith have made shipwreck: Of whom is Hymenaeus and Alexander; whom I have delivered unto Satan, that they may learn NOT to BLASPHEME" (I Timothy 1:19, 20)*. Really people, you cannot possible think God is going to usher you into His Kingdom if your spirit goes around using His name as a curse word! If the Holy Spirit lived inside your heart, you would NEVER speak God's name in vain; the mere mention (breath) of "God" or "Jesus" would perk up your ears into a heightened sense of alertness, causing a Holy, righteous, reverent (fear)-of-God to flood your soul! But today I hear so-called "born-again" Christians use "Jesus" or "Geesh"—which is just (Jēs-us) shortened!—continually in conversations where God or Jesus is NOT the subject matter. In other words, they are using God's name in vain (or as a curse word). Friend, God will NOT hold a soul guiltless who curses the very "being" that gave it life! Their future will definitely be the 2nd Death unless they repent (change their ways)! Paul wrote: *"For which things' sake the WRATH of God cometh on the children of DISOBEDIENCE…but now ye also put off ALL these…blasphemy, filthy communication out of your mouth" (Colossians 3:6, 8)*.

Instead, Paul described how our conversation should flow: *"And be NOT drunk with wine, wherein is excess; but be filled with the Spirit; Speaking to yourselves in psalms and hymns and spiritual songs, singing and making melody in your heart to the Lord; Giving thanks always for ALL the things unto God and the Father in the name of our Lord Jesus Christ" (Ephesians 5:18-20)*. Again, Paul wrote: *"be thou an EXAMPLE of the believers, in WORD, in CONVERSATION, in charity, in spirit, in faith, in purity" (I Timothy 4:12)*. Certainly, the 3rd Love Commandment "Thou shall NOT take the Lord's name in vain" is still in affect today with the same resulting consequence of death for its disobedience. Rather, glorify, magnify, and honor the name of the only one, true, Almighty, Creator God!

The **4th Love Commandment** is *"Remember the Sabbath day, to keep it HOLY. Six days shalt thou labour, and do all thy work: But the seventh day is the Sabbath of the LORD thy God…For in six days the LORD made heaven and earth, the sea, and all that in them is, and RESTED the seventh day: wherefore the LORD blessed the*

226

Sabbath day, and hallowed it" (Exodus 20:8-11). God told Moses the punishment for the <u>sin</u> of "disobeying the 4th Love Commandment" was to be sure death: *"Ye <u>shall keep the sabbath</u> therefore; for it is HOLY unto you: <u>**every one that defileth it shall surely be put to death**</u>" (Exodus 31:14)*. Friend, the Sabbath is a sign of God's covenant with mankind, culminating with His sanctifying (making Holy) the righteous at Christ's 2nd Coming: *"Verily my Sabbaths ye shall keep: for <u>it is a SIGN between me and you</u> throughout your generations; <u>that ye may know that I am the LORD that doth sanctify you</u>" (Exodus 31:13)*. During the 40 year wilderness journey the Bible recounts the story of a man who was found working on the Sabbath: *"And while the children of Israel were in the wilderness, <u>they found a man that gathered sticks upon the Sabbath day</u>. And they that found him gathering sticks brought him unto Moses and Aaron…And the LORD said unto Moses, <u>The man shall be surely put to death</u>…And <u>all the congregation brought him with-out the camp, and stoned him with stones, and he died</u>" (Numbers 15:32-36)*. See, God's feelings about the Sabbath day are candid and clear-cut!

In the Biblical record of Paul, there is NO doubt he observed the 7th day Sabbath: *"And Paul, **<u>as his manner was</u>**, went in unto them, and <u>three Sabbath days reasoned with them out of the scriptures</u>" (Acts 17:2)*. Realize, there were Jews AND gentiles present at these 7th day weekly Sabbath meetings. But in the centuries following Christ's ascension, Lucifer worked a truly amazing deception on mankind to ensure the majority of people (for the most part unknowingly) sin by not keeping God's 4th Love Commandment: <u>He falsely switched the 7th day (sundown Friday to sundown Saturday) Sabbath to the 1st day of the week (sundown Saturday to sundown Sunday)</u>! So today most of the religion of "Christianity" holds church services on Sunday, <u>thinking THAT day is the Lord's Holy Sabbath</u>! Now please understand it is OK to congregate with folks in a building and talk about the Bible & God ANYDAY of the week, <u>but to believe Sunday is God's Sabbath day is a lie, FOR IT IS NOT</u>!!! Imagine the man working *"gathering sticks"* in the story above saying to Moses, "Look Moses, I'm out here collecting wood on the weekly DAY God commanded us to rest because it suits <u>my</u> life and <u>my</u> schedule. You go and tell your God I'll *"rest"* on the 1st Day of the week!" Are you kidding me? Good luck with that proposition! Friend, time scholars have verified the "7 day week" has **NEVER** gotten out of sync; thus, there is only ONE blessed & Holy day each week—the 7th day (Friday sundown till Saturday sundown) Sabbath—because God makes the rules, not us!!! Personally, I am extremely saddened by Lucifer's momentous con because he and I know what he has stolen from mankind, for I have personal proof of the great ANOINTING that rests on God's TRUE Sabbath day, and I will share that with you later in the "*Holy Spirit*" chapter.

I would love nothing more right now than to write a lengthy discourse on how (and through whom) Lucifer accomplished his "Sabbath day switcheroo" and to make convincing note of the prophetic Scripture in the Old Testament book of Daniel foretelling that he would do that one day, but this is not the purpose of this book! Furthermore, there is much good reading material out there on the subject, and I encourage you to read it. But what I do want to do is take you on a behind-the-scenes look (into the invisible spirit world) at an ongoing "occurrence"—which is VERY real, though the Bible only seldom mentions it!—and show you how it relates to Satan's "Sabbath day sham".

Here is the "occurrence": However the spirit world is constructed (or laid out), it allows for direct discussion to occur between God and Lucifer, even now after Lucifer's sin! The Bible first unveils this truth in the book and story of Job—possibly occurring around 2,000 BC—where God and Satan discussed thoughts about Job that then influenced his future: "*And the LORD said unto Satan, Whence comest thou? Then Satan answered the LORD, and said, From going to and fro in the earth, and from walking up and down in it. And the LORD said unto Satan, Hast thou considered my servant Job…*" *(Job 1:7)*. Later, during Christ's day on Earth, Jesus informed Peter: "*Simon, Simon, behold, Satan hath desired to HAVE you, that he may sift you as wheat*" *(Luke 22:31)*. Here is the point: You need to realize "what happens to mankind (you) on Earth" is an ongoing "Game" between God and Lucifer! And the stakes are DEADLY for us!!! But more importantly, you need to realize Satan's ONLY objective in this "Game" is to get you & me (and all mankind) to sin against God—which is COMPLETELY wrapped up in disobeying God's 10 Love Commandments. Please, please

228

understand **THAT** is **ALL Satan now cares to accomplish on Earth**, for he knows the end result of the souls who <u>DO</u> THAT (sin against God) will be banishment to the "*lake of fire*" with him, forever. And if you end up in the "*lake of fire*" one day, Lucifer and his demonic cohorts will laugh their heads of at YOU for being so foolish (stupid) as to listen to their lies while you lived on Earth, and thus missing out on your opportunity to obtain eternal life!

With that being said, you should <u>now</u> be able to clearly see the satanic force behind the "Sabbath day transfer". Friend, IT IS ALL A GAME! God wants us to obey Him and Lucifer wants us to disobey God. Therefore, Satan will do EVERYTHING within his power to get us to defy God's wishes, <u>even if it requires trickery</u>!!! I have NO doubt if you could hear Lucifer's cackling at God over his "Sabbath day sham" and listen to his prideful taunting of how he has deceived the whole world into sin because of it, you would IMMEDIATELY start respecting and observing God's true 7th day (sundown Friday to sundown Saturday) Sabbath. In fact, I believe you would be SO appalled at what Satan has done you would never again <u>want</u> to go to a church on a Sunday! You would frantically desire and demand your church hold service on God's true Sabbath day. But since people have not heard the exchange or know of the battle between God and Lucifer over the 4th Love Commandment, they do not care!

Allow me to enlighten you on some of the facts behind the "Sabbath Day battle" being waged between God and Satan, for it goes back to the beginning of time! After Lucifer coerced Adam & Eve into sinning against God, he immediately began his next deception into the hearts (spirits)—thoughts, desires, & emotions—of mankind. What was it? He persuaded mankind to turn their backs on God by getting them to worship God's CREATION instead of the Creator. Paul revealingly wrote: "*Instead of believing what they knew was the truth about God, they deliberately chose to believe lies. **So they prayed to the THINGS God made**, but wouldn't obey the blessed God who made these things*" *(Romans 1:25)*. Now, friend, it did not take long for the SUN to become the most exalted and venerated object of all God's creation. All ancient pagan cultures, long before Jesus came to Earth, had their specific name(s) for the bogus sun god—e.g. the Canaanites sun god was Baal

229

(Beelzebub). And long before Jesus' day on Earth, the 1ˢᵗ day of the week (sundown Saturday to sundown Sunday) was established for pagan sun worship—hence, the name <u>Sun</u>-day was attached to the 1ˢᵗ day of the week.

God loathed the ancient heathen's practices of adoring, revering, and deifying His creation. And since the Egyptians were famous for their sun-god worship, God explicitly told Moses to warn the Israelites to <u>NOT</u> worship the sun: *"<u>Take ye therefore good heed unto yourselves</u>...lest thou lift up thine eyes unto heaven, and <u>when thou seest the sun</u>, and the moon, and the stars...<u>shouldest be driven to worship them, and serve them</u>" (Deuteronomy 4:15, 19)*. See, God was NOT going to put up with this abomination, and He told Moses to kill anyone who worshipped the sun: *"If there be found among you...man or woman, that <u>hath wrought wickedness in the sight of the LORD thy God, in transgressing his covenant</u>, And hath gone and <u>served other gods, and worshipped them, either the sun, or moon, or any of the host of heaven</u>, which I have not commanded...**<u>Then shalt thou bring forth that man or that woman...and shalt stone them with stones, till they die</u>**" (Deuteronomy 17:2-5)*. Friend, Lucifer knew/knows God's intense hatred of sun worship, and he connected it to the 1ˢᵗ day of the week. Thus, I can almost see Satan's evil grin as he watches most of the world today "worship" God on the venerable day of the sun! Undoubtedly, Lucifer is gloating to God about his incredible deceptive achievement.

Inevitably though, Lucifer will be locked up for a thousand years and EVERYONE living in Christ's millennial Kingdom will worship God on the true 7ᵗʰ day Sabbath, for planet Earth will keep on spinning and every day will be accounted for right through the devastation of Jesus Christ's 2ⁿᵈ Coming. Isaiah prophetically wrote about ALL those living in Christ's eternal Kingdom: *"And it shall come to pass, that from one new moon to another, and <u>from one Sabbath to another, shall ALL flesh come to worship before me, saith the LORD</u>. And they shall go forth, and look upon the carcases of the men that have <u>transgressed against me</u>: for their worm shall not die, netiher shall their fire be quenched; and they shall be an abhorring unto all flesh" (Isaiah 66:23, 24)*. Friend, their will be NO more false Sunday (1ˢᵗ day) worship in Christ's eternal Kingdom! And now that you have been confronted with

230

the truth, it is your choice if you want to obey God and keep His 7th day (sundown Friday to sundown Saturday) Sabbath Holy or continue lovingly stroking Satan's back by paying respect to his wicked Sabbath transference.

By the way, here are God's Biblical requirements for observing the Sabbath and His amazing blessing for doing so: *"If thou turn away thy foot from the Sabbath, from doing thy pleasure on my holy day; and call the sabbath a delight, the holy of the LORD, honourable; and shalt honour him, not doing thine own ways, nor finding thine own pleasure, nor speaking thine own words: THEN shalt thou delight thyself in the LORD; and I will cause thee to ride upon the high places of the earth, and feed thee with the heritage of Jacob thy father: for the mouth of the LORD hath spoken it" (Isaiah 58:13, 14).* Notice, "keeping the Sabbath day Holy" is a MAJOR way in which one *"delights thyself in the Lord"*. And do you know what God promises to those that "delight in the Lord"? The Bible states: *"Delight thyself also in the Lord; and he shall give thee the desires of thine heart" (Psalms 37:4).* Do you know what this verse truly means? Friend, this passage of Scripture does not mean God will shower you with worthless, dirt possessions to satisfy your greedy, materialistic heart! This verse literally means: the desires (thoughts) in your head will COME from God!!! Wow, did you get that? Read it again. In other words, your spirit (thoughts, desires, & emotions) will be Godly because God (love) will be controlling them. What does that mean? It means your heart has been *"born again"* of God's Holy Spirit! Now THAT is a truly PRICELESS blessing because that means eternal life is residing inside you. And just think…ALL for simply honoring and keeping God's Sabbath day holy!!!

Friend, I am Biblically and personally convinced God will COMPLETELY change the lives of those people willing to "delight themselves in God's Sabbath day". Realize God can control your thoughts! See, God's Holy Spirit can MAKE you no longer crave money, possessions, pornography, cigarettes, alcohol, or whatever. It can COMPEL you to be patient, kind, longsuffering, gentle, self-controlled, etc. God's Holy Spirit can FURNISH you with a spirit (thoughts, desires, & emotions) that continually longs to feed the hungry, visit the imprisoned, and give drink to the thirsty. Again, the battle for your eternal destiny is being waged in your mind (heart), and God PROMISES those who "delight in His Sabbath Day" a new heart with His desires! THAT is how important obeying the 4th Love Commandment is, and THAT is what Satan has stolen from mankind!

Gander at the Sabbath day from God's perspective: Imagine you are the father of two children. One of them can hardly wait for the weekend to arrive to get to spend a whole day with you; in fact, during the week they even drop little hints to you about how excited they are for Saturday to arrive. The other child could care less about spending a day with you; they are too busy with their own agenda to care about you. They smugly snort, "I'm not under any law. I don't have to spend a day with dad!" Now which child do you think the father is going to bless? Which child puts a smile on their dad's face when he thinks about them? Which child's actions prove they love their father? See, I cannot make you love your heavenly Father—the one who actually hung the moon and stars!—I can only tell you how you are breaking His heart when you do not want to spend time with Him.

Friend, God created the Sabbath day to be a blessing to mankind. It was never intended to be a day of drudgery. God loved us so much that He planned a day for us to rest from our struggle with work—which was the result of sin! Thus, Sabbath-keeping symbolizes "rest" from our battle with sin, and it is a mini foretaste of God's coming 7th millennial Sabbath day, where rest and peace will blanket planet Earth. By observing the Sabbath, one pays homage to God's 7 day (7,000 year) master time plan for mankind on Earth. Really, what could be better than taking a day off from work to rest your body and reflect on God? Do not be legalistic about the day. It is a fun day to rest, help others, visit widows, read God's word, take a nature walk to enjoy God's creation, etc. Or get online and study God-related things—e.g. creation vs. evolution, history of the Bible, Israelite history, history of other religions, scientific evidence of Noah's flood, etc. Keep a list during the week of questions that pop into your head about God, and then use the Sabbath day to search out answers. That is how you seek God! There are literally thousands of things to do on the Sabbath day, but stay focused on discovering and loving your Creator. You will be immensely rewarded for this!

Always remember, God does not miss anything His spirit children are doing. He sees your every move and knows your every thought, desire, & emotion: *"The LORD knoweth the thoughts of man"* *(Psalms 94:11)*. He will take notice when someone is serious about seeking Him, and He will visit them! He will also know if during the Sabbath you are really thinking, "When is this day going to be over so I can get back to my business of making money!" God prophesied angrily through Amos: *"Listen, you merchants who rob the poor, trampling on the needy; you who long for the Sabbath to end and the religious holidays to be over, so you can get out and start cheating again"* *(Amos 8:4, 5, Living Bible)*. See, keeping the Sabbath is up to you, but you will not fool God. So search your own heart and ask God to help you love Him. Personally, I still get butterflies in my stomach when I see the sun setting in a Friday sky! Friend, God is anxiously watching to see who loves Him, and the Sabbath day is part of that test!

In the wilderness, God supplied the Israelites with manna for food, and He instructed them to gather enough manna for 2 days on the 6th day of the week in preparation for the 7th day Sabbath and to not go out looking for food on the Sabbath day. But some Israelites went out to gather manna on the 7th day: *"And it came to pass, that there went out some of the people on the seventh day for to gather, and they found none. And the LORD said unto Moses, **How long refuse ye to keep my commandments and my laws**?"* *(Exodus 16:27, 28)*. See, their disobedience infuriated God! (Incidentally, this incident occurred BEFORE God spoke the 10 love Commandments to the Israelites at Mount Sinai, again proving mankind had/has always known God's 10 Love Commandments.) Furthermore, clay tablets unearthed in ancient Babylonia—from before Abraham's time!—tell of the 7th day as a "Holy Day" in which mankind should "cease from all business". Friend, God's 7th day Sabbath has ALWAYS been a test to ALL mankind to see if they will obey Him: *"Then said the LORD unto Moses, Behold, I will rain bread from heaven for you; and the people shall go out and gather a certain rate every day, that I MAY PROVE THEM, whether they will walk in my law, or no"* *(Exodus 16:4)*. Will you obey God's Law? Will you prove you love Him?

Undeniably, the Sabbath was created for ALL mankind for Jesus said: *"The Sabbath was made for MAN, and not man for the Sabbath"* *(Mark 2:27)*. Do you see? If the Sabbath day was made for just Jews, Jesus would have said the Sabbath was made for "Israel" instead of "man". But you already know the Israelite story (parable) is really a skit being controlled by God to teach <u>ALL</u> mankind His message, so obviously the 10 Love Commandments are for everyone. And take note; <u>God created the Sabbath day FOR US, not the other way around!</u> We need the Sabbath day! We need a day a week to get to know our Creator God. We need a day of rest to rejuvenate our physical body every 7th day. Thus, we were NOT created for the Sabbath day; <u>it was created for us</u>: *"The works of his (God's) hands are verity and judgment; <u>ALL</u> his commandments are sure. <u>They stand fast for ever and ever, and are done in truth and uprightness</u>" (Psalms 111:7, 8)*. Certainly, the 4th Love Commandment "<u>Remember the Sabbath day, to keep it Holy</u>" is still in affect today.

The **5th Love Commandment** is ***"<u>Honour thy father and thy mother: that thy days may be long upon the land which the LORD thy God giveth thee</u>" (Exodus 20:12)***. God told Moses the punishment for sin of "disobeying the 5th Love Commandment" was certain death: *"For **every one that curseth his father or his mother shall be surely put to death**: he hath cursed his father or his mother; his blood shall be upon him" (Leviticus 20:9)*. That is plain enough: God did not take lightly to this sin!

So what about today? Paul wrote: *"<u>Children, obey your parents in the Lord: for this is right</u>. <u>Honour thy father and mother; which is the first commandment with promise</u>; That it may be well with thee, and thou mayest live long on the earth" (Ephesians 6:1-3)*. No doubt Paul believed the 5th Love Commandment was still in affect. He wrote about disobedient children: *"Being filled with all unrighteousness... **disobedient to parents**...who knowing the judgment of God, that **they which commit such things are worthy of death**" (Romans 1:29-32)*. Again Paul penned: *"This know also, that in the last days perilous times shall come. For men shall be lovers of their own selves...<u>disobedient to parents</u>, unthankful, unholy...<u>from such turn away</u>" (II Timothy 3:1-5)*. Yes, certainly, the 5th Love Commandment "<u>Honor thy father and thy mother</u>" is still in affect today with the same resulting consequence of

234

death for its disobedience. Rather, you should obey, thank, appreciate, respect, and take care of (if they need it) your biological parents on this Earth.

The **6ᵗʰ Love Commandment** is ***"Thou shalt not kill" (Exodus 20:13)***. God told Moses the punishment for the sin of "disobeying the 6ᵗʰ Love Commandment" was to be death: *"And **he that killeth any man shall surely be put to death"** (Leviticus 24:17)*. God was not talking about deaths that occur during war in self defense; He was talking about senseless killing out of anger or hatred: *"if he thrust him of hatred, or hurl at him by laying of wait, that he die; Or in enmity smite him with his hand, that he die: **he that smote him shall surely be put to death; for he is a murderer**: the revenger of blood shall slay the murderer, when he meeteth him" (Numbers 35:20, 21)*. See, the 6ᵗʰ Love Commandment is about envious murder! And God was/is not playing around with the wicked sin of murder.

So how did Paul feel about murder? He wrote: *"Now the works of the flesh are manifest, which are these…hatred, variance, emulations, wrath, strife…**murders**…of the which I tell you before, as I have also told you in time past, that they which do such things shall NOT inherit the kingdom of God" (Galatians 5:19-21)*. Is that clear enough? Paul believed willful murderers will not enter the Kingdom of God. And Jesus' beloved disciple John felt the same way: *"He that loveth not his brother abideth in death. Whosoever hateth his brother is a murderer: and **ye know that no murderer hath eternal life abiding in him**" (I John 3:14, 15)*. Do you see? If you just hold hatred towards someone on Earth—which is un-forgiveness held towards someone that offended you—the Bible says you are a MURDERER and will NOT enter the Kingdom of God! See, a person *"born again"* of God's Holy Spirit of Love does not hate anyone!

Jesus confirmed the same thing: *"Ye have heard that it was said by them of old time, Thou shalt not kill; and whosoever shall kill shall be in danger of the judgment: But I say unto you, That **whosoever is angry with his brother without a cause shall be in danger of the judgment**" (Matthew 5:21,22)*. Look, no matter how horrible you feel someone—sibling, friend, business partner, or whomever—has wronged you…FORGIVE THEM because your eternal destiny depends on it!

235

Remember, God will have to forgive ALL your <u>many</u> transgressions (sins) you did against Him at the Judgment to allow you entrance into His Holy Kingdom. So if you cannot forgive someone of the "little" thing(s) they have done against you, WHY do you suppose God will forgive ALL your many wicked sins? Friend, the Bible is very clear: <u>you reap what you sow</u>—forgiveness for forgiveness, or un-forgiveness for un-forgiveness! Certainly, the 6th Love Commandment "<u>Thou shall not kill</u>" is still in affect today with the same resulting consequence of death for its disobedience.

Instead of murdering people through unrighteous anger, hatred, arguing, fighting, complaining, and impatience, Jesus taught we should "turn the other cheek" and always show mercy towards others: ***"<u>Love your enemies, bless them that curse you, do good to them that hate you, and pray for them which despitefully use you, and persecute you</u>***; *That ye may be children of your Father which is in heaven: <u>for he maketh his sun to rise on the evil and on the good, and sendeth rain on the just and the unjust</u>" (Matthew 5:44, 45)*. Always remember, God is Spirit and we are ALL His spirit children—in other words, our spirit (soul) is made in the image of God!—and it is our "spirit material" that thinks, feels, remembers, loves, hates, etc. Consequently, we ALL come face to face with God everyday of our lives. He is <u>everyone</u> we meet!!! Do you love the people you meet? Then you love God. Do you hate someone for something they have done to you? Then you hate God! If you harbor bitterness towards someone, then you are bitter towards God. Are you impatient with people's driving? Then you are being impatient with God! Continually monitor the thoughts in your spirit (mind) towards other people, because one day you will answer directly to God for them.

The **7th Love Commandment** is ***"<u>Thou shalt NOT commit adultery</u>" (Exodus 20:14)***. God told Moses the punishment for the sin of "disobeying the 7th Love Commandment" was to be sure death: *"And <u>the man that committeth adultery with another man's wife, even he that committeth adultery with his neighbour's wife</u>, **<u>the adulterer and the adulteress shall surely be put to death</u>**" (Leviticus 20:10)*. That is uncomplicated, right? So how about lesbianism & homosexuality? God commanded Moses: *"<u>If a man also lie with mankind, as he lieth with a</u>*

236

woman, both of them have committed an abomination: ***they shall surely be put to death;*** *their blood shall be upon them" (Leviticus 20:13).* You will discover Biblically that God forbids <u>ALL</u> sexual activity—even sexual fantasy in the mind!—except for that between "a man and a woman" that have entered into a marriage covenant. THAT is the <u>only</u> acceptable place for sex in God's eyes.

So how did Paul feel about adultery? He declared: *"Now the works of the flesh are manifest, which are these;* ***Adultery, fornication, uncleanness, lasciviousness****...of the which I tell you before, as I have also told you in time past, that* ***they which do such things shall NOT inherit the kingdom of God"*** *(Galatians 5:19-21).* Therefore, Paul rightfully believed people living in <u>willful</u> sexual sin will NOT enter the Kingdom of God! John the Revelator wrote: *"But... whoremongers...shall have their part in the lake which burneth with fire and brimstone: which is the second death" (Revelation 21:8).* The English word "whoremonger" was translated from the original Biblical manuscript's Greek word *"pornos"*—where we derive the term "pornography"—and it means: <u>one who is sexually immoral</u>. Today, the world has embraced and (for the most part accepted) ever kind of sexual sin—from homosexuality & lesbianism to fornication (premarital sex) & adultery and from masturbation (solo sex) & pornography to threesomes and drunken orgies—but in <u>NO WAY</u> has God's view ever changed! Today non-married, scantly-clad actresses sit on late night TV shows and boast about their sexual escapades, flaunting the deadly message that premarital sex is OK. Yet, God has plainly declared ALL willful fornicators will perish! Peter wrote: *"But these, as <u>natural brute beasts</u>...SHALL UTTERLY PERISH in their own corruption...Having eyes full of adultery, and that cannot cease from sin" (II Peter 2:12, 14).*

Jesus said: *"Ye have heard that it was said by them of old time, <u>Thou shalt NOT commit adultery</u>: But I say unto you,* ***That whosoever looketh on a woman to lust after her hath committed adultery with her already in his heart****. And <u>if thy right eye offend thee, pluck it out, and cast it from thee: for it is profitable for thee that one of thy members should perish, and not that thy whole body should be cast into hell</u>" (Matthew 5:27-29).* Do you grasp how serious God is about

237

sin? This is not a joke, my friend! It is CRYSTAL clear from the above passage Jesus believed a willful sexually immoral person will end up in hell. According to Jesus, a <u>wise</u> <u>person</u> would take whatever drastic measures necessary to stop sexually sinning—gouging one's eyes out if necessary!—so they might enter the Kingdom of God. Friend, if you plan on obtaining eternal life, <u>YOU MUST CHOOSE TO STOP WILLFUL SIN—which is to repent</u>! See, Jesus would never have uttered the above Scripture's radical words if one was "born again" by simply muttering some words in a church. No, you must conquer sin!!! Thus, certainly, the 7ᵗʰ Love Commandment "<u>Thou shall NOT commit adultery</u>" is still in affect today with the same resulting consequence of death for its disobedience.

If you want to enjoy sex, get married! If you want to entertain sexual thoughts, get married and only have those thoughts about your wife or husband. You can hate me all you want for saying that, but I will NOT stand in front of God one day having to answer for writing a book with some lackadaisical message that contradicts the VERY words of Jesus Christ and sends people to hell. I will NOT have your blood on my hands! The Bible is unmistakably black & white about the eternal destiny of those committing willful sexual sin: They will perish!!! I only love you enough to tell you this truth: *"<u>Marriage is honourable in all, and the bed undefiled</u>: **<u>but whoremongers and adulterers GOD WILL JUDGE</u>**" (Hebrews 13:4)*. Now, obviously, we can all make a mistake and commit a sexual sin, but here is the proper response: Hit your knees and beg God's forgiveness, then get up and reenter the *"narrow way"* leading to eternal life by absolutely PURPOSING in your spirit (thoughts, desires, & emotions) you will never again sin sexually! See, that is how a spiritually *"born again"* person reacts to sexual sin: <u>They fight it and get victory over it</u>. So <u>DO</u> whatever it takes! Stop watching and supporting filthy TV shows and sitcoms filled with sinful sexual innuendos—i.e. promoting premarital sex, pornography, homosexuality, etc. You will <u>never</u> get victory over sexual sin if you feed your soul (through your eyes) with Satan's vile vomit!

Listen, you MUST have God's Holy Spirit living inside your heart to enter the Kingdom of God. And God's Spirit is <u>HOLY</u>: It is clean, pure, and righteous. It will not live inside of a person's body

238

who commits willful sexual debauchery. It lives inside clean temples! Remember Paul's words: *"Know ye not that ye are the temple of God, and that the Spirit of God dwelleth in you?* ___If any man defile the temple of God, him shall God destroy;___ *for the temple of God is holy, which temple ye are"* (I Corinthians 3:16, 17). See, asking God's Holy Spirit to live inside of a sexually impure body is like asking you to live inside of an old dilapidated house crawling from floor to ceiling with snakes, worms, and rats, while stinking like feces. Would you live there? No!!! Well, neither will the Holy Spirit live inside an unclean temple. So if you are willfully committing sexual sins, I am warning you to clean up your act before your time expires!

The **8ᵗʰ Love Commandment** is *"Thou shalt not steal" (Exodus 20:15).* God told Moses the punishment for the sin of "disobeying the 8ᵗʰ Love Commandment" was to be death. For instance: *"If a man be found stealing any of his brethren of the children of Israel, and maketh merchandise of him, or selleth him; then that thief shall die; and thou shalt put evil away from among you"* (Deuteronomy 24:7). God instructed the Israelites to seek to return something they knew was lost and not to hide it from its owner: *"If you see someone's ox or sheep wandering away, don't pretend you didn't see it; take it back to its owner. If you don't know who the owner is, take it to your farm and keep it there until the owner comes looking for it, and then give it to him. The same applies to donkeys, clothing, or anything else you find. Keep it for its owner"* (Deuteronomy 22:1-3, Living Bible). Yes, God hates thievery!

So how did Paul feel about a willful thief's chance of entering the Kingdom of God? He stated: *"Know ye not that the unrighteous shall NOT inherit the kingdom of God? BE NOT DECIEVED...__Nor thieves...nor extortioners, shall inherit the kingdom of God__"* (I Corinthians 6: 9, 10). That is as lucid as a flashing neon sign! The Holy Spirit talking through Paul gave a willful thief <u>NO</u> chance at entering God's Kingdom (obtaining eternal life). Without repentance (change of ways) a thief's soul will perish. Certainly, the 8ᵗʰ Love Commandment "Thou shall NOT steal" is still in affect today with the same resulting consequence of death for its disobedience.

Instead of stealing, the Bible teaches we should <u>GIVE</u>! Give of

239

your time, money, and anything you have to help others, all the while desiring nothing in return. THAT is the mindset of a righteous, loving, godly person! THAT is how a follower of Christ lives. Jesus preached: *"Give to him that asketh thee, and from him that would borrow of thee turn not thou away" (Matthew 5:42)*. The Bible is replete from front to back with the message of "give to others". Friend, God is scrutinizing everything you do, and He will notice your selfless charity done out of a pure heart and repay you personally: *"When you help the poor you are lending to the LORD—and he pays wonderful interest on your loan!" (Proverbs 19:17, Living Bible)*. How awesome! Paul wrote: *"God loveth a cheerful giver" (II Corinthians 9:7)*.

The book of Acts contains an exhilarating story about a man named Cornelius (who was a non-Jew living in Caesarea) that gave generously to the poor: *"A devout man, and one that feared God with all his house, which gave MUCH alms to the people, and prayed to God always" (Acts 10:2)*. I love what the Bible says about his "giving of alms": *"Thy prayers and thine alms are come up for a memorial before God" (Acts 10:4)*. Is that not splendid! I say again; God does not overlook your charity. And what was Cornelius' reward for his giving? *"...the Holy Ghost fell on all them" (Acts 10:44)*. He received the Holy Spirit!!! Yes, God always rewards a giver: *"I the LORD search the heart, I try the reins, even to give every man according to his ways, and according to the fruit of his doings" (Jeremiah 17:10)*. And the Holy Spirit is by FAR the best gift you can receive!

Yes, instead of doing evil by thieving the Bible teaches we should give "life" to others. Jesus suggested feeding the hungry, quenching the thirsty, clothing the naked, and visiting the sick, widowed, and imprisoned. All of these activities give "life" to people's spirits (souls). At the Judgment, Jesus revealed it will be like this for those who "gave NOT to others": *"Then shall he (God) say also unto them on the left hand, Depart from me, ye cursed, into everlasting fire, prepared for the devil and his angels: For I was an hungred, and ye gave me no meat: I was thirsty, and ye gave me no drink: I was a stranger, and ye took me not in: naked, and ye clothed me not: sick, and in prison, and ye visited me not" (Matthew 25:41-43)*. The people will cry "When did we see YOU in these conditions, Lord?" And God will say, "I was the "spirit material" in everyone on planet Earth! But you were too busy with your own life, ambitions, and materialism to help me. Now get away from me, forever, ye cursed children!" Friend, I urge you to stop stealing, robbing, and ripping-off people, companies, and organizations and make your life about "giving to others": feed the hungry, quench the thirsty, clothe the naked, entertain strangers, and visit the sick, imprisoned, & widows! These are the deeds (works) that manifest out of the loving thoughts dancing around in the head of a people "*born again*" of God's Holy Spirit.

The **9ᵗʰ Love Commandment** is "***Thou shalt NOT bear false witness against thy neighbor" (Exodus 20:16)***. This means do NOT lie! God instructed Moses to punish those who sin by "disobeying the 9ᵗʰ Love Commandment" with death. For example: *"If a false witness rise up against any man to testify against him that which is wrong...**Then shall ye do unto him, as he had thought to have done unto his brother: so shalt thou put the evil away from among you"** (Deuteronomy 19:16, 19)*. In other words, if someone sought to have another man killed for something he falsely accused him of...then the liar was to be killed! Yes, God's fury rests on the head of a liar.

How did Paul feel about the sin of lying? He maintained: *"Being filled with all unrighteousness...debate, DECEIT ...whisperers, backbiters...who knowing the judgment of God, that they which commit such things are worthy of death" (Romans 1:29-32)*. In other words, Paul believed a willful, continual liar will not inherit the Kingdom of God! God proclaimed the same through John the revelator: "***ALL liars, shall have their part in the lake which burneth with fire and brimstone***: *which is the second death" (Revelation 21:8)*. No, the eternal future does not look bright for a person who is a deceiving, scheming, and conniving liar! Certainly, the 9ᵗʰ Love Commandment "Thou shall NOT bear false witness" is still in affect today with the same resulting consequence of death for its disobedience.

Instead of lying, the Bible teaches we are to ALWAYS tell the truth. Paul wrote: *"Provide things honest in the sight of men" (Romans 12:17)*. Again he instructed: *"that we may lead a quiet and peaceable life in all godliness and honesty" (I Timothy 2:2)*. Friend, continually seek to tell the truth and be honest in every situation with everyone!

And of course, share the Gospel every chance you get because it is TRUTH! Testify (witness) the Truth to others in how God has changed your life.

The **10ᵗʰ Love Commandment** is *"__Thou shalt not covet thy neighbour's house, thou shalt not covet thy neighbour's wife, nor his manservant, nor his maidservant, nor his ox, nor his ass, nor any thing that is thy neighbour's" (Exodus 20:17)__*. I call this the "dirt law" because I have told you over and over again in this book that everything you "see" in this world is just dirt. And it is plain old FOOLISHNESS to lust for dirt! Even a human being's physical body is just dirt. Therefore, it is folly to lust after that, too! When drooling out your mouth feasting on the beauty of someone's physical body, allow your mind to switch over and picture every atom making up their physique coming from the food they ate, which grew out of brown dirt that lay on planet Earth for thousands of years. Silly, is it not? Yet, people continue to willfully lust (covet) over dirt with their eyes and heart. Friend, the 10ᵗʰ Love Commandment is actually the "desire that breeds in one's spirit", which then leads them to disobey all of the other 10 Love Commandments! Do you understand? In other words, "coveting dirt" leads people to love money (idolatry), steal, kill, commit adultery, etc. And we already know God declared the punishment of death for those sins; therefore, the consequence for covetousness (if acted upon) was death also.

So how did Paul feel about covetousness? He said: *"__Know ye not that the UNRIGHTEOUS shall NOT inherit the kingdom of God? BE NOT DECEIVED__...__nor covetous__, nor drunkards...__shall inherit the kingdom of God"__ (1 Corinthians 6:9, 10)*. That is blunt and direct enough, right? Paul fully believed covetous people will end up in hell. Again, he wrote: *"For this ye know, that __NO...covetous man, who is an idolater, hath ANY inheritance in the kingdom of Christ and of God"__ (Ephesians 5:5)*. Thus, certainly the 10ᵗʰ Love Commandment "Thou shall NOT covet" is still in affect today with the same resulting consequence of death for its disobedience.

See, instead of coveting dirt, we should love, help, and pray for our brothers and sisters all across the world. Do you understand the difference? This means we remove our love and affection from what we see (atoms) and onto what we do not see (spiritual things)—people's

242

hearts (souls)! It is essential that you grasp this point. Stop loving dirt and love God, who is the invisible "spirit material" inside people! Paul wrote: "*we look NOT at the things which are seen, but at the things which are not seen: for the things which are seen are temporal; but the things which are not seen are eternal*" *(II Corinthians 4:18)*. Amen.

Well there they are my friend: the 10 Love Commandments God placed INSIDE the Ark of the Covenant!!! If we choose to live our daily lives in obedience to these 10 Love Commandments we will obtain eternal life (not experience the 2nd spiritual death), for they have power to transform a soul: "***The LAW of the LORD is perfect, CONVERTING the soul***" *(Psalms 19:7)*. This word "converting" was translated from the original Hebrew word "*šûb*" meaning: to turn back, return; restoration of relationship, as when one returns in repentance to God. In other words, our willful choice to obey God's Law (10 Love Commandments) will restore our soul's relationship with God! Do you understand? That is how the "*Law of the Lord*" converts a soul!!! Remember, Peter preached: "*REPENT ye therefore, and be CONVERTED,* ***THAT your sins may be blotted out***, *when the times of refreshing shall come from the presence of the Lord; And he shall send Jesus Christ*" *(Acts 3:19, 20)*. See, your repentance (conversion) is what will prompt God to blot out your sins at Christ's 2nd Coming. Jesus confirmed this also by saying: "*Except ye be converted...ye shall NOT enter into the kingdom of heaven*" *(Matthew 18:3)*.

Yes, God's story (parable) of the Israelites was flawlessly accurate, and the "wilderness part" perfectly represented the condition ALL mankind's souls had/have been in since Adam & Eve's sin. Look, God's "salvation (from bondage to sin) part" for mankind through the Messiah, Jesus Christ, was a done deal before Earth was even created! Thus, ALL mankind's souls on Earth had been and still are in the "wilderness" and reaching the Promise Land (Kingdom of God) was ALWAYS possible. All mankind ever HAD TO DO—no matter where or when they lived on Earth or under what Country—was choose to follow the WAY of love (Good) over the WAY of sin (evil) as outlined by obedience to the 10 Love Commandments, and God would allow their souls to receive eternal life by entering the Kingdom of God. Subsequently, God proclaimed to the Israelites in the wilderness: "*That*

243

which is altogether JUST shalt thou follow, THAT thou mayest LIVE, and INHERIT the land which the LORD thy God giveth thee" (Deuteronomy 16:20). Likewise, if you follow after the WAY of justice by obeying the 10 Love Commandments, you will <u>live</u> forever by INHERITING the Kingdom of God!

When I was a child it was obvious to me the 10 Love Commandments were meant to be obeyed by <u>ALL</u> mankind, but I was always puzzled as to why God prefaced them with these words: ***"I am the LORD thy God, which have BROUGHT THEE OUT of the land of Egypt, out of the house of bondage..."*** *(Exodus 20:2)*. Then, after saying that, God began speaking His 10 Love Commandments to the Israelites: *"Thou shalt have no other gods before me...etc., etc." (Exodus 20:3)*. Confused, I often wondered, "What is the big deal, God? How does your freeing the Israelites out of Egyptian <u>bondage</u> have ANYTHING to do with <u>ME</u> keeping your 10 Love Commandments?" See, I could not make the connection. Well, thankfully, God personally answered my lifelong question that blessed Sabbath morning of December 8, 2007! For now I know—and you know, too!—Israel's bondage in Egypt and subsequent deliverance by God through Moses was meant to be a <u>prophetic</u> story (parable), <u>directed towards ALL mankind</u>, explaining how He would deliver <u>ALL</u> mankind's souls out of bondage to sin.

Thus, God's <u>introductory</u> words kicking off the 10 Love Commandments were/are actually saying to <u>ALL</u> mankind, "I am the Lord thy Father God. Out of love, I sent my only Son, Jesus, to die for you. He laid down his sinless soul, enduring horrific torture and spiritual separation from me on the cross to pay your soul's death penalty, for sin had you in bondage, permanently cut off from me. Yes, your souls were spiritually dead—separated from my life giving force. But I wanted you back with me: I wanted you to live with me forever! <u>Thus, I did my part and freed your souls from your spiritual bondage to sin & death through Christ</u>. So, since I did THAT for you (making forgiveness for your sins available) here is what you <u>MUST</u> **DO** for me to receive it: <u>I want you to live your Earthly journey in obedience to my 10 Love Commandments</u>!!! If you will do this for me, I will take care of you and lead you into the Promise Land (Kingdom of God),

244

where you will receive eternal life and experience pleasures you cannot possible dream of right now. But if you refuse to live your Earthly life in obedience to my 10 Love Commandments, then you will make void the very salvation I provided you through Christ! Your disobedience (sin) will make a mockery of the love I showed you!!! And for this wicked evil, I will curse you into the pit forever! You will certainly taste the full fury of my wrath, experiencing the 2nd spiritual Death (outer darkness), where your soul will be permanently cut off from mine and there will be weeping and gnashing of teeth!"

Wow, thank you Father God for opening up my spiritual eyes to the Truth of your Word. Friend, do you see the connection between God's deliverance through Christ and our need to obey the 10 Love Commandments (repent of sin) to obtain eternal life? Listen, if God has NOT delivered us from sin's bondage, then we are still spiritually dead!!! If that is the case, then there is absolutely NO benefit in us obeying God's 10 Love Commandments, because we are all going to perish anyway. Do you understand? This is why Paul wrote: *"And if Christ be not raised, your faith is vain; YE ARE YET IN YOUR SINS. Then they also which are fallen asleep in Christ are perished"* (I Corinthians 15: 17, 18). See, God's deliverance through Jesus Christ and our obedience to the 10 Love Commandments go hand-in-hand; either way you slice it, one is worthless without the other. Read that last sentence again, for truer words could not be written!!! See, if we continue to live in sin (DO EVIL by disobeying the 10 Love Commandments) then Jesus Christ died in vain, because we will perish anyway. And vice versa, if we forsake sin (DO GOOD by obeying the 10 Love Commandments) but Jesus never died for us, then we will perish also because we ALL sinned at one time or another and just one sin separates a soul from God forever: *"For ALL have sinned, and come short of the glory of God"* (Romans 3:23). Consequently, only both (God's supernatural deliverance through Jesus and our obedience to the 10 Love Commandments) will yield a soul eternal life. Therefore, Paul sternly wrote: *"**Get some sense and quit your sinning**"* (I Corinthians 15:34, Living Bible).

Another way the Bible explains all of this is through use of the "Law concept". If you remember, I broached this subject in chapter

3: God, THE sovereign authority, has the absolute right to make the Law(s) and enforce it; disobeying God's (10 Love Commandment) Law is the very definition of sin: *"for sin is the transgression of the law" (I John 3:4)*; and there is ALWAYS a "consequence to be paid" for disobeying a Law. Well, remember God's initial Law to mankind was to "NOT eat from the Tree of the Knowledge of Good & Evil" or the consequence would be spiritual death (spiritual separation from God). And remember, Adam & Eve disobeyed God's Law (sinned), which immediately placed ALL (future) mankind's souls UNDER the death penalty of God's Law! In other words, the Bible reported all mankind was now *"under the Law"*, which simply meant mankind's souls were in bondage to the Law of sin & death.

Then, I clarified this "Law concept" via an analogy which I will now further develop to include this chapter's message. Here was the analogy: A certain country with a law stating "someone convicted of 1st degree murder will receive the death penalty" had a man who disobeyed that law and was sentenced to death. And I explained…while the man is sitting on death row he is considered *"under the law"*. In other words, he is UNDER the consequence of disobeying the Law—namely, the death penalty! Simply put, the man is in bondage to the law, sitting in a jail cell awaiting his day of execution! He has no hope and no way out. Once again, THAT is truly, completely, and utterly the definition of being *"under the law"*, and the souls of ALL mankind were in that exact condition after Adam & Eve's sin.

Oh, but then something wonderful and amazing happened: While sitting on death row (under the Law), one day several guards came to the man, unlocked his cell door, and said, "You are FREE to go!" The man was stunned and asked, "How could that be?" They said, "Someone came and chose to die in your place, and they have already been executed for you!" Wow, do you see? Someone freed the man from the curse of the law. Someone freed him from his bondage! He was now no longer under the death sentence for disobeying the law. In other words, he was no longer *"under the law"*. HE WAS FREE!!! Friend, this is precisely what God did for us through Jesus' sinless death on the cross! God paid our death sentence, opened our cell door, and freed us from our bondage to the Law of sin. In other words, we are NO longer under the consequence of "spiritual death" for disobeying the Law. Simply and Biblically put; we are "free from the Law". So Paul wrote: *"For the… Spirit of life in Christ Jesus **hath made me FREE from the law of sin and death**" (Romans 8:2).* Do you understand? This amazing act of love by God (on behalf of His spirit children) is Biblically termed "God's grace" or "God's mercy". In other words, THAT was how God showed his great love, grace, and mercy towards the souls of ALL mankind!

But now lets return to the man in the parable…does his freedom (from the law) mean he can now go out on a full-fledged murdering spree without any consequence to the law? Absolutely NOT!!! **For the country's law still remains**! If the man goes out and continues to murder, he will be caught again and now face the death penalty himself. Do you see? Likewise, God's salvation (from the Law) through Jesus Christ is NOT a free gift card to sin, for the Law of sin & death still remains!!! Jesus said, *"Think NOT that I am come to destroy the law… For verily I say unto you, Till heaven and earth pass, one jot or one tittle shall in NO wise pass from the law, till all be fulfilled" (Matthew 5:17, 18).* See, God did NOT destroy the law, it still exists and states: *"For the wages of sin is death" (Romans 6:23).* And since "sin" is "disobeying the 10 Love Commandments", if we willfully continue to live our lives in disobedience to THAT Law, we will ultimately pay the death penalty ourselves, killing our own soul!

Now, you should be able to clearly and perfectly understand Paul's incredibly wise words: *"For sin shall NOT have dominion over you: for ye are not under the law, but under grace. What then? Shall we sin, because we are not under the law, but under grace? **GOD FORBID**. Know ye not, that to whom ye yield yourselves servants to obey, his servants ye are to whom ye obey; **whether of sin unto death**, or **of obedience unto righteousness**?" (Romans 6:14-16).* Do you see? If we continue to sin (disobey the 10 Love Commandments) we are servants to sin, and our soul will perish! Jesus said: *"Verily, verily, I say unto you, Whosoever committeth sin is the servant of sin" (John 8:34).* But if we willfully choose to stop sinning (obey the 10 Love Commandments) we are servants to obedience, and our soul will be made righteous at Christ's glorious return, whereby we will obtain eternal life by God's grace through Jesus' atonement (forgiveness of our sins).

My friend, it is like this; if you keep right on willfully sinning, you are behaving like you are still a slave to sin! In other words, you are behaving like God has <u>not</u> set you free from the death penalty of the Law of sin. Do you understand? Relating this back to the Israelite story (parable), here is a graphic picture of how preposterous "continual, willful sin" in a spirit child's life appears from God's perspective: It is like an Israelite, in the wilderness, wanting and begging Moses to get a group of guys together to force him/her to carry heavy bricks daily until he is so tired he can barely stand, while whipping his/her back until it is bloody raw. (Remember, that was the <u>work</u> the Israelites had to do because of their bondage in Egypt!) Can you comprehend the absurdness of this Israelite's desire? What kind of a fool would still want to DO the work of a slave after being set free? <u>Yet, that is exactly what you DO when you continue to do the works of sin (disobey the 10 Love Commandments) after having been set free from sin's bondage through Jesus Christ</u>! It is TRULY like you are laughing at the very freedom God provided. You might as well stand beside Jesus, while he was being bound to the cross on the ground, and spit on him yourself! For THAT is what you DO every time you willfully sin (disobey the 10 love Commandments)! What a dangerous thing to DO in front of the eyes of a Living God.

Yes, friend, our lives are a spiritual journey through a "wilderness", where God is testing each and every one of us. You should now recognize why "*the wilderness*" was a common place for many Biblical stories to occur—i.e. because it represented what planet Earth had become after sin entered the world. The word "wilderness" is in the Bible 305 times. Jesus was tempted 40 days and 40 nights in "a wilderness" because God wanted a physical (seeable) scenario to occur in his life making known to mankind he had undergone the same temptations we ALL face on Earth, yet he never sinned once: *"For we have not an high priest (Jesus) which cannot be touched with the feeling of our infirmities; <u>but was in ALL points tempted like as we are, yet without sin</u>" (Hebrews 4:15)*. See, a "wilderness" location was the perfect symbolic place for Jesus to be tempted—yet, never sin—to mirror the meaning behind God's ancient Israelite parable's "wilderness

248

part"—where the Israelites were <u>tempted</u> to see if they would enter the Promise Land: *"Then was Jesus led up of the spirit <u>into the wilderness</u> to be tempted of the devil" (Matthew 4:1).*

John the Baptist dwelled in "a wilderness" while he prepared the world for the Savior. John was mankind's forerunner of Jesus, and he was crying out for mankind to repent of their sins: *"He said, **<u>I am the voice of one crying in the wilderness</u>**, Make straight the way of the Lord" (John 1:23).* Mark records: *"John did baptize <u>in the wilderness</u>, and preach <u>the baptism of repentance FOR the remission of sins</u>" (Mark 1:4).* Yes, we will all have to repent in the "wilderness"—during this present age on planet Earth—if we intend to be forgiven of our sins! Therefore, again, do you see what a perfect location it was for John the Baptist to carry out his Godly assignment in "a wilderness"?

Furthermore, we know the Bible likens mankind's souls to "sheep that have gone astray": *<u>"All we like sheep have gone astray; we have turned every one to his own way"</u> (Isaiah 53:6).* This just means, again, ALL mankind has sinned. But Jesus uttered a parable demonstrating how he is like a Shepard searching to rescue his lost sheep. And where do you think was the "location of the sheep" in the parable? That is right…they were in the "wilderness"!!! Jesus said: *"What man of you, having an hundred sheep, if he lose one of them, doth not leave the ninety and nine <u>in the wilderness</u>, and go after that which is lost, until he find it?" (Luke 15:4).* Do you see? A "wilderness" location Biblically always represents "this sinful age on planet Earth".

The Apostle Paul understood perfectly that God had <u>created</u> the Israelite's 40 year "wilderness journey" as an <u>example</u> (parable) to <u>teach</u> ALL mankind how they should live on Earth to obtain eternal life—i.e. reach and enter the Promised Land (Kingdom of God). He wrote: *"But with many of them (Israelites) God was NOT well pleased: for they were overthrown in the wilderness. **<u>Now these THINGS were our EXAMPLES</u>**, <u>to the intent we should not lust after evil things (sins), as they also lusted</u>" (I Corinthians 10:5, 6).* Paul went on to talk about their specific "evil lusts (sins)" of idolatry, fornication, etc.—ALL 10 Love Commandments things—and said: *"**<u>All these things happened to them as examples</u>**—as object lessons to us—**<u>to warn us against DOING the same things</u>**; they were WRITTEN DOWN so that WE could read* *about them and learn from them in these last days as the world nears its end" (I Corinthians 10:11, Living Bible)*. Wow! See, friend, the Bible confirms the Israelite story was exactly what God had revealed to me on December 8, 2007: A prophetic story (parable) God caused to happen in real life, with real people, that was then written down so mankind could read about it and learn EVERYTHING involved in a "soul's journey back to God"!

In the following chapters I will clear up many Biblical terms and concepts that have caused much confusion today concerning what a soul MUST DO to obtain eternal life. When you see the picture clearly you are going to be amazed, because the concepts and terms all point to the same conclusion: Repentance (obeying God's 10 Love Commandments) yields eternal life! The concepts are all so completely synergistic that you will be stunned how simple and concise the Bible's message is! The concepts are: Love, Truth, Holy Spirit, Bearing Fruit, Faith, Love of Money, Will of God, Word of God, and the Fear of God.

Chapter 11

LOVE

"Thou shalt LOVE the Lord thy God with all thy heart...
Thou shalt LOVE thy neighbor as thyself.
On these two commandments hang ALL the LAW"
(Matthew 22:37-40)

What a seemingly daunting subject for an author to tackle...
Love! Yet, Biblically the term "love" is clearly defined, and I have been
ostentatiously displaying its definition throughout this entire book by
calling the 10 Commandments the "10 LOVE Commandments". Friend,
simply put, <u>love is SHOWN by obeying the 10 Love Commandments</u>.
It is that uncomplicated! Realize it, learn it, internalize it, and engrain it
into your spirit to the point that whenever you hear one term you instantly
think of the other. Thus, when you see or hear the word "love" you
should automatically think "obeying the 10 Commandments". And vice
versa, when you see or hear the phrase "obey the (10) Commandments"
you should automatically think "love". Or, like I do, just combine the
two terms so you will forever know love is demonstrated by obeying
the 10 Love Commandments!

Consider it logically; do you love God when you blaspheme
(curse) His name? Do you love God when "money" is your idol? Do you
love God when you refuse to spend the Sabbath day with Him? Do you

251

love someone when you steal from them? Do you love someone when you murder (hate) them? Do you love someone when you lie to them? And on and on I could go with the 10 Love Commandments. Friend, the answer to all of these questions is a big, fat...**NO**! We "love" only by DOING the things on the "do side" of the 10 Love Commandments chart and by NOT DOING the things on the "do not side". It is that straightforward! So instead of cursing God, love magnifies and glorifies His name; instead of idolizing money (dirt possessions), love idolizes God (the "spirit material" inside everyone); instead of working on God's Sabbath day, love can't wait to spend a restful day with God each week. Instead of stealing, love gives (feeds the hungry, clothes the naked, etc.); instead of murdering, love forgives (shows mercy); instead of lying, love tells the truth—and on and on with the 10 Love Commandments.

Honing in closer on the 10 Love Commandments, an amazing thing is revealed: The first 4 Love Commandments are "how to love God" and the last 6 Love Commandments are "how to love our neighbor"! And what is "loving God with all our heart and loving our neighbor as ourselves" called? **It is the GOLDEN RULE**!!! In other words, the 10 Love Commandments are simply an exploded (or more detailed) version of the Golden Rule [See Figure #8, page 221]. And, in fact, God had actually given Moses the VERY words of the "Golden Rule", and he wrote them in Scripture: *"And thou shalt love the LORD thy God with all thine heart, and with all thy soul, and with all thy might" (Deuteronomy 6:5)*. And: *"thou shalt love thy neighbor as thyself" (Leviticus 19:18)*.

Ok, so we <u>love</u> God by:

1. Having no other God's before Him
2. Not worshiping idols
3. Not blaspheming His name
4. Keeping His Sabbath day Holy

And we <u>love</u> our neighbor by:

Honoring our father & mother
Not murdering (hating)
Not commit adultery (lusting sexually)
Not stealing
Not lying
Not coveting

In the previous chapter we learned Jesus replied to a man's question of "what MUST I <u>DO</u> to obtain eternal life" by listing the 10 Love Commandments and saying, *"Keep (DO) them!"* Well, is there an example in the Bible of Jesus answering the SAME question with *"obey the Golden Rule"*? If so, this would prove what I am telling you—namely, the Golden Rule is equal to the 10 Love Commandments. And yes, there is such an exchange in the Bible! One day a lawyer stood up and asked Jesus, *"Master, <u>what shall I DO to inherit eternal life?</u>" (Luke 10:25)*. Jesus inquired of the man, *"<u>What is written in the law? how readest thou? (Luke 10:26)</u>*. Notice, Christ's replying question to the Lawyer's question <u>confirms</u> the ANSWER to "what MUST I <u>DO</u> to obtain eternal life" is found in the <u>LAW</u>, which is the Torah (first 5 books of the Bible)!!! The lawyer answered, ***"<u>Thou shalt love the Lord thy God with all thy heart, and with all thy soul, and with all thy strength, and with all thy mind; and thy neighbor as thyself</u>" (Luke 10:27)***. Jesus replied, *"<u>Thou hast answered right: this DO, and thou shalt LIVE</u>" (Luke 10:28)*. Wow, so it checks out! The "Golden Rule" is merely a truncated (condensed) summary of the 10 Love Commandments. Friend, if you choose to live your Earthly life by the "Golden Rule" your soul will live forever!

Now, of course, Jesus knew EXACTLY what the ancient story (parable) of the Israelites—God's message to ALL mankind about EVERYTHING involved in a soul's journey back to God—in the Jewish Scrolls represented, so whenever someone asked him "what MUST I <u>DO</u> to obtain eternal life" he was probably thinking, "People, do you NOT know what the Scriptures are about? I am the prophet *'like unto Moses'*, and I am finally here on planet Earth to lead your (mankind's) souls out of bondage during Earth's 4,000[th] year! As far as what **YOU** people MUST <u>DO</u> to obtain eternal life—it has never changed!—you must L.O.V.E., which means you MUST repent of your sin (non-loving ways) by obeying the 10 Love Commandments. THAT is what the "40 year wilderness scene" in the Israelite story (parable) is all about! THAT is why my Father spoke and wrote the 10 Love Commandments on stone tables and put them in an Ark! Why do you people not understand this? Why do you still try and act like you do not know what YOU must <u>DO</u> to enter the Promise Land (Kingdom of God) when the road that travels there is already written in your heart? You know what is good (love) and you know what is evil (sin); thus, follow after the way of good (love) and stop doing evil (sin). That is EXACTLY what your fathers in the wilderness needed to DO to enter the Promise Land (Kingdom of God), and it is still what you need to <u>DO</u> today! Mankind needs to obey the 10 Love Commandments or they will perish in the wilderness."

As we analyze the Golden Rule's condensed <u>summary</u> of the 10 Love Commandments God's impeccable wisdom shines forth in the ORDER in which He <u>originally</u> listed (spoke & wrote) the 10 Love Commandments for Moses and the Israelite's at Mount Sinai, for He listed the 4 on "how to love God" first and the 6 on "how to love your neighbor" second. How perfect and beautiful was that order in 1334 BC when it would not be until Jesus' day on Earth that God would officially anoint (or teach mankind) the special 2 Commandments (Golden Rule) as the shortened form of the 10 Love Commandments—i.e. the 1st and Greatest Commandment is "to love God" and the 2nd Greatest Commandment is to "love our neighbor"? Friend, God had the "Golden Rule" in mind from before Creation.

One day a certain lawyer asked Jesus, *"Master, which is the great commandment in the law? (Matthew 22:36).* Jesus answered, *"<u>Thou shalt love the Lord thy God with all thy heart, and with all thy soul, and with all thy mind</u>. **<u>This is the FIRST and great commandment</u>**. And <u>the SECOND is LIKE UNTO IT, Thou shalt love thy neighbor as thyself</u>. <u>**On these two commandments hang ALL THE LAW and the prophets**</u>"* (Matthew 22:37-40). Wow, did you hear what Jesus said? <u>ALL</u> the <u>LAW</u> (the Torah) hangs on these 2 Commandments, which POSITIVELY verifies the 10 Love Commandments hang on the Golden Rule! Do you see? Once again Jesus <u>proved</u> in this exchange the "10

254

Love Commandments" are simply a more detailed version of "how to love God with all your heart and your neighbor as yourself". And no wonder they are the <u>Greatest of Commandments</u> because Jesus declared our "obedience to them" will ensure us eternal life! That makes perfect sense, right?

Now observe in the above passage of Scripture that Jesus said (in the "Golden Rule") the second Commandment is *"LIKE UNTO"* the first! Now how can that be? How can "loving your neighbor as yourself" be like "loving God"? Friend, I have already answered that question in this book: We are <u>all</u> God's children with His "spirit material" inside of us, for we are made in the image of God and He is Spirit. Thus, when you "love your neighbor" you are loving "spirit material", which is God!!! Jesus' Judgment Day parable substantiated this truth by God saying, *"<u>Inasmuch as ye have done it unto one of the least of these my brethren, ye have done it unto me</u>" (Matthew 25:40)*. Honestly, my friend, could the Bible's message be any more harmonious? The 2nd Commandment of the "Golden rule" is *"like unto the 1st"*, because "loving our neighbor" is like "loving God"!

The Apostle Paul validated "the 10 Love Commandments" are "love defined" and even gave credence to the fact that the last 6 Love Commandments are the one's concerned with "loving our neighbor": *"Owe no man any thing, but to LOVE one another: for <u>he that loveth another hath fulfilled the law</u>. For this, <u>Thou shalt not commit adultery, Thou shalt not kill, Thou shalt not steal, Thou shalt not bear false witness, Thou shalt not covet; and if there be any other commandment</u>, it is briefly comprehended in this saying, namely, <u>THOU SHALT LOVE THY NEIGBOR AS THYSELF. Love worketh no ill to his neighbor: therefore love is the fulfilling of the law</u>" (Romans 13:8-10)*. Do you see? Do you think Paul thought the 10 Love Commandments were obsolete? Not a chance my friend! Paul knew perfectly well that <u>all</u> a person had/has to <u>DO</u> to obtain eternal life is to "live a life of love towards God and their neighbor (which is everyone on Earth) by continually obeying the 10 Love Commandments". Thus, I say to you again; if you want to live eternally…LOVE!!!

Jesus spoke a parable about a rich man and a beggar named Lazarus who lay at the rich man's gate. During their Earthly lives, the rich man <u>refused to love</u> hungry Lazarus by not even giving him crumbs to eat from his table. Eventually, they both died, and the rich man went to hell for his willful sin (lack of love) and Lazarus went to paradise. The rich man, being in torment, begged Abraham to send Lazarus to warn his 5 brothers about the reality of hell and what they should **DO** to NOT end up there (By the way, notice how Jesus' parable <u>proves</u> our spirit is still alive after we physically die on Earth.) Listen to Abraham's reply: *"THEY have **MOSES AND THE PROPHETS**; <u>let them hear them</u>" (Luke 16:29)*. Say what? Are you kidding me? Is Jesus' parable of truth telling us the ANSWER to "<u>ALL</u> <u>WE</u> need to KNOW and <u>DO</u> to NOT end up in hell" is contained in the Old Testament Scriptures? You better believe it!!! But the story of the Earthly man Jesus Christ is contained in the New Testament! I thought we needed to know that? Nope, NOT AT ALL!!! Jesus' parable here proves MANKIND DOES **NOT** NEED TO KNOW <u>ANYTHING</u> ABOUT THE STORY OF CHRIST'S EARTHLY "DELIVERANCE MISSION" TO ESCAPE HELL AND OBTAIN ETERNAL LIFE, for no one knew anything about the Earthly man Jesus in the Old Testament Scriptures, and yet Abraham said, "Let them hear Moses and the prophets." Do you understand?

So what <u>IS</u> the "Eternal Life obtaining Truth" contained in the writings of *"Moses and the prophets"*? (Remember, again, Moses wrote the first 5 books of the Old Testament Scriptures called the Law or the Torah which contained the Israelite's story (parable), and the prophets like Isaiah, Jeremiah, Ezekiel, Jonah, etc. wrote the prophetic books in the Old Testament Scriptures.) So again I ask you; what information is nestled in the *"Law and the prophets"* that can <u>save a soul from hell</u>? The answer is contained in Jesus' reply to the lawyer's question I cited 4 paragraphs above: *"<u>On these two commandments hang ALL the LAW AND THE PROPHETS</u>" (Matthew 22:40)*. What 2 Commandments? <u>The GOLDEN RULE</u>!!! And, again, the "Golden rule" is just a brief summation of the 10 Love Commandments which were/are written in the Law. <u>So OBEYING God's 10 Love Commandments (which He wrote through Moses in Scripture) was/is the key to obtaining eternal life</u>! Is this not easy? In other words, Abraham was correct in Jesus' parable above to tell the rich man, "Your brothers have '*Moses and the prophets*' let them hear (obey) them if they want to escape hell!" Friend,

256

the Bible's message could not be anymore congruous on "the <u>WAY</u> that leads to heaven" from Old Testament to New Testament…WE MUST REPENT OF SIN BY CHOOSING TO LOVE!!! The rich man in hell finally got it; he finally understood what he SHOULD have <u>DONE</u> on Earth to ensure he escaped hell and obtained eternal life: *"<u>No, Father Abraham</u>, they (my brothers) won't bother to read them. But if someone is sent to them from the dead, **<u>then they will TURN FROM THEIR SINS (REPENT)</u>**" (Luke 16:30, Living Bible)*. So, how about you? Have you repented of your sins (by choosing to obey God's 10 Love Commandments) to ensure you will obtain eternal life? Or will you be like the rich man and only acknowledge that truth after your hopelessly wailing in torment in hell?

Let me say it again; the <u>WAY</u> to obtain eternal life has remained the same for the souls of ALL mankind since Adam & Eve first learned the difference between good & evil in the Garden of Eden. For the first 4,000 years of mankind, NO ONE fully understood who the Messiah (Jesus) was or what he was coming to Earth to do. But did that matter? No! The KNOWLEDGE of "THAT" was not important at all!!! And it still does not matter! You can know every detail of the story of Jesus from his birth to ascension and even think (or believe) it is all true, but that head knowledge **CANNOT** obtain your soul eternal life. Only a willful decision of <u>repentance</u> (to live a sinless life of love by obeying the 10 Love Commandments) will prompt God to forgive your past sins through Christ's blood, which will garner your soul entrance into the Kingdom of God and eternal life.

Alright, let me tie this "message of love" up—the Bible's message!—and relate it TO GOD in concluding this chapter. The Apostle John penned: *"Beloved, <u>let us love one another</u>: **<u>for LOVE is OF GOD</u>**; and <u>EVERY ONE that LOVETH is **BORN of GOD**, and KNOWETH GOD</u>. He that loveth NOT knoweth not God; for **GOD IS LOVE**" (I John 4:7, 8)*. Now remember, every time you see the word "love" you can replace it with "obey the 10 Love Commandments". Consequently, by making THAT substitution in the above verses we learn *"everyone who obeys the 10 Love Commandments is born of God and knows God"*! Furthermore, we learn *"he/she that disobeys the 10 Love Commandments does NOT know God, for God is love."* Do you

257

see? But wait…does the Bible come right out and plainly say what I have just substituted? Yes, it most certainly does! John wrote: *"And hereby we do know that we KNOW him (GOD), IF we keep his (10 Love) commandments. He that saith, I know him (God), and keepeth not his (10 Love) commandments, is a liar"* (I John 2:3, 4). Wow, so I ask you…do you KNOW God (love)? Are you keeping (obeying) His 10 Love Commandments? Or are you a liar?

Friend, again, the Bible's message about "what we MUST DO to obtain eternal life" is clearer than the blue sky on a fall day: We must choose to love (obey the 10 Love Commandments). If we willingly do NOT obey the 10 Love Commandments (the Golden Rule) we do NOT know or love God! You can sit in a church building, raise your hands, jump around, and sing pretty songs till the cows come home, but if you are NOT obeying the 10 Love Commandments, you DO NOT KNOW OR LOVE GOD, and your soul will perish on Judgment Day! See, in that condition, you are nothing but a willful, wicked sinner, and your religion is worthless. God wants to see second-by-second, minute-by-minute, hour-by-hour, day-by-day, week-by-week, month-by-month, and year-by-year love pour out of your spirit. He wants to witness you DOING the things on the "do side" of the 10 Love Commandment chart and NOT DOING the things on the "do not side" of the 10 Love Commandment Chart. THAT is exactly how you please, honor, worship, know, and love God!

Jesus said frankly, *"IF ye love me, keep my (10 Love) commandments"* *(John 14:15).* So I ask you again; do YOU love Jesus (God)? Do NOT say you do if you are a greedy-minded, money-loving idolater who cares nothing about helping the needy, for that makes you disobedient to the 2nd, 8th, and 10th Love Commandments. See how simple this is? Look, your actions (works) say it all!!! Do NOT say you love Jesus (God) if you willingly watch pornography, commit adultery in your mind, or indulge in premarital sex. If you do those things you are disobeying the 7th Love Commandment, and "doing those things" while saying you love God only makes you a liar! Do not fool yourself people, for this is not a joke! Jesus' words in the above Scripture verse are truth. Do NOT say you love Jesus (God) if you willingly steal things from your workplace, hook cable up illegally, etc. And on and

258

on you can go with each of the 10 Love Commandments. Friend, if you TRULY love God (love), your heart will want to obey His 10 Love Commandments!

Jesus declared, *"By THIS shall ALL men know that ye ARE my disciples,* **IF YE HAVE LOVE ONE TO ANOTHER***" (John 13:35)*. Do you see? THIS is HOW you detect a "disciple of Christ (love)"! You cannot tell a "disciple of Christ" from a person's church attendance record: You can ONLY tell a "disciple of Christ" by observing who keeps (obeys) God's 10 Love Commandments, for that is how mankind shows love! Friend, a "disciple of Christ" may never step inside of a church building in their lifetime, and some may never have heard the name of Jesus or know his story, yet they are 100% "*born again*" of God (love) if they have chosen to live a life of love over a life of sin by obeying the 10 Love Commandments. Therefore, if you TRULY want to know if someone is a "disciple of Christ" watch if they obey God's 10 Love Commandments. It is that easy! If their mouth and actions reveal they are prideful, money-loving, possession-lusting coveters… you got your answer. If their mouth and actions reveal they commit willful sexual sin….you got your answer, etc.

Standing on a hill about to ascend into heaven, Jesus gave his last instructions for EXACTLY what he wanted his disciples to "*go into all the world*" and preach. Do you know what it was? Listen to his words: "*Go ye therefore, and teach ALL nations…**Teaching them to OBSERVE all things whatsoever I have COMMANDED you*" *(Matthew 28:19, 20)*. The word "observe" is from the original Greek word "*tēreō*" meaning: to keep, guard, OBEY, observe. So do you get it? Jesus wanted/wants his disciples to go into the entire world and teach people to OBEY the 10 Love Commandments—which means to teach people to stop their willful sinning!!! THAT is what ministers should be preaching and teaching: They should be commanding people to love (to do good)! Now why would Jesus have wanted his disciples to teach "that" to people? Do you really need to ask? Because Jesus (God) knew/knows those people who willingly choose to "obey the 10 Love Commandments" will obtain eternal life. Shoot, Jesus had been saying such his entire Earthly ministry! And although you may be offended at this "message of love", I am fulfilling Jesus' exact wish in this very book.

259

Now you should recognize why (in these last days) Satan is ripping the 10 Love Commandments off school and court walls. He hates them for he knows they are the WAY to eternal life. He knows they are the deeds (works) of love, and he hates love because he hates God (love)! Friend, I wish I could plaster the 10 Love Commandments on every billboard in every town across the entire world. I want to write them on flags and fly them high on the top of every flagpole. I want to shout them from the rooftops. I want to sing them in the streets. They are the WAY of God, for they are the WAY of Love. They are glorious, magnificent, splendid, and wonderful! Oh, how I love God's Law of Love!

Friend, we have been born on planet Earth to see if we will choose the "way of love (good)" over the "way of sin (evil)". Each of us is a player in God's Game of Life, and eternal life will be bestowed upon those souls who chose to love God. James wrote: *"Blessed is the man that endureth temptation: for when he is tried, he shall receive the crown of life (eternal life), **which the Lord hath PROMISED to them that LOVE him**" (James 1:12)*. The Lord promised "eternal life" to whom? Those that LOVE Him!!! And HOW do we know if we love Him? ONLY if we keep His 10 Love Commandments, or else we are liars! Friend, it does not matter where you look in the Bible, the answer to "what MUST I DO to obtain eternal life" is always "willingly choose to live a life of love"—which means to repent of sin by obeying God's 10 Holy Love Commandments. The Apostle Paul wrote: *"Eye hath not seen, nor ear heard, neither have entered into the heart of man, the things which God hath prepared for them that LOVE him" (I Corinthians 2:9)*. God has prepared unimaginable pleasures for whom? Those that LOVE Him! And HOW do we know if we love God? I think you get the point.

See, the ONLY thing God will have against a soul on Judgment Day is if they "willingly did NOT love Him (disobey the 10 Love Commandments)" for that is sin! The Apostle John wrote: *"**For THIS is the LOVE OF GOD, that we keep his (10 Love) commandments**" (I John 5:2)*. In other words, if the "love of God" is inside your heart, you will "keep His 10 Love Commandments". You will DO the things on the "do side" of the 10 Love Commandment list and NOT

DO the things on the "do not side". Listen to <u>precisely</u> what Jesus had against certain of the Jews: *"<u>But I know you, that ye have NOT the **LOVE OF GOD** in you</u>" (John 5:42).* How did Jesus know that? Obviously, <u>BECAUSE THEY DID NOT KEEP (OBEY) GOD'S 10 LOVE COMMANDMENTS</u>! And you will find verse after verse in the Gospel's showing how Jesus pointed out people's—Religious leaders, included!—specific "disobeying of the 10 Love Commandment" sins. Watch for them as you read the Gospels.

Friend, the word "love" or some derivative of it (loved, loveth, etc.) is used over 500 times in the Bible, and it is always a "good report" for those who love God: *"<u>The LORD preserveth all them that LOVE him:</u> but all the wicked will he destroy" (Psalms 145:20).* The Lord saves who? Look, if you seriously want to go to heaven…OBEY God's 10 Love Commandments. I pray the Holy Spirit rises up inside your heart (thoughts, desires, & emotions) driving you to desire to obey God's 10 Love Commandments. Personally, I love them WAY more than money: *"**<u>I love thy commandments above gold</u>**; <u>yea, above fine gold</u>" (Psalms 119:127).* Why is that? Because I <u>know</u> my obedience to them will yield my soul eternal life!

Truly, the <u>WAY</u> leading to eternal life in the Promise Land (Kingdom of God) is just as God had revealed in the story (parable) of the Israelites in the wilderness. All they had to <u>DO</u> was keep God's 10 Love Commandments—choose the "way of love"—and all would have gone well for them. But instead they rebelled and <u>disobeyed</u> God's wishes and all but two (Joshua & Caleb) that came out of Egypt perished in the wilderness!!! (I have more to say about that later.) Friend, God's message still calls out identical today: Follow the WAY of LOVE by obeying the 10 Love Commandments and you will obtain eternal life in God's Kingdom or disobey them and perish.

Chapter 12

Truth

"Thy LAW is the TRUTH…
and all thy (10 Love) COMMANDMENTS are TRUTH"
(Psalms 119:142, 151)

The day Jesus was crucified, he told Pilate, *"To this end was I born, and for this cause came I into the world, that **I should bear witness unto the TRUTH**. Every one that is of the TRUTH heareth my voice" (John 18:37)*. A confused Pilate muttered, *"What is TRUTH?" (John 18:38)*. Ah, the million dollar question! Yet, it is so simple. Do you know what "truth" is? The Bible is clear on its meaning: The "truth" is love (God)! Jesus came to bear witness of love, and everyone that loves hears God's voice.

Since "truth" is love, then "truth" is displayed by "obeying the 10 Love Commandments". THAT is why John wrote (and I am now going to finish the verse from the last chapter): *"And hereby we do know that we know him (God), if we keep his (10 Love) commandments. He that saith, I know him (God), and keepeth not his (10 Love) commandments, is a liar, and **the TRUTH is not in him**" (I John 2:3, 4)*. Wow, WHAT is not in him? The TRUTH!!! This verse proves the "truth" is love, for "love" is shown by "obeying the 10 Love Commandments". Show me a person who disobeys the 10 Love Commandments, and I will show

263

you a person who is devoid of "truth (love)"!

Jesus said: *"And this is the condemnation, that light is come into the world, <u>and men loved darkness rather than light, because their deeds were evil. For every one that doeth evil hateth the light,</u> neither cometh to the light, lest his deeds should be reproved. **<u>But he that DOETH TRUTH cometh to the light</u>**<u>, that his DEEDS may be made manifest, that THEY are wrought in God (Love)"</u> (John 3:19-21)*. Friend, how can someone "<u>DO</u> truth"? And what are these "*deeds (works) wrought in God (love)*"? Come on, reader, how could it be any CLEARER!!! They are the "deeds (works)" of "obeying the 10 <u>LOVE</u> Commandments". Someone who does the things on the "do side" of the 10 Love Commandment chart and does not do the things on the "do not side" <u>DOES truth</u> (love)! In other words, people who live sinfully (do evil by disobeying the 10 Love Commandments) hate the "truth (love)". But people who live righteously (do good by obeying the 10 Love Commandments) love the "truth (love)".

The Apostle Paul penned: *"<u>And with all deceivableness of unrighteousness in them that perish; because</u>* **<u>they received not the LOVE of the TRUTH, that they might be saved</u>**<u>...That they all might be damned who believed not the TRUTH, but had pleasure in unrighteousness"</u> (II Thessalonians 2:10,12)*. Ah, come on! It is glaringly obvious again in this verse what "truth" is! Notice the Bible's juxtaposition: "*believing not the truth (love)*" equals "*having pleasure in unrighteousness (sin)*". Friend, I cannot be anymore straightforward; the "truth" is literally shown by "obeying the 10 Love Commandments"! Do you see? People who willfully sin (disobey the 10 Love Commandments) are those who live in unrighteousness—meaning they <u>do not believe nor will receive God,</u> who IS Love (Truth)—and therefore, they will perish! They CANNOT be saved because they do not <u>DO</u> Truth (love); they would rather enjoy their wicked sin.

Remember Lucifer was the original sinner—which denotes he was the first one to defect from "truth". Addressing the Pharisees, listen to Christ's harsh words: *"Ye are of your father the devil, <u>and the LUST of your father ye will DO</u>. He was a murderer from the beginning, and **<u>abode NOT in the TRUTH, because there is no TRUTH in him</u>**. When he speaketh a lie, he speaketh of his own: for he is a liar, and*

264

the father of it" (John 8:44). Do you recognize how Jesus is naming (listing) "disobedience to 10 Love Commandment things—namely, the 6ᵗʰ (Thou shalt not Murder) & 9ᵗʰ (Thou shalt not lie)" as evidence the *"truth is not in Lucifer"*? In other words, there is literally NO Love in Satan!!! Yes, those who disobey the 10 Love Commandments *"abide NOT in the truth (love)"*! And Lucifer chose to do THAT (sin) by telling a lie and murdering the souls of mankind! Friend, by now you should be completely convinced the "truth" = "love", indicating the "truth" is shown by "obeying the 10 Love Commandments". And, in fact, the 3 things are identical: "truth" = "love" = "obey the 10 Love Commandments".

Moreover, Jesus referred to the Holy Spirit as the "Spirit of Truth": *"But when the Comforter (Holy Spirit) is come, whom I will send unto you from the Father, **EVEN the SPIRIT OF TRUTH,** which proceedeth from the Father" (John 15:26).* See, if one truly becomes *"born again"* of God (Love), they will be compelled to DO truth (obey the 10 Love Commandments) because the "Spirit of Truth" comes from God. This should be no surprise to you because God the Father, Jesus, and the Holy Spirit are all the same: They are all LOVE!!! So, if you willingly disobey the 10 LOVE Commandments, you prove you are NOT *"born again"*, for a *"born again"* person is spiritually reborn of the Spirit of Truth (Love). Are you starting to see how all these Biblical terms are centered around (on) the 10 Love Commandments—i.e. love, truth, and the Holy Spirit? Friend, they are all the same thing! In other words, if you are NOT willfully obeying the 10 Love Commandments… you do not know God (love), the truth is not in you, and you are not *"born again"* of the Holy Spirit!

You should now be able to discern the correct meaning of Jesus' words: *"**IF ye CONTINUE in my WORD,** THEN are ye my disciples indeed; And **YE shall KNOW the TRUTH, and the truth shall make you free"** (John 8:31, 32).* In other words, ONLY by DOING the things Jesus said to DO—which was all based on the 10 Love Commandments—do you prove you *"know the truth"*!!! Do you understand? I know you know what Jesus taught: He taught love (obeying the 10 Love Commandments) was the PATH to obtaining eternal life. Thus, in this verse Jesus is saying we MUST CONTINUE

265

in his word (which again confirms "obtaining eternal life" is a daily journey!) to "*know the truth*" and to have IT "*set us free*". To be blunt, Jesus is declaring "if we <u>constantly</u> obey the 10 Love Commandments (know the truth), we WILL obtain eternal life." This is simple, right? Friend, if we live a life of love, our deeds will prove we "*know the truth*" and that we have been <u>set</u> <u>free</u> from the bondage of sin. "Love" literally sets us free!!! Listen to the result of someone who <u>continues</u> in Christ's words: *"Verily, verily, I (Jesus) say unto you, <u>If a man KEEP my saying, he shall never see (spiritual) death</u>" (John 8:51).*

I pray something is changing inside your spirit (thoughts, desires, & emotions) as you read these life-giving, spiritual words God wrote. I hope a desire is bubbling up inside of your heart compelling you to want to religiously obey God's 10 Love Commandments. We all need to take a long, hard look at our lives and correct everything we are doing wrong! Are you stealing cable illegally? Are you watching pornographic videos? Do you lie to business costumers? Are you cheating on your taxes? The list is endless, but I am warning you to clean (rid) your spiritual temple of <u>all</u> sin. Prepare to meet the Messiah, Jesus Christ, because he is almost here! Then, after making the decision to clean up your life, NEVER go back to sin—i.e. <u>continue</u> in love and you will "*know the truth*", and that WILL set you free!

Peter confirms the "truth" is "love"—something which needs to be <u>obeyed</u>—by instructing: *"<u>Seeing ye have purified your souls in OBEYING the TRUTH through the SPIRIT unto unfeigned LOVE of the brethren, see that ye love one another with a pure heart fervently</u>" (I Peter 1:22).* What can I say? Peter's words tie all these concepts together: If we "*obey the truth (the 10 Love Commandments)*" we prove we have been "*born again*" of the "*Spirit of Truth*" and "*purify our souls*" through love of God and our neighbor! Then, ALL we have to <u>DO</u> to obtain eternal life is <u>continue</u> journeying in love—"*continue to love with a pure heart fervently*". THAT is the "*narrow WAY*" which leads to eternal life that few will find, because most people do NOT want to love (obey the 10 Love Commandments). Most people want to enjoy the pleasure of "not loving (sin)". How about you?

In wrapping up this chapter, I saved the <u>definitive</u> Biblical proof "the 10 Love Commandments" are the "truth" until the end, for the psalmist cried: *"**Thy LAW is the TRUTH**...and **all thy COMMANDMENTS are TRUTH**" (Psalms 119:142, 151)*. Wow! Yes, the "truth" = "obey the 10 (Love) Commandment LAW". One time in Scripture, God even called His 10 Love Commandments the *"Law of Truth"* while speaking through His prophet Malachi: *"The LAW OF TRUTH was in his mouth, and iniquity was not found in his lips: he walked with me in peace and equity, and did turn many away from iniquity (sin)" (Malachi 2:5, 6)*. I pray I can persuade you to turn away from iniquity (sin), for your soul's eternal future is riding on your decision! Truly, obeying the "Law of Truth" can set you free, which means if you "obey the 10 Love Commandments" you will obtain eternal life!

The Psalmist sung: *"**I have chosen the WAY of TRUTH**...**I will run the WAY of thy COMMANDMENTS**...**I shall keep thy LAW**; yea, I shall observe it with my whole heart" (Psalms 119:30, 32, 34)*. Whomever you are reading this book, I want you to know that I love you. My spirit often groans for everyone living on the face of planet Earth, for I long for everyone to know God (love). I do not want ANYONE to end up in the fires of hell, which means I avidly desire for people to follow the *"WAY of TRUTH"*—to obey the 10 Love Commandments— and obtain eternal life: *"Search me, O God, and know my heart; test my thoughts. Point out anything you find in me that makes you sad, **and lead me along the PATH of eternal life**" (Psalms 139:23, Living Bible)*.

Chapter 13

Holy Spirit

"The fruit of the (Holy) Spirit is love, joy, peace, longsuffering,
gentleness, goodness, faith, meekness, temperance:
AGAINST SUCH THERE IS NO LAW"
(Galatians 5:22, 23)

The Holy Spirit is the name of God's Spirit because _"God is_
Spirit" and _"He is holy"_. "Holiness" connotes moral purity, which is
completely satisfied by love. (This is why the Bible states _"God IS_
Love".) Consequently, the "Holy Spirit" must be the "Spirit of Love"—
or as we learned in the last chapter...the Spirit of Truth! Webster
defines "Holy Spirit" as the active presence of God (love) in human
life. The Bible also calls the "Holy Spirit" the "Holy Ghost" because
it is invisible. But even though invisible, it is very, very real! For it is
spirit, which means it affects one's thoughts, desires, & emotions.

Jesus told Nicodemus, _"**Except a man be BORN AGAIN**, he_
cannot see the kingdom of God" (John 3:3). The phrase _"born again"_
literally means "reborn, spiritually, of God's Holy Spirit". When this
happens to a person, their spirit (heart)—thoughts, desires, & emotions—
change. Jesus described the immaterial, infilling process of the Holy
Spirit to Nicodemus as such: _"The wind bloweth where it listeth, and_
thou hearest the sound thereof, but canst not tell whence it cometh,

269

and wither it goeth: **_so is every one that is BORN of the SPIRIT_** _(John 3:8)_. In other words, we cannot tell how the Holy Spirit enters (or leaves!) a soul, but we <u>can</u> tell when it is present in someone—just like we can <u>hear</u> the sound of the wind—because we can see its affects.

And what are the visible affects of the Holy Spirit having invaded someone's soul? Love, love, love!!! Friend, people with the Holy Spirit dwelling inside them cherish obeying the 10 <u>Love</u> Commandments. THAT is the change that occurs in their heart! John wrote: _"<u>little children, abide in him</u>; that, when he (Jesus) shall appear, we may have confidence, and not be ashamed before him at his coming. If ye know that he (Holy Spirit) is righteous, **<u>ye know that every one that DOETH righteousness is BORN of him</u>**" (I John 2:28, 29)_. What does _"doeth righteousness"_ mean? It means "obey the 10 Love Commandments"! THOSE thoughts and deeds manifesting in someone's life <u>prove</u> they have been _"born again"_ of God's Holy Spirit: _"Beloved, <u>let us love one another</u>: for <u>love is of God</u>; and <u>every one that loveth is BORN of God</u>, and knoweth God" (I John 4:7)_.

Subsequently, in searching our spirit (thoughts, desires, & emotions) it is <u>easy</u> to detect if we have been _"born again"_ of God's Holy Spirit. If you have an overwhelming desire in your spirit to "obey the 10 Love Commandments," you are born again!!! If you are a business owner and you cringe at even the thought of lying (falsifying the books) on your taxes, your spirit is "born again". If you hate idolatry (love of money), your spirit is "born again". If a sense of dread envelopes your spirit when confronted with an adulterous (pornographic material) situation, your spirit is "born again"! If you feel a sickening feeling in your stomach when someone uses God's name in a derogatory manner, you are "born again". Do you understand? The change is in your heart (thoughts, desires, & emotions)! God's Holy Spirit will drive you to love (obey the 10 Love Commandments), which is to forsake evil: _"**<u>We know that whosoever is BORN of GOD sinneth not</u>**; but <u>he that is begotten of God keepeth himself</u>, and that wicked one toucheth him not" (I John 5:18)_.

Furthermore, since the Holy Spirit (Ghost) is spirit, it can form words in your spirit (mind) and speak them out your mouth! Jesus spoke about Israel's king David, who lived around 1,000 BC: _"For_

270

David himself said by the Holy Ghost..." (Mark 12:36). Do you see? God's Holy Spirit can speak through your lips! Jesus, knowing the persecution the Disciples would encounter after he left, comforted them by saying, *"But when they shall lead you, and deliver you up, take no THOUGHT before hand what ye shall speak, neither do ye premeditate: but whatsoever shall be given you in that hour, that speak ye: **for it is not ye that speak, but the Holy Ghost***" *(Mark 13:11).* The Old Testament prophets spoke under the unction of the Holy Ghost: *"For the prophecy came not in old time by the will of man: but holy men of God spake as they were moved by the HOLY GHOST" (II Peter 1:21).*

Obviously, the "Holy Spirit" has always existed because it is God's Spirit. John the Baptist received the Holy Ghost while yet in his mother's womb: *"For he shall be great in the sight of the Lord, and shall drink neither wine nor strong drink; and he shall be filled with the HOLY GHOST, even from his mother's womb" (Luke 1:15).* Wow! The Holy Ghost gave Simeon a wonderful message about the coming Messiah: *"And it was revealed unto him by the HOLY GHOST, that he should not see death, before he had seen the Lord's Christ" (Luke 2:26).* Friend, it is the Holy Ghost that has revealed to me the things I have written in this book. I could have perused the Bible's stories a thousand times over and never deciphered the true spiritual meaning behind the many details. The Biblical secrets I have disclosed in this book were given to me by the Holy Ghost to alert the world of Jesus Christ's imminent return and to make-ready a holy people prepared to meet him. So please do not take this book's message lightly!

The book of Acts is chocked-full of stories of the Holy Ghost being poured out on people in the most dramatic way! It appears a deeper power of the Holy Spirit was attainable to mankind after Jesus conquered Satan's power over mankind's spiritual death. The first believers to be baptized with the Holy Ghost began speaking in foreign languages they did not know! In other words, the Holy Ghost was literally controlling their heart and tongue: *"And they were all filled with the HOLY GHOST, and began to speak with other tongues, as the Spirit gave them utterance" (Acts 2:4).* Wow!!! I know for an absolute fact the Holy Ghost still comes in this spectacular way, because it happened to me!!! Allow me to share my experience with you.

271

After my deceased father's shadowed profile appeared on my refrigerator door on May 6th, 2005, God immediately began dealing with me to correct certain obvious sins in my life. An inner voice inside of me desired I live right, and thankfully I continued to make all the right decisions! (Now at the time I did not realize my sins were ALL encompassed by the 10 Love Commandments, for God had not yet given me the revelation that ALL sin is based on "disobedience to the 10 Love Commandments".) But if you will remember from the *Introduction*, at the same time I was also ferociously researching everything I could get my hands on relating to God and His Bible—creationism, archaeology, astronomy, etc—and, amazingly, everywhere I turned I found evidence supporting the truth behind God's 7th day (sundown Friday to sundown Saturday) Sabbath. When I finally discovered time scholars profess the 7 day week is an unbroken cycle—traceable back to the time of Moses!—I was convinced of my sin. Simple, honest rational said, "Something sinister is behind the Sabbath day transfer, but now I know I can keep the Sabbath on the EXACT day of the week God intended it from Creation, the same day Jesus and all the prophets did": *"And he (Jesus) came to Nazareth, where he had been brought up: and, as his custom was, he went into the synagogue on the Sabbath day" (Luke 4:16).* (Little did I know, God simply wanted me to obey His 4th Love Commandment, too!)

By this time, it was May 2006—only 1 year after God's dramatic visitation with me—and I had come a long way in aligning my life up to God's 10 Love Commandments (repenting by ridding my life of sin!), but now the final piece to the "righteousness-puzzle" was about to fall into place. Fully persuaded and extremely thrilled to honor and respect God's wishes by observing His Holy 7th day Sabbath, I anxiously awaited for the sky to turn dark on a Friday night. When it did, I turned off the lights in my apartment, lit a single red candle, and knelt down close to it on my living room floor. With butterflies in my stomach, I told God, "Here I am, Lord." The love and joy I felt in my heart towards God that night is beyond description, for I absolutely KNEW in my heart that I was doing something the Creator of the entire universe wanted me to DO. Then slowly, by the candle's light, I began reading in my Bible: *"In the beginning God created the heaven and the*

272

earth..." My joy has never ceased!

A Sabbath or so later, in June 2006, I was lying on the living room carpet on a Saturday morning listening to a preacher cassette in my karaoke tape deck. (Yep, the same tape deck, sitting in the same place, which played the Joe Diffie song the night dad's profile appeared a year earlier!) Knowing the sermon was nearly finished, I got up to walk over to the tape deck to remove it. As I approached the karaoke box I was instantaneously arrested by an unseen force. It hit as quick as a lightning bolt! Immediately, my legs and feet felt like they weighed 100 pounds a piece and I remember thinking, "My God, I can't move my feet!" I was rooted to the floor. Then, slowly, an invisible weight began increasing pressure on my shoulders until I was unable to withstand it. Still standing, but being bent forward from the waist, I wondered what was happening to my trembling body.

After what must have lasted 5 to 10 minutes, the powerful pressure gradually let up and I was able to stand up straight again. But I had to concentrate real hard to make my feet move, and eventually I was able to gingerly take a couple of steps back toward the center of my living room. Then, all of a sudden, my mouth burst forth in some African tribal sounding language! It poured out of my belly like a river's flowing water. It was uncontrollable and unstoppable. Circling the living room floor with hands raised, I was now speaking in other tongues!!! Only then did I grasp what had happened to me, because I knew the story in the book of Acts...I had been baptized in the Holy Ghost!

From that day onward I could feel the change in my spirit (thoughts, desires, & emotions). I could literally feel LOVE inside of me! All the fruits (characteristics) of the Holy Spirit Paul listed in his letter to the Galatians were oozing out of me: *"But **the fruit of the (Holy) Spirit is love, joy, peace, longsuffering, gentleness, goodness, faith, meekness, temperance**: AGAINST SUCH THERE IS NO LAW. And they that are Christ's have crucified the flesh with the affections and lusts"* (Galatians 5:22-24). I received a patience (longsuffering) never before imaginable: I could feel it inside me when driving in my car, for nothing anyone did in their car—e.g. slow driving in front of me, not moving when the light turned green, etc.—upset me anymore! Being single, I used to have moments of loneliness, but now I had only pure joy! I could write endlessly on the heart-transformation that occurred inside of me after the Holy Spirit possessed me, and yet I still could not accurately do it justice. But I <u>know</u> it is Love! Take note: the 9 "fruits" of the Holy Spirit manifested in the heart of someone "*born again*" are really just the personality traits of someone who keeps (obeys) God's 10 Love Commandments—think about it!

Around 6 months later, I ran across Jesus' words in the book of John and instantly knew <u>WHY</u> I had been baptized in the Holy Spirit: ***"If ye love me, keep my (10 Love) commandments. And I (Jesus) will pray the Father, and he shall give you another Comforter, that he may abide with you for ever; Even the Spirit of truth****...He that hath my commandments, and keepeth them, he it is that loveth me: and he that loveth me shall be loved of my Father, and I will love him, AND WILL MANIFEST MYSELF TO HIM" (John 14:15-21).* Wow, did you get that? Jesus said **IF** <u>we willingly choose to keep his 10 Love Commandments</u>—which is to love him—**THEN** <u>he will personally ask God to give us the Holy Spirit</u>!!! Do you see it? Friend, you ought to be shouting by now, for THERE is the Biblical key to receiving the Holy Ghost! Is that not awesome? If there ever was a motivating reason to obey **ALL** of the 10 Love Commandments, there it is!

Eventually I began to find other Bible verses supporting the correlation between "obeying the 10 Love Commandments" and "receiving the Holy Ghost". Not long after Jesus' ascension, the Apostle Peter identified the connection while speaking the truth boldly to the high priest and council in Jerusalem,: *"We are his (Jesus) witnesses of these things; and **so is also the HOLY GHOST, whom God hath given to them that OBEY him**" (Acts 5:32).* Do you see? Friend, it does not get any clearer! God gives his Holy Spirit to whom? To those that obey him! Obey what? The 10 Love Commandments, just like Jesus said to <u>DO</u>.

The first martyr, Stephen, made the connection, for he understood perfectly well "<u>disobeying</u> the 10 Love Commandments" is actually "<u>resisting</u> the Holy Ghost"—which is exactly what many of the Pharisees were doing! See, you can be extremely religious, go to church every time the doors are open, and know every name and date in the Bible, but if you refuse to quit sinning, you are REJECTING the Holy Spirit and the "*born again*" process! The reason the Pharisees hated Jesus so much was because he continually called them out on their "disobedience to the 10 Love Commandments"—e.g. pride, love of money, adultery, thievery, etc. They were so sure they were God's children because they were pious and religious, yet they did not know God (Love) ! With a face glowing full of the Holy Ghost, Stephen fatally called them out on their wickedness one last time: *"Ye stiffnecked and uncircumcised in heart and ears, ye do always RESIST the HOLY GHOST...Who have received the law by the disposition of angels, and have NOT KEPT IT"* *(Acts 7:51, 53)*. Do you see? HOW were they resisting the Holy Ghost? By NOT keeping the 10 Love Commandment Law of God given to them by Moses!!! Friend, could it be any more apparent? If you want to be *"born again"* of the Holy Ghost, OBEY God's 10 Love Commandments and Jesus will ask the Father to send it to you air mail express! But if you continue making excuses to justify your "disobeying of the 10 Love Commandments"... YOU are resisting the Holy Ghost's (God's Spirit of Love's) desire to come into your heart.

Inflamed at Stephen's words, the Pharisees (church leaders) went wild in a demonic rage and ran upon him, stoning him to death: *"When they heard these things, they were CUT to the heart, and they gnashed on him with their teeth...and stopped their ears, and ran upon him with one accord...and stoned him"* *(Acts 7:54-58)*. But even at the point of death, the Holy Ghost (Love) was glowing like the noon day sun on Stephen's face as he cried out, *"Lord, lay not this sin to their charge"* *(Acts 7:60)*. Wow, what kind of a "spirit in a man" can love like THAT while men are busting open his head with rocks? Friend, ONLY one full of the Holy Ghost!!! The "Holy Spirit" is pure love, and when it is inside of you it is impossible to conceal, for it will flow out of your heart like rivers of living water.

Lastly, in absolute definitive proof of the link between "keeping the 10 Love Commandments" and "receiving the Holy Spirit," is the meaning behind and fulfillment of God's 4th Feast day which He instituted with the Israelites in the wilderness. (Remember the first 3 Feasts—Passover, Unleavened Bread, & First Fruits—were all fulfilled by Jesus the week he died.) Well, the 4th Feast was called the "Feast of Weeks" and God instituted it with the Israelites in the wilderness to commemorate, yearly, the day He gathered them around the base of Mount Sinai and boomingly spoke the 10 Love Commandments to them. THAT day was 50 days after the "Feast of First Fruits", which occurred during Passover week. The fulfillment of this Feast came the year of Jesus' death—mankind's 4,000th year—when exactly 50 days after Christ's resurrection around 120 believers were gathered in an Upper Room, praying, and the Holy Ghost descended on them in flames of fire, filling them all with the Holy Ghost with the evidence of speaking in other tongues! In other words, the Holy Spirit was given on the SAME (yearly) day that God had given (spoke) the 10 Love Commandments! Do you see the link? Friend, the events are intimately connected: "obeying the 10 Love Commandments" is the path to receiving the Holy Ghost!

Let us take a closer look at God's 4th Feast: In the wilderness, 1334 BC, God instructed Moses on WHEN to keep the **Feast of Weeks**: *"And ye shall count unto you from the morrow after the sabbath, from the day that ye brought the sheaf of the wave offering (First Fruits); seven sabbaths shall be complete: Even unto the morrow after the seventh sabbath shall ye number FIFTY DAYS; and ye shall offer a new meat offering unto the LORD" (Leviticus 23:15, 16).* In other words, the "Feast of Weeks" was celebrated 50 days after the "Feast of First Fruits". The Greeks renamed the "Feast of Weeks" to "Pentecost" because that means "fifty". That name has stuck, and today Christians still refer to the Feast of Weeks as "Pentecost", but it is really God's 4th special Feast He instituted with Israel, commemorating the giving of the moral Law (the 10 Love Commandments) and eventually the Holy Ghost [See Figure #5, page 182].

Let us now delve, intelligently, into the Biblically recorded action immediately following the Israelites exodus out of Egypt on the night of Passover, the 14th of Nissan. Pharaoh's army drowned in the Red Sea most likely 7 days later on the 21st of Nissan, which was the last day of God's "Feast of Unleavened Bread". Three days after the "Red Sea incident" the Israelites were desperate for water: *"So Moses brought Israel from the Red Sea...and they went THREE days in the wilderness, and found no water" (Exodus 15:22).* So God provided water for them that day by sweetening bitter water they later found and

276

said to them: *"If thou wilt diligently hearken to the voice of the LORD thy God, and __wilt DO that which is right in his sight, and wilt give ear to his commandments__..."* *(Exodus 15:26)*. Now how could God ask the Israelites to *"__DO__ that which is right in His sight and give ear to his Commandments"* when they still had not reached Mount Sinai and received the 10 Love Commandments? Friend, this is just more proof the Israelites ALREADY knew (and ALL mankind had/has ALWAYS known) God's 10 Love Commandments. (Remember, Abraham kept them all over 600 years earlier!)

But what happened next positively verifies mankind even knew about God's 4th Love Commandment (Keep the 7th day Sabbath Holy) before God officially spoke and wrote the 10 Love Commandments on stone. Listen, within one month after leaving Egypt the Israelites had run out of food provisions, and they were hungry: *"And they took their journey...and all the congregation...of Israel came unto the **wilderness of Sin**...on the FIFTEENTH DAY of the SECOND MONTH after their departing out of the land of Egypt. And the whole congregation... murmured against Moses...ye have brought us forth into the wilderness, to kill this whole assembly with hunger" (Exodus 16:1-3)*. So it is now only (exactly) 1 lunar month after the night they escaped Egypt; it was here and now that God began supernaturally feeding the Israelites with *"manna from heaven"*—which He would continue to do for their entire 40 year wilderness journey!

But watch, God told the Israelites to gather enough manna for 2 days on the 6th day of the week because there would be no manna on the ground during the 7th day Sabbath: *"Six days ye shall gather it; but on the seventh day, which is the sabbath, in it there shall be none" (Exodus 16:26)*. Now wait a minute, the Israelites still have NOT reached Mount Sinai—where God will thunderously speak the 10 Love Commandments to them! So this "7th day Sabbath thing" should have confused the Israelites, right? No!!! I told you mankind had/has always known about God's 7 day week and 7th day Sabbath—even since Creation! But unfortunately, some Israelites went out to collect manna on the Sabbath: *"And it came to pass, that there went out some of the people on the seventh day for to gather, and they found none" (Exodus 16:27)*. God was extremely disappointed: *"And the LORD said unto*

277

Moses, ___How long REFUSE ye to keep my commandments and my___ ___laws"___ *(Exodus 16:28).* See, the Israelites STILL had NOT reached Mount Sinai, yet God inquired of them <u>again</u> why they would NOT obey His laws!

Finally, in the 3rd month after leaving Egypt, the Israelites reached Mount Sinai: *"In the third month, when the children of Israel were gone forth out of the land of Egypt...they...were come to the desert of Sinai, and had pitched in the wilderness; and there <u>Israel camped before the mount</u>" (Exodus 19:1, 2).* It was here and now that God descended on Mount Sinai in a thick cloud with thunder, lightning, and fire, making the mountain tremble while speaking the 10 Love Commandments! The Jews today celebrate this as having occurred on the 50th day after exiting Egypt on the 14th day of the 1st month of Nissan—do the math. Thus, God's "<u>giving</u> of the 10 Love Commandment Law day" in the wilderness was to be the same day He would and did "<u>give</u> the Holy Ghost (Spirit of Truth) to the believers in the Upper Room! No wonder Jesus declared, "***If ye love me, KEEP MY COMMANDMENTS. And I will pray the Father, and he shall give you another Comforter, that he may abide with you for ever; Even the Spirit of truth***" *(John 14:15-21).* Friend, the two concepts—"receiving (obeying) the 10 Love Commandments" & "receiving the Holy Spirit"—are intrinsically linked, for the two amazing events happened on the same day of the Jewish year!

The church today <u>desperately</u> needs to get back to some old fashioned, sin-fleeing, 10-Love-Commandment keeping, Law of Love abiding preaching. Friend, God is testing each and every one of us! He is proving whether you will walk in His laws or not. I can picture Jesus turning to the Father God and saying, "Do you see Gabriel down there Father? Look at him keeping our Holy 7th day Sabbath! In a world that now predominately believes 'obeying our 10 Love Commandments' is worthless, he has received the <u>truth</u> and <u>loves</u> us enough to <u>keep</u> <u>ALL</u> of our 10 Love Commandments. Let's send him a gift, Father, and fill him with the Holy Ghost!" (By the way, at the time I was filled with the Holy Ghost in June of 2006 I knew NOTHING about God's 7 Holy Feasts, but when I did learn about them, one day it hit me in 2008 that I must have been filled with the Holy Ghost around the time

278

of Pentecost! So I looked up online the day of Pentecost in 2006 and found it occurred on Saturday June 3rd of 2006! Searching in my diary for the exact Saturday in June that I was filled with the Holy Ghost I noticed I did not log it. But other factors—too involved to mention—lead me to believe (around 99% sure) that June 3rd was the very day of my infilling! Yes, friend, I believe I was filled with Holy Ghost on the very day of Pentecost, only a few weeks after making the decision to obey God's 4th Love Commandment, and did not even know it at the time!!!) Listen, do yourself a huge favor and please take the time to research and learn HOW God's Holy 7th day Sabbath got switched to the 1st day of the week and who did it. Here is your Biblical clue: *"And* **_he (Satan) shall_** *speak great words against the most High, and shall wear out the saints of the most High, and **_think to change TIMES and LAWS_**" (Daniel 7:25).*

Friend, Satan detests God's 10 Love Commandment Law because he knows our obedience to IT will ensure us eternal life in God's Kingdom. Therefore, Satan continually tries to change them, hide them, and tear them off walls. Do you want to enrage Satan? Just determine in your heart, "Satan, I will no longer listen to and believe your lies that God's 10 Love Commandments are obsolete!" Then, start obeying **ALL** of the 10 <u>Love</u> Commandments, devotedly. It would be horrifying to Lucifer to find the whole world "repented of sin" and turned back to keeping God's true 7th day Sabbath—ignoring the *"time"* he worked so hard to change—for Satan knows God's promise of <u>blessing</u> to those who *"delight themselves in the Lord"* by keeping His 7th day Sabbath Holy. He also knows God will fill everyone with the Holy Spirit, if they will only repent of sin by willingly choosing to obey His 10 Love Commandments. And THAT is, truly, Satan's worst nightmare…a world full of people that love!!!

Chapter 14

Bearing Fruit

"Ye shall know them by their fruits…
every good tree bringeth forth GOOD FRUIT;
but a corrupt tree bringeth forth EVIL FRUIT"
(Matthew 7:16, 17)

"Bearing fruit" is another Biblical concept that relates to whether someone will obtain eternal life or not: For only those folks who "bear <u>GOOD</u> fruit" will obtain eternal life! (Note: In the Bible, the word "good" is usually dropped, but understood, in the phrase "bearing fruit".) And what does the phrase "bearing fruit" really represent? It is simply a Biblical analogy describing the works (or deeds) of someone who "obeys the 10 Love Commandments". In other words, it is an expression describing the actions of someone who DOES the things on the "do side" of the 10 Love Commandment chart and DOES NOT DO the things on the "do not side". Thus, "bearing fruit" depicts those people who LOVE—e.g. honor God's name, keep the Sabbath, tell the truth, feed the hungry, forgive, etc. See, THESE are the eternal-life-rewarding deeds of someone "bearing the good fruit of love". Are you starting to see how these Biblical terms are all about the same thing? Friend, the Biblical concept of "bearing fruit" is just another way Jesus Christ confirmed "obeying the 10 Love Commandments" is the WAY to eternal life!

One day Jesus spoke an analogy, *"I AM the true vine...Abide in me, and I in you. **As the branch cannot BEAR FRUIT of itself, except it abide in the vine**; no more can ye, except ye abide in me. I am the vine, ye are the branches: **He that abideth in me, and I in him, the same bringeth forth much FRUIT**: for without me ye can do nothing (John 15:1-5)*. Are you confused? Look, this analogy is ALL SPIRITUAL in meaning! Do you understand? To *"abide in Christ"* means to abide in the Spirit of the man. And what is that? It is LOVE!!! Jesus came from God, and God is Love; thus, Christ was nothing but love, too. And of course, because he was SINLESS! (Remember sin is just anything that is NOT love.) So, to "bear fruit"—bear the good fruit of love—a soul must *"abide in (the Spirit of) Christ (love)"* just as fruit can only produce on a branch that is connected to a vine which feeds it nutrients and water from the soil. Did you ever see fruit growing on a branch not connected to anything?

Listen to Christ explain his own analogy as he continues: *"**If ye abide in me, and my WORDS abide in you**...that ye BEAR MUCH FRUIT; so shall ye be my disciples...continue ye in MY LOVE. **If ye keep my (10 Love) commandments, ye shall abide in my love**; even as I have kept my Father's commandments, and abide in his love"* (John 15:7-10). Ah, THERE IT IS: It all goes right back to "obeying the 10 Love Commandments!!! To *"abide in Christ"* means to *"abide in his words of love"*, which means to "keep (obey) his 10 Love Commandments!" Do you see? I told you these Biblical concepts ALL center on "obeying the 10 Love Commandments"! Look, the vine is love, which is the Spirit of Christ (or God); thus, if a soul attaches itself to the "vine of love", it produces good fruit—i.e. obeys the 10 Love Commandments. So to *"abide in Christ"* really just means to "keep (obey) the 10 Love Commandments". Notice, Jesus said, *"If ye BEAR MUCH FRUIT, ye are my DISCIPLES."* But remember what Jesus said earlier: *"By THIS shall all men know that ye are my DISCIPLES, if ye have LOVE one to another"* (John 13:35). Do you see? These two Scriptures prove "bearing fruit" simply means "to love", which is only shown by obeying the 10 Love Commandments. Yes, the two concepts are precisely the same!

On the flip side of the coin, to *"NOT abide in Christ"* means

282

to "NOT obey the 10 Love Commandments". And sure enough, the Apostle John wrote: *"**Whosoever transgresseth (disobeys the 10 Love Commandments), and ABIDETH NOT in the doctrine of Christ, hath NOT God**. He that abideth in the doctrine of Christ, he hath both the Father and the Son"* (II John 1:9). Here, John calls Christ's words the *"doctrine of Christ"*. What is that? It is "to obey the 10 Love Commandments"! Christ's doctrine was/is for mankind to love God and their neighbor. Therefore, John declares those souls who love (obey the 10 Love Commandments) *"abide in Christ,"* having both God and Jesus!

Now we learned when Adam & Eve ate the forbidden fruit of the Tree of the Knowledge of Good & Evil, all the souls of mankind were born knowing the difference between good (love) & evil (sin)—defined by obeying or disobeying the 10 Love Commandments, respectively: *"And the LORD God said, **Behold, the man is become as one of us, to know good and evil**"* (Genesis 3:22). Understanding this, John wrote: *"**Beloved, follow NOT that which is EVIL, but that which is GOOD**. HE THAT DOETH GOOD IS OF GOD: but he that doeth evil hath not seen God"* (III John 1:11). See, God's message has NEVER changed since the very dawn of time: do good (love) and live, or do evil (sin) and perish! In other words, stop living your life in disobedience to the 10 Love Commandments (doing evil) and start living it in obedience to them (doing good)! This same message rings out loud and clear down through the entire corridor of time.

Around 800 BC, God vehemently warned Israel through the prophet Amos: *"For many and great are your sins. I know them all so well...**Be good, flee evil—and live!** ...Hate evil and love the good...I want to see a mighty flood of justice—a torrent of doing good"* (Amos 5:12, 14, 15, 24, Living Bible). Yes, ALL mankind has known the difference between good & evil, and they have ALL had a chance (choice) to either obey God and obtain eternal life or disobey Him and perish. Remember, Paul wrote: *"He (God) will punish sin (evil) wherever it is found. He will punish the heathen when they sin, even though they NEVER had God's written laws, **for down in their hearts they know right from wrong. God's laws are written within them**; their own conscience accuses them, or sometimes excuses them. And God will punish the Jews for sinning because they HAVE his written* *laws but don't obey them. They know what is right but don't do it.* ***After all, salvation is not given to those who know what to do, UNLESS THEY DO IT****.* *The day will surely come when at God's command Jesus Christ will judge the secret lives of everyone, their inmost thoughts and motives" (Romans 2:12-16 Living Bible).* Yes, friend, God has not changed His way of thinking over time! He still passionately hates sin (evil) and will destroy all those who <u>willfully</u> continue sinning (disobey His 10 Love Commandments)!

So, with respect to *"bearing fruit"* or *"abiding in Christ"* (during mankind's first 4,000 years on Earth) here is the truth: <u>Anyone</u> who lived a life in obedience to God's 10 Love Commandments—chose the WAY of good (love) over the WAY of evil (sin)—was "bearing fruit" and *"abiding in Christ"* even though they never heard the name of the Earthly man Jesus Christ! Do you understand? See, <u>anyone</u> who lives a life of love *"abides in the Spirit of Christ,"* because he is love. Is there Biblical evidence to support this? Yes, of course! The Apostle Paul, writing in reference to the Israelites 40 year wilderness experience (which occurred over 1,300 years before mankind knew anything of the <u>Earthly</u> man Jesus Christ) wisely said: *"Moreover, brethren, <u>I would not that ye should be ignorant</u>, how that all our fathers (Israelites) were under the cloud, and all passed through the sea; and were all baptized unto Moses in the cloud...<u>And did all eat the same SPIRITUAL meat;</u> <u>And did all drink the same SPIRITUAL drink:</u> **<u>for they drank of that SPIRITUAL Rock that followed them: and that ROCK WAS CHRIST</u>***" (I Corinthians 10:1-4).* Ah, do you see? The Israelites ate and drank of the SPIRIT of CHRIST? What does that mean? It means "LOVE". God gave them the Law of Love (the 10 Love Commandments) yet, even after continually hearing (drinking and eating) the message of love (Christ), they still disobeyed it and DID NOT LOVE!

In the Israelite story (parable), the supernatural manna and water God supplied the Israelites with in the wilderness was a type of the "spiritual food & water" we are all to eat and drink to live eternally. That food and drink is "love," which is the Spirit of Christ! This truth has never changed since the dawn of time. THAT is why Jesus said, *"<u>I am the bread of life</u>. Your fathers did eat manna in the wilderness, and are dead. This is the bread which cometh down from heaven, that a man*

284

may eat thereof, and not die. I am the living bread which came down from heaven: if any man eat of this bread, he shall live for ever" (John 6:48-51). Friend, ANYONE living throughout history who obeyed the 10 Love Commandments was eating and drinking of "spiritual Christ" and becoming love, for LOVE was/is the living bread that comes from God, which if ate will sustain a soul for eternity!

Look, eating physical food only sustains your physical body, which keeps your spirit attached to it. But the <u>real</u> food we are to eat is God's WORDS, which are the 10 Love Commandments. If you eat THAT food you will live forever! Jesus said, *"It is written, <u>Man shall not live by bread alone, but by every WORD that proceedeth out of the mouth of God" (Matthew 4:4).</u>* Jesus was quoting here what Moses wrote in Deuteronomy 8:3. Remember, God's (spoken & written) WORDS to mankind were/are to "obey the 10 Love Commandments." It is very sad to see people deeply concerned about getting and having physical food to eat, but caring little about obeying God's words! Yet, obeying God's 10 Love Commandments is the "spiritual food" that would sustain their soul forever! Friend, you should be a million times more concerned about aligning your life up to God's 10 Love Commandments, then concerned about having and eating physical food!

And what did Christ confirm will happen to a soul who *"does NOT abide in Christ"* (does NOT keep the 10 Love Commandments)? Jesus said: *"If a man abide <u>NOT</u> in me, <u>he is cast forth as a branch, and is withered</u>; and men gather them, and **cast them into the fire, and they are burned"** (John 15:6).* Do you understand what Jesus is saying? He is referring to Judgment Day and the *"lake of fire"* prepared for the Devil and his angels. All who do not walk in love (obey the 10 commandments) will be thrown into the fire and perish! Again, Jesus said, *"**<u>Ye shall know them by their fruits</u>**. Do men gather grapes of thorns, or figs of thistles? Even so <u>every good tree bringeth forth GOOD FRUIT; but a corrupt tree bringeth forth EVIL FRUIT.</u> A good tree cannot bring forth evil fruit, neither can a corrupt tree bring forth good fruit. **<u>Every tree that bringeth NOT forth good fruit (love) is hewn down, and cast into the fire"</u>** (Matthew 7:16-19).* What a clear, concise, harmonious message the Bible paints!

And of course, John the Baptist preached the same message:

*"**Bring forth therefore (good) fruits meet for repentance**...And now also the axe is laid unto the root of the trees: **therefore every tree which bringeth NOT forth good fruit is hewn down, and cast into the fire**" (Matthew 3:8, 10).* Do you understand what John meant by saying, *"Bring forth (good) fruits MEET for repentance"*? The word "meet" was translated from the Greek word *"axios"* meaning: worthy, deserving, in keeping with, corresponding to. Do you see? John's words prove TRUE REPENTENCE is ONLY proved by "bearing fruit"!!! Again, I told you these Biblical terms are all related, for "turning away from sin" (or to stop sinning) by choosing to obey the 10 Love Commandments is "bearing fruit"—which IS repentance! Therefore, "REPENTENCE" IS the good fruit mankind is to bear. John knew a person had to "stop sinning" and "start loving" to PROVE they had repented. In other words, if you are still willfully sinning (disobeying the 10 Love Commandments), you have NOT repented, you are NOT "bearing fruit", and you have a future date in a hellish inferno if you do not change! THIS is what John the Baptist was warning the people of his day about.

Certain ones asked John what they should DO to prove they had repented of sin; listen to John the Baptist's "do side of the 10 Love Commandment chart" answers in the following dialogue: *"The crowd replied, "What do you want us to DO?" "If you have two coats,"* he replied, *"give one to the poor (8th Love Commandment). If you have extra food, give it away to those who are hungry (8th Love Commandment)." Even tax collectors—notorious for their corruption—came to be baptized and asked, "How shall we prove to you that we have abandoned our sins?" "By your honesty (9th Love Commandment),"* he replied. *"Make sure you collect no more taxes than the Roman government requires you to (2nd Love Commandment)." "And us,"* asked some soldiers, *"what about us?" John replied, "Don't extort money by threats and violence (6th Love Commandment); don't accuse anyone of what you know he didn't do (9th Love Commandment); and be content with your pay (10th Love Commandment)!"* (Luke 3:10-14, Living Bible). Wow, what a beautiful passage of Scripture—one of my favorite in the whole Bible!!! John knew EXACTLY what a soul MUST DO to obtain eternal life; they MUST prove they have repented of sin by "obeying the 10

286

Love Commandments", and then God will one day forgive their past sins through Christ's sinless, sacrificial, spiritual death on the cross.

In summary, the "<u>GOOD</u> fruit" Christ commands our souls to bear is to "obey the 10 Love Commandments" and the "EVIL fruit" we are to avoid producing is "disobeying the 10 Love Commandments. Obedience leads to righteousness and eternal life, while disobedience leads to sin and eternal death. Paul penned: *"For <u>when ye were the servants of sin, ye were free from righteousness</u>. **<u>What FRUIT had ye then in those things whereof ye are now ashamed? For the end of those things is death</u>**. But now being made <u>free from sin, and become servants to God (Love), ye have your (good) FRUIT unto holiness, and the end everlasting life</u>" (Romans 7:20-22)*. Could it be any simpler? If you want words describing the "(good) fruit" we are to bear, they are the "fruits" of the Holy Spirit we learned about in the last chapter: *"But the **<u>FRUIT of the (Holy) Spirit is love, joy, peace, longsuffering, gentleness, goodness, faith, meekness, temperance</u>**" (Galatians 5:22)*. Friend, these are the "(good) fruits" we MUST bear to obtain eternal life! Are these fruits blooming out of your spirit? I pray they are: *"That ye might walk worthy of the Lord unto all pleasing, **<u>being FRUITFUL in every GOOD WORK</u>**, and <u>increasing in the knowledge of God (love)</u> ... unto <u>all patience and longsuffering with joyfulness</u>" (Colossians 1:10, 11)*.

Chapter 15

Faith

"WHAT DOTH IT PROFIT, my brethren,
though a man say he hath faith,
and have not works?"
(James 2:14)

The word "faith" is probably the most misunderstood word in the entire Bible. We <u>must</u> return to the original Greek word used in the ancient New Testament manuscripts to ascertain its correct meaning. The word "faith" was translated from the Greek word "*pistis*" meaning: <u>faith, faithfulness, BELIEF, trust,</u> **with an implication that ACTIONS based on that trust may follow**. Ah, so the original Greek word translated "faith" denoted an "<u>action</u> based faith"!

Notice also "faith" means "belief". Consequently, when you come across the word "believe" in the Bible, it is IDENTICAL in meaning to the word "faith", for faith is believing! Therefore, the original Greek word translated "believe" in the Bible is "*pisteuō*" meaning: <u>to believe, put one's FAITH in, trust,</u> **with an implication that ACTIONS based on that trust may follow**. Do you see? The word "faith" is equal to the word "believe"; and both words are based on actions (works). In other words, the <u>Biblical</u> terms "faith" and "believe" signify whatever we have "faith in" or "believe in" will <u>CHANGE the way we live</u>!

One day God furnished me with a wonderful story illustrating the ACCURATE meaning of the Biblical words "faith" and "believe": A certain man was diagnosed with a painful stomach ulcer, and one day (over the phone) he told a friend about his affliction. Excited, the friend said, "Oh, man, I have the cure for you! All you have to <u>DO</u> is drink 16 ounces of carrot & cabbage juice daily for a week or two and your pain will be gone and your ulcerous tissue will heal. In fact," the friend continued, "I'll even let you borrow my juicer."

Well, a month went by and the man never came for the juicer, so the friend called him up one day and inquired, "How's your ulcer doing?"

"Oh, it hurts terrible," the man groaned.

Amazed, the good friend asked, "Well how come you never came over for my juicer? You do <u>believe</u> what I told you would cure your pain don't you?"

"Yes!" the man indignantly replied. (But he still never came for the juicer.)

A year later the man with the juicer had a female friend who was diagnosed with the same affliction. After giving her the same wise advice he had given his male friend a year earlier, he asked her, "Do you <u>believe</u> me?"

The woman said, "No, not really."

But later that night the man with the juicer heard a knock on his door, and he opened it up to find the ailing lady crying on his porch asking, "Can I take your juicer home with me?" Not two weeks later, the man with the juicer received a phone call from the woman, and she ecstatically shouted, "My ulcer is gone! I have no pain anymore!"

Now I ask you; which sick person "believed" (or had faith in) the WORDS of the man who owned the juicer? If you said the woman, you are correct!!! See, the man's words were worthless, his LACK OF ACTION (the fact that he did not come for the juicer) <u>proved</u> he DID NOT BELIEVE in his friend's cure—even though he said he did! On the other hand, the woman's ACTION (the fact that she came for the juicer) <u>proved</u> somewhere deep down inside her spirit (thoughts, desires, & emotions) she had FAITH in the cure—even though she said she did not. **THAT**, my friend, is the <u>correct</u> meaning behind the original Greek

290

words translated "faith" or "believe" in the Bible.

Therefore, when the Bible states those who "*believe in Christ*" will receive eternal life…what does that mean? In other words, what are the ACTIONS that back up a "*belief or faith in Christ*"? Friend, again, this is all SPIRITUAL in meaning: It has nothing to do with believing in the earthly man Jesus Christ, for that would require a person to have heard or know the story of Jesus Christ (which only few have throughout history)! Friend, I have already told you Christ represents the "Spirit of Love", which is God; thus, to "believe in love (God)" means to "obey the 10 Love Commandments"!!! See, the man Jesus Christ was simply the spiritual embodiment of love. So, once again, this is all the same thing: You cannot say you "believe" or "have faith in" Jesus Christ (the Spirit of Love) while simultaneously disobeying the 10 Love Commandments. That would make you a liar like the Apostle John wrote! Friend, "believing in, knowing, and loving Christ" is all the same thing; the 3 terms are <u>ONLY</u> proved through our ACTIONS of obeying the 10 love Commandments.

Now you can truly understand the plethora of Biblical New Testament verses like: "*<u>Whosoever liveth and BELIEVETH in me (Christ) shall never die</u>*" *(John 11:26)*. And: "*Verily, verily, I (Christ) say unto you, <u>He that BELIEVETH on me hath everlasting life</u>*" *(John 6:47)*. Do you understand there is NO contradiction between Jesus making these statements in regards to "how to obtain eternal life" or answering someone's questions of "*what must I <u>DO</u> to receive <u>eternal life</u>*" by naming off the 10 Love Commandments (Golden Rule) and saying keep them? Both declarations are identical in meaning, because to "*believe in Christ*" means to "believe in love", which means to obey the 10 Love Commandments! See, both statements accurately reveal the WAY leading to eternal life in the Promise Land. Friend, Jesus preached nothing but LOVE. Consequently, his words (instructions) to mankind were to "continually obey the 10 Love Commandments". Thus, he would also say things like: "*Verily, verily, I say unto you, <u>If a man KEEP my saying (words), he shall never see death</u>*" *(John 8:51)*. Do you see? You will receive eternal life because you willingly chose to <u>keep</u> Jesus' words to "obey the 10 Love Commandments". For these are the <u>ACTIONS (or works)</u> that prove you truly have FAITH in GOD (Love).

To be perfectly frank, the original Greek words translated "faith" and "believe" would have been better served if translated "obey". In other words, he who *"obeys Christ's words of love"* will receive eternal life! And, as a matter of fact, the Bible actually uses the word "obey" several times in relation to "how to obtain eternal life": *"And being made perfect,* **he (Jesus) became the author of eternal salvation unto all them that OBEY him** *" (Hebrews 5:9)*. Ah, do you see? Friend, there is NOTHING conflicting here in Scripture! Thus, this verse proves to *"believe in Christ"* really means to *"obey him"*. And the "10 Love Commandments" are what we are to obey—i.e. DO the things on the "do side" of the list and DO NOT DO the things on the "don't" side of the list. THAT is the WAY to eternal life.

Consequently, to *"believe NOT in Christ"* really means to *"disobey him"*. Disobey what? The 10 Love Commandments!!! Jesus said, *"He that believeth on the Son hath everlasting life: and he that* **BELIEVETH NOT the Son shall not see life***; but the wrath of God abideth on him" (John 3:36)*. Here, the English phrase *"believeth not"* was translated from a SINGLE Greek word in the original New Testament manuscripts *"apeitheo"*, which literally means: <u>to disobey, be disobedient</u>! Do you see? To *"believe NOT the Son"* literally means to "disobey him"! Friend, people who disobey Christ's (God's) unswerving message of "Love God with all your heart and your neighbor as yourself by keeping the 10 Love Commandments" are those who *"do NOT believe in Christ (Love)"*! Thus, if you willingly <u>disobey</u> the 10 Love Commandments, you prove you *"do not believe in the Son"*, and you will **NOT** reap eternal life but will endure the wrath of God!!! In acknowledging the first half of the above verse then, the ONLY way to prove you *"believe on the Son (Christ)"* is by <u>obeying</u> God's Law of love (10 Love Commandments) and THAT is how you obtain eternal life. Yes, Christ's (God's) message of "how to obtain eternal life" was consistent and true throughout Scripture, for "obeying the 10 Love Commandments" is the WAY!

Knowing the proper meaning behind the Biblical word "believe", one can now finally understand the real meaning of the famous verse: *"For God so loved the world, that he gave his only begotten Son, <u>that whosoever BELIEVETH IN HIM should not perish, but have everlasting</u>*

life" (John 3:16). See, it took Jesus' sinless, spiritual death to free us from sin's power of death (make forgiveness for our sins available), but then it takes our following the WAY of love ("believing in Christ") by obeying the 10 Love Commandments to receive eternal life. In fact, Christ said this immediately after the famous verse above: _"He that believeth on him (Christ who is love) is not condemned: but **he that BELIEVETH NOT is condemned already**" (John 3:18)._ What are the _"believeth not"_ people <u>DOING</u> that proves they do not believe in Christ and thus condemns them? Living evilly (disobeying the 10 Love Commandments)!!! Their <u>actions</u> (deeds) prove they do NOT believe in LOVE! Jesus confirmed this point as he continued speaking, _"And THIS is the <u>condemnation</u>, that light is come into the world, **and men loved darkness rather than light, because their DEEDS WERE EVIL**. For every one that doeth evil hateth the light, neither cometh to the light, lest his deeds should be reproved. But <u>he that DOETH truth cometh to the light, that his DEEDS may be made manifest, that they are wrought in God (Love)</u>" (John 3:19-21)._ This full discourse by Jesus makes it obvious, again, that it is our good deeds (obeying the 10 Love Commandments) that validates our "belief in Christ"! And these are the people who fulfill the word "believe" in John 3:16, and therefore are not condemned (will not perish) but will receive eternal life.

James argued well that only someone's "obedience to the 10 Love Commandments" proves they have "faith in Christ (love)": _"Dear brothers, <u>what's the use of saying that you have FAITH and are Christians if you aren't proving it by helping others</u>? <u>Will that kind of faith save anyone</u>? If you have a friend who is in need of food and clothing, and you say to him, "Well, good-bye and God bless you; stay warm and eat hearty," and then don't give him clothes or food, what good does that do? So you see, it isn't enough just to have faith. **<u>You must also DO GOOD (do love) to prove that you have it</u>. <u>Faith that doesn't show itself by good works (bearing fruit) is no faith at all—it is dead and useless</u>" (James 2:14-17, Living Bible)._ Wow! James confirms the original Greek word translated "believe" is actually an "action based faith in love"! Did you notice the example "action of love" James used to demonstrate "belief in Christ (God)"? It was the DO side of the 8th Love Commandment—i.e. do not steal but give to the poor, feed the hungry, clothe the naked, etc. In other words, James is saying…if you are NOT keeping the 10 Love Commandments (walking in love towards God and your neigbor), you do not have true faith (belief) in Christ (love), and your soul will perish on Judgment Day! See, James words perfectly agree with Jesus' Judgment Day parable, where he revealed God pronouncing, "You did not feed me or give me clothing, so away with you into outer darkness." I told you the Bible's message was beautifully congruent!

Let us now inspect some greatly misinterpreted Bible verses that "preachers" often cite in an attempt to make "obtaining eternal life" sound effortless. Paul wrote: *"That **if thou shalt confess with thy mouth the LORD Jesus**, and shalt BELIEVE in thine heart (spirit) that God hath raised him from the dead, thou shalt be saved" (Romans 10:9).* Do you know what it means to "*confess Jesus (God) as your LORD*"? It means to "OBEY Him"; it means to obey his words of love (obey the 10 Love Commandments)! See, if someone is your LORD and MASTER, YOU DO WHAT THEY TELL YOU TO DO! See, you cannot say you have "confessed Jesus as your LORD" when you DO NOT DO the things he said! Jesus said this himself: *"And **why call ye me, Lord, Lord, and DO NOT the things which I say?**" (Luke 6:46).* Do you see? If you are not "obeying the 10 Love Commandments," YOU HAVE NOT CONFESSED JESUS AS YOUR LORD!!!

But today, "ministers" love to quote Paul's verse above— conveniently glossing over the true meaning behind the "*confessing Jesus as Lord*" part—and then misinterpret the word "*believe*" to simply mean "think". This is a deadly doctrine!!! Yet, many people have bought the lie "If you think Jesus was a real man and God sent him to die on a cross for your sins, and if you think he was resurrected; then you are saved and on your way to eternal life in God's Kingdom! Do you see the gross error in this doctrine? The word "*believe*" has been downgraded to only mean "think". This is dead WRONG!!! To hold to this erroneous belief you must ignore the truthfulness of every Bible verse I have discussed in this book so far, with respect to what a soul MUST DO to obtain eternal life. You have to throw away most of the Bible as a lie! Please do not wrest Paul's words to your own destruction! Peter knew people were doing this with Paul's words even

294

back in his day: *"Our wise and beloved brother PAUL...**Some of his comments are not easy to understand**, and there are people who are deliberately stupid...they have TWISTED his letters around to mean something quite different from what he meant, just as they do the other parts of Scripture—and **the result is DISASTER for them**" (II Peter 3:15, 16, Living Bible)*. Amen and Amen!

It is from the above "incorrect doctrine" that we get inane questions like, "I wonder what happens to all the people who never heard about Jesus?" Friend, EVERYONE has heard about Christ for <u>he is love</u>! Anyone who "obeys the WAY of love (good)" knows the Spirit of Christ (God), no matter when or where they lived in history or if they ever heard the name of Jesus! But if you are fortunate enough to have heard the story of how the man Jesus Christ came to Earth to deliver mankind's dead spirits from sin's death grasp through his sinless death and resurrection, then you ought to (all the more) want to <u>make him the LORD of your soul</u> by obeying his words of love (keeping the 10 Love Commandments) in order to lay hold on eternal life! Jesus said: *"<u>Not every one that saith unto me, Lord, Lord, shall enter into the kingdom of heaven; but **he that DOETH the will of my Father**</u> which is in heaven" (Matthew 7:21)*. Yes, Jesus' words prove the only people who can truly call God or Christ their "Lord" are those who are <u>DOING</u> God's (love's) will.

Another misrepresented verse of Paul's (making obtaining eternal life sound easy) occurs because "ministers" neatly pluck it out of Scripture without exposing Paul's very next words: *"For whosoever <u>shall call upon the name of the Lord shall be saved</u>" (Romans 10:13)*. This effortless WAY to the Promise Land is trumpeted everywhere you look these days. But what does it mean to truly *"call upon"* the name of the Lord? Well, you have to read the entire Bible for that answer, or just read Paul's very next words: *"<u>How then shall they call on him in whom they have not BELIEVED?</u>" (Romans 10:14)*. Wow, do you see? You cannot *"call upon the Lord to save you"* if you *"do not believe in love"*—i.e. want to turn from your sins and obey God's 10 Love Commandments. I am warning you to not twist Paul's words to your own peril! Paul was not confused in his doctrine of salvation; he knew perfectly well a person MUST "<u>turn</u> from sin" to be saved. Listen to him: *"For God sometimes uses sorrow in our lives **to help us turn away*** *from sin and SEEK eternal life*. *We should never regret his sending it" (II Corinthians 7:10, Living Bible)*. See, eternal life is something we seek, because it is a *"narrow path"* we MUST follow in order to obtain entrance into the Promise Land. Therefore, genuine *"calling on the Lord to be saved"* refers to someone seriously meaning business with God by wanting to quit sinning (repent). So, I urge you to turn from your sins of disobeying the 10 Love Commandments and "work out" your eternal salvation, laying hold on eternal life.

Here is my great concern: It appears we have a vast generation of people, today, who enjoy sitting in church buildings and listening to someone talk! But all this "activity" amounts to is "hearing". That is why the deed of "church attendance" will count for nothing (a big fat Zero!) on Judgment Day. Please do not think you are <u>doing</u> God's will because you "attend church", for that is simply a hearing (listening) activity. And only "hearing" is useless in obtaining eternal life. Jesus said, *"And <u>every one that heareth these sayings of mine, and DOETH THEM NOT, shall be likened unto a foolish man</u>, which built his house upon the sand: And the rain descended, and the floods came, and the winds blew, and beat upon that house; <u>and it fell: and great was the fall of it"</u> (Matthew 7:24-27)*. Friend, Jesus did not preach "church attendance"; he preached "self-sacrificial love towards God and others by obeying the 10 Love Commandments". I beg you to start aligning your life up to God's 10 Love Commandments, for that is how you become a <u>DOER</u> of Jesus' words of love!

In conclusion then, our *"faith"* or *"belief"* in Christ is only demonstrated or actuated by our willful choice to obey the 10 Love Commandments, meaning our "faith" or "belief" in God (love) is confirmed only by our willful choice to walk in love towards God and our neighbor—which is the very definition of REPENTENCE. <u>Paul</u> described what the Biblical words *"faith"* or *"belief"* meant with a few powerful words: *<u>"faith</u> (which) <u>worketh by love"</u> (Galatians 5:6)*. How about that? Is that not awesome? In other words, "<u>Faith</u> in God (or Christ)" means to BELIEVE IN LOVE. See, ONLY by our WORKS OF LOVE (obeying the 10 Love Commandments) do we prove we have FAITH in GOD! THAT is the true saving, Promise-Land-entering, kind of faith (belief) we must possess to obtain eternal life! Do you

296

understand? And it will be faith (working by love) that lands a soul in the Kingdom of God, for that act of repentance will activate God to forgive their sins through Christ's redemptive work.

Yes, friend, salvation is a journey. It is an everyday, minute-by-minute decision. Once you make the decision to actively keep God's 10 Love Commandments (repent of sin) do not ever go back to disobeying them again! Follow the *"narrow way"* until your last dying breath, and you will reap eternal life. It is really a simple matter of "reaping what you sow": If you willingly sow "love" you will justly reap love! Listen to Paul's Scripture fully explaining how a person's continuance in traveling the "narrow way" is the KEY to leading them to the Promise Land: *"he (God) will SAVE their SOULS if they trust (believe) in him, living quiet, good, and **loving** lives"* (I Timothy 2:15, Living Bible). The King James Bible says: *"if they CONTINUE in faith (belief) and charity (love) and holiness (10 Commandments) with sobriety (mental soundness)"* (I Timothy 2:15). THAT is the truth about "HOW to obtain eternal life"—show continual goodness (love) towards God and everyone else on the face of planet Earth!

Let us listen to more Scripture passages penned by Paul confirming PERSISTANT faith (shown by love) is the key to obtaining eternal life: *"And let us not be weary in **well doing**: for in due season we shall reap, if we faint not"* (Galatians 6:9). Again, Paul wrote; *"Who (God) will render to every man according to his deeds: To them who by PATIENT CONTINUANCE in **well doing** seek for glory and honour and immortality, **eternal life**. But unto them that are contentious, and do NOT obey the truth, but obey unrighteousness, indignation and wrath, Tribulation and anguish, upon every soul of man that doeth evil"* (Romans 2:6-9). How can the point be any clearer! Even Peter wrote: *"Wherefore let them that suffer according to the will of God commit the keeping of their souls to him in **well doing**, as unto a faithful Creator"* (I Peter 4:19). Clearly, if we continue to obey the 10 Love Commandments, which is *"well doing"* or *"doing good"*, we will reap eternal life by entering the Kingdom of God.

Now, let us return to the *"example"* God made of the Israelites in the 40 year wilderness journey portion of the grand salvation parable, revealing the truth of what all mankind MUST DO to obtain eternal life (enter the Promise Land). The New Testament writer of the book of Hebrews perfectly summed up the REASON most Israelites PERISHED in the wilderness, having never entered the Promise Land: *"But with whom was he (God) grieved forty years? Was it not with them **that had SINNED**, whose carcases fell in the wilderness? And **to whom sware he that they should NOT enter into his rest, but to them that BELIEVED NOT**? So we see that they could not enter in because of unbelief"* *(Hebrews 3:17-19)*. Wow, do you see? The message is perfectly clear: The Israelite's willful SIN (disobedience to the 10 Love Commandments) PROVED their *"unbelief in God, Christ, and Love"*! And for THAT reason, they perished in the wilderness, having never entered God's rest in the Promise Land.

Yes, unmistakably, in the above passage of Scripture we see again the Biblical word *"believe"* really signifies *"to sin not"*, which means "to love by obeying God's 10 Love Commandments". And to *"not believe"* signifies *"to sin"*, which means "to not love by disobeying God's 10 Love Commandments. Therefore, you should now recognize God's Israelite story (parable) was exactly what I told you it was; it was God's message to all mankind revealing EVERYTHING involved in a soul's journey back to God! In other words, it revealed EVERYTHING it took/takes for a soul to obtain eternal life by entering the Promise Land (Kingdom of God). And here is what it took/takes: it took God supernaturally delivering mankind from sin's bondage of spiritual death through Jesus, which placed us in a wilderness where it was now possible to reach the Promise Land; then, it only takes our *"FAITH in love (God)"*, which means to repent of sin by willingly choosing to follow the WAY of love (obey the 10 Love Commandments). Yes, friend, it will only be because of *"unbelief in love (God)"*—shown by a soul's willful desire to continue sinning (disobey the 10 Love Commandments)—that a soul will perish in Earth's wilderness and NEVER obtain eternal life in the Kingdom of God.

The Hebrew writer truly understood the reason God had led the Israelites on a 40 year journey through the wilderness. Let us hear more of his beautiful, divinely-inspired words revealing what it takes for a soul to obtain eternal life: *"The Holy Spirit warns us to listen to him, to be careful to hear his voice today and not let our hearts become*

298

set against him, as the people of Israel did. ***They steeled themselves against his LOVE*** and complained against him in the desert ***while he was testing them***...God says, "I was very angry with them, for their hearts were always looking somewhere else instead of up to me, and ***they never found the PATHS I wanted them to follow***"...***Beware then of your own hearts, dear brothers, lest you find that they, too, are EVIL and UNBELIEVING and leading you away from the living God***. Speak to each other about these things every day while there is still time, so that none of you will become hardened against God, ***being blinded by the DECEITFULNESS of SIN***. For if we are FAITHFUL to the END...we will share in all that belongs to Christ...But now is the time. Never forget the warning, "***Today if you hear God's voice speaking to you, do not harden your heart against him***, as the people of Israel did when they rebelled against him in the desert." And who were those people I speak of, who heard God's voice speaking to them but then rebelled against him? They were the ones who came out of Egypt with Moses their leader. And who was it who made God angry for all those forty years? ***These same people who SINNED and as a result DIED in the wilderness***. And to whom was God speaking when he swore with an oath that they could NEVER go into the land he had promised his people? ***He was speaking to all those who DISOBEYED him***. And why couldn't they go in? ***Because they didn't TRUST (BELIEVE) him***." (Hebrews 3:7-19, Living Bible). Ah, it is so obvious: willful sin = disobeying the 10 Love Commandments = unbelief in God (Love); and repentance = obeying the 10 Love Commandments = belief in God (Love).

Jude was given the same revelation: "*I will therefore put you in remembrance, though ye once knew this, how that the LORD, having SAVED the people out of the land of Egypt, afterward destroyed them that BELIEVED not*" (Jude 1:5). The Living Bible writes: "*Remember this fact—which you know already—that the LORD SAVED a whole nation of people out of the land of Egypt, and then killed every one of them who did NOT TRUST and OBEY him*" (Jude 1:5, Living Bible). Do you see? Look, the truth is God saved ALL mankind from the bondage of sin & death through Jesus' redemptive work on the cross, but sadly MOST people's souls will still perish because they will refuse to repent of sin and live a life of love toward God and their neighbor, as outlined by obedience to God's 10 Love Commandments!!!

By now, you should be able to clearly understand Paul's writings like: "*NOT by works of righteousness which WE have done, but according to his mercy (love) he (God) saved us...through Jesus Christ our Savior...**THAT they which have BELIEVED in God (Love) might be careful to maintain GOOD WORKS (obey the 10 Love Commandments)***" *(Titus 3:5-8)*. See, there it is, again: God's 2 part process that leads a soul to eternal life! Do you want to hear it again from Paul? Ok: "*But God, who is rich in mercy (love), for his great love wherewith he loved us, even when we were dead in sins, hath quickened us together with Christ...**For by grace are ye saved through FAITH**; and that not of yourselves: it is the gift of God: Not of works, lest any man should boast. **For we are his workmanship, created in Christ Jesus UNTO GOOD WORKS (obeying the 10 Love Commandments), which God hath before ordained that we should walk in them**" *(Ephesians 2:4-10)*. Friend, we can obtain eternal life ONLY because of our "Faith in God (Love)"—which is proved only by our willful decision to repent of sin and live a life of love (obey the 10 Love Commandments).

Please, please, listen to me, reader! Today is the day. Now is the time to repent! If you are still breathing air on planet Earth, you have a chance at eternal life! Do not harden your heart (thoughts, desires, & emotions) to the truth, but turn from your wickedness (evil) and choose to love God. For if you harden your heart, stiffen your neck, and never stop your willful sinning, you will seal your soul's doom for all eternity! And I promise you THAT will be the biggest mistake you ever make!!! It is insanity to trade eternal life for the lousy, fleeting pleasures of sin. You must willfully eliminate idolatry (love of money), blasphemy, murder (hatred), sexual immorality, thievery, lying, covetousness, etc. out of your heart. We are in the wilderness, my friend, and God is testing every one of us! He is finding out "whether we love him or not" by every choice we make every day of our lives. I am in the same battle as you are reader, fighting for my eternal destiny; therefore, let us forsake sin while there is still a chance, proving we are BELIEVERS!!!

Chapter 16

Love of Money

"No servant (soul) can serve two masters...
Ye cannot serve God and mammon"
(Luke 16:13)

Alright, by now it is abundantly obvious that <u>we MUST love</u> (obey God's 10 Love Commandments) if we plan on obtaining eternal life, for "obedience to the 10 Love Commandments" is love defined, the truth revealed, the Holy Spirit described, the good fruit we are to bear, and the works (actions) that prove our faith (belief) in Christ (love)! To "disobey the 10 Love Commandments" is the consummate definition of sin: *"Whosoever committeth sin transgresseth also the law: for **SIN is the transgression of the law (10 Love Commandments)**" (I John 3:4)*. Therefore, once again, "sin" is simply "to not love".

Since "obeying the 10 Love Commandments" (loving God and our neighbor as ourselves) is the key to obtaining the incredible reward of eternal life with pleasures unknown for our soul, why would anyone in their right mind want to live a life of sin (to not love) and perish in a *"lake of fire"*? Did you ever think about that? In other words, what is the <u>motivating</u> <u>force</u> driving people to want to sin (to <u>not</u> love God and to <u>not</u> love their neighbor)? What could possibly be so tempting and attractive to someone to cause them to trade "eternal life" for it?

Oh, the Bible has the answer! But here is where things are going to get very uncomfortable for those of you who are not *"born again"* of God's Spirit of love, because I must talk about the very heart and soul of sin—i.e. the very lifeblood or root that feeds ALL sin.

I assure you this chapter (discussion) on sin is extremely important and necessary, for one day God gave me a graphic parable describing what it is like to <u>NOT</u> talk about sin with people. It proceeds as follows: A certain man sustained a massive leg injury in a war, and after several days his gaping wound became infected and blood poisoning set in. It was obvious without reopening and cleaning the man's wound, he would die! But some people—not wanting to cause the dying man any discomfort—gingerly approached the wounded man, patted him lightly on the shoulder, and laid cool rags on his forehead, all the while saying encouraging words to him like, "I hope you get to feeling better! You're doing great!" But then along came a man who quickly and anxiously removed the injured man's bandages, poured a bottle of peroxide in his wound, and while the man howled and screamed, writhing in pain, he scrubbed his infection clean and saved his life. God then asked me, "Gabriel, <u>who</u> showed the GREATEST love towards the wounded (dying) man?"

"The one who saved his life," I replied.

Do you understand the parable? Friend, we absolutely <u>MUST</u> talk about sin with people if we TRULY love them (care about saving their soul) <u>for sin is a soul killer</u>! "Sin" is like the fatal blood poisoning coursing through the wounded man's veins in the parable above. If the deadly poisoning (sin) is not purged from our spirit, it will cause our soul to be banished to *"outer darkness"* for all eternity. Paul wrote: *"For **the wages of sin is (spiritual) death**" (Romans 6:23)*. So here is the deal; if you are living in willful sin (disobeying the 10 Love Commandments), then a discussion on "sin" is going to cause you great spiritual (in your thoughts, desires, & emotions) discomfort, but it is critical that we address it. If you cast this book aside as it gets uncomfortable to read, you will be like the injured man in the parable above pushing away the very hands of the loving man trying to clean his wound to save his life! Oh, yes, the spiritual discomfort may stop in your mind, but the end result—if you <u>never</u> purge your life of sin (repent)—will be eternal

302

spiritual death! Friend, "sin" is the disease we are ALL fighting, and it is 100% fatal if not eradicated from a spirit (soul). Therefore, let us get to scrubbing.

Alright, if "sin" was a tree, the "evil fruit" hanging off of its branches would be "disobeying 10 Love Commandment things"— e.g. idolatry, blasphemy, murder, adultery, lying, covetousness, etc. With that analogy in mind, the Bible maintains the ROOT feeding or nourishing that "tree of sin" is the "LOVE OF MONEY"! How about that? Paul wrote: *"**For the LOVE OF MONEY is the ROOT of ALL EVIL (sin)**" (I Timothy 6:10).* In other words, I can say with absolute certainty the underlying cause of EVERYONE who ends up in hell will be the *"love of money"* rooted in their heart (thoughts, desires, & emotions), for IT is the spiritual source that produces ALL of sin, and we already, clearly know only those individuals who live continual, willful lives of sin (evil) go to hell. Consequently, if you care at all about your eternal destiny, this TRUTH ought to make you want to stand up, turn around, and take a triple look into your heart, accurately and honestly discerning your attitude towards money.

The Biblical phrase *"love of money"* was translated from a single Greek word *"philargyria"* in the original New Testament documents meaning: love of money, avarice, greed. So what makes a person "greedy for money"? In other words, what is it about "money" that makes people desire it? Let me even ask it another way; what can money do for you? Friend, all it can do is buy dirt (atoms)!!! "Money" is the legal means whereby we can obtain dirt. Ah, so the driving ambition behind the *"love of money"* is really the acquisition of materialistic possessions, which are made of dirt (atoms). But the atoms have all been here since Creation, and they will all be here after our spirits leave planet Earth: *"For **we brought nothing into this world, and it is certain we can carry nothing out**" (I Timothy 6:7).* So what is the big deal? Does "acquiring dirt" have any eternal value? NO!!! It is worthless! Thus, the very ROOT of ALL sin (love of money)—the driving spiritual force inside people's hearts (thoughts, desires, & emotions) causing them to sin—is all one colossal lie! Jesus called it: *"the DECEITFULNESS of riches" (Matthew 13:22).* Look, how can someone with a big pile of dirt (a lot of money & materialistic possessions) maintain they are rich when the dirt they are in "control" of during their temporary Earthly life cannot be taken with their soul into eternity? They cannot, it is a sham! Only things that are ETERNAL have true value! Thus, the "*love of money*" is a deceiving desire, and the sin (non-loving actions) it produces is foolishness. Subsequently, the Bible refers to "sin" as: "*the deceitfulness of sin*" *(Hebrews 3:13)*. Get it through your head, reader; "lusting for dirt (money)" is pointless! Millions and millions of people are going to end up in hell over an illusory craving. How sad is THAT?

So what is the attraction (pull)? Why would someone allow their heart (thoughts, desires, & emotions) to be consumed with "greed for dirt (money)? Because "obtaining money (dirt)" brings pleasure! In other words, the sin that evolves out of a heart full of "greed for money (dirt)" is to pleasure one's self. But, sadly, the pleasure can only be temporary, for our lives on Earth (in this age) are but a "*vapor of smoke*". Thus, a desire for "fleeting pleasure" is really the draw of ALL sin. As you get more money, you can obtain more dirt possessions (houses, cars, boats, electronics, etc.) and your head swells with pride. You actually start to believe you really are somebody—i.e. you think you are successful, and you think you are better than the next guy. Yet, it is all a foolish lie, because your "dirt" can only be possessed momentarily. Moses understood "dirt pleasures" on planet Earth are temporary, and the Bible says when he became a <u>man</u> he refused to enjoy the "*riches of Egypt*" and left off being called Pharaoh's daughters son: "<u>*Choosing rather to suffer affliction with the people of God*</u>*, than to <u>enjoy the pleasures of sin for a season</u>*" *(Hebrews 11:25)*. See, sin's pleasure is only a temporary thing; then, our spirits leave planet Earth and <u>must</u> stand in front of God to give account for what we did with our time and life He gave us on Earth!

You ask, "Gabriel, how do I know if I love money?" Oh, it is not hard to discern! Does "making money" consume your time and thoughts? Is "obtaining dirt possessions" the predominate goal on your mind? Do you only want to "do for others" if you get paid? These are key signs that your heart loves money! Then, I would instruct you to check and see if your "greed for money (dirt)" has progressed to the point where you are lying, cheating, stealing, etc. in your passion for money. In other words, do you cheat on taxes, lie to clients to make a sale, hook cable up illegally, refuse to honor God's Holy Sabbath day because your heart feels you need to make money on that day, too! There are hundreds of specific sins I could list, but honestly search your heart and record how often you are "disobeying God's 10 Love Commandments (sinning)" because of a lust for money.

Then, I want you to realize there is NO <u>love</u> shown towards God or your fellow man—whom the "spirit material" inside them is God!—when you are "disobeying the 10 Love Commandments" to make money. Remember, when you lie to someone, you are lying to God. When you steal from someone, you are stealing from God. When you are devising ways to swindle and take advantage of people, you are doing it to God! When you flip the middle finger at someone in their car because your impatient heart is revving like your car's engine, rushing to your job to make money, you did it to God. When you hate someone, you hate God. Friend, as I have already said in this book…the way you treat other people is the way you are treating God. Never forget that!

Jesus accurately said, *"No servant (soul) can serve two masters: for either he will <u>hate the one, and love the other; or else he will hold to the one, and despise the other.</u> **Ye cannot serve God and mammon"** (Luke 16:13).* "Mammon" comes from the Greek word *"mamōnas"* and it literally means: <u>wealth, assets</u>. Wow, is that not amazing? In other words, it is <u>impossible</u> to love both God and money (wealth, assets, & possessions), because the two entities are diametrically opposed to each other. And everyone living on planet Earth is serving one or the other! Listen very carefully to Jesus' words of truth, for there is only two possibly scenarios in your heart: <u>Either you love God (spirit) while hating (despising) wealth & assets, or you love wealth & assets while hating God (spirit)</u>. Do you understand? <u>There is no middle ground!!!</u> Either the Creator God is the God you love and serve, or wealth & assets is the God you love and serve!

Satan's BIG lie today—even in the church!—is to convince people they can love both! Yet it is a terrible deception which will lead millions and millions of people to hell and destruction! Allow me to present you with a simple example of how loving one (God or wealth & assets) <u>automatically</u> makes you hate (despise) the other. I have explained to you in this book that God is the "spirit material" living inside everyone on planet Earth, for we are all His "spirit children". So, think about this; while you lay down to go to sleep tonight in your grossly-oversized, luxurious house with thoughts dancing in your spirit (thoughts, desires, & emotions) about the new draperies you want, or that new huge sectional couch you desire, or the extra property you just bought, God is the "spirit material" laying inside some African (or wherever) child, starving to death, with every rib showing through His thinly stretched skin and distended stomach, crying for a crumb of food and a drop of water! Yet, your prideful heart believes you "love God" because you attend church on Sunday, but you cannot see He is the "spirit material" breathing inside everyone on planet Earth. You are blind to the fact that while your heart (thoughts, desires, & emotions) is fixated on Earthly, worthless, dirt treasure, you are simultaneously ignoring, hating, and despising God!

Remember the Golden Rule: *"Thou shalt love the Lord thy God with all thy heart, and with all thy soul, and with all thy mind. This is the first and great commandment. And the second is LIKE UNTO IT, **Thou shalt love thy neighbour as thyself**. On these two commandments hang all the law and the prophets" (Matthew 22:37-40)*. Listen, it is impossible to say you *"love your neighbor (who is every soul on Earth) AS YOURSELF"* when you live in flagrant lavishness, knowing your brothers and sisters across the world are starving to death and homeless. If you say you do, you are lying, for your lifestyle and actions are screaming out, "ALL I LOVE IS MYSELF AND MY INSIGNIFICANT, VALUELESS DIRT!" And I assure you, this type of heart will <u>never</u> hold water on Judgment Day!

One day, Jesus summed up the Golden Rule like this: *"Therefore all things whatsoever ye would that men should do to you, DO ye even so to them: for this is the law and the prophets" (Matthew 7:12)*. In other words, <u>DO unto others, as you would have them DO unto you</u>. Do you understand if you make the decision to follow this ONE simple rule, daily, you will (without a doubt) obtain eternal life? THAT is ALL you have to <u>DO</u>!!! So think about this; if the tables were reversed and God had birthed your spirit inside a physical body somewhere on planet Earth where there was no food or water and no opportunity for work, you would be the one lying there begging and wishing someone would help you! So why do you not help them? Paul wrote: *"**Look not every man on his own things, but every man also on the things of others.** Let this mind be in you, which was also in Christ Jesus"* (Philippians 2:4, 5). Do you want the *"mind of Christ (love)"* to be inside you? He was our example of how to live our lives on Earth. And how did he live his life? Did he use his daily, spiritual (mental) energy running around Earth seeing how much dirt he could pile up for himself? No, my friend! He went around <u>helping, giving, serving, healing, and teaching</u> every person he could, trying to turn their hearts to the WAY of truth (love), in hope that their soul would follow the *"narrow path"* leading to eternal life. THAT should be our goal and purpose in life, also!

Now, on the other hand, someone who truly DOES love God (every human soul in the world) can hardly rest knowing God is starving, thirsty, imprisoned, naked, etc. Consequently, <u>they DO everything within their power to help Him</u>, for their heart (thoughts, desires, & emotions) is full of the love of God! They sacrifice themselves, take up their cross of suffering, and live a simple, humble life, while using their time, energy, and resources (money, food, clothing, etc.) to DO everything they possibly can to help those who are in need. Their "loving deeds" confirm they hate money, because if they loved money they would keep it and use it for themselves. THAT is what "serving (loving) God" is truly all about! That is why Jesus uttered the Judgment Day parable, which got straight to the heart of truth about how to obtain eternal life: *"Then shall the King say unto them on his right hand, <u>Come, ye blessed of my Father, inherit the kingdom</u>...For **I was an hungred, and ye gave me meat: I was thirsty, and ye gave me drink: I was a stranger, and ye took me in: Naked, and ye clothed me: I was sick, and ye visited me: I was in prison, and ye came unto me**...Verily I say unto you, <u>Inasmuch as ye have done it unto one of the least of these my brethren, ye have done it unto me</u>"* (Matthew 25:34-40). Make no mistake about it friend, you cannot have it both ways: You cannot love God (spirit) AND your wealth (money) & assets (possessions) at the same time, for while you are holding on to the one, you are automatically despising the other!!!

Today, people incorrectly think "loving God" is expressed by going to church, singing songs, and (if they are not embarrassed) raising their hands to Him. But friend, that is NOT how you serve (love) God! Truthfully, God could care less if you frequent a church building or not. God wants to see a soul "sold out"—meaning at the expense of your money!—to daily helping others, which is Him! He wants to see your love shown continually by "obeying the 10 Love Commandments"—DO the things on the "do side" and DO NOT DO the things on the "do not side". THAT is how you love, know, and worship God…by your loving thoughts & deeds! Listen to God's righteous anger boiling through the prophet Amos: *"**I HATE your show and pretense**—your hypocrisy of "honoring" me with your religious feasts and solemn assemblies (church functions) …Away with your hymns of praise—they are mere noise to my ears. I will NOT listen to your music, no matter how lovely it is. **I want to see a mighty flood of justice—a torrent of DOING good (obeying the 10 Love Commandments)**" (Amos 5:21-24, Living Bible)*. Wow, can you feel God's heart?

Listen to God continue: *"You push away all thoughts of punishment awaiting you, BUT BY YOUR DEEDS you bring the Day of Judgment near. **You lie on ivory beds surrounded with luxury**, eating the meat of the tenderest lambs and the choicest calves…You drink wine by the bucketful and perfume yourselves…**caring nothing at all that your bothers need your help**…I despise the pride and false glory… and HATE your beautiful homes…And just as stupid is your rejoicing in how great you are, when you are less than nothing! And priding yourselves on your own tiny power!" (Amos 6:3-13, Living Bible)*. Friend, this same disgusting hypocrisy is prevalent everywhere today! But I promise you Jesus will soon be here to *"weed out the (evil) tares from the (good) harvest wheat"*.

Listen to the Apostle James frightening, prophetic words about materialistically rich people who do not care about others: *"**Look here, you RICH men**, now is the time to cry and groan with anguished grief because of all the terrible troubles ahead of you. **Your wealth is even now rotting away, and your fine clothes are becoming mere moth-eaten rags**. The value of your gold and silver is dropping fast, yet **IT WILL STAND AS EVIDENCE AGAINST YOU**, and eat your flesh like fire. THAT is what you have stored up for yourselves, to receive on that coming day of judgment…**You have spent your years*** *here on earth having fun, satisfying your every whim, and NOW YOUR FAT HEARTS ARE READY FOR THE SLAUGHTER. You have condemned and killed good men who had no power to defend themselves against you"* (James 5:1-6, Living Bible). Do you understand that when it is within your power (meaning you have the money and resources) to help hurting and dying people and you do not do it...YOU CONDEMNED THEM TO DEATH!!! Do you comprehend that? You are like a judge who held the power of life or death over them, and you chose to sentence them to death! And for what? So you could get those new granite kitchen counter tops? Or maybe buy another piece of property? Are you kidding me? Good luck explaining your heart to God on Judgment Day!

Listen to me friend, read James' words again in the above Scripture; do you see a person's "wealth & assets" will literally be the EVIDENCE God will use to convict them on Judgment Day? Wow!!! In other words, a person's "money & possessions" will stand as ABSOLUTE PROOF they loved dirt more than God (their own hurting brothers and sisters in the world)! Yet, the stone-cold truth is most materialistically rich people are proud as peacocks over their extravagant homes and possessions, when they ought to be embarrassed and terrified by them! Someone living in excessive opulence ought to walk out of their home in the morning with their hands covering their reddened, shameful face! But no, instead you hear them crowing on the street corners to anyone and everyone they meet about their money & possessions. Meanwhile, they attend churches where devil-inspired "ministers" stand behind pulpits (tickling their greedy ears) encouraging them to desire all the more wealth & assets. SHAME ON THEM!!! Hell will be full of these satanic preachers!!! If they knew truth (love), they would preach the words of Christ, encouraging their flock "be content with what you have" and "help the poor"—which is a Godly mindset and lifestyle which builds up spiritual treasure in heaven against the coming Day of Judgment.

The Apostle John understood perfectly well the unbreakable separation that exists between "loving God (spirit)" and "loving wealth & assets (dirt)" as he wrote: *"Love NOT the world, neither the THINGS (wealth & assets) that are in the world. If any man love the world, the*

309

love of the Father is NOT in him" (*I John 2:15*). Do you see again how opposed the two "loves" are? Read it again; John is literally saying those people (souls) who love wealth & assets (dirt) ARE NOT "*born again*" of God's Spirit of love! See, this Scripture is absolute proof the Holy Spirit of God ("*love of the Father*") is NOT inside the heart of someone who loves Earthly "wealth & assets". Listen sensibly; a person who truly loves God only loves "spirit material" inside of every person and animal on planet Earth. Thus, a person whose spirit (thoughts, desires, & emotions) is focused on worldly things (wealth & assets) proves they do NOT love God.

John continues (in the above passage of Scripture) by clarifying exactly what "*loving the world*" consists of: "*For ALL that is in the world, the lust of the flesh, and the lust of the eyes, and the pride of life, is NOT of the father, but is of the world*" (*I John 2:16*). Here, John breaks down the three desires involved in "*loving the world*". Note keenly that each desire involves "loving dirt"—i.e. flesh is dirt, eyes only see dirt, and the pride of life has to do with the smugness that comes from acquiring dirt! The word "lust" was translated from the Greek word "*epithymia*" meaning: to desire, long for, covet, and crave. Let us now analyze each "worldly desire" in detail—keeping in mind that these spirit cravings are NOT of God but are "*of the world*", and THEY are the root desire (lust) in a person's heart causing ALL sin (disobedience to the 10 Love Commandments)!

In the phrase "*lust of the FLESH*", the word "flesh" was translated from the Greek word "*sarx*" meaning: flesh, physical body. Thus, the "*lust of the flesh*" has to do with all sexual sin. In other words, it describes a spirit (thoughts, desires, & emotions) that desires, craves, and covets flesh. Yet, physical bodies are just made of dirt (atoms)! Consequently, the "*lust of the flesh* is just worthless dirt worship. Yes, those people (souls) caught up in "sexual sins" actually worship flesh— i.e. they have made "flesh" their god. And, in these last days, Satan has gripped the entire world with the sick, perverted sins of the "*lust of the flesh*"…and I assure you they are soul killers!!!

Listen to God: "*My son, keep my words, and lay up my commandments with thee. Keep my (10 Love) commandments, and live; and my law as the apple of thine eye…That they may keep thee* *from the strange woman...For at the window of my house...I discerned among the youths, a young man void of understanding...And, behold, there met him a woman with the attire of an harlot...So she caught him, and kissed him, and...said...I have perfumed my bed...Come, let us take our fill of love until the morning...With her much fair speech she caused him to yield...**He goeth after her straightway, as an ox goeth to the slaughter**...Till a dart strike through his liver...Hearken unto me now...Let not thine heart decline to her ways...For she hath cast down many wounded: yea, many strong men have been slain by her. **HER HOUSE IS THE WAY TO HELL, going down to the chambers of DEATH**"* (Proverbs 7:1-27). Today, this deadly, lustful scene is occurring in people's minds as they stare licentiously at pornographic magazines and videos! Yet, the result is the same...willful, worldly *"lust of the flesh"* deeds will kill your soul for all eternity.

In the phrase *"lust of the eyes"*, the word "eyes" was translated from the Greek word *"ophthalmos"* meaning: eye, organ of sight. Since our eyes can only see dirt, this is also just dirt worship. In reality, the *"lust of the FLESH"* is part of the *"lust of the eyes"*, but the phrase *"lust of the eyes"* branches out past "flesh" to include all types of dirt worship, for everything we SEE is made of dirt—e.g. houses, vehicles, televisions, computers, or whatever. So *"lust of the eyes"* is the lust for ANY type dirt possession! "Eyeful lust" is such a massive soul killer that Jesus made a point to say: *"And if thine eye offend thee (cause thee to sin), pluck it out: **it is better for thee to enter into the kingdom of God with one eye, than having two eyes to be cast into hell fire**"* (Mark 9:47). Friend, it is essential that you quit lusting for dirt with your eyes! See, it takes eyeballs to fester a love of possessions. Do you see? If you had no eyes, you would hardly be interested in materialistic possessions! In other words, people's EYES is the main instrument (organ) causing them to love dirt—which causes them to sin (disobey the 10 Love Commandments)—ultimately sending them to hell itself. Wow!

Think about it; would you desire a plush, splendid, colossal house if you were blind? Nope! You would care less about it. But because of their EYES people think a big, beautiful house or brand new vehicle or whatever is necessary. But they are wrong. It is just the prideful, worthless desire of the *"lust of the eyes"*. And IT is NOT of GOD!!! It is *"of the world"*. Jesus' harsh sounding words of instruction above were full of love! For it honestly would be better for most people if they would gauge both their eyes out and live in darkness on Earth. Lost in ONLY their thoughts, maybe then they could learn how to truly love God (the spirit in people) and not worthless, dirt possessions.

In the phrase *"pride of life"*, the word "pride" was translated from the Greek word *"alazoneia"* meaning: boasting, pretension, arrogance; and the word "life is from the Greek word *"bios"* meaning: (everyday) life; what one lives on, property, possessions. So, the phrase *"pride of life"* literally refers to people who are all puffed up about their "wealth & assets"!!! These are people who live to make money and gain possessions. When you talk to them all you hear rolling and frothing out of their heart is "money talk" or "possession talk"—e.g. how much money they are making or what they just bought or are going to buy. But read my Biblical lips, friend, this type heart (thoughts, desires, & emotions) is NOT of God (love); it is of the world!

Jesus wisely said, *"Lay NOT up for yourselves treasures upon earth, where moth and rust doth corrupt, and where thieves break through and steal: **But lay up for yourselves treasures in heaven**, where neither moth nor rust doth corrupt, and where thieves do not break through nor steal" (Matthew 6:19-20).* Do you know how to *"lay up treasure in heaven"*? Friend, by DOING the "things" on the "do side" of the 10 Love Commandment list—e.g. feed the hungry, quench the thirsty, clothe the naked, etc. Look, whenever you "show love towards another person" it is like placing a deposit inside of a heavenly bank account for yourself! And THAT is a wise place to *"lay up treasure"* for it will last forever. No one can steal away from you the "love you show" God and other people. Do you understand? Remember: *"He that hath pity upon the poor LENDETH UNTO THE LORD; and that which he hath given will he (God) pay him again" (Proverbs 19:17).* If only people would DO Christ's words!

Listen, we are ALL going to be judged according to the deeds we DO: *"And the dead were judged out of those things which were written in the books, ACCORDING TO THEIR WORKS...and **they were judged EVERY man (woman) according to their works**" (Revelation*

20:12, 13). Friend, God is keeping an accurate record of everything you DO, and if you plan on standing in front of God having done nothing for others or God…it is NOT going to be a good Judgment Day for you! Jesus prophesied, *"And, behold, I come quickly; <u>and my REWARD is with me</u>, **<u>to give EVERY man (woman) according as his work shall be</u>**" (Revelation 22:12)*. I am urging, pleading, imploring, and begging you today to start "loving God and your neighbor as yourself"!

After advising people to *"lay up treasure in heaven and NOT on Earth"*, Jesus declared: *"**<u>For where your treasure is, there will your HEART be also</u>**" (Matthew 6:21)*. What did Christ mean by this? Is Christ warning here that there is something wrong with having a heart (thoughts, desires, & emotions) that loves (continually thinks about) Earthly (dirt) "wealth & assets"? Yes!!! Remember, that which defiles a man comes out of his heart. Friend, what your heart thinks about is what you love, and a heart fixated on "acquiring money & possessions" is a heart full of idolatry (disobeying the 2nd Love Commandment). Remember, Paul wrote: *"You can be sure of this: <u>The Kingdom of Christ and of God will NEVER belong to anyone who is impure or greedy</u>, **<u>for a greedy person is really an idol worshipper—he loves and worships the good things of this life more than God</u>. <u>DON'T BE FOOLED BY THOSE WHO TRY TO EXCUSE THESE SINS</u>**, <u>for the terrible wrath of God is upon all those who DO them</u>. <u>Don't even associate with such people</u>" (Ephesians 5:5-7, Living Bible)*. I am warning you to search your spirit, friend, because if you love *"wealth & assets"* you will NOT enter the Kingdom of God. And I counsel you to <u>RUN AS FAST AS YOU CAN</u> from any "preacher" who is encouraging the "love of money & possessions". Do not be <u>fooled</u> by these satanic preachers, who try and downplay the "root of all sin"…the "love of wealth & assets".

Another word the Bible uses to describe the phrase *"love of money"* is "<u>covetousness</u>", and it was translated from the Greek word *"pleonexia"* meaning: <u>greediness, avarice</u>. Thus, the 10th Love Commandment *"Thou shall not covet"* is actually the "root of all evil" when disobeyed! Do you see what God did in the way he numbered (ordered) the sin list (10 Love Commandments)? He sandwiched ALL OF SIN between the 1st Love Commandment *"Thou shall have NO other gods before me"* and the 10th Love Commandment *"Thou shalt*

NOT covet" knowing they both deal with loving God (spirit) if obeyed, or loving dirt (wealth & assets) if disobeyed. Do you understand? In other words, ALL mankind serves one of two Gods: the Creator God (Spirit of Love) or the God of money (dirt), and God encompassed this fundamental truth in the first and last Love Commandments. Thus, if a soul obeys these 2 "outside" Love Commandments it leads to obedience to ALL the Commandments in the middle, or if a soul disobeys these 2 "outside" Love Commandments it leads to disobedience to ALL the Commandments in the middle. Pretty clever, huh? So I want you to realize anyone disobeying the 10th Love Commandment is automatically disobeying the 1st Love Commandment (for their God is dirt) and the 2nd Love Commandment (for their dirt worship is idolatry). Do you see? To say it bluntly; a covetous person's God is dirt, and they worship that God in their spirit (thoughts, desires, & emotions) as they continually think about making money to obtain dirt possessions.

Friend, Jesus did not joke around with people about the nasty sin of covetousness. One day a naïve man asked Jesus to talk to his brother about dividing up an inheritance (wealth & assets) with him. Can you imagine? Jesus barked (and I am paraphrasing), "Are you kidding me, man. I don't care about that stuff!" But then—knowing what ruled the man's heart (thoughts, desires, & emotions)—Jesus gave him a solemn warning about something far more important than money, for it dealt with the eternal destiny of the man's soul: *"**Take heed, and BEWARE of covetousness**: for a man's LIFE consisteth NOT in the abundance of the things which he possesseth" (Luke 12:15)*. Why do you think Jesus sternly cautioned, *"Beware of covetousness"*? Friend, because he knew THAT sin is the ROOT of all sin (evil), which leads to eternal destruction in hell! I am telling you the truth, reader; unrepentant covetousness (love of money & possessions) will kill your soul for all eternity!

So how is the soul scrubbing going so far? Is your spirit (thoughts, desires, & emotions) twisting and writhing in emotional agony while reading these Bible verses? If you are NOT a money-loving, dirt (possession) lusting, covetous idolater, then your spirit should be quiet and unruffled. In fact, a person's heart full of the love of God will actually enjoy hearing these words about forsaking "wealth &

314

assets", because they already automatically hate them! Yes, a person's heart "*born again*" of God's Holy Spirit of Love will actually rejoice over these words of love. But if your spirit is in emotional distress, then you need to wake up and take a long look into your heart; for if you love "wealth & assets" your soul is infected with a deadly poison which will ultimately lead to your soul's demise. Friend, greed ("*the love of money*") is the deepest, nastiest, fetid part of sin's wound. But if you can endure the emotional torment (letting the Bible's loving words of wisdom penetrate your soul) and become willing to change, you will purge your spirit of sin and save your soul for all eternity! So please, please, do not stop reading now!

Do you remember the man (I wrote about in chapter 10) who asked Jesus, *"Good Master, what shall I DO that I may inherit eternal life?" (Mark 10:17)*? And Jesus answered with: *"Thou knowest the commandments, Do not commit adultery (# 7), Do not kill (# 6), Do not steal (# 8), Do not bear false witness (# 9), Defraud not (# 9), Honour thy father and mother (# 5)" (Mark 10:19)*. Notice, Jesus did not initially list ANY of the first 4 Love Commandments—those DIRECTLY related to loving God, which includes the 1ˢᵗ (Have no other gods) and the 2ⁿᵈ (Worship no idols) Love Commandments—nor did he list the 10ᵗʰ (Do not covet) Love Commandment. Does this mean these 5 Love Commandments do not need to be obeyed to obtain eternal life? Are you kidding me? OF COURSE they need to be obeyed! But Jesus knew the sin ruling this man's heart (thoughts, desires, & emotions) so he was simply setting him up! Friend, God knows our sins because He knows our heart (thoughts, desires, & emotions) and the sins of covetousness and idolatry take place in the heart.

See, on the outside, this man would have appeared to be a good man because he answered Jesus: *"Master, ALL these have I observed from my youth" (Mark 10:20)*. This leads me to believe he was probably even a church (synagogue) going fellow! But then Jesus hit him with the truth about love! Jesus said, *"One thing thou lackest: go thy way, SELL whatsoever thou hast, and give to the poor, and thou shalt have treasure in heaven: and come, take up the cross, and follow me" (Mark 10:21)*. Ah, this was just too much for the man to DO, and he lowered his head and walked away depressed: *"And he was sad at* *that saying, and went away grieved: for he had great possessions. And Jesus looked round about, and saith unto his disciples, **How hardly shall they that have riches (money, wealth, & possessions) enter into the kingdom of God** (Mark 10:22, 23)*! Can you imagine? Here was a man who apparently got his money & possessions honestly and did not commit sexual immorality—he did not steal, lie, cheat, murder, commit adultery, etc.—but it was still not good enough to enter the Kingdom of God!!! He was on his way to hell because his heart (thoughts, desires, & emotions) was wrapped up in his Earthly, materialistic wealth & assets, which meant he was sinning by disobeying the 1st, 2nd and 10th Love Commandments. Friend, you CANNOT go to heaven willfully sinning like that!

The Disciples were shocked at Christ's words, as you may be too! I am sure they thought, "How can this man's love of his 'wealth & assets' keep him from obtaining eternal life? But Jesus confirmed his verdict: *"How hardly shall they that have (materialistic) riches enter into the kingdom of God! **It is easier for a camel to go through the eye of a needle, than for a rich man to enter into the kingdom of God**."* (Mark 10:23). Astonished, the Disciples asked, *"WHO then can be saved?" (Mark 10:26).* Jesus answered, *"With men it is impossible, but not with God: for with God all things are possible" (Mark 10:27).* Friend, here now is the plain hard truth; a heart that "does NOT love money & possessions" HAS TO COME FROM GOD!!! Do you understand? God has to put His heart inside of you! THAT is what being *"born again"* means. When this happens, God literally changes your thoughts, desires, & emotions. And I promise you, God's heart of love beats for the poor! That is why you should avidly seek after and ask God for His Holy Spirit of Love.

One day, God gave me a stunning comparable picture further illustrating the infeasibility of a rich man obtaining eternal life—meaning it is virtually impossible to possess riches (money & possessions) and not be sinning by being a coveting idolater. God said, "Gabriel, it is literally as impossible as lining the inside walls, floor, and ceiling of a man's house with triple X-rated pornographic DVD's, and then telling him to NOT commit the sin of adultery." My jaw dropped!!! How could a man NOT lust sexually in his mind when surrounded by graphic sex

316

scenes? It is virtually impossible!!! So, too, it is nearly impossible to be surrounded by luxury, riches, and materialistic possessions and not be a prideful, coveting idolater. THAT is why Christ said DO NOT seek to lay up materialistic wealth for yourself on Earth, for if you DO, YOUR HEART WILL BE FIXATED ON THOSE THINGS. And covetousness will send a person to hell faster than adultery! Please reread the *"Wilderness"* chapter and internalize the Apostle Paul's words—**NO** adulterer, coveter, nor idolater will <u>ever</u> enter the Kingdom of God and obtain eternal life!

See, from the analogy God gave me above, you would most certainly tell the man with the pornographic DVD's that <u>HE HAS TO GET RID OF THEM</u> if he wants to conquer the sin of adultery. There really is no other way! But what is sad is people cannot see the <u>same</u> goes for money & possessions. If someone truly wants to get victory over the sins of covetousness and idolatry, <u>THEY MUST GET RID of their money & possessions</u>!!! Do you see? NOW you know why Jesus continually instructed people to *"sell their possessions, give the money to the poor, and take up their cross of suffering"*. Christ was not being mean, nor was he giving out absurd advice: His wise words were/are the key to obtaining eternal life, for (if obeyed) they will KILL the root of ALL sin in a person's life! Peter recognized the wisdom in Jesus' words and said: *"<u>Lord, to whom shall we go?</u> **Thou hast the WORDS of eternal life**" (John 6:68)*. But just hearing Jesus' words will not gain you eternal life, <u>YOU MUST DO WHAT HE SAID</u>!!!

Look, the encounter with the rich man above was NOT the only time Jesus told people to sell their possessions! He said it over and over again to <u>all</u> people: *"**SELL that ye have, and give alms**; provide yourselves bags which wax not old, <u>a treasure in the heavens that faileth not</u>, where no thief approacheth, neither moth corrupteth" (Luke 12:33)*. Friend, do you not see you are playing with fire by being (and wanting to be) materialistically rich? Your odds of going to heaven are almost zero. The wicked sins of covetousness and idolatry are some of the most overlooked sins, yet they are soul killers. That is why Paul wrote: *"**Don't be FOOLED by those who TRY TO EXCUSE these sins**, <u>for the terrible wrath of God is upon ALL those who DO them</u>. **Don't even associate with such people**" (Ephesians 5:5, 6, Living Bible)*. See, if you hang out with greedy people—continuing to listen to their incessant, money-loving, moneymaking, and possession acquiring talk—soon that same "spirit of greed" will worm its way into your heart! And the next thing you know, your spirit (thoughts, desires, & emotions) will be spinning wildly with lusts, ideas, and plans to try and get rich to obtain dirt possessions. It is a wicked, nefarious poison, (which spreads by the "*pride of life*") compelling a soul to jealously compete with their neighbor, seeing how they can out do them or "one-up" them. Yet, the end result of that kind of loveless mentality will be eternal spiritual death! So Paul was wise to say: "*do NOT even associate with those kinds of people.*" In other words, STAY CLEAR OF THEM!!!

Are you starting to recognize (from stories like the rich man above) we can ONLY obtain eternal life by making a willful decision to repent of sin—i.e. stop disobeying and start obeying the 10 Love Commandments! That is why the stone tables containing the 10 Love Commandments were placed INSIDE the Ark of the Covenant, representing the place of rest in the Kingdom of God! Yes, the rich man's disobedience to the 1st, 2nd & 10th Love Commandments had him on the path to hell! I mean really, could the truth be any more obvious? To obtain eternal life we must CHANGE our heart: We must choose the WAY of love (good) over the WAY of sin (evil)—which means to begin obeying the 10 Love Commandments.

But in today's diabolically-twisted church world, the rich man who met Jesus in the story above would be nauseatingly fawned over, ushered into a padded pew, fed a steady diet of false preaching that stroked his materialistic ego (have his ears tickled with sugary, prosperity words about how God wanted him to be Earthly rich) and then told he would be on his way to heaven if he simply paid lip service to some prayer of "accepting Jesus into his heart". I can almost hear the Devil laughing at this insanity! Do you recognize the deceit? The church has put blinders on towards sin!!! They no longer want to talk about sin (hmmm…I wonder who is behind that ideology?). They cannot or will not recognize the sin in people's lives that has them on the path to destruction. Therefore, the church is going to be responsible for sending millions of people to hell! We MUST get back to straight-talk, warning people of sin. Friend, we must willfully STOP sinning,

318

there is NO other way to obtain eternal life!

By the way, have you noticed "prosperity-gospel" churches grow huge! You can spot them a mile away. All someone has to do to achieve a <u>massive</u> church congregation is STOP talking about sin and START telling people God wants them to be materialistically rich. It is really quite pathetically easy! Then complement your act by writing and selling books containing stories like "if you see an enormous, beautiful house on a hill somewhere, you should desire (lust after) that house: You should think big of God and not limit Him!" Are you kidding me? What a twisted pile of deceptive devil's dung! Can you NOT see this is just Satan preaching greed (covetousness) or the "love of mammon"? Yes, friend, Satan is advocating *"the love of money"* from pulpits all over the world today! He is inside the spirits (thoughts, desires, & emotions) of "ministers" and he is out to <u>deceive</u> the entire world. He has been peddling the same old crap from the beginning of time—the love of dirt! But Jesus forewarned: *"**<u>WOE unto you that are rich! FOR YE HAVE RECEIVED YOUR CONSOLATION</u>**. <u>Woe unto you that are full! for ye shall hunger</u>. <u>Woe unto you that laugh now! for ye shall mourn and weep</u>. Woe unto you, when all men shall speak well of you! for so did their fathers to the false prophets"* (Luke 6:24-26). Amen and amen.

Let us juxtaposition the current fake church scene with a REAL story of salvation in the Bible. It is the story of another materialistically rich man named Zacchaeus: *"there was a man named <u>Zacchaeus,</u> which was the chief among the publicans, and <u>he was rich</u>"* (Luke 19:2). Zacchaeus had heard about Jesus and was extremely excited to meet him, so one day he climbed up a sycamore tree to get a look at him as he passed by. Jesus noticed Zacchaeus and said, *"Zacchaeus, make haste, and come down; for <u>today I must abide at thy house</u>"* (Luke 19:5). And the Bible records: *"he made haste, and came down, and <u>received him joyfully</u>"* (Luke 19:6). Friend, this is how we should ALL receive the "Word of God (Christ)—with joy!

But while dining at Zacchaeus' house, all of a sudden Zacchaeus jumped up and declared, *"Behold, Lord, the **<u>HALF of my goods I (will) give to the poor</u>**; <u>and if I have taken any thing from any man by false accusation, I restore him fourfold</u>"* (Luke 19:8). Wow, are you kidding?

What on Earth do you think Jesus was talking about that prompted that kind of a response out of Zacchaeus? I think you can correctly guess…Christ was talking about "the root of all sin"—the Love of Money (dirt). And what was Christ's reply to Zacchaeus' amazing (repentant) declaration? He said, *"**This day is SALVATION come to this house** forsomuch as he also is a son of Abraham. For the Son of man is come to seek and to save that which was lost" (Luke 19:9, 10).* Wow, Zacchaeus was SAVED right there on the spot! (And Christ had not even gone to the cross yet, nor did Zaccheaus understand that he would have to do that!!!) Zacchaeus was SAVED because he had done mankind's part in the "salvation equation". His words (and deeds) of repentance (love) proved he was instantly *"born again"*. What made the difference? Zacchaeus' complete change of heart about greed was the KEY to obtaining eternal life (salvation)! His new heart was saying (and I am paraphrasing), "Ok, Lord, I will no longer love my money (dirt), and I'll prove it by giving half of mine away. I will right every wrong I have ever done, and in the future I will treat people fairly (obey the 10 Love Commandments)!"

Friend, THAT is the absolute Biblical truth about how to obtain eternal life! Do you understand? A total change took place in Zacchaeus' spirit (thoughts, desires, & emotions). It was his thought process that entirely changed with respect to right living: HE REPENTED! Remember, Christ said; *"except ye repent, ye shall ALL likewise perish" (Luke 13:3).* Thus, the very moment Zacchaeus "changed his mind" about his *"love of money"*—the root of all evil—he was saved. Then, all he had to DO was continue living that WAY till the day he died, and he would receive eternal life in God's Kingdom.

Did you notice (in the story) there was no need to recite some "accepting Jesus into your heart" prayer to obtain eternal life? And there was no "church attendance" needed? But what WAS necessary was a heart transplant; a brand new way of thinking that conquers sin by saying, "I will no longer live for money. I will chop down, mutilate, and uproot the 'love of wealth & assets' out of my spirit (thoughts, desires, & emotions). I will choose to walk in love towards God and my fellow man—obey all of the 10 Love Commandments—for the rest of my Earthly life." THAT is what SALVATION is about, my friend!

Salvation will happen for you, too, the moment you decide to quit loving money and choose to follow the "*narrow path*" of righteousness.

Let me ask you a question; do you know of a church around today where people jump up under conviction of sin during the sermon and proclaim from a repentant heart, "Ok, preacher, I will sell half of my possessions (land, houses, etc.) and <u>give</u> the money to the poor, and I will make right four times over everyone I have cheated in the past!" Are you kidding me? There is NO chance to hear that <u>REQUIRED</u> "change-of-heart salvation response" out of congregants today, because "God's message" has somehow changed (that is me being sarcastic)! Today, it seems God wants everyone to be materialistically rich, just listen to "His preachers" inundating people's ears with how He wants to bless them more financially (materialistically). Hogwash!!! And today's pompous church-goers are swallowing that devilish message hook-line-&-sinker. They are already on there way to hell (living in greed) and are getting their money-loving, self-indulgent spirits pumped up with hopes that God will give them more money & possessions. It is really a sickening situation! Who would possibly jump up today and say what Zacchaeus said, when Christ's message in the Bible is NO longer the message in the church?

Yet, after Christ's ascension, what were the <u>first</u> TRUE believer's spirits like that were turning to the Apostle's message? Listen to what the new converts were DOING: *"And <u>they continued stedfastly in the apostles' doctrine</u>...and <u>fear came upon every soul</u>: and many wonders and signs were done by the apostles. And <u>ALL THAT BELIEVED</u> were together, and <u>had ALL things common</u>; **And SOLD their possessions and goods, and parted them to all men, as every man had need**...And <u>the Lord added to the church daily such as should be SAVED</u>" (Acts 2:42-47).* Are you kidding me? Did you hear what the TRUE SAVED <u>BELIEVERS</u>—meaning on their WAY to obtaining eternal life!—were DOING? They were **<u>DOING</u>** the very words Christ had preached his entire 3½ year ministry—namely, selling their possessions and giving the money to the poor—which obviously means the Apostles were preaching Christ's SAME message! To my knowledge this is unheard of in today's church world. What has happened? Friend, God's message of truth (love) is gone!!!

321

Listen to another early-church passage: *"And the multitude of them that BELIEVED were of one heart and of one soul: **neither said any of them that ought of the things which he possessed was his own**; but they had all things in common...Neither was there any among them that lacked: for AS MANY AS WERE POSSESSORS OF LANDS OR HOUSES SOLD THEM, and brought the prices of the things that were sold, And laid them down at the apostles' feet: and distribution was made unto every man according as he had need"* (Acts 4:32-35). Friend, I am extremely disheartened at what Satan has done: He has had almost 2,000 years to distort the truth of Christ's words, and he has done a stunning job! And most church goers today are Biblically illiterate. But I thank God for recording these early-church passages of Scripture for a permanent record of what TRUE BELIEVERS DO, and what God's TRUE church (people) are like.

Friend, the original believers were rightly "selling out" to God! Undoubtedly, they were hearing the undiluted truth from the disciples about God (love), how to obtain eternal life, and what living in this Earthly life is all about. My friend, they KNEW truth (love)! They were actually obeying Jesus' words: *Whosoever he be of you that forsaketh NOT ALL he hath, **he CANNOT be my disciple**"* (Luke 14:33). Friend, they WERE forsaking ALL!!! They were giving up their materialistic (dirt) life—land, houses, & possessions—and their worthless, selfish Earthly dreams to follow Christ and his WAY of selfless love towards others. They TRULY loved their neighbor as much as themselves, because their deeds proved it! How about you, today? (By the way, notice the Apostles—the preachers—did not suck up the money for themselves so they could live high-on-the-hog. No, the money went to help the poor and the needy!)

Amazingly, though, the Holy Spirit speaking through Peter knew the time of today's prosperity church age would come: *"But there were false prophets, too, in those days, just as there will be false teachers among you. **They will CLEVERLY tell their lies about God**... Many will follow their evil teaching that there is nothing wrong with sexual sin. And because of them Christ and his way (of love) will be scoffed at. **These teachers in their GREED will tell you ANYTHING to get hold of your money**. But God condemned them long ago and* *their destruction is on the way"* (II Peter 2:1-3, Living Bible). Wow!!! The King James Version says it like this: *"And **through covetousness shall they with FEIGNED (lying) words make merchandise of you"*** (II Peter 2:3). Friend, this is happening right before our eyes! If you do not believe me, turn on your TV and listen to the greedy minded "prosperity gospel preachers", then send your money in for their evil products. But this should be no surprise to you, because Christ's 2ⁿᵈ Coming is right around the corner!

Coming is right around the corner!

If we would all just sit down and think rationally about the Scriptures, we would easily <u>KNOW</u> that God does NOT want people to be materialistically rich, for what kind of a God would want us to be Earthly rich when he said, forthrightly, *"Rich people have almost NO CHANCE of obtaining eternal life"*? Think about that, seriously: That would make God a monster! If God wants us all to be materialistically wealthy, then I guess He wants us ALL to have the best chance possible of winding up in hell! Does that make any sense at all? No, my friend!!! God does not wish <u>ANYONE</u> to perish: *"The Lord is...<u>NOT willing that any should perish, but that all should come to REPENTANCE"</u>* (II Peter 3:9). Do you see? God does not want to lose any of His children. Therefore, logical deduction leads us to the correct conclusion that God could not possibly want people to be Earthly rich, because He does not want them to perish!

Rather, the Bible says: *"**LABOUR NOT TO BE RICH**: <u>cease from thine OWN wisdom. Wilt thou set thine eyes upon that which is not? For riches certainly make themselves wings; they fly away as an eagle toward heaven"</u>* (Proverbs 23:4, 5). See, from an Earthly (worldly) viewpoint it appears to be sagacious to spend your days striving and struggling for "wealth & assets"—get all you can and prepare for your retirement. All these thoughts and ideas seem so right, but they are not!!! THAT is why God said, *"<u>Cease from your OWN wisdom and do NOT labor to be rich</u>"*. Are you laboring to be monetarily and materialistically rich? Is that what drives your spirit on a daily basis? The Bible says: *"<u>There is a WAY that seemeth right unto a man, but the end thereof are the ways of death"</u>* (Proverbs 16:25). See, it <u>seems</u> right to a man, but it is not. It is actually foolishness!

You ask, "Gabriel, but how could that be? I thought I was smart by preparing for my future?" Ah, you think you are preparing for your FUTURE, but you are not! You are preparing for an Earthly future by hoarding up money to buy food, clothing, and shelter; **YET, you do NOT know if you will even be living on Earth TOMORROW**! Do you see? A wise person gives his money away, daily—e.g. feeding the hungry, giving drink to the thirsty, clothing the naked, etc—storing up treasure in heaven against the coming Day of Judgment, which prepares their soul for their TRUE future—THEIR ETERNAL DESTINY!!! See, people think they are smart and intelligent to stockpile money, but they are really dumb and stupid.

Paul wrote: *"Tell those who are (materialistically) rich not to be proud and not to trust in their money, which will soon be gone, but their pride and trust should be in the living God...**Tell them to USE their money to DO GOOD**. They should be rich in GOOD WORKS and should GIVE HAPPILY to those in need, always being ready to share with others whatever God has given them. **By DOING THIS they will be STORING UP real treasure for themselves in heaven**—it is the ONLY safe investment for eternity! And they will be living a fruitful Christian life down here as well"* (I Timothy 6:17-19, Living Bible). The King James Bible says: *"**Laying up in store for themselves a good FOUNDATION against the time to come, THAT they MAY lay hold on eternal life**"* (I Timothy 6:19). Friend, as I said earlier; God is watching what you DO, and only your "good works" deeds prove your love, worship, and belief in God (love), and THAT is what God will assess in deciding your eternal fate!

If your spirit (mentality) is only concerned about *"saving your life"* down here on planet Earth, you will surely lose your soul's eternal destiny. This is what Jesus meant when he said, *"Whosoever shall seek to save his life shall lose it; and whosoever shall lose his life shall preserve it"* (Luke 17:33). See, God's wisdom is all backwards with respect to conventional, fleshly wisdom. Here is the trap; if your spirit (thoughts, desires, & emotions) is greatly concerned about your future here and now on Earth, you will DO almost nothing in cheerful, selfless service (love) towards others. You just cannot because you are too worried about *"saving your own life"*! But who are you? Do you have ANY control over your life? No! God can have you dead tonight, and you will stand in front of the Creator of the universe having lived a worthless, selfish, fruitless life, only concerned about yourself. And if that is the case...I guarantee your spiritual knees will be knocking uncontrollably at that time!

Friend, God wants you to live fearlessly. He wants you live one day at a time, doing everything possible to help your fellow man. THAT is being a wise person! Jesus instructed *"**Take NO thought for your life**, what ye shall eat; neither for the body, what ye shall put on. **The life is more than meat, and the body is more than raiment**" (Luke 12:22, 23)*. Do you see? God does not even want you to be anxious about food and clothing! So why are you worried about your retirement? You SHOULD be worried that your spiritual bank account is broke because you are not loving God with all your heart and your neighbor as yourself—i.e. obeying the 10 Love Commandments.

Jesus said, *"If any man will come after me, let him DENY himself and take up his cross, and follow me. For whosoever will save his life shall lose it: and whosoever will lose his life for my sake shall find it. **For what is a man profited, if he shall GAIN the whole world, and LOSE his own soul?**" (Matthew 16:24-26)*. Do you see? *"Losing your life for Christ's (loves) sake"* has to DO with "giving up your wealth & assets". And likewise *"denying yourself"* has to DO with "denying yourself money & possessions". That is why (immediately after those two statements) Jesus said, *"For WHAT is a man profited, if he shall GAIN THE WHOLE WORLD, and lose his own soul?"* See, it is obvious Jesus had one train-of-thought in his words above—namely, for people to not worry about dirt (making money to obtain possessions) or they would be traveling the path towards eternal destruction! So, how about you? Are you DENYING yourself Earthly riches and taking up your cross of suffering, or are you seeking to save (love) your immediate Earthly life by storing up wealth & assets?

Friend, our life here on Earth is just a tiny blip on the radar screen of eternity. James wrote: *"Go to now, ye that say, To day or to morrow we will go into such a city, and continue there a year, and buy and sell, and get gain: Whereas ye know not what shall be on the morrow. **For what is your life? It is even a VAPOUR, that appeareth for a little time, and then vanisheth away**. For that ye OUGHT to say,*

*If the Lord will, we shall live, and do this, or that. But now ye rejoice in your boastings: **ALL such rejoicing is EVIL**" (James 4:13-16).* Are you getting it? Live for God daily (put Him first in EVERYTHING) and forget worrying about your Earthly life now. Jesus instructed: *"So don't be anxious about tomorrow. God will take care of your tomorrow too. **LIVE ONE DAY AT A TIME**" (Matthew 6:34, Living Bible).*

One day Jesus told a sobering parable about a rich man who was ONLY concerned about himself and his future here and now on Earth: *"The ground of a certain rich man brought forth plentifully: And he thought within himself, saying, What shall I DO, because I have no room where to bestow my fruits? And he said, This will I DO: I will pull down my barns, and build greater; and there will I bestow all my fruits and my goods. And I will say to my soul, **Soul, thou hast much goods laid up for many years; take thine ease, eat, drink, and be merry**. But God said unto him, **THOU FOOL, this night thy soul shall be required of thee**: then whose shall those things be, which thou hast provided? **So is he that layeth up treasure (dirt) for himself, and is not rich toward God**" (Luke 12:16-21).* Do you recognize the selfishness of this man's thoughts? He only cared about himself! He could have cared less that his brothers and sisters in the world were starving and that he had the resources to help them. Do you know how many people think like this today? Do you know how many people have the Earthly goal to get monetarily rich so they can then take it easy in life? This is the mindset of a FOOL!!! This attitude GREATLY displeases the Lord God Almighty! Friend, we do NOT know what day God is going to require our soul to stand before Him, so we better be continuously helping (loving) people—i.e. getting rich towards God (spirit)—everyday of our lives.

Remember Jesus' parable of the rich man and Lazarus the beggar? THAT parable again confirms the hellish fate awaiting monetarily rich people who will not help monetarily poor people during their time on Earth. If you remember, the rich man lived in luxury while Lazarus did not: *"There was a certain rich man, which was clothed in purple and fine linen, and fared sumptuously every day: And there was a certain beggar named Lazarus, which was laid at his gate, full of sores, and desiring to be fed with the crumbs which fell from the rich man's table" (Luke 16:19-21)*. Sure enough, the rich man wound up in anguish in hell and the poor man went to paradise! In hell, the rich man now begged for Lazarus to <u>HELP</u> him by cooling his tongue with a drop of water, but Abraham rebuked the rich man by saying: *"<u>Son, remember that thou in thy lifetime receivedst thy good things, and likewise Lazarus evil things</u>: but <u>**now he is comforted, and thou art tormented**</u>" (Luke 16:25)*. Can you perceive truth? Do you recognize the rich man's wicked sin of "covetousness" and refusal to <u>DO</u> the "do side" of the 8th Love Commandment (Thou shall not steal, but give) sent him to hell? Without a doubt, we will ALL reap <u>exactly</u> what we have sown during our Earthly life!

Some of Jesus' parables are explained (interpreted) in the Bible, but his parable of the *"talents"* was not. Allow me to divulge to you its true meaning. Jesus began: *"For <u>the kingdom of heaven</u> is as a MAN traveling into a far country, <u>who called his own servants, and delivered unto them his goods</u>. And unto one he gave <u>five talents</u>, to another <u>two</u>, and to another <u>one</u>; <u>**to every man according to his several ability**</u>; and straightway took his journey" (Matthew 25:14, 15)*. When Jesus starts a parable with *"the kingdom of heaven is (like)..."*—which he often did—it means he is either going to reveal the Kingdom of God's characteristics or he is about to reveal to mankind what it takes to ENTER the Kingdom of God and obtain eternal life. This parable is for the latter cause, <u>for IT was told to reveal (or give) a PROFOUND explanation of the TRUE PURPOSE for mankind's souls being placed down here on planet Earth</u>. In other words, IT is a "big-picture" look at the real reason why we are all here and what God is looking for out of each of our lives in order to obtain eternal life.

In the parable, God refers to mankind (His spirit children) as His servants, and the *"<u>Man</u> traveling into a far country"* is God. So take note, GOD delivered to each one of us *"a certain amount of <u>HIS</u> goods"* and then *"took <u>HIS</u> journey"*. This represents the fact that we live on Earth and God is in heaven watching us from afar: *"<u>The heaven, even the heavens, are the LORD'S</u>: but <u>the earth hath he given to the children of men</u>" (Psalms 115:16)*. God is intently examining what we <u>DO</u> with what He gave us so He can later reward us (negatively or positively) at the Judgment. But **WHAT** did **GOD** give each of us? In other words, WHAT do the "*talents*" in the parable represent? (Remember, in a parable a physical thing always represents a spiritual thing). Friend, the "*talents*" represent our spirit (soul or heart)—i.e. that invisible, <u>invaluable</u> part of us that houses our thoughts, desires, & emotions!!! THAT is why the parable states "*God gave us HIS goods*". Do you understand? God is spirit; thus, He gave us a part of <u>Himself</u> for we are ALL His "*spirit children*".

The word "talent" is from the Greek "*talanton*" meaning: <u>talent (weight and MONETARY unit; about **57** to **80 lbs.**); a talent of silver was about 6,000 day's wages (denarii) of a common laborer and a talent of gold was about 180,000 day's wages, **often implying a vast, unattainable amount**</u>! Do you recognize the gargantuan <u>value</u> of a talent? No doubt, the Disciples and people living in Jesus' day would have known how much a talent of metal was worth. At 250 working days a year, <u>1 talent of silver represents the wages of 24 years of work;</u> and <u>1 talent of gold represents the wages of 720 years</u>! Friend, this is MORE than a lifetime's worth of money—and that is only **1** talent!!! Do you see then in Jesus' parable of the talents, a "talent" accurately represented the <u>priceless</u> value (or worth) of a human soul?

Now notice in the parable God gave some people 1 talent, some 2 talents, and some 5 talents. The difference in "value" is related to the disparity God gave each of our <u>spirits</u> with respect to our creativity, intelligence, and talent (no pun intended). Do you understand? For example, we each have varying degrees of mental abilities—i.e. some of us were born retarded, while some of us were born geniuses (some have IQ's of 60, while others have an IQ of 200). Do you see? But either way, God loves us ALL the same, and our spirit (soul) is still priceless! Remember Jesus fumed, *"WHAT shall a man give in exchange for his soul?" (Mark 8:37).* Friend, there is <u>nothing</u> you can give in exchange for your soul!!! One spirit (soul) is worth more than all the dirt on planet Earth! It is **BY FAR** the most valuable thing YOU possess, and yet most people treat it as if it is worthless.

Adding to the dissimilarity in "value" (or potential) God bestowed upon each of our spirits is the place and time period we were born into. For instance, some countries have jobs in every town, while others have few! To take it even further, there are even differences in the <u>specific</u> family we were each born into—i.e. some of us were born into Royalty, while others of us were born in the slums. All of these factors combined give credence to the *"different amount of goods"* God initially bestowed upon each of our spirits. But I want to say it again, in NO WAY is one soul any more important or valuable to God then another, because we are <u>ALL</u> His dearly beloved *"spirit children"*!

The parable proceeds by disclosing the man (God) returned at a later time to inquire (or add up) the "usefulness" of each servant with respect to the *"goods"* they were given and then to reward them equivalently. In other words, they each gave an account of what they had done with their *"goods"*: *"<u>After a long time</u> <u>the Lord of those servants cometh, and reckoneth with them</u>" (Matthew 25:19)*. I think you know what this represents…Judgment Day! It may feel like a long time off, but it is <u>inevitable</u> for each and every one of us. We will ALL stand there someday and give account as those burning, all-knowing eyes of the Father pierce our soul. And friend, a one-time "salvation prayer" at some point in your life is NOT what God will be looking for! That is <u>not</u> what is going to decide your eternal fate (unless God allowed you to die in such a way that you had time to truly repent of your sins while dying, like the man on the cross beside Jesus). <u>PLEASE DO NOT COUNT ON THAT OPPORTUNITY</u>, for it is probably an extremely rare occurrence! Rather, this parable more accurately reveals the truth about the Judgment Day scene and our eternal future. And at the Judgment God will be looking to see how we did in increasing (or gaining) spirits (souls) for Him!!!

You ask, "Gabriel, what are you talking about? How can <u>I</u> <u>gain</u> spirits (souls) for God?" Friend, it is accomplished by using your life as a beacon of light (love) to turn other people's spirits to the *"WAY of righteousness"*—i.e. persuading others to walk in love towards God and their neighbor (obey the 10 Love Commandments) which will save their soul for all eternity. In other words, your continual, daily light (life of love) has the power to turn other people's hearts to God (love), which will in turn save their souls and yield them <u>eternal</u> life. Consequently, <u>YOU just increased spirit (souls) for God</u>!!! Do you understand? Yes, you can literally use your spirit (thoughts, desires, & emotions)—the *"goods God gave you"*—to love God and your neighbor as yourself (<u>DO</u>

the Golden Rule) to help other people's spirits learn to love God and others. I could write an in depth 200 page dissertation on all the ways we can use our spirits to help encourage and increase other people's spirits everyday of our lives (from simply smiling at someone to dying for them!) but it will always boil down to <u>DOING acts of love</u>, which means to obey the 10 Love Commandments.

The Bible states: *"<u>The FRUIT of the righteous is a tree of life</u>; and <u>**he that winneth souls is wise**</u>" (Proverbs 11:30).* Do you see? Look, in this book I am not trying to get you to mouth some "sinner's prayer": I am trying to get you to LIVE RIGHT (obey the 10 Love Commandments). I want you to live a life of love towards God and others. THAT is what is important! THAT is how you use your spirit (life) to shine like a lighthouse (leading others to safety in a dark, evil world) influencing them to live a life of love, which will save their soul. Listen to the prophet Daniel reveal truth about the Judgment Day scene: *"And many of them that sleep in the dust of the earth shall awake, some to everlasting life, and some to shame and everlasting contempt. And <u>they that be WISE shall shine as the brightness of the firmament</u>; and <u>**THEY THAT TURN MANY TO RIGHTEOUSNESS**</u> as the stars for ever and ever" (Daniel 12:2, 3).* And you know the verse: *"My tongue shall speak of thy WORD: <u>for ALL thy (10 Love) commandments ARE righteousness</u>" (Psalms 119:172).* So who are the wise? Those that *"turn others to obeying the 10 Love Commandments"* or to follow the WAY of love! How does that make one wise? Because it will SAVE other people's souls! It is <u>precisely</u> what Jesus meant when he told Peter and Andrew: *"Follow me, and <u>I will make you fishers of men (souls)</u>" (Matthew 4:19).*

Listen to Paul explain what we are to <u>DO</u> and <u>BE</u> in our few short years here on Earth: *"Dearest friends, when I was there with you, <u>you were always so careful to follow my instructions</u>. And now that I am away <u>you must be even more careful to DO the GOOD THINGS that result from being saved</u>, <u>**OBEYING GOD with deep reverence, shrinking back from ALL that might displease him**</u>. For God is at work within you, <u>helping you WANT TO OBEY HIM, and then helping you DO what he wants</u>. In everything you <u>DO</u>, stay away from complaining and arguing, so that no one can speak a word of blame against you.*

330

You are to live clean, innocent lives as children of God in a dark world full of people who are crooked and stubborn. **SHINE OUT AMONG THEM LIKE BEACON LIGHTS, holding out to them the Word of Life (love)**" *(Philippians 2:12-16)*. Friend, get it through your head; you are a "beacon of light of God's love" ONLY when you "obey the 10 Love Commandments". THAT is the light of God's love. So speak them and DO them, continually.

If you are skeptical, allow me to give you just one example of how "obeying the 10 Love Commandments" at ALL times during your life can help others obtain eternal life; thus, increasing spirits (souls) in God's Kingdom! Friend, you must realize people are watching and listening to you continually, and your deeds and words are continually influencing them—whether good or bad! Even when you did not know it, someone saw you pick up a $20 dollar bill and hand it back to a person who unknowingly just dropped it. The individual who noticed you DO that was touched in their spirit (thoughts, desires, & emotions) by your act of love—i.e. obeying the 8th Love Commandment "*thou shall not steal*". Later that night, as they lay in bed, they remembered your "good deed" and decided to get out their Bible and read it! They were hooked. And as the months passed they kept on reading the Bible's words of love until their spirit became "*born again*" and now they too follow the WAY of love (righteousness). And to think…the whole ball got rolling all because of your willingness to walk in love (obey God's 10 Love Commandments! See, your "good deeds and words" are preaching all the time, leading others towards repentance and salvation. THAT is why it is most important to live a life of love, continually! That is how you increase spirits for God. In fact, YOU just might be the only person God had planned for someone else to get to know Him (love).

Now on the other hand, disobeying the 10 Love Commandments (sinning) leads to the exact opposite result! It is a vicious cycle that kills people's spirits (souls). It can range from simply not keeping God's Sabbath day Holy (which tells others you do not have time for God so why should they) all the way to having an adulterous affair with someone (which leads them to kill their spouse in order to be with you!) See, "disobeying the 10 Love Commandments (sinning)" always influences others toward death and destruction for their soul. If this is how you live your life—e.g. loving money (dirt), cursing God, stealing, lying, etc.—then you are Satan's preacher of "non-loving deeds and words"! You are helping people to NOT know God (love). You are literally using your spirit (the "*goods*" God gave you) to help kill souls! And THAT will be a colossal mistake come Judgment Day.

Returning to the "*talent*" parable, we find the man returned to settle up with each of his servants. The servant given 5 talents earned 5 more talents, and the man said, "***Well done, thou good and faithful servant***...*ENTER thou into the joy of the Lord*" *(Matthew 25:21)*. From the man's language we recognize this as God's <u>rewarding</u> Judgment Day talk. Thus, the man given 5 talents must have repented of sin and lived a good life (obeyed the 10 Love Commandments), having influenced other spirits to follow the Way of love too, which won their spirits (souls) into God's Kingdom! Likewise, the servant given 2 talents gained 2 more talents, and God was just as pleased with him as the first servant, "*<u>Well done, GOOD and faithful servant</u>; thou has been faithful over a few things, I will make thee ruler over many things: <u>enter into the joy of the lord</u>*" *(Matthew 25:23)*.

But WHAT did the servant given 1 talent do with his spirit? The Bible says: "*But he that had received <u>one</u> went and **DIGGED IN THE EARTH, and hid his lord's money***" *(Matthew 25:18)*. Wow!!! Do you get it? Do you understand what Christ is saying he did? Friend, this servant HID his spirit in dirt!!! Say what? Look, he used his spirit (intelligence, creativity, & talent) only to acquire "money & possession" <u>WHICH ARE ALL JUST DIRT</u>! Do you understand? In other words, he <u>buried</u> his priceless soul in dirt, which is the ROOT of all evil! He even told God <u>why</u> he did it: "***I WAS AFRAID**, and went and hid thy talent in the earth: lo, there thou hast that is thine*" *(Matthew 25:25)*. Friend, do you understand this truth? Listen, people who are <u>anxious</u> they will not have food, clothing, and lodging during their lifetime on Earth live in FEAR!!! And this fear stifles their ability to love God and others. This fretful, worried mentality drives people to hoard up wealth & assets (dirt) ONLY for themselves. But one day they will show up at the Judgment Day scene spiritually bankrupt, with no treasure in heaven awaiting them in the form of acts of love shown towards God and their neighbor. Truly, they will have buried their spirit in dirt, living

332

a useless and pointless life on Earth!

And what was God's response to this man's life? He despised it!!! God shouted, *"**Cast ye the UNPROFITABLE servant into outer darkness: there shall be weeping and gnashing of teeth**" (Matthew 25:30)*. Friend, I am warning you to stop worrying about your puny life down here on Earth! Make your life useful and profitable to God by loving Him and others (which is Him, too) as yourself! Stop *"loving your life"* and trying to *"save your life"* by ambitiously, greedily striving to obtain *"mammon"*. Remember Christ's words: *"He that loveth his life shall lose it; and he that HATETH HIS LIFE in this world shall keep it UNTO LIFE ETERNAL" (John 12:25)*. *"Hating your life in this world"* means living a fearless, self-less life in service and love towards God and others. It means being concerned about other's future as much as your own! Live courageously, giving what you have to those who need everyday of your life. You are not promised tomorrow, friend, so stop worrying about it!

One day the Lord gave me a striking image of how He views people who are all wrapped up in their pursuit of obtaining Earthly (dirt) riches (money & possessions). He said when He looks at them He sees a diaper-clad baby—devoid of any wisdom—sitting in a field, clumsily flopping dirt around with a plastic shovel. I was stunned at the visual, for it is a purposeless life! Yet, what is heartbreaking is these greedy, worldly people usually feel they are the top of the heap (the cream of the crop). As they acquire more money and more dirt possessions, they get more and more bigheaded, thinking they are extremely successful. But God views them as a baby without any understanding at all! They are actually among the least successful (poorest) people on planet Earth! It is the classic case of the *"deception of riches"*.

On a Sunday morning May 20, 2007—only 9 days before I was to start my 40 day fast—I was jarred out of a deep sleep by a resounding voice! With my eyes suddenly opened, I struggled to adapt to the fact that I was now wide awake and conscious. Slowly, my senses righted me, and I marveled over the words still rattling in my head, for I clearly remembered the simple sentence the voice had just proclaimed, *"Esau TRADED his birthright for a 'right-now' gratification!"* That was it!!! I was baffled. I had NEVER heard anything like that in my life: The statement was way out of left field to me. But I had a hunch it was from God, so I asked, "God, what does that mean?" Then, like magic (as I lay in bed now wide awake and fully conscious) Scripture verses began to pass before me in my mind. It was like an angel of the Lord began communicating Scriptures to me till I knew EXACTLY what was meant by the amazing, divine sentence that had orally woke me up. Within about 30 minutes the experience was over, but I was so astounded at the message that I got up, grabbed my Bible, and read the story of Jacob & Esau in Genesis.

If you remember, it was about two brothers Jacob & Esau: *"Esau was a cunning hunter, a man of the field; and Jacob was a plain man, dwelling in tents" (Genesis 25:27).* One day, Esau came in tired from a long day of hunting and was very hungry. He saw Jacob cooking pottage (stew) and asked him for some: *"Feed me, I pray thee, with that same red pottage; for I am faint" (Genesis 25:30).* Jacob replied, "I will give you some food (dirt) if you sell (trade) me your birthright for it!" (See, in those days the firstborn son received the father's blessing, and Esau was Isaac & Rebekah's firstborn son.) Esau said, *"Behold, I am at the point to die: and **what profit shall this birthright do to me?**" (Genesis 25:32).* Jacob insisted: *"Swear to me this day; and **he (Esau) sware unto him: and he sold his birthright unto Jacob**" (Genesis 25:33).* After this: *"Then Jacob gave Esau bread and pottage of lentils; and he did eat and drink, and rose up, and went his way: **thus Esau DESPISED his birthright**" (Genesis 25:34).*

Now here was/is what the story (parable) is REALLY all about as the angel of the Lord revealed it to me that Sunday morning. The *"birthright"* or *"spiritual blessing"* in the story represents "eternal life in the Kingdom of God"! Look, we are ALL spiritually separated from God the Father because of sin, but God reconciled us to Himself through Christ's blood, giving us ALL a CHANCE at being reunited with Him! In other words, it is EVERY single human beings "birth-RIGHT" to be reunited with God someday in His Kingdom. Do you understand? THAT is the legal "spiritual blessing" we ALL have a RIGHT TO as God's *"spirit children"*. It is our BIRTH-RIGHT! But Esau traded his wonderful, priceless birthright blessing for a measly "right-now gratification" of a bowl of food (dirt).

334

Do you comprehend <u>now</u> the amazing spiritual truth behind the incredibly revealing sentence spoken in my ear? The angel said, "Gabriel, there is only <u>ONE</u> underlying reason why people (souls) will NOT receive their birthright (eternal life): It will be because they <u>traded</u> it to be "gratified (satisfied) right-now" by dirt on planet Earth! Remember sin is pleasurable; subsequently, "sin" stems from a need for "self-gratification" which is the EXACT opposite of love. And again, what is the ROOT SOURCE for ALL sin (self-gratification)? <u>It is the "love of money" which is the "love of dirt"</u>!!! See, obtaining "wealth & assets" can gratify (delight) your soul "right now" on Earth, giving rise to the ugly *"pride of life"* oozing out of your spirit, but it will only be temporary (the length of your lifespan on Earth). Do you understand? Consequently, people who are enjoying the "pleasures of sin" on Earth are trading their "birthright of eternal life" for a worthless, short-lived, self-gratification! It is a horribly sad situation.

See, people who live to acquire "wealth & assets" are actually living life like the "here and now" is all there is? Do you see that? Most people do not realize it but their "greed-for-dirt" spirit and lifestyle is the quintessential NON-believer attitude. In other words, their self-centered, dirt-worshiping lifestyle PROVES their unbelief in God (Love) and the afterlife! Oh, they may go to church and swear up and down they know, love, and worship God, but their "get-all-you-can-get-because-you-only-live-once" attitude proves they do not! Their selfish mentality screams, "I do NOT believe in God or heaven…I believe only in the here and now, and therefore I am going to self-gratify myself NOW all I possibly can!" This outlook on life is a surefire way to kill your soul for all eternity because you will live your Earthly life to save it, which is <u>exactly</u> what Jesus said NOT to DO!

I am warning you…do not trade your "birthright of eternal life" for some fleeting "right-now" gratification, or it will be the biggest blunder you ever make! Friend, life is about sacrifice: It is about dying to ourselves and our own selfish, evil, fleshly-gratifying desires. Once you die to your own fleshly needs, desires, and wants for money & possessions, you will then have all the time in the world to help, love, and care for others. And if you die to yourself, you will live eternally!!! This is what Paul meant when he wrote: ***"Set your affection on things*** *above, NOT on things on the earth. For ye are dead, and your life is hid with Christ in God...Mortify therefore your members which are upon the earth; fornication, uncleanness, inordinate affection, evil concupiscence, and covetousness, which is idolatry. For which things' sake the wrath of God cometh on the children of DISOBEDIENCE"* (*Colossians 3:2-6*). See, we are to MORTIFY (kill) all sinful pleasures and "right-now gratifications" on Earth, setting our love on obtaining entrance into the Kingdom of Heaven.

Listen to the above passage in the Living Bible: *"Set you sights on the rich treasures and joys of heaven...Let heaven fill your thoughts; don't spend your time worrying about things down here.* ***YOU SHOULD HAVE AS LITTLE DESIRE FOR THIS WORLD AS A DEAD PERSON DOES****...Away then with sinful, earthly things; deaden the evil desire lurking within you; have nothing to do with sexual sin, impurity, lust and shameful desires; don't worship the good things of life, for that is idolatry.* ***God's terrible anger is upon those who DO such things***" (*Colossians 3:1-6, Living Bible*). Wow! Did you hear that? Our desire for "things" in this world should be on par to a dead person!!! Is that how you live? Or are you running helter-skelter, striving and struggling to "get all you can get" in this world? See, it is a funny thing; everybody wants to go to heaven but nobody wants to die! They want to have their cake and eat it too. But it does not work that way. You MUST die to this world if you plan on receiving eternal life.

Then on July 11, 2007, I ran across a New Testament verse absolutely confirming the Old Testament story of Jacob & Esau was TRULY all about how <u>NOT</u> to miss out on eternal life. It read: *"Follow peace with all men, and HOLINESS, without which no man shall see the Lord: Looking diligently lest any man fail of the grace of God; lest any root of bitterness springing up trouble you, and thereby many be defiled; Lest there be any fornicator, or profane person,* ***as Esau, who for one morsel of meat sold his birthright.*** *For ye know how that afterward, when he would have inherited the blessing,* ***HE WAS REJECTED****: for* ***he found NO PLACE of REPENTANCE, though he sought it carefully with tears***" (*Hebrews 12:14-17*). Wow, do you see? Afterward, Esau sought the birthright blessing with <u>copious tears</u>, but it was to no avail! It fell on deaf ears!!! THIS is exactly what Jesus said will take place with those people who end up in hell: *"**There shall be WEEPING and gnashing of teeth**, when ye shall see Abraham, and Isaac, and Jacob, and all the prophets, in the kingdom of God, and **you yourselves thrust out**"* *(Luke 13:28)*. Oh, my! In other words, in the 19th century BC, God gave mankind a dramatic, visual display—through the story (parable) of Jacob & Esau—of the desperate reaction of those souls who wind up in hell through Esau's tearful reaction to losing his birthright!

Yes, on Judgment Day the tears are going to flow like a river just like they did for Esau. They will be impossible to stop as the gut-wrenching realization sets in to those in hell that they traded eternal life (with eternal pleasures!) for a silly, worthless, "right-now Earthly gratification". Never forget the pleasures of sin are only temporary, but their consequence is eternal!!! The prophet Ezekiel wrote: *"**The soul that sinneth, it shall DIE**"* *(Ezekiel 18:20)*. You can laugh at me if you want to, but I love you enough to tell you, "You must stop sinning (repent) now! You must turn from wickedness now!" It is all so very real my friend. You only get one chance: *"**it is appointed unto men ONCE to die**, **but after this the judgment**"* *(Hebrews 9:27)*. So it is your choice! This is your ONE big shot at eternal life, and I pray you make the right decision and choose righteousness.

By the way, did you notice in the story (parable) of Jacob & Esau, Esau lamented to Jacob that his hunger was so great <u>he was about to die</u>, so what use was the birthright? Friend, even at the point of physical death God demands your faithfulness! John the Revelator wrote: *"Fear none of those things which thou shalt suffer...**be thou faithful unto death, and I will give thee a crown of life (eternal life)**"* *(Revelation 2:10)*. Do you understand? <u>Nothing</u> is more precious than your eternal birthright!!! DO NOT DESPISE IT LIKE ESAU!!! Be prepared to suffer in this life, and do not sin even at the point of death.

"Suffering" is almost a lost message in today's church age, yet the Bible CLEARLY states that a <u>TRUE</u> follower of Christ (love) will suffer here and now on Earth! Why is that you ask? Well, think about it logically; since sin has pleasure, then to <u>STOP SINNING</u> means to "deny oneself the temporary, Earthly pleasures that come from sinning". "Denying yourself of pleasure" <u>IS</u> "SUFFERING" my friend!!! Do you

337

understand? Peter got it: *"Forasmuch then as <u>Christ hath suffered for us</u> <u>in the flesh, ARM YOURSELVES LIKEWISE WITH THE SAME MIND:</u> for <u>**he that hath suffered in the flesh hath ceased from sin**</u>"* (I Peter 4:1). Wow, do you see? Anyone who "ceases from sin" automatically suffers in the flesh!

This is precisely what Jesus meant when he told people over and over again to *"take up their cross of <u>suffering</u> and follow him"*. He simply meant for people to cease from sinning! The way of love is a self-sacrificing life...It is a life of suffering! It means you love others so much that you are willing to *"deny yourself"* the temporary pleasures that come from "loving money & possessions" so you can fully love others. Listen again to Jesus' words: *"<u>If any man will come after me,</u> <u>**let him DENY himself, and take up his cross DAILY, and follow me**</u>. <u>For whosoever will save his life shall lose it:</u> but whosoever will lose his life for my sake, the same shall save it"* (Luke 9:23, 24). Do you see it now? *"Saving your life"* means enjoying all the pleasures of sin that come from loving money. But *"losing your life"* means denying yourself the pleasures of sin that come from loving money. Those that *"lose their life"* will suffer now on planet Earth, but one day they will obtain eternal life with pleasures galore. Peter understood the end result of our suffering: *"But the God of all grace, <u>who hath called us</u> <u>unto his eternal glory (eternal life) by Christ Jesus,</u> <u>**after that ye have**</u> <u>**SUFFERED a while**</u>, make you perfect, stablish, strengthen, settle you"* (I Peter 5:10). Yes, quitting sin means you will suffer now, but the end result of your suffering will be sweet eternal life with pleasures unknown: *"For <u>I reckon that the SUFFERINGS of this present time are</u> <u>NOT worthy to be compared with the glory which shall be revealed in</u> <u>us</u>" (Romans 8:18)*. I pray you are willing to SUFFER (quit sinning) to obtain eternal life!

Christ uttered another phrase accurately describing what our "decision to quit sinning to obtain eternal life" is like. He called it *"counting the cost"*. How about that? Is that not a perfect way to express it, since the root <u>source</u> of all sin is the "love of money"? Look, when we think "cost" we usually think in terms of "money". And Jesus knew a true follower of Christ (love) will have to "deny themselves the pleasure that comes from loving money; thus, <u>there is a COST to</u>

338

obtaining eternal life! Listen to Jesus: *"For which of you, intending to build a tower, sitteth not down first, and **counteth the cost**, whether he have sufficient to finish it? Lest haply, after he hath laid the foundation, and is not able to finish it, all that behold it begin to mock him, Saying, This man begun to build, and was not able to finish...So likewise, **whosoever he be of you that forsaketh not ALL he hath, he CANNOT be my disciple***" *(Luke 14:28-33)*. Do you see? Friend, you must *"count the cost"* of the journey to the Promise Land. It is a self-sacrificing journey of love taken only by obeying the 10 Love Commandments. So count the cost, forsake all of sin, and take up your cross of suffering to lay hold on eternal life! (By the way, Christ's analogy here again confirms that it is quite possible to be traveling down the path towards eternal life, and then quit. Do you see it?)

God's story (parable) of the Israelites in the wilderness again (even with respect to loving money) perfectly exposed the correct way to view our situation on Earth as we try to obtain entrance into the Promise Land (Kingdom of God). Look, when the Israelites were in bondage in Egypt they had access to all the riches of Egypt but they had to live as a slave to receive that temporary Earthly pleasure. But now free and in the wilderness the Israelites lived in tents, relying totally on God to feed and clothe them. Likewise, our complete trust should be in God to take care of us, not the false comfort that comes from living as a slave to sin when trusting in money! See, the truth is our attitude towards "money" is THE MAJOR WAY God is testing us on Earth, for we will either "love money" and put our trust and hope in it, proving we are an "unbeliever" who only believes in the here and now, or we will "love God" and put our trust and hope in Him, proving we are a "believer" who cares about eternal life!

Listen to Moses sum up what God was looking for out of the Israelites during their 40 year journey: *"Thou shalt remember all the WAY which the LORD thy God led thee these forty years in the wilderness, to humble thee, and **to PROVE thee, to KNOW WHAT WAS IN THINE HEART, whether thou wouldest keep his commandments (10 Love Commandments), or no**. And he humbled thee, and suffered thee to hunger, and fed thee with manna...that he might make thee know that man doth not live by bread only, but by every WORD that proceedeth* *out of the LORD doth man live. Thy raiment waxed not old upon thee, neither did thy foot swell, these forty years. Thou shalt also consider in thine heart, that, as a man chasteneth his son, so the LORD thy God chasteneth thee. Therefore thou shalt keep the commandments of the LORD thy God, to walk in his ways, and to fear him" (Deuteronomy 8:1-6).* Friend, this is what our life on planet Earth is all about. God is testing each and every one of us. We are His spirit children and He is proving who fears Him by observing who obeys His 10 Love Commandments in order to obtain eternal life, or who could care less about Him (love) by observing who disobeys the 10 Love Commandments to obtain eternal damnation!

Yes, believe it or not, your eternal destiny is actually going to be decided by your attitude towards money, because "loving it" is the ROOT of all sin (evil)—disobedience to the 10 Love Commandments! So I am urging you to "NOT love money" and to be content with what you have, ceasing from striving to be materialistically rich. Instead, put the same fervor and energy into living righteously (obeying God's 10 Love Commandments) for they are God's words you can live by in order to obtain eternal life. Paul wrote: *"And **having food and raiment let us be therewith content**. But they that will be rich fall into temptation and a snare, and into many foolish and hurtful lusts, which drown men in destruction and perdition" (I Timothy 6:8, 9).* The living Bible sums up beautifully Paul's words about the correct attitude we should hold of money: *"Do you want to be TRULY rich? **You already are if you are happy and GOOD**. After all, we didn't bring any money with us when we came into the world, and we can't carry away a single penny when we die. **So we should be well satisfied WITHOUT money if we have enough food and clothing**. But people who long to be rich soon begin to do all kinds of wrong things to get money, things that hurt them and make them evil-minded and finally send them to HELL itself. **For the love of money is the first step towards ALL kinds of sin**" (I Timothy 6:6-10, Living Bible).* I cannot say it any better or clearer…the "love of money" is the WAY to hell!!!

Lastly, allow me to say a few candid words about the tempting money-trap Satan has set up in these last days, for it is a deceptive, soul-killing snare!!! I am referring to the ease in which someone can purchase things (dirt) on credit. In today's world, people can entertain their greed (love of money & possessions) by legally obtaining new houses, cars, furniture, property, etc. on a good-faith nod that they will pay for it later. Then their soul becomes a slave to that greed. They say, "I cannot help the poor for I have bills to pay!" Yet, it never once crosses their mind that they could and should have bought a much smaller house, used car, cheaper furniture, and fewer possessions! See, their greed—desire to be filled with the "pride of life"—ensnares them, and they jump on the hamster wheel and spin like crazy, struggling to support their greed for worthless dirt!

Eventually, their naïve, mammon-loving spirits (thoughts, desires, & emotions) become fixated on their dirt possessions. They worry about how their going to pay for them; they worry about thieves breaking in and stealing them; they worry about maintaining them from rust and decay. And it is all a useless, vicious cycle that sucks up their spirit's time here on Earth, leading to a worthless, fruitless, "buried-in-the-dirt" life. Then, in the end they will stand in front of God on Judgment Day having to answer for using their soul's precious time on Earth to only obtain and maintain dirt. They will be the epitome of the wicked servant who buried his talent (spirit) in the ground in Jesus' parable of the talents. I am pleading with you to NOT make that mistake!

When it comes to purchasing things on credit, Paul wrote wonderful, simple words of advice: *"**Owe no man any thing**, but to love one another" (Romans 13:8)*. See, we should live humble and content lives—not lusting for worthless, materialistic, dirt possessions—so we can then use our spirit's time on Earth to love others (help those in need). THAT is how someone lives and what someone <u>DOES</u> who truly has God's heart of love beating inside their chest. THAT is the evidence of someone "born-again" of God's Holy Spirit of love. Paul wrote: *"Let him that stole steal no more: but rather <u>let him labour, working with his hands the thing which is GOOD, **that he may have to give to him that needeth**</u>" (Ephesians 4:28)*. See, there is why you should work for money, so you can give to others! Again, Paul wisely penned: *"**Let no man seek his own, but every man another's wealth**" (I Corinthians 10:24)*. Can you imagine living in a world where everyone had this mindset towards others and lived accordingly? Wow, it would be heaven on Earth. God help mankind today, for God's message of love is almost dead. Friend, do not seek your own dirt, but seek to serve your neighbor!!!

In conclusion, here is the Biblical truth about the END of the "*lust of the flesh*", the "*lust of the eyes*", and the "*pride of life*"—which are all worldly, dirt worship: *"For all that is in the world, the lust of the flesh, and the lust of the eyes, and the pride of life, is NOT of the Father, but is of the world. And **THE WORLD PASSETH AWAY, AND THE LUST THEREOF**: but **he that DOETH the WILL OF GOD abideth for ever**"* (I John 2:16, 17). Friend, ALL evil (sinful) lusts that stem from the "love of money (dirt)", and the fleeting pleasure they bring, are <u>ALL</u> going to pass away one day very soon. I promise you from the bottom of my heart, they will NOT be a part of God's Kingdom of Love. So I ask you, "Why would you want to enjoy them now?"

Chapter 17

Will Of God

"And the world passeth away, and the lust thereof:
but he that DOETH the WILL OF GOD
ABIDETH FOR EVER"
(I John 2:17)

I have heard people ask, "I wonder what the 'will of God' is for my life?" And every time, I am stunned at that question, for the Bible is abundantly clear concerning God's will for every one of us! The "will of God" for every human being (soul) who ever lived—from Adam to you— is to *"love God with all their heart and their neighbor as themselves"*, which is precisely carried out by obeying the 10 Love Commandments! Boy that was a big surprise, huh? Friend, it is just the same thing all over again. We were put on planet Earth to love! And God is meticulously scrutinizing our lives to see if we choose the WAY of love or not. If we <u>DO</u> love, we will receive eternal life, and THAT <u>IS</u> the ultimate "will of God" for everyone: *"The Lord is not slack concerning his promise (of eternal life), as some men count slackness; but is longsuffering to us-ward, **NOT WILLING that ANY should perish**, but that all should come to REPENTANCE"* (II Peter 3:9). Do you see? God's basic, fundamental <u>will</u> is for mankind's souls to repent (turn from doing evil to DOING good) to obtain eternal life.

So the "will of God" for you and all mankind is to "obey the 10 Love Commandments"—i.e. <u>DO</u> the things on the "do side" of the list and <u>DO NOT DO</u> the things on the "do not side". Thus, allow me to add up all these Biblical terms, once again, comprehensibly: "<u>Obedience to the 10 Love Commandments</u>" is <u>love defined, the truth revealed, the Holy Spirit described, the good fruit produced, a belief (or faith) in God displayed, money hated, and the will of God observed</u>! Wow, now that is a mouthful…but oh so very, very true!

I concluded the last chapter with the Apostle John's words: *"<u>And the world passeth away, and the lust thereof</u>: but **he that DOETH the WILL OF GOD abideth for ever**" (I John 2:17)*. Who will live forever (obtain eternal life)? Those who <u>DO</u> the "will of God"! Verses like this put a terrible kink in the "one-time sinner's prayer" method to eternal life. Friend, to obtain eternal life you MUST turn from sin to the WAY of love, which is to <u>DO</u> the "will of God". You must hate mammon, while bravely loving God and your neighbor as yourself during your few brief years watching the sun rise and fall down here on planet Earth.

Jesus proclaimed, *"<u>Not every one that saith unto me, Lord, Lord, shall enter into the kingdom of heaven</u>; but **he that DOETH the WILL OF MY FATHER which is in heaven**. Many will say to me in that day, Lord, Lord, have we not prophesied in thy name? And in thy name have cast out devils? And in thy name done many wonderful works? And then will <u>I profess unto them, I NEVER KNEW YOU: depart from me, ye that work INIQUITY (sin)</u>" (Matthew 7:21-23)*. Listen, let me say this again; it is pointless to call Jesus your "Lord" if you are not <u>DOING</u> the words he spoke! And the words God (Christ) <u>spoke</u> for all of us to <u>DO</u> (obey) are the 10 Love Commandments. If you are not <u>DOING</u> them, you are merely a willful worker of <u>iniquity</u> (sin), and God (Christ) is <u>NOT</u> your Lord! Listen, nothing else will count on Judgment Day. You can be a pastor, deacon, secretary, lawyer, doctor, painter, or the Pope, but if you willfully disobey the 10 Love Commandments, God only sees you as wicked, evil, godless person that He <u>does not know</u>, for He is love!

One day the multitudes informed Jesus that his Earthly mother and brothers had come to see him. Always thinking spiritually, Jesus replied, *"**Whosoever shall DO the WILL OF GOD**, <u>the same is my brother, and my sister, and mother</u>" (Mark 3:35)*. Do you understand

344

what Christ meant? See, Jesus always looked at the heart (soul) of mankind! Remember, our physical dirt body is just a tent housing the real us, our spirit. Some of our spirits are in male physical tents and some are in female physical tents—no big deal there—but we are really and truly spirit beings first and foremost. Our spirit (soul) is the real us! Thus, Jesus knew these physical (dirt) terms—like mother, brother, sister, etc—are really unimportant but our spirit is ALL important. So he said whoever on Earth obeyed the 10 Love Commandments (DID the will of God) was intimately connected with him (love) spiritually, because he was love. Love knows love. So realize a physical "tent" name like mother, uncle, sister, etc. is meaningless.

Peter instructed: *"Since Christ suffered and underwent pain, you must have the same attitude he did; you must be ready to suffer, too. For remember, when your body suffers, sin loses its power, and you won't be spending the rest of your life chasing after evil desires, but* ***will be anxious to DO the WILL OF GOD****. You have had enough in the past of the evil things the godless enjoy—sex, sin, lust, getting drunk, wild parties, drinking bouts, and the worship of idols, and other terrible sins. Of course, your former friends will be very surprised when you don't eagerly join them any more in the wicked things they DO, and THEY WILL LAUGH AT YOU in contempt and scorn.* ***But just remember that they must face the Judge of all, living and dead; they will be punished for the WAY they have lived"*** *(I Peter 4:1-5, Living Bible)*. Do you see? These verses make it perfectly clear the "will of God" for us is to forsake the WAY of sin and to follow the WAY of love by living righteously (obeying the 10 Love Commandments).

But you say, "Gabriel, if I obeyed the 10 Love Commandments all the time I would be perfect!" Yes, yes, yes…you are exactly right!!! And THAT is precisely what God wants for each and every one of us. That is God's will for every soul who was every born. Jesus said, *"**Be ye therefore PERFECT**, even as your Father which is in heaven is perfect"* (Matthew 5:48). My friend, you CAN live righteously! Paul wrote: *"All scripture is given by inspiration of God, and is profitable for doctrine, for reproof, for correction, for instruction in righteousness:* ***That the man of God may be PERFECT, thoroughly furnished unto ALL GOOD WORKS"*** *(II Timothy 3:16, 17)*. Yes, God's will for each

345

and every one of us is to walk in love towards Him and our fellow man all the days of our lives. That is perfection!

I believe as someone starts correcting things in their life they know they are doing wrong, God looks down from heaven and sees their repentant heart and progressively fills them more and more with His Holy Spirit of love, driving them further towards perfection (perfect love). That is the WAY that leads to eternal life! The Bible states: *"Now the God of peace...__Make you PERFECT in every GOOD WORK to DO HIS WILL__, working in you that which is well pleasing in his sight"* (Hebrews 13:20, 21). Friend, the change takes place in your spirit (thoughts, desires, & emotions). Consequently, Paul wrote: *"be not conformed to this world: but be ye TRANSFORMED by the renewing of your MIND, __that ye may PROVE what is that good, and acceptable, and PERFECT, WILL OF GOD__"* (Romans 12:2). Amen.

I implore you to begin DOING the "will of God". In other words, start aligning your life up to His 10 Love Commandments. Do not just say you will and then do not do it, for that will make you an unbeliever. Listen to Christ: *"But what think ye? A certain man had two sons; and he came to the first, and said, Son, go work to day in my vineyard. He answered and said, I will not: but afterward he REPENTED, and went. And he came to the second, and said likewise. And he answered and said, I go, sir: and went NOT. __Whether of them twain DID the WILL of his FATHER?__"* (Matthew 21:28-31). The chief priests and the elders answered Jesus: *"The first"* (Matthew 21:31). Christ then scolded the religious leaders: *"Surely evil men and prostitutes will get into the Kingdom of God before you do. For John the Baptist told you to REPENT and TURN TO GOD, and you wouldn't, while evil men and prostitutes DID. And even when you saw this happening, you refused to REPENT, and so you couldn't BELIEVE"* (Matthew 21:31, 32, Living Bible). Do you see? I cannot be any more emphatic about this eternal life obtaining fact: You MUST start DOING God's will (obeying the 10 Love Commandments), for nothing else will matter in the end!

Chapter 18

Word of God

"But be ye DOERS of the WORD, and not hearers only,
deceiving your own selves"
(James 1:22)

With the Israelites gathered at the base of Mount Sinai, 1334 BC, God thunderously <u>spoke</u> WITH AN <u>AUDIBLE</u> <u>VOICE</u> the 10 Love Commandments to them. Moses would later write: *"And ye came near and stood under the mountain…And the <u>LORD SPAKE</u> unto you out of the midst of the fire: <u>ye HEARD the **VOICE of the WORDS**</u>, but saw no similitude; <u>only ye heard a voice"</u> (Deuteronomy 4:11, 12).* Friend, the "10 Love Commandments" <u>ARE</u> the "Word(s) of God"! They are the <u>ONLY</u> word(s) God <u>spoke</u> to the Israelites DIRECTLY: *"**These WORDS** <u>the LORD SPAKE unto all your assembly in the mount out of the midst of the fire, of the cloud, and of the thick darkness, with a great voice: and **he added no more**. And <u>he wrote them in two tables of stone"</u> (Deuteronomy 5:22).* Yes, unquestionably, the "Word of God" to mankind is "<u>DO</u> the 10 Love Commandments".

But God further cemented His "Word" to mankind by writing the 10 Love Commandments on stone tables. How much more proof could/can He give that they are His <u>words</u> and His <u>will</u>. And by now you know they are simply the deeds and thoughts that define (explain) "how we LOVE God and our neighbor as ourselves", which means they are God's character for He is Love! Furthermore, you also know this "Mount Sinai scene" was just one act in God's massive story (parable) that was intended as a MESSAGE to all mankind to explain everything involved in their journey back to Him. Thus, I have already explained when God spoke the 10 Love Commandments to the Israelites in 1334 BC...**THEY were NOT something NEW to mankind**!!! For God had placed His "Word" into the hearts of all mankind from the moment Adam & Eve sinned in the Garden of Eden. Therefore, <u>everyone</u> who has ever lived has known the "Word of God", for obedience or disobedience to "the 10 Love Commandments" is the difference between good & evil, respectively!

Now in the Bible, God refers to Jesus as *"the Word"*. John wrote: *"<u>In the beginning was the Word, and the Word was with God, and the Word was God...And the Word was made flesh, and dwelt among us...full of grace and truth"</u> (John 1:1, 14).* Do you understand this? The "Spirit of Love (God)" was made flesh in the person of Jesus Christ! See, the real Jesus was/is the spirit that was inside his physical body—just like the real you is the spirit inside you—and THAT spirit in him was EXACTLY the Spirit of God for God had impregnated Mary with His seed (the Holy Spirit). In other words, Christ was simply the "embodiment of the Spirit of Love". What does that mean? It means he was a walking, talking, doing embodiment of the 10 LOVE Commandments!!! He was perfectly sinless, meaning he loved at ALL times. It was the first time mankind had ever scene anything like this...a man who loved purely and perfectly at all times! Wow. Thus, Jesus Christ IS, WAS, & HAS ALWAYS BEEN the "Word of God (love)". Do you see? John the revelator, witnessing a vision of Jesus 2nd Coming, wrote: *"And I saw heaven opened, and behold a white horse; and <u>he (Jesus) that sat upon him was called Faithful and True</u>, and in righteousness he doth judge and make war. His eyes were as a flame of fire...And he was clothed with a vesture dipped in blood: and <u>his name is called **The WORD of GOD**</u>" (Revelation 19:11-13).* Earlier, John had wrote: *"For <u>there are three that bear record in heaven, the Father, the WORD, and the Holy Ghost: and these three are ONE</u>" (I John 5:7).* Friend, the REAL Jesus is the "spirit of Love", which is the "Word of God".

348

Now you should easily understand why Jesus said, *"**IF ye love me, keep my (10 Love) commandments**" (John 14:15)*. Do you see? Since Jesus was/is the "Word of God"—the 10 Love Commandments personified—then it is impossible to truthfully say you know, love, or worship the REAL Jesus while disobeying the 10 Love Commandments. That would make you a liar!!! Because to know Jesus is to know the Word of God (love)! Therefore, John accurately wrote: *"He that saith, I know him, and keepeth NOT his (10 Love) commandments, is a liar, and the truth is not in him" (I John 2:4)*. It is really quite simple!

John said: *"I have written unto you, fathers, because **ye have known him (Christ) that is from the BEGINNING**. I have written unto you, young men, because ye are strong, and the **WORD of GOD abideth in you**, and ye have overcome the wicked one" (I John 2:14)*. Again here, the *"Word of God"* is the "spirit of love". And the "spirit of love" (Jesus Christ) has always existed from the beginning. So to know Jesus is to know love, which is to obey the 10 Love Commandments. Friend, folks who have chosen to live their life in obedience to the 10 Love Commandments have <u>known</u> Christ (love)—the Spirit of God (love)—all throughout history, even during the first 4,000 years before he came to planet Earth in the form of a baby. Consequently, when the *"Word of God* (love)" <u>ABIDES</u> in you, you are overcoming evil (sin). Paul penned: *"Be not overcome of evil, but <u>overcome evil with good</u>" (Romans 12:21)*. See, evil (sin) is trying to kill your soul for all eternity, but if you conquer it by following the WAY of good (love)—obey the 10 Love Commandments—you will overcome sin's (evil) destruction and obtain eternal life.

Understanding the "Word of God" is really "the 10 Love Commandments" allows us to comprehend the Bible's clear assertion that the "Word of God" is something to be <u>obeyed</u>. Subsequently, we find Bible verses declaring: *"But <u>be ye **DOERS of the WORD**, and not hearers only, deceiving your own selves</u>" (James 1:22)*. Do you see? We must <u>DO</u> (obey) the 10 Love Commandments. In other words, we must DO (obey) the "Word of God"! James intelligently preceded the above verse with these words: *"<u>Wherefore lay apart all filthiness and superfluity of naughtiness, and **receive with meekness the ENGRAFTED WORD, which is able to SAVE your souls**</u>" (James*

1:21). Let me boil James words down for you: <u>DOING</u> the 10 Love Commandments—the Words God (Christ) spoke—will SAVE your soul!!! Notice the contrasting of good & evil? Friend, the "Word of God" is something that has to be engrafted into your spirit, which will then change your thoughts, desires, & emotions to WANT to follow the WAY of love, thereby saving your soul.

On the other hand, if you hardheartedly refuse to obey God's Word, you will lose your soul. God told the Israelites: *"Because he hath DESPISED the **WORD of the LORD**, **and hath broken his commandment(s)**, that SOUL shall utterly be cut off; his iniquity shall be upon him"* (Numbers 15:31). Solomon wrote: *"Whoso DESPISETH the WORD shall be DESTROYED: but he that feareth the commandment shall be rewarded"* (Proverbs 13:13). Simple enough, right? Look, whenever you sin (disobey the 10 Love Commandments) you are actually <u>despising</u> the "Word of God (Christ)"! If you steal, your thievery is saying, "I hate you Jesus!" When you lust sexually after strange flesh, your sexual immorality is saying, "I despise you Christ!" If you yearn for wealth & assets, your covetous and idolatrous heart is saying, "I abhor you God!" Do you see? Your evil (sinful) deeds are on par with spitting on Christ's face, yourself!!!

The Bible informs us the "Word of God" is something that will endure <u>forever</u>. And of course it will, for love (God) will never die!!! Jesus said, *"Heaven and earth shall pass away, but **my WORDS** shall not pass away"* (Matthew 24:35). Do you see? God's (Christ) words are the "words of love", and love is eternal because God is eternal! Therefore, the "Word of God" has always been God's word for mankind to fulfill, and someday the righteous, forgiven souls will live forever— never pass away!—like the Spirit of God. This was the thrust of God's message through the ancient prophets. God continually warned mankind to REPENT (turn from their wicked sins of disobeying the 10 Love Commandments) and follow the WAY of God (love) and live. That was Jonah's message to Nineveh, Jeremiah's message to Israel, and John the Baptists message in the wilderness. Even today, nothing has changed! Any <u>true</u> prophet of God shouts the same message: REPENT and obey God's 10 Love Commandments to obtain forgiveness for your sins and receive eternal life!

Alright, let me tie all these Biblical concepts together once again: "Obeying the 10 Love Commandments" is showing love, knowing truth, displaying the Holy Spirit, bearing fruit, exhibiting faith in God, despising money, fulfilling the will of God, and following the Word of God. Wow, do you grasp the entirety of the Bible's message in regards to what mankind MUST DO to obtain eternal life (with its many terms and concepts) is all wrapped up in "obeying the 10 Love Commandments"? That is because they are the heart of the Law! Obey them and live forever; disobey them and perish!!!

Understanding the above paragraph is no small revelation for it unlocks and clarifies the meaning behind a plethora of Scripture verses. Listen to a complicated passage written by Peter combining many of these elements. You should now be able to clearly understand everything Peter is saying: *"Seeing ye have purified your souls in obeying the truth through the Spirit unto unfeigned love of the brethren, see that ye love one another with a pure heart fervently: Being born again, not of corruptible seed, **but of incorruptible (seed)**, by the Word of God, which liveth and abideth for ever. For all flesh is as grass, and all the glory of man as the flower of grass. The grass withereth, and the flower thereof falleth away: But the Word of the Lord endureth for ever"* (I Peter 1:22-25). Wow, how about the incredible wisdom of the Holy Spirit displayed behind those words? Friend, Peter knew the truth was all centered around L-O-V-E, which is God! Allow me to summarize Peter's words: "Since the world is passing away and only love is eternal…if you want to live forever, you must obey the truth—the Word of God (the 10 Love Commandments)—to purify your soul. If you DO love God with all your heart and your neighbor as yourself it will prove your soul has been "born again" of God's eternal Holy Spirit of love.

Comprehension of the link between all these Biblical concepts (all focused on obeying the 10 Love Commandments) allows us to now truly understand a very powerful parable Jesus told. The parable describes the four dissimilar heart responses people produce when confronted with the "Word of God"—i.e. the message that they MUST stop sinning and OBEY the 10 Love Commandments. It is the parable of the seed sower. With his brain swimming in wisdom, Jesus opened

351

his mouth: *"Behold, a sower went forth to sow; And when he sowed, (1) __some seeds fell by the way side__, and the fowls came and devoured them up: (2) __Some fell upon stony places__, where they had not much earth: and forthwith they sprung up, because they had no deepness of earth: And when the sun was up, they were scorched; and because they had no root, they withered away. And (3) __some fell among thorns__; and the thorns sprung up, and choked them: But (4) __others fell into good ground__, and brought forth (good) FRUIT, some an hundredfold, some sixtyfold, some thirtyfold" (Matthew 13:3-8).*

Fortunately, Jesus' interpretation of the spiritual meaning behind this striking parable was included in the Bible. And I want you to pay particular close attention to two overlooked truths that come out of it. One, the parable <u>clearly</u> confirms again that "obtaining eternal life" is NOT a one-time decision but a continual, daily journey. And secondly, the parable <u>clearly</u> and unmistakably reveals the fact that someone can be following the "narrow path" leading to eternal life for awhile and then get off course and begin traveling the "wide path" leading to destruction (hell)! Let us take a detailed look at the amazing parable.

Jesus began explaining the parable to his Disciples: *"Now the parable is this: __The SEED is the word of God__" (Luke 8:11).* Nice! We have plainly learned by now the "*Word of God*" to mankind is for them "<u>to willingly DO (obey) the 10 Love Commandments</u>". Next in the parable, we notice the "seed" the sower was scattering is landing in different places—i.e. way side, stony place, thorny place, and good ground. These "different places" represent the four unique hearts (or spirits) people posses in <u>reaction</u> to HEARING the "Word of God". In other words, folk's spirits (thoughts, desires, & emotions) will react differently—initially and over the course of time!—when confronted with God's Word which commands them to stop sinning (repent) and choose to follow the WAY of love by obeying the 10 Love Commandments. Out of the 4 heart responses, 3 lead to eternal damnation and only 1 leads to eternal life! Therefore, this parable takes a meticulous look into the heart conditions of mankind, shining a revealing light on EXACTLY <u>WHY</u> most souls will perish on Judgment Day while only a few will obtain eternal life. Let us take a comprehensive look at the four hearts.

Jesus taught: *"__Those by the WAY SIDE are they that HEAR__;*

then cometh the devil, and taketh away the WORD out of their hearts, lest they should BELIEVE and be SAVED" (Luke 8:12). Ah, see, by now these Biblical words should leap off the page with spiritual meaning! For instance, you know exactly what the Biblical term "believe" means…it really implies "obeying the 10 Love Commandments"! (Go back and read the *"Faith"* chapter if you need to refresh your memory.) Thus, wayside-hearted people are so hardened toward God (love) that they instantly <u>refuse</u> to repent of sin. Consequently, their lack of repentance—turning from sin (evil) to obeying God's 10 Love Commandments—proves they <u>do not believe</u> in God (love)! Therefore, they cannot be saved and will perish on Judgment Day.

When these type people are told they need to stop loving money & possessions (dirt), stop being sexually immoral, start keeping the Sabbath day holy, etc, their spirit (thoughts, desires, & emotions) immediately rise up and angrily growl, "No one's going to tell me how to live my life! I'll do whatever I want!" Can you hear the words of a calloused heart? Can you hear the words of a rebellious heart towards God? The devil's grip on these people's spirits (thoughts, desires, & emotions) is so severe that he literally sucks the soul-saving truth of God's words of love right out of their mind the moment they hear or read it! Satan is like a black crow in their mind devouring God's word like seed falling on a hard, trodden-down path! If these people's spirits (hearts) never soften towards God (love) and repent, their continual, willful, wicked sin (refusal to love) will kill their soul.

Jesus continued: *"They on the ROCK are they, which, when they HEAR, **receive the word with joy**; and these have no root, **which for a while BELIEVE, and in time of temptation fall away**" (Luke 8:13).* Wow, do you see? These people *"FOR A WHILE BELIEVED"*! The original Greek word translated "believe" here is the <u>same</u> Greek word used in the plethora of Biblical verses stating, *"He who BELIEVES shall be saved."* Therefore, there is <u>NO</u> disputing that these people were on their way to obtaining eternal life, for they BELIEVED!!! And what really <u>proved</u> their belief and <u>caused</u> their joy? Without a doubt, they turned from their sins and began obeying the 10 Love Commandments. Jesus said, *"<u>If ye keep my (10 Love) commandments, ye shall abide in my love</u>…These things have I spoken unto you…**that YOUR JOY might*** *be full" (John 15:10, 11)*. See, they repented!!! They heard the message of God's word (Word of God) just like Jesus instructed us to preach: *"Go ye therefore, and teach all nations...* **Teaching them to OBSERVE (OBEY) all things whatsoever I have COMMANDED (the 10 Love Commandments)"** *(Matthew 28:19, 20)*—and they were delighted! They were willing to change their life to the WAY of righteousness (love).

Oh, but then look what happens. Listen to Christ's explanation of the stony-hearted person in Mark's Gospel: *"And these are they likewise which are sown on STONY ground; who, when they have heard the word, <u>immediately receive it with gladness</u>; And have NO ROOT in themselves, and <u>SO ENDURE BUT FOR A TIME: afterward, when affliction or persecution ariseth for the Word's sake, immediately they are offended"</u> (Mark 4:16, 17)*. Do you understand this? When wicked folks start making fun of them for not wanting to go out drinking in the bars any more, or laughing at them for not wanting to look at pornographic images on their cell phones, or ridiculing them for keeping the Sabbath day holy, etc, they are saddened! The list of persecutions for "living righteously" is endless, but eventually stony-hearted people say, "Enough of this, I'm tired of people making fun of me and deriding me! I'm going back to my old sinful ways to fit in and be accepted by the world." At that point, they return to the wide path that leads to destruction, for they go back to "disobeying the 10 Love Commandments" proving they NO LONGER BELIEVE in love (God). In other words, they were saved for awhile, but then they are not!

These people's spirits are just like Jesus' parable of the sower revealed; the soil of their heart is stony and shallow, not allowing the "Word of God" to take deep enough root! Thus, the HEAT of persecution withers away their initial, spiritual emotion of joy—which stemmed from following the WAY of love towards God and their fellow man—and the maltreatment becomes too much for their spirit (thoughts, desires, & emotions) to handle, and so they cave in to the pressure and return to the sinful crowds way of life. What a sorry fate these type people will face! Do you remember Peter's words about them? Listen: **"For if after they have escaped the pollutions of the world through the KNOWLEDGE of the Lord and Saviour Jesus Christ (which is to know love or to obey the 10 Love Commandments)**, *they are again entangled therein,*

354

*and overcome (return to their sinful ways of disobeying the 10 Love Commandments), **THE LATTER END IS WORSE WITH THEM THAN THE BEGINNING**. For it had been better for them not to have known the WAY OF RIGHTEOUSNESS, than, after they have known it, to turn from the HOLY (10 Love) COMMANDMENT(S) delivered unto them. But it is happened unto them according to the true proverb, **The dog is turned to his own vomit again; and the sow that was washed to her wallowing in the mire**" (II Peter 2:20-22).* Ugghhhh…how very, very sad!!!*

After learning this passage of Scripture, HOW can anyone refute the ONLY <u>WAY</u> to obtain eternal life is by TURNING from sin—which is to obey the 10 Love Commandments? It is so barefacedly obvious!!! Look at the verse again; Peter said these people *"escaped the pollutions (sins) of the world through the **KNOWLEDGE** of the Lord Jesus"*. Remember, to <u>know</u> Jesus is to know love, which is to obey the 10 Love Commandments! Listen to John's words, again: *"**And hereby we do KNOW that we KNOW him (Jesus), IF we keep his (10 Love) commandments**. He that saith, I know him, and keepeth not his commandments, is a liar, and the truth is not in him"* (I John 2:3, 4). Honestly, friend, how much clearer can the truth be? The Bible is perfectly lucid on what it means to truly KNOW Christ! It means to know LOVE by ceasing to disobey the 10 Love Commandments! Do you see? And it has meant THAT down throughout <u>all</u> of history—even for the first 4,000 years when mankind never heard the name of the Earthly man Jesus Christ! Consequently, to "cease sinning' by coming to "know Christ (love)" and then turn back to a sinful lifestyle—to NOT know Christ (love)—is a catastrophic decision! These people's punishment will be severe in the end.

Hear me reader; even if the WHOLE world denies Christ's WAY of love (mocking you and calling you a fool for keeping God's 10 Love Commandments), you arch your back, thrust out your chest, and shout, "I <u>WILL</u> love my God with all of my heart and my neighbor as myself! Even if I'm the last man on Earth who will do so, then so be it!" Friend, you have NO idea how pleased and joyous the Father God in heaven is over one of His spirit children possessing this type mindset! They will SURELY reap a bountiful harvest of eternal life in

God's heavenly Kingdom one day for following after the WAY of love, hearing God say, *"Well done my GOOD and faithful servant!"*

Jesus continued, *"And that which fell among THORNS are they, which, when they have HEARD, go forth, and **are choked with cares and riches and pleasures of this life, and bring NO (good) FRUIT to perfection**"* (Luke 8:14). Ah, do you see? Here, Jesus uses the *"bear good fruit"* phrase! But by now you know the "good fruit" we are to bear is also "obeying the 10 Love Commandments". Therefore, what stops thorny-hearted people from obeying the 10 Love Commandments (showing love)? The LOVE OF MONEY—which is the root of all evil! They are covetous and idolatrous people who cannot bring themselves to feed the hungry, quench the thirsty, or clothe the naked, etc, because they want to store up worthless dirt (money) for themselves! They most likely lie, cheat, steal, murder, etc, in their pursuit of money, but even if they do not "money (dirt)" is still their god (what they trust in), and that idolatry is enough to send their soul to hell!

Listen to Jesus interpretation of the thorny-hearted person in Mark's Gospel: *"And these are they which are sown among THORNS; such as HEAR the WORD, And the **cares (concerns, worries, anxieties) of this world**, and the **deceitfulness of riches**, and the **lusts of other things entering in, choke the word, and it becometh unfruitful"*** (Mark 4:18, 19). I cannot say it any better; this is the *"Love of Money"* chapter's message summed up in a nutshell! Worrying about *"saving your (fleshly) life"* on planet Earth is a waste of time. But these people are all wrapped up in their busy everyday lives, as if the materialistic possessions they are obtaining actually matter. And it is an extremely useless existence! Thorny-hearted people are stressed to the max over an immediate future they have absolutely no control over, and these silly concerns will strangle any chance of them displaying continual, daily, selfless "deeds of love (good fruit)".

When your heart loves mammon (wealth & assets) you will NOT selflessly help other people. You just cannot DO it! Your time will be spent obtaining more and more money and dirt possessions. You will acquire "things" you do not need—only lust after!—on credit plans, hopping on life's mad hamster wheel. Round and round you will run, as year after year of your life fades away, accomplishing NOTHING

356

of purpose. All your spirit's energy (thoughts, desires, & emotions) will be totally used up supporting your greed. It is a worthless WAY of life. Thus, the *"thorns"* in Jesus' parable are actually "wrong thought processes and beliefs in a person's heart (spirit) about what is truly important in life". To be blunt; Satan has DECEIVED these people!!! And their foolish worries and cares will choke out the small opportunity they had to "love God and their neighbor" during their brief lifetime on Earth, sending their soul to hell in the end!

Finally, Jesus said, *"And these are they which are sown on GOOD GROUND; such as HEAR the WORD, **and receive it, and bring forth FRUIT, some thirtyfold, some sixty, and some an hundred"** (Mark 4:20)*. Friend, this is the ONLY response to God's Word that leads to eternal life! These people's hearts are like soft, rich, fertile ground. They hear the message of love (obey the 10 Love Commandments!) and the seed grabs deep root in their spirit (heart). They start "living righteously (bearing good fruit)". They <u>DO</u> the things on the "do side" of the 10 Love Commandments chart and <u>DO</u> <u>NOT</u> <u>DO</u> the things on the "do not side". They tell the truth and do not lie. They honor and keep God's Holy Sabbath and do not run around that day chasing the almighty dollar. They give to the poor and do not steal. They are content with what they have and do not covet "money & possessions". And their REPENTANT heart (righteous living or "bearing the good fruit of love") will cause God to reward them in the end with eternal life by allowing them entrance into the Promise Land!

Yes, friend, "to obey the 10 Love Commandments (<u>DO</u> good rather than evil)" has always been the "Word of God" to all mankind, for disobeying them is sin. ALL God truly desires out of you during this age on Earth is "TO LOVE by obeying the 10 Love Commandments". Yet, this is the very message that offends wicked people because it cuts right to the core of their evil heart (thoughts, desires, & emotions). The Bible says: *"The WORD of GOD is quick, and powerful, and sharper than any two-edged sword, piercing even to the dividing asunder of soul and spirit, and of the joints and marrow, and is a discerner of the thoughts and intents of the heart" (Hebrews 4:12)*. Do you see? The Word of God (the message instructing and commanding souls to obey the 10 Love Commandments) upsets folks! Tell people to cease their sexual immorality, and you will see the devil rage in their eyes. Tell people to stop loving money, sell their possessions, and take up their cross of suffering to follow God's WAY of love, and you will find yourself attacked by diabolical spirits spewing a barrage of venomous, pride-filled words. Do you understand? The "Word of God" is like a knife, cutting deep into the thoughts, desires, & emotions of a person's heart!

Listen to the above verses in the Living Bible: *"For the **WORD of GOD is full of living power: it is sharper than the sharpest dagger, cutting swift and deep into our innermost thoughts and desires with all their parts, EXPOSING US FOR WHAT WE REALLY ARE**. He (God) knows about everyone, everywhere. Everything about us is bare and wide open to the all-seeing eyes of our living God; **NOTHING can be hidden from Him to whom we must explain all that we have done**"* (Hebrews 4:12, 13, Living Bible). Wow, the "Word of God" is powerful!!! Friend, you MUST make a conscious effort to obey God's Word—stop sinning (repent) and obey the 10 Love Commandments— if you want to obtain eternal life, for God is watching everything you DO and you <u>WILL</u> answer to Him for it all!

A good test to know what condition your heart is currently in is to perceive your response to the message "you <u>MUST</u> willfully choose to OBEY the 10 Love Commandments to obtain eternal life". Does that offend you? If so, you are probably still willfully sinning! Do you not believe it? If so, you are severely deceived by Satan! Friend, those who live their life in accordance to the 10 Love Commandments are not offended by the "Word of God". Do you understand? It does not cut their soul! They can hear the "Word of God" preached all day long (about the sins of loving money & possessions, blasphemy, not keeping the Sabbath day holy, hatred, sexual immorality, lying, etc, and never once be offended, <u>because they are NOT sinning</u>. Do you see? Oh, what peace and joy there is in "living right"!!! Listen to the Psalmist: *"**Great PEACE have they which LOVE thy LAW (the 10 Love Commandments): and NOTHING SHALL OFFEND THEM**. Lord, I have hoped for thy salvation, and DONE thy commandments"* (Psalms 119:165, 166). Do you love obeying God's 10 Love Commandment law? Or are you offended by it? You MUST obey God's "Law of Love" to receive eternal life in the end. The Apostle Paul knew such and wisely penned: *"For <u>not the HEARERS of the law are just before God</u>, but **<u>the DOERS of the LAW shall be JUSTIFIED</u>**" (Romans 2:13)*. Friend, if you strive on a continual, daily basis to obey the Word of God (obey the 10 Love Commandments)—which is to seek after righteousness—your repentant soul <u>WILL</u> enter the Kingdom of God and live forever.

Chapter 19

Fear of God

"Let us hear the conclusion of the whole matter:
FEAR GOD, and KEEP HIS COMMANDMENTS:
for this is the WHOLE DUTY of man"
(Ecclesiastes 12:13)

From all we learned so far in this book, it is painfully obvious that WILLFUL sinning (willful disobedience to the 10 Love Commandments) is ultimately what will send a person to hell. The REFUSAL to <u>repent</u> of wickedness and follow God's WAY of love (obey the 10 Love Commandments) will cause a soul to experience the condemnation of the 2nd spiritual death at the Great White Throne Judgment. Furthermore, the Bible has taught us "greed" or the "love of money"—which can only buy dirt!—is the underlying factor or root that produces all sin. So the "love of money (dirt)" will be the common denominator in everyone's heart that ends up in hell! Therefore, Life's gameboard is plainly laid out for each of us: We can choose to "love our Earthly life" with all its fleeting dirt possessions and obtain eternal death, or we can choose to "hate our Earthly life" desiring sin's pleasure as much as a dead man and obtain eternal life.

Now, in this chapter, we will discuss the major ROOT that feeds all holy living (obedience to the 10 Love Commandments). In other words, like "greed for money (dirt)" in a person's heart is the origin (or cause) of all disobedience to the 10 Love Commandments, this "factor" in a person's heart will be the origin (or cause) of all <u>obedience</u> to the 10 Love Commandments. What is it? It is the "fear of God". Think about it! Friend, a healthy fear of God will drive a spirit (soul) to <u>NOT</u> sin against God. And I will prove this Biblical fact to you in this chapter. But at the outset, please realize a person who willfully sins (disobeys the 10 Love Commandments) <u>PROVES</u> by their evil conduct that they have NO "fear of God"!!! Consequently, someone who willfully disobeys the 10 Love Commandments proves they neither fear God, nor believe in Him (love), for the two go hand in hand.

The Greek word translated "fear" in the Bible is *"phobeō"*, meaning: <u>to fear, be afraid, alarmed; to reverence, respect, worship</u>. In other words, it actually means to <u>FEAR</u>! Listen to Christ's advice: *"I say unto you my friends, <u>be NOT afraid of them (humans) that kill the body, and after that have no more that they can do. But</u> **<u>I will forewarn you whom ye shall fear</u>**: **<u>FEAR him (God), which after he hath killed hath power to cast into hell; yea, I say unto you, FEAR HIM</u>**" (Luke 12:4, 5)*. How plain is that? Jesus is clearly warning us to fear God because He holds the power of death over our soul. In other words, God can KILL our <u>priceless</u> soul! <u>THAT</u> is why we should fear ONLY Him. Listen to Christ's words in Matthew's Gospel: *"And <u>fear not them (humans) which kill the body, but are NOT able to kill the soul</u>: but **<u>rather FEAR HIM (God) which is able to DESTROY both soul and body in hell</u>**" (Matthew 10:28)*. Do you understand? God can destroy your soul! He can wipe out that part of you that has thoughts, desires, & emotions. Nothing else can do that!

Listen, it is <u>healthy</u> and <u>wise</u> to fear anything that has power over you! With this in mind, allow me to elucidate the correct meaning behind the phrase "fear of God" with an analogy. Consider a famished lion trapped in a barred cage. Would it be a smart decision to go strolling into his cage? Of course not! It is healthy and wise to <u>fear</u> (respect) the consequences of what the lion can DO to your physical body. Do you see? That is the gist behind what it truly means to "<u>FEAR</u> (respect) God". (Incidentally, in the grand scheme of eternity, Jesus was saying we actually do <u>NOT</u> need to fear a lion or mankind, because they can

362

ONLY kill our physical dirt body—which merely releases our spirit into the spirit world—but cannot touch our invaluable soul!)

Now, do I walk around terrified every second of the day thinking about what a famished lion can do to me? Of course not! Neither, do I walk around all day long terrified of God. In both cases, I simply have a healthy fear tucked away in my spirit (thoughts, desires, & emotions) knowing the power they hold over me. In the lion's case, my healthy fear (respect) restrains me from walking up to touch one, which is wise. In God's case, my healthy fear (respect) restrains me from disobeying His 10 Love Commandments, which is extremely wise! Do you see? "Disobeying God's 10 Love Commandments" is like physically walking into a lion's cage: It is a stupid thing to DO! If someone walked into a hungry lion's cage and you watched them scream in agony as they were gruesomely mutilated, you would say that person was a fool. Well I say to you, "A person who willingly disobeys God's 10 Love Commandments is a FAR worse fool, because they will mutilate their priceless soul!"

Yet, ironically, people do fear what mankind and wild animals can do to them, but they do not fear God!!! How daft is that? The one thing they should fear above all else in the universe, they do not fear. And why is that? It is because deep down in their heart they really, truly do NOT believe in God, and thus they go on willfully enjoying sin's pleasure! See, people have all kinds of wrong thought patterns causing them to not fear God, and they are ALL deceptions from Satan. I hear people say, "If there is a God, He would never send people to hell!" (Do you hear the unbelief in this heart?) Are you kidding me? Who do you think has sold them that lie? It is Satan, my friend!!! This is the same lie he has been peddling since the Garden of Eden. Do you remember what Lucifer told Eve? He said, "Did God say you will die if you sin by eating of that tree? Well, no you won't, Eve. God would never do that to you. God is a god of love! So go ahead now and eat the forbidden fruit." Did Adam & Eve die? OF COURSE!!! For God is NOT a liar. And God is not lying about the consequences of sin now either! The Bible, written by God's Holy Spirit, clearly states if we continue in willful sin (disobeying the 10 Love Commandments) God will annihilate our soul in the lake of fire! But Satan says, "No, He won't! God would never do that to His children. So go on now and enjoy the pleasures of sin, just have fun and DO whatever you want." Friend, <u>WHO</u> do you think is telling the truth this time? I am warning you to not believe Satan's lies.

Incidentally, <u>punishment for sin IS love</u>, for it is JUSTICE!!! Remember from my "*Introduction*" of this book, a father that does not punish his child when they do wrong DOES <u>NOT</u> LOVE THEM. So in the End, even when God sentences an unrepentant sinner's soul to ETERNAL PUNISHEMENT—which is eternal death—He will still love them! Do you see? Seriously, you did not think God was going to let you willfully treat Him and others (which is Him, too!) with NO love (sin) during your Earthly life, and then reward you with the wonderful pleasures of eternal life did you? Come on!

Other people—even some "preachers"—say, "There is no hell!" Again, are you kidding me? Think about it logically; if there is NO hell, then there was NO need for the Bible, period! Do you see? If there is no place of torment, then why did Jesus come to Earth and die a horrific death? <u>What was he trying to save us from</u>? And what is the purpose of God writing the Bible (commanding us to obey the 10 Love Commandments) when we are all going to heaven anyway? That would be pointless, too. We might as well live like we want to. Just do what you want because everything is going to be fine. Friend, who do you think is selling these ridiculous lies? It is Satan!!! And frankly, I do not see how people can buy such nonsense?

Friend, I assure you there is a place of torment. Jesus talked about it over and over again. And sadly, most people are going to go there. Life is about sowing and reaping, my friend, and the Lord God Almighty <u>loves</u> justice: "*<u>I the LORD love judgment</u>*" (Isaiah 61:8). We will all receive our <u>JUST</u> reward for the wickedness or love we have shown, and God will be the perfect, righteous Judge of us all. Therefore, if you find a truly <u>wise</u> person on planet Earth, you will do so ONLY if they possess a "fear of God" in their heart, because the Bible says wisdom only begins with a healthy fear of God: "***<u>The fear of the LORD is the beginning of WISDOM</u>***" (Proverbs 9:10). So, do you want to be wise? Then be greatly concerned about your soul's eternal destiny, fear the power God holds over it, and willingly <u>DO</u> (obey) His every Word (the 10 Love Commandments).

Some people wonder, "Why would a loving God kill His own

364

spirit children in hellfire?" Because it is part of the Game of Life He has created! Without the option to lose our soul, there would be no chance to <u>win</u> eternal life for our soul; therefore, there would be no pleasure to be received by God and the angels when a soul repents of sin and chooses the WAY of love! Do you see? In a game there has to be the option to lose, and in God's Game of Life the losing souls will be burned up in the lake of fire! Consequently, God laid out the rules (or laws) in His Game of Life for His spirit children to obey to win, or disobey to lose. So it really all comes down to His "Law of love"!

Now, I want you to understand God's spiritual "Law of love" is His word, it is truth, it is love, and it is eternal. In other words, it cannot be changed! To understand this concept, compare God's spiritual law to a physical law He made such as gravity. On planet Earth the law of gravity is always present. It is always binding, for it is truth! If you jump off the top of a high rise building, the law of gravity will be in effect to crash you to the ground in a world of hurt, probably killing you. See, God does not change the law to save your life if you are foolish enough to test it, for a law is a law. And going against (disobeying) laws always has consequences!!! Likewise, God's "Law of love" cannot be changed, for it is truth: It maintains if we <u>willfully</u> disobey the 10 <u>Love</u> Commandment Law, our soul will perish! And God has been very fair to all mankind, for He wrote His "Law of love" on all His spirit children's hearts. Thus, they are clearly known, and all mankind has had a chance to win in the Game of Life!

Consequently, the only hope God has in getting His spirit children to NOT hurt themselves is for Him to continually warn them of the consequences of disobeying His spiritual "Law of love" (the 10 Love Commandments). Thus, God is like a parent on planet Earth who screams at their child to get off the road because they could get hit by a vehicle and severely hurt themselves or die. Do you see? The parent puts <u>FEAR</u> in their child by forcibly grabbing their arm, yanking them off the road, and shouting in their ear to never do that again! Even though the child burst into tears, the parent has shown the highest love for their child, for they have instilled <u>fear</u> into the child's heart to save its life. Hopefully, in the future, when the child considers wandering out into the middle of the road they will remember the awful experience and horrified look on their parent's face and decide not to go into the street. See, this kind of fear is very healthy!

Likewise, a righteous "fear of God" should be instilled inside of us when it comes to <u>deciding</u> to DO evil (disobey God's 10 Love Commandments). The Bible says: *"The **FEAR of the LORD is to hate evil**" (Proverbs 8:13)*. Do you understand this verse? It means "fearing God" = "hating evil (hating disobeying the 10 Love Commandments)". In other words, the terms are synonymous! See, if someone truly "fears God" they instinctively <u>hate</u> evil, because they know, understand, and <u>believe</u> the dreadful consequences that result from DOING evil (disobeying the 10 Love Commandments). This is just like if you truly fear a lion, you will <u>hate</u> to go into his cage! Do you see? Your fear causes you to hate to <u>DO</u> the "thing" that will cause you immense suffering. This is what it truly means to "fear God". Therefore, when presented with the opportunity to gawk at pornographic material, an instinctive "fear of God (hatred of evil)" ought to well up in your heart (thoughts, desires, & emotions) propelling you to flee the dangerous situation, yelling, "No, I will NOT lust sexually and commit adultery in my mind, because I know the law of God says <u>no</u> adulterer will enter into the Kingdom of God!" See how a healthy "fear of God (hatred of evil)" can save your soul? A "fear of God" will drive you to not love money, not steal, not lie, not disobey the Sabbath, etc. Friend, a true "fear of God" in your spirit is a wonderful blessing from God, because it will save your soul!

Moreover, a "fear of God" in your heart is actually evidence of the Holy Spirit in you. Listen to Isaiah: *"And <u>the SPIRIT of the LORD shall rest upon him</u>, the **spirit of wisdom, and understanding, the spirit of counsel and might, the spirit of knowledge and of the FEAR of the LORD**" (Isaiah 11:2)*. Do you see? Wisdom, understanding, counsel, might, knowledge, and a "fear of God" are all attributes of the Holy Spirit. How about that? In other words, if you have been truly *"born again"* of the Holy Spirit, you WILL "fear God (hate evil)". Without a doubt, it is a godly trait to have a healthy "fear of God" so strong inside your spirit (thoughts, desires, & emotions) that it drives you to live righteously. Oh, that God would give everyone a heart like that, for then they would flee evil and win eternal life: *"**A wise man FEARETH,** *and DEPARTETH from evil: but the fool rageth, and is confident"* *(Proverbs 14:16).*

Alright, let us return to God's Israelite story (parable)—God's ALL INCLUSIVE message detailing everything involved in a soul's journey back to God—to learn more about this concept of "fearing God". (Remember, in the "wilderness scene" God is revealing everything concerning MANKIND'S PART in the salvation equation to be able to enter the Promise Land and obtain eternal life.) Thus, it is here in the wilderness that we find the emotion God instilled in the children of Israel at the base of Mount Sinai when speaking the 10 Love Commandment Law to them was FEAR. How about that? This part of the story (parable) could not be anymore accurately informative. Listen to the account: *"And mount Sinai was altogether on a smoke, because the LORD descended upon it in fire: and the smoke thereof ascended as the smoke of a furnace, and the whole mount quaked greatly" (Exodus 19:18).* This "event" terrified the Israelites: *"And all the people saw the thunderings, and the lightnings, and the noise of the trumpet, and the mountain smoking: and **when the people saw it, they removed, and stood afar off**" (Exodus 20:18).* Later, Moses wrote about the people's fear: *"I (Moses) stood between the LORD and you at that time, to shew you the WORD of the LORD: **FOR YE WERE AFRAID** by reason of the fire, and went not up into the mount" (Deuteronomy 5:5).* Do you see?

While the Israelites trembled in fear, Moses told them WHY God demonstrated himself with such power on the mountaintop: *"**God is come to PROVE you**, and **that his FEAR may be before your faces, THAT YE SIN NOT**" (Exodus 20:20).* Oh, reader, can you hear truth? This verse is powerful in understanding the correct mindset you MUST possess of God if you want to obtain eternal life. God was like a loving parent watching out for His children, and He wanted to instill raw, hardcore FEAR in the Israelite's hearts, so they would NOT SIN (disobey the 10 Love Commandments) and harm themselves! Friend, the best motivation for keeping yourself from sinning against God is to retain a healthy "fear of God" in your heart. Do not ever forget that fact. God WANTED the Israelites to truly FEAR Him!!! And God wants you and me to fear Him as well, so we will not hurt ourselves by disobeying His 10 Love Commandment Law and destroy our souls. See, a "fear of

God" is for your own well being!

But, unfortunately, the Israelites soon forgot their fearful experience at Mount Sinai and began disobeying God's 10 Love Commandments, and for that they perished in the wilderness having never obtained entrance into the Promise Land! Their disobedience proved their disbelief in God's Word. Please do not make the same mistake! You should now be able to clearly understand Paul's wisely written admonition: *"**WORK OUT your own salvation with FEAR and TREMBLING**" (Philippians 2:12)*. See, your salvation (obtaining eternal life) will be a result of your "fearing God" and choosing to turn from sin. In other words, it is just as Paul said *"you work out your own salvation through fear and trembling"*! This is a continual, daily journey on planet Earth. Everyday you choose to either obey or disobey God's Law.

Satan does not want you to understand this. He wants you to believe in a "one-time salvation prayer" method to obtain eternal life. Then he can divert your attention away from the truth! He takes all the importance off a DAILY need to "sin not (obey God's 10 Love Commandments)" to obtain eternal life. Meanwhile, he continues to tempt you to sin because he knows God's Law (if willfully disobeyed) still has the death consequence!!! He knows if you continue to willfully sin, you will lose your soul. Friend, Satan knows the truth better than you do! That is why he has been twisting it for millennia. If he can get you convinced you are on your WAY to heaven because of some little, one-time prayer, he almost certainly has you! You will soon have NO "fear of God" in your heart, believing you can live like you want to because you "accepted Jesus". What a load of garbage! Do not believe Satan's lie, my friend. You must always "fear God", which means to willingly obey his 10 Love Commandments always. THAT is the ONLY *"narrow way"* that leads to eternal life. Listen to Christ: *"And, behold, I come quickly; and my reward is with me, to give every man according as his WORK shall be...**Blessed are they that DO his (10 Love) commandments**, THAT THEY may have right to the tree of life, and MAY ENTER IN through the gates into the city" (Revelation 22:12, 14)*. Yes, "fear God" and "obey His 10 Love Commandments" and you will one day eat from the tree of life in His Kingdom and obtain eternal life!

King Solomon, in all his sagacity, summed up the ONLY "thing" mankind needs to DO (or accomplish) during his sojourning here on Earth: *"Let us hear the conclusion of the WHOLE matter:* ***FEAR GOD, and KEEP HIS (10 LOVE) COMMANDMENTS: for this is the WHOLE DUTY of MAN***. For *God shall bring every work into judgment, with every secret thing, whether it be good, or whether it be evil"* (Ecclesiastes 12:13, 14). Wow, that is IT my friend! Can you hear wisdom? There is nothing else you need to DO during your time down here on planet Earth but to Fear God and obey His 10 Love Commandments. NOTHING else matters! If you are not DOING this, YOU ARE A FAILURE!!! Whatever you think you are accomplishing by buying, selling, and trading (shuffling around) dirt is pointless. Only the love you show God and your neighbor by obeying the 10 Love Commandments has value. Obtaining materialistic (dirt) possessions is worthless, but obtaining eternal life is priceless! Solomon's words show he truly did possess the highest of wisdom in his mind, but only when you DO what he said are you considered among the wisest people on Earth, for anyone who *"fears God and obeys His 10 Love Commandments"* is the wisest.

The message to "fear God and turn from sin" is prevalent throughout the Bible. It is the genuine heart of ALL God's instruction to mankind. It is truly ALL you have to know and DO to obtain eternal life. For example, listen to the Proverb: *"Be not wise in thine own eyes:* ***FEAR the LORD, and depart from evil"*** *(Proverbs 3:7)*. The Psalmist sung: *"The **LORD taketh pleasure in them that FEAR him***" (Psalms 147:11). Do you see? This message is everywhere in the Bible. So be on the lookout for it when reading God's word. God asked Satan about Job: *"Hast thou considered my servant Job, that there is NONE like him in the earth, **a PERFECT and UPRIGHT man, one that FEARETH God, and escheweth (to turn away, depart from) evil?**" (Job 1:8)*. Would you like to hear God talk about YOU like that? I tell you the truth; God longs for people that still fear Him, running from sin (evil) to the WAY of love (good)! Unfortunately, they are an extremely rare breed of people on planet Earth today.

One day in AD 2007, I was working as a carpenter installing crown molding and baseboard in a room at a retirement center. Suddenly,

God began speaking to me and asked, "Gabriel, do you know WHY people continue willfully sinning against me?" I was still thinking of an answer when he answered for me, "It is because they do not fear me, Gabriel! They have no concept or reality of the horrifying fire of hell!" At those words, I was taken aback!!! I questioned, "Lord, is this really you speaking to me, because your words seem harsh?"

But He plowed on, "Listen to me, son, as I explain what I am saying. If you ignited a massive bonfire on Earth and told people when they sinned (disobeyed the 10 Love Commandments) they will be captured, bound, and held for 15 minutes with their feet 5 inches from the roaring flames, how much sin do you think would still be occurring? Take for instance the sin of premarital sex," He continued, "If you warned people that I will point their sexual immorality out to you—in other words, no one will be able to hide their sin and escape the 15 minutes of fiery punishment—how much premarital sex do you think would still be happening? After everyone watched the first person caught sinning be held close to the scorching fire, screaming, writhing, and hollering in agony, with their eyes bulging in horror as the heat burned deeper and deeper into their boiling flesh, do you think people would still be itching to sin by having premarital sex?"

By now I was shocked! But I answered, "No, Lord, they would be scared to death to fornicate. But Lord," I said, "this is too cruel! Why are you telling me something like this? If I told this story to people they would say I am a fear-monger. They would arrogantly chide back, 'God is love'!"

He fumed, "I am love!!! I am trying to save their soul, but they will not stop sinning! And it is ONLY because they <u>DO NOT FEAR ME</u>, Gabriel. The truth is the fire of hell is already burning! The punishment is already awaiting all those who disobey my Word, but people do not truly "believe" it strong enough to deter them from sinning. Many people say they "believe in Me", but by their continual, willful sin they prove they do not. They say they cannot help themselves for they are just sinners, but I say nonsense! One 15 minute hellish encounter beside that bonfire and I guarantee the next time the opportunity to have premarital sex arose they could and would control themselves. You would be amazed at how quick their spirit (mind) would recall the terrifying, painful experience, and they would run with their charred feet like a wild person from that potentially sinful situation. THAT is the "fear of Me" that is missing in people's hearts today Gabriel! THAT is the kind of '*fear and trembling*' that could and would work out my spirit children's salvation (obtain them eternal life), but they do not possess it! A raw "fear of Me" is absent from my children. Willful sin will kill their soul, but they do not believe it!"

I got to tell you, I was startled and dumbfounded by the time God finished speaking to me, but His alarming words would not leave my head. They churned in my spirit like a slow moving hurricane. No matter how I viewed it, I knew He was right! People do not "believe in God (love)" like that, I thought. Their "fear of God" is no where near that kind of intensity. Yet I knew the strong fear the Lord had described to me was the correct "fear of God" that would produce perfection (continual obedience to the 10 Love Commandments) in His spirit children's hearts, which is the real action-based "*faith*" and "*good works*" we MUST <u>DO</u> to obtain eternal life. I drove home from work that afternoon with the Lord's message still ablaze in my mind.

When I got home the phone rang. It was my next door neighbor's daughter Labrina. She lived about 2 miles away from her parents and me and was calling from her house just to chat. Well since God's words still satiated my heart, I shared with her what God had told me that morning and she was silent. (But when I told her the story I personalized it by saying, "If I built a big bonfire in <u>MY</u> front yard…") Needless to say, the story's gruesomeness and graveness put a quick damper on any kind of frivolous chitchat, so we talked briefly and hung up. Then, I lied down for an afternoon nap. But within less than an hour the phone's ringing woke me up, and I was surprised to hear Labrina's voice again! Turns out, she had driven over to her parent's house and was sitting in their driveway in her car on her cell phone. "Look out your front door!" she said excitedly to me.

When I opened my front door my jaw dropped! I stood in shock beholding the sight about 80 feet from my eyes. A car was sitting on the street across from my house <u>completely</u> engulfed in flames. (I am not talking just the hood area, I mean the ENTIRE car!) The massive flames were leaping 30 feet into the air!!! The bonfire God had spoke about to

371

me earlier that morning (and that I had just spoken about to Labrina less than an hour earlier) was now burning in front of my house! A few people were calmly standing far back away from the car—obviously the car's occupants—so I knew no one was being hurt. Therefore, I left my front door open and sat down in the living room. I sat there for over 10 minutes in astonishment and horror, watching the gigantic fire through my storm door until the fire-trucks arrived. In those few miraculous minutes, I realized God was physically confirming what He had told me earlier that day was 100% directly from Him! Consequently, I am warning you today with a heavy heart to FEAR GOD and OBEY HIS 10 LOVE COMMANMENTS for unbearable hellfire is awaiting all unrepentant sinners.

In time, I realized the harsh tone of God's message to me that day was not unlike the harsh tone of His message He spoke through His only begotten son, Jesus: *"Ye have heard that it was said by them of old time, Thou shalt not commit adultery: But I say unto you, That whosoever looketh on a woman to lust after her hath committed adultery with her already in his heart (spirit). And if thy right eye offend thee (cause thee to sin), PLUCK IT OUT, and cast it from thee: for it is profitable for thee that one of thy members should perish, and not that thy whole body should be cast into HELL. And if thy right hand offend thee (cause thee to sin), CUT IT OFF, and cast it from thee: for it is profitable for thee that one of thy members should perish, and not that thy whole body should be cast into hell"* (Matthew 5:27-30). Do you see? These words are equally ghastly and gruesome as what the Lord told me. But please do not miss the fact that God's message is FULL of LOVE! (By the way, note it was the same sin God used as an example to me—namely, sexual immorality—that prompted Jesus to say what he did!) Friend, there is NO other way to interpret Christ's words; he is pointblank warning, "We MUST REPENT—meaning STOP our willful sinning—or we will end up in unthinkable hellfire one day!" So, again, I am warning you to honestly FEAR God and take whatever measures necessary to quit sinning, because your decision to live righteously (obey the 10 Love Commandments) is your duty in obtaining eternal life.

More Biblical proof a "fear of God" in a person's spirit is the

372

mindset that has the potential to save their soul from hell comes from Bible verses concerning children. Listen carefully to the following proverb: "*Withhold NOT correction from the child: for if thou beatest him with the rod, he shall not die. **Thou shalt BEAT him with the ROD, and shalt DELIVER his SOUL from HELL***" *(Proverbs 23:13, 14)*. Wow, how about that? How could that be? How can "*beating a child*" SAVE his/her soul from hell? Well, what does "*beating a child with a rod*" instill in a child? Fear, people, fear…It puts the "fear of God" in them!!! And it is this FEAR that will drive them away from doing evil (disobeying the 10 Love Commandments)—which the Bible is CLEARLY saying in this verse will SAVE their SOUL from hell. Friend, even this little proverb contains the absolute truth about what mankind MUST DO to obtain eternal life: We must flee evil (sin)! But unfortunately in today's wicked world, Satan is even hampering parents from being able to instill a "fear of God" in their children by applying the above verse's Godly, soul-saving technique. In other words, today parents can go to prison for punishing their child for doing wrong! How sad is that? Friend, you should be acutely aware that Satan is doing everything possible in these last days to foster a generation of people that are on their WAY to hell! For He is ripping the 10 Love Commandments off every wall possible, while actively trying to abolish child punishment!

Satan's goal is to eliminate any trace of the "fear of God" in people's hearts. See, if he can get a person to "NOT fear God" he will soon have them sinning! And he starts his soul-killing work right from childhood by not allowing parents to punish their children: "*Foolishness is bound in the heart of a child; but **the rod of correction shall drive it far from him**" (Proverbs 22:15).* Do you see? "*Fear and trembling*" in a child's heart (from understanding the painful punishment received for DOING evil) will drive foolishness (sin) out of their spirit, meaning it will propel them to DO good and AVOID evil! But instead, we have a generation of kids growing up today without any fear of wrongdoing. Is it any wonder it is such a grossly wicked, sexually immoral, money (dirt)-loving, God-hating world?

The concept of "fearing God = eschewing evil (sin)" has been around since the fall of Adam & Eve in the Garden of Eden. The story of Abraham and Abimelech in the 20ᵗʰ century BC confirms this fact. Abraham told king Abimelech of Gerar that Sarah, his wife, was his sister—which was actually not lying for she was his half-sister!—because he was afraid king Abimelech would kill him and take his beautiful wife. Abimelech took Sarah into his court, but when he found out in a dream by God that she was Abraham's wife he was distraught, and he brought Abraham in for questioning. Abraham said: *"**I thought, Surely the FEAR of GOD is not in this place**; and they will slay me for my wife's sake" (Genesis 20:11)*. See, even then—700 years before Moses received the 10 Love Commandments—mankind understood that someone who "obeyed the 10 Love Commandments" like *"thou shall not murder"* or *"thou shall not commit adultery"* was someone who "feared God"! Do you see? But Abraham was wrong because Abimelech did fear God. He knew murder and adultery were evil (sin), and he was <u>scared</u> to sin against God. How about you? Do you fear God? Are you terrified to sin against God by disobeying His 10 Love Commandments?

Friend, God is our loving Father. He is out to protect you from harm. He wants you to FEAR the hellish punishment that will come from disobeying His unchanging 10 Love Commandment Law. He is no different than an Earthly parent who tries to protect their young by instilling fear in them to not play in the street, swim in an alligator infested pond, or put their hand on a hot burner. Do you see? He is avidly and passionately trying to save you from pain and hurt! Are you listening to him? God says: *"**By the FEAR of the LORD men DEPART from EVIL**" (Proverbs 16:6)*. So how about you? Do you fear God? Or are you living an Earthly existence fearless of God, ignoring His WAY of love that leads to eternal life (by disobeying the 10 Love Commandments) and spiraling towards a world of torment in hell?

Here is the type person God desires: *"**but to this man will I look, even to him that is POOR and of a CONTRITE spirit, and TREMBLETH at my WORD**" (Isaiah 66:2)*. The word "poor" is from the Hebrew word *"ānî"* meaning: <u>needy, poor, afflicted, oppressed, often referring to a class of persons of low status and lacking resources</u>. I told you God's heart beats for the materialistically poor. Does yours? The word "contrite" is from the Hebrew word *"nākeh"* meaning: <u>lame,</u>

crippled; contrite, crushed, humbled. Friend, God loves a humble, materialistically content person with a spirit that truly FEARS Him by fleeing from evil (obeys His 10 Love Commandments). THAT is the type people who will obtain eternal life one day in God's Kingdom: *"The LORD is nigh unto them that are of a broken heart; and **SAVETH such as be of a contrite spirit**" (Psalms 34:18)*. But it is the worldly-minded, selfish-minded, money-loving, possession-lusting, self-gratifying, arrogant, prideful, overfed, materialistically rich people who disgust God and are headed for eternal destruction! (And, sadly, many of these people sit in church buildings every Sunday unaware that they are on their WAY to hell because their "pastor" is full of Satan himself—i.e. full of greed and unable to reveal the truth about the Love of God!)

I will close this chapter with an excerpt from a King David psalm and an excerpt from a letter of Peter displaying God's parent-like mindset over His spirit children and what He is looking for out of them: *"**Like as a father pitieth (shows mercy or compassion on) his children, so the LORD pitieth them that FEAR him**. For he knoweth our frame; he remembereth that we are dust. As for man, his days are as grass; as a flower of the field, so he flourisheth. For the wind passeth over it, and it is gone; and the place thereof shall know it no more. **But the MERCY of the LORD is from everlasting to everlasting upon them that FEAR him**...To such as keep his COVENANT, and **TO THOSE THAT REMEMBER HIS (10 Love) COMMANDMENTS TO DO THEM**" (Psalms 103:13-18)*. Truly, the people God will have mercy on and allow into His wonderful Kingdom of Heaven (obtaining eternal life) will be those who "fear Him" enough to always "obey His 10 Love Commandments" during their brief existence on planet Earth: *"OBEY God because you are his children; don't slip back into your old ways—doing evil...But be holy now in everything you DO, just as the Lord is holy...And remember that your heavenly Father to whom you pray has no favorites when he judges. He will judge you with perfect justice for EVERYTHING you DO; **so ACT in reverent FEAR OF HIM from now on until you get to heaven**" (I Peter 1:14-17, Living Bible)*. Amen and amen.

Chapter 20

Joshua

"When the people heard the sound of the TRUMPET,
and the people shouted with a GREAT SHOUT…
the wall fell down flat"
(Joshua 6:20)

Well, my friend, we have reached the concluding scene (or act) of God's 440 year long Israelite story (parable) that secretly explained—but now has been revealed to you!—<u>EVERYTHING</u> involved in mankind's spiritual journey back to God. The message (or meaning) behind the story prophetically and clandestinely described how the souls of mankind would be supernaturally delivered out of bondage to "sin & death" through the Messiah (Jesus) during the 4,000th year of mankind's history, and then it <u>confirmed</u> exactly what the souls of ALL mankind MUST **DO** to obtain entrance (eternal life) in the Promise Land (Kingdom of God)—namely, REPENT of sin (evil) by willingly choosing to follow (continue journeying along) the WAY of love by obeying God's 10 Love Commandment Law.

In this concluding scene—the action of which transpires at the END of the Israelites 40 year wilderness journey—God finally allows the Israelites to enter into the Promise Land! And it is here, through the DETAILS of this part of the story (parable), that God again prophetically revisits the topic of Jesus Christ's 2nd Coming (or mankind's 6,000th year), for that is when ALL the righteous souls will finally be physically resurrected and officially ENTER the Kingdom of God (Promise Land). In other words, God is about to secretly prognosticate more information concerning Jesus' 2nd Coming and subsequent "setting up" of his Earthly Kingdom for the fulfillment of God's restful (7th millennial) Sabbath day reign. Is that not incredible? Let us take a look.

Remember, God initiated the prophetic topic of the Messiah's 2nd Coming in parabolic form through the story of Noah in mankind's 1,656th year (2316 BC). In that account (parable), God foretold that "one house" of people—only Noah's house in the parable—will be "lifted up" off of planet Earth while its surface is simultaneously being totally destroyed! The Ark represented the ONLY place of safety available for the souls of mankind during the (soon coming) terrifying day of God's wrath—i.e. it embodied the Kingdom of God with its 3 levels, rooms, windows, and door. And the destructive flood commenced when Noah was 600 years old to signify Christ's return will absolutely, positively happen during mankind's 6,000th year (or exactly 2,000 years from the YEAR Jesus died on the cross)! THAT is the 7 day (7,000 year) master plan of God for mankind on planet Earth. It is a divine plan that is impossible to stop! Friend, Christ's 2nd Coming WILL occur somewhere around the year AD 2028, and very likely during that exact year!!!

Next, God prophetically revisited the topic Of Jesus' 2nd Coming through the story of Sodom & Gomorrah during mankind's 2,048th year (1924 BC). In that story (parable), we learned FIRE will be the physical vehicle of choice God will use to destroy the entire surface of planet Earth, along with ALL the ungodly people's flesh, at Christ's return. Furthermore, God again verified only "one house" of people will be saved from the fiery destruction—only Lot's house in the parable—and that they would be "lifted up" off of planet Earth by God's holy angels!

So here we are in mankind's 2,678th year (1294 BC, 1334 BC – 40 years) at the closing stages of God's massive Israelite story (parable). It is still 1,322 years till the all important 4,000th year when Jesus will die on the cross for the sins of mankind, and yet God is about to reveal more intricate truths (facts) about the events surrounding Jesus' 2nd Coming! Look, at this point in time the Israelites still do not even know the NAME of the coming Messiah (nor that he will come to planet Earth first as the "sacrificial Lamb of God"), and yet God is going to lead them through detailed events that secretly prophecy more about the Messiah's 2nd Coming! Oh, but one thing is about to change, for <u>now</u> is the time and scene where God will prophetically clue the unsuspecting and unknowing Israelites into the Messiah's name!

Here is the setting; during the Israelite's 40th year in the wilderness, Moses died: *"And Moses was an <u>hundred and twenty years old</u> when he died" (Deuteronomy 34:7)*. But before Moses expired he turned the <u>commanding</u> position over to a man named Joshua: *"And **<u>JOSHUA the son of Nun was full of the spirit of wisdom</u>**; for Moses had laid his hands upon him: and the children of Israel hearkened unto him" (Deuteronomy 34:9)*. The original Hebrew name translated "Joshua" in English is *"yᵉhôšua"* meaning: <u>Yahweh saves</u>! It would be almost 1,300 years later until the angel Gabriel informed Mary: *"Behold, thou shalt conceive in thy womb, and bring forth a son, **<u>and shalt call his name JESUS</u>**" (Luke 1:31)*. The original Greek word translated "Jesus" in our English Bibles was *"Iēsous"* meaning: <u>Jesus, JOSHUA, Yahweh saves</u>! Do you see? The Greek name for "Jesus" is equal to the Hebrew name for "Joshua"! In other words, at this stunning point in the Israelite's story (parable), God was actually revealing the future name of the coming Messiah by raising up a man named "Joshua" to lead the army of Israelites into the Promise Land.

Friend, during the Messianic 2nd Coming, <u>JESUS</u> will be the <u>captain</u> of the spiritual army that conquers Satan (the Antichrist) to set up God's millennial Kingdom on Earth. Thus, the Israelite story (parable) could not be any more prophetically perfect in its name sake, for we see a man named Joshua (Jesus) is about to lead the army of Israelites INTO the Promise Land! Yes, during year 6,000, the Kingdom of God will finally arrive on planet Earth with Jesus Christ reigning as King, and we know at that time <u>REST</u> will be restored on Earth because Satan will be bound for 1,000 years. So listen to God's description of what will happen to those Israelites who ENTER the "Promised Land" Joshua is about to conquer: *"**<u>Until the LORD have given your brethren REST...and they also have possessed the land</u>** which the LORD your God giveth them" (Joshua 1:15)*. Do you see? God refers to the

"Promise Land" as the "place of REST"! Friend, this is EXACTLY what will happen to planet Earth at Jesus' 2nd Coming: Planet Earth will be transformed into a peaceful, restful "Promise Land" for ALL the righteous souls to inhabit.

Now, the actual physical location on Earth God set up to represent the "Promise Land" in this scene of the Israelite's story (parable) was a city called Jericho that resided on the land where Israel exists today. In other words, Jericho was located on the SAME land Abraham & Sarah had traveled to after Sarah was freed from Pharaoh and the SAME land Jacob traveled to after escaping Laban. Jericho sat west of the Jordan River in Canaan, and it was a worldly, heathenish place. Consequently, Jericho accurately represented what ALL of planet Earth will be like right before Christ's 2nd Coming—namely, it will be full of wicked, godless people, and "one small house" of righteous people! Oh, but Joshua (Jesus), as captain of the army, was about to lead a battle to conquer Jericho and inhabit the Promise Land! So, next, we see in the story (parable) that God lays out specific DETAILS of exactly how He wants Joshua to conquer Jericho. And I must say, in that situation and at that time (1294 BC) not knowing God was prophesying about the future, Joshua and the Israelites must have thought God flew over the cuckoo's nest, for His detailed battle plan seems like borderline insanity.

Listen to God's war plan: *"And ye shall compass the city, all ye men of war, and go round about the city once. Thus shalt thou do SIX DAYS. And **SEVEN priests shall bear before the ark (of the covenant) SEVEN trumpets of rams' horns**: and the SEVENTH DAY ye shall compass the city SEVEN TIMES, and the priests shall blow with the trumpets. And **it shall come to pass, that when they make a LONG BLAST with the RAM'S HORN, and WHEN YE HEAR THE SOUND OF THE TRUMPET, all the people shall SHOUT WITH A GREAT SHOUT; and the wall of the city shall fall down flat,** and the people shall ASCEND UP every man straight before him"* (Joshua 6:3-5). How about that craziness? The Israelite army was to march around the city of Jericho once for each of 6 days and then march around it 7 times the 7th day! All the while, 7 priests were to be marching and blowing their trumpets before the Ark of the Covenant (housing the 2 tables etched with the 10 Love Commandments!) which was also being carried around the city. Then, on the 7th day after the 7th time around the city, the 7 priests were to blow one long, sustained trumpet blast, and the people were to make a *"great shout"*! After which, the walls of Jericho would fall down, and Joshua and his army would conquer the land by *"ascending up"*—let him that reads understand. Wow, if I were Joshua back then, I would have thought, "Good Lord in Heaven, what is this madness? How did you come up with this crazy, yet specific, plan?"

Oh, but Glory to God, around 1,400 years later (near 90 AD) God's reason and motive for His outrageous, detailed battle plan for Joshua was revealed (although there is no evidence anyone made the connection)! On the Isle of Patmos, God began showing John the Revelator a <u>detailed</u>, behind-the-scenes vision in the spirit world of the final battle that will take place on Earth at Christ's 2nd Coming, when he conquers Satan's (the Antichrist) rule on planet Earth and sets up His Kingdom, regenerating Earth into the restful Promise Land! John wrote the vision in the Bible's book "The Revelation". Watch how it perfectly mirrors the battle plan God gave Joshua to conquer Jericho.

In the vision, John saw a book containing 7 seals that needed to be opened right before Jesus' 2nd Coming: *"And I saw in the right hand of him that sat on the throne a book written within and on the backside, **sealed with SEVEN SEALS**" (Revelation 5:1)*. No one was worthy to open the 7 seals except Jesus: *"Behold, <u>the Lion of the tribe of Judah</u>, the Root of David, <u>hath prevailed to open the book, and to LOOSE the SEVEN SEALS</u> thereof" (Revelation 5:5)*. So, one by one, Jesus opens each seal, paralleling each day Joshua and the army of the Israelites walked around the city of Jericho! Each seal represents terrible "events" that are coming to planet Earth right before Christ's return. (Please read them sometime in Revelation chapters 6 & 7.)

Then, when the Lamb of God (Jesus) opens the 7th seal—which mirrors day 7 in Joshua's battle plan—look what happens: *"And when he had opened the <u>seventh seal</u>...<u>I saw the SEVEN ANGELS which STOOD BEFORE GOD; and to them were given SEVEN TRUMPETS</u>" (Revelation 8:1, 2)*. Are you kidding me? Friend, I cannot make this stuff up! When the 7th seal is opened, 7 angels appear EACH having to sound their trumpet in successive order, in which each of these 7 successive trumpet blasts brings farther specific devastation to planet

Earth, all the while leading up to Christ's 2nd Coming. Subsequently, God wanted Joshua to walk around Jericho 7 times on the 7th day with 7 priests each blowing their trumpet!

Finally, in John's "The Revelation" the <u>seventh</u> angel from the 7th seal blows his trumpet and listen to what happens: *"And the <u>seventh</u> <u>angel sounded</u>; and there were great voices in heaven, saying, **<u>The</u>* *<u>kingdoms of this world are become the kingdoms of our Lord, and of</u>* *<u>his Christ; and he shall reign for ever and ever</u>" (Revelation 11:15).* Do you see? THIS is precisely when Jesus' 2nd Coming will take place with the resurrection (rapture) of the saints to meet him in the air, after which he will set up his eternal Earthly kingdom, transforming Earth into the Promise Land. At that time, the 7th millennial day of God's 7,000 year master plan will begin. In other words, it will be mankind's 6,000th year of history since the Creation of the world!

Now, listen again to exactly what God told Joshua's men to do with their mouths during the 7 days they marched around Jericho: *"<u>Ye</u>* *<u>shall NOT shout, nor make any noise with your voice, neither shall any</u>* *<u>word proceed out of your mouth</u>, **<u>until the day I bid you shout; THEN</u>* *<u>SHALL YE SHOUT</u>" (Joshua 6:10).* See, they were to be completely <u>silent</u> until completing the 7th lap around Jericho on the 7th day. THEN, they were only to <u>shout</u> at the <u>hearing</u> of the <u>last trumpet</u>! And they did: *"So the people <u>shouted</u> when the priests blew with the trumpets: and it came to pass, **<u>when the people HEARD the sound of the TRUMPET,</u>* *<u>and the PEOPLE SHOUTED WITH A GREAT SHOUT, that the wall</u>* *<u>fell down flat...and they took the city</u>" (Joshua 6:20).* WHY was God adamant about Joshua's army conquering Jericho after the "sound of a trumpet and a great shout"? Because, unknowingly to them, this was a precise, prophetic picture of exactly how Jesus Christ's <u>RAPTUROUS</u> 2nd Coming will transpire!

Almost 1,400 years later, the Holy Spirit prophetically described the scene of Christ's 2nd Coming through the Apostle Paul: *"For **<u>the</u>* *<u>Lord himself shall descend from heaven WITH A SHOUT, with the</u>* *<u>voice of the archangel, and WITH THE TRUMP OF GOD</u>: and <u>the</u>* *<u>dead in Christ shall rise first: Then we which are alive and remain shall</u>* *<u>be caught up together with them in the clouds to meet the Lord in the</u>* *<u>air: and SO SHALL WE EVER BE WITH THE LORD</u>" (I Thessalonians*

382

4:16, 17). Do you see? The Joshua battle scene was perfection! The entire incident was <u>exactly</u> how Jesus' 2nd Coming will occur—i.e. <u>with a trumpet blast and a great shout</u>! Friend, is God's prophetic wisdom not stunning in these ancient Bible stories? I told you every detail had purpose and meaning!

By the way, notice how the RAPTURE of the saints happens at the <u>END</u> of the tribulation (7 seals) period, with the sounding of the 7th angel's trumpet from the opening of the 7th seal—NOT 7 years before!!! Comprehension of God's prophetic meaning behind Joshua's story of conquering Jericho and how it relates to John's revelation of the 7 seals—which EVERYONE knows is the great tribulation period—absolutely, 100 % ends the argument over the PRE-tribulation rapture theory. Do you see? The *"trumpet blast and the shout"*—which everyone knows is the "rapture verse" in the Bible of I Thessalonians 4:16, 17—of Joshua's army happens at the <u>END</u> of the 7 day marching period. Think about this until you understand it clearly! Friend, the whole "secret vanishing theory of the saints 7 or more years before Christ comes back to Earth" is nothing but a SATANIC LIE!!!

Now, did you notice the <u>WALLS of Jericho fell down</u> after the priest's trumpet blast and Israel's shout? THAT is because THAT is exactly how it will be ALL OVER EARTH at Christ's 2nd Coming!!! Listen to God prophesy directly about "the day" through Ezekiel in the 6th century BC: *"<u>It shall be in the latter days</u>...<u>Surely in that day there shall be a great shaking in the land of Israel; So that the fishes of the sea, and the fowls of the heaven, and the beasts of the field, and all creeping things that creep upon the earth, <u>and ALL the men that are upon the face of the earth, shall SHAKE at my presence, and the mountains shall be thrown down, and the steep places shall fall</u>, and EVERY WALL SHALL FALL TO THE GROUND...and <u>I will rain upon him (mankind)...an overflowing rain (think Noah!), and great hailstones, fire, and brimstone"</u>* (Ezekiel 38:16-22). Do you see, my friend? Joshua and the Israelite army's "conquering of Jericho" was a precise, prophetic picture of Christ's 2nd Coming!

Oh, but God included even more revelation about Christ's 2nd Coming in the act of Joshua conquering Jericho. (Hint: the story (parable) would not be complete without "one house" of people being saved <u>ABOVE</u> the ensuing destruction!) So watch how God develops this part of the story. Before the Israelites began their 7 day march around the city of Jericho, God asked Joshua to send out <u>2</u> spies (messengers) into Jericho: *"And <u>Joshua the son of Nun SENT OUT of Shittim TWO MEN to spy secretly, saying, Go view the land"</u> (Joshua 2:1).* While in the city, the two men were received and protected from harm in a harlot's house! Her name was Rahab. Guess where she lived? On <u>TOP</u> of the high wall surrounding Jericho: *<u>"for her house was UPON the town wall,</u> and <u>**she dwelt UPON the wall**"</u> (Joshua 2:15).* Can you perceive how God is already setting up the "one house of people to be saved <u>ABOVE</u> the destruction" part of the parable?

When trouble passed, Rahab kindly let the two men down Jericho's wall by a <u>scarlet</u> colored rope hanging out the window of her house: *"Then <u>she let them down by a cord through the window"</u> (Joshua 2:15).* The men told her to gather her "<u>household</u>" into her house, because the city was about to be destroyed and her family would be SAVED only if she left the red colored rope dangling from her window: *"Behold, when we come into the land, <u>thou shalt bind this line of scarlet thread in the window</u> which thou didst let us down by: and <u>**thou shalt bring thy father, and thy mother, and thy brethren, and all thy father's HOUSEHOLD, home unto thee**"</u> (Joshua 2:18).* So, there it is again my friend...only "one HOUSE" of people would be <u>saved</u> above the destruction of Jericho! The <u>red</u> colored rope symbolized the blood of the Lamb (Jesus) who would die for mankind's sins—just like the red blood symbolized on the doorposts of the Israelite's houses in Egypt the night the death angel passed over them 40 years earlier. Remember, people who willingly choose to REPENT OF SIN (obey the 10 Love Commandments) prove by their deeds that they have love (Jesus Christ) living inside their heart; thus, their body is part of the HOUSE of Jesus Christ's spirit, and the righteous, red blood of the Lamb will be applied to their soul to atone for their sins.

When the moment of truth arrived (after the Israelite's marched around Jericho 7 times on the 7th day) Joshua cried, *"**SHOUT**; for the LORD hath given you the city. And <u>the city shall be accursed, even it, and ALL that are therein,</u> to the LORD: <u>**ONLY rahab the harlot shall live, SHE and ALL THAT ARE WITH HER IN HER HOUSE**</u>, because* *she hid the **messengers** that we sent" (Joshua 6:16, 17).* In other words, the portion of Jericho's wall where Rahab's house lived, amazingly and supernaturally, did not fall down!!! Consequently, her household was saved <u>ABOVE</u> the resulting destruction! Therefore, once again, God was perfect with His prophetic detail. And what happened to the city? The Bible records: *"And **they UTTERLY DESTROYED ALL that was in the city**, both man and woman, young and old, and ox, and sheep, and ass, with the edge of the sword...And **they BURNT the city with FIRE, and ALL that was THEREIN**" (Joshua 6:21, 24).* There you have it...<u>everything</u> was destroyed with FIRE, while only "one house" of souls was saved above the mayhem. It, again, could not have been a more perfect, prophetic picture of Jesus' 2nd Coming, just like the stories of Noah and Lot!

By the way, notice the word change God used above to describe the <u>2</u> SPIES Joshua sent into Jericho: *"And Joshua saved Rahab the harlot alive, and her father's household, and all that she had...**because she hid the (two) MESSENGERS, which Joshua sent to spy out Jericho**" (Joshua 6:25).* See, they are now called "messengers"! The original Hebrew word used in the Scriptures translated "messengers" was *"mal'āk"* meaning: <u>messenger, a human representative; angel, a supernatural representative of God, sometimes delivering messages, sometimes protecting God's people</u>. So what was God's purpose in sending out "<u>2</u> messengers" into Jericho to <u>warn</u> Rahab's house of the coming destruction? The answer came clandestinely to John the Revelator almost 1,400 years later, for he probably did not make the connection between his prophetic vision of Christ's 2nd Coming and the story of Joshua. But God revealed to him in "The Revelation" that right before Christ's 2nd Coming He will send out not 1, not 3, not 4, not 12, but <u>TWO</u> witnesses (messengers) to planet Earth: *"And **I will give power unto my TWO WITNESSES, and they shall prophesy a thousand two hundred and threescore days, clothed in sackcloth**" (Revelation 11:3).* Do you see? Joshua's <u>2</u> messengers he sent into Jericho foretold of God's <u>2</u> witnesses He will send to Earth right before Jesus' 2nd Coming to <u>warn</u> Earth's inhabitants of the soon coming fiery destruction!

Friend, have you acquired an appreciation for the incredible prophetic purpose God had behind <u>every</u> detail He "caused to occur" in the ancient Bible stories? God's ability to "know the future" is truly breathtaking to comprehend! (And to think; God did it all <u>ONLY</u> for provable EVIDENCE He exists, so that YOU might believe in Him, Love!!!) But let me say a word about the reason God picked a <u>harlot</u> (Rahab) to be saved. Listen, her "harlotry" represented the entirety of mankind's spiritual condition, because we have <u>ALL</u> "gone astray" from God's WAY of love—in other words, we have ALL "played the harlot" for we have ALL sinned: *"<u>All we like sheep have gone astray; we have</u> <u>turned EVERY ONE to his own way; and the LORD hath laid on him</u> <u>the iniquity of us all</u>" (Isaiah 53:6).* Thus, Rahab's sinful occupation was to perfectly represent how we all have turned our backs on God (love) at one time or another.

So what, then, <u>really</u> saved Rahab? The Bible says: ***"<u>By FAITH</u>*** ***<u>the harlot Rahab perished not</u> with them that BELIEVED NOT, when*** ***<u>she had received the spies with PEACE</u>" (Hebrews 11:31).*** Do you see what it was? It was the "<u>love</u> she <u>showed</u>" towards the messengers! Her <u>action-based</u> love proved her faith in God (love). Incidentally, I find it very hard to believe that she continued to DO the deeds of a prostitute in those final weeks, once the messengers told her of Jericho's impending destruction. I believe she truly repented to God of ALL her sins! And the scarlet rope hanging out of her window pictured the coming blood of Jesus that would atone for her past sins, saving her soul from death. But the rest of the city's inhabitants continued "DOING evil deeds"— i.e. "not showing love" by disobeying the 10 Love Commandments— which proved their "<u>unbelief</u> in God (love)", and thus they perished in the fire!

Alright, so after 3 times of visiting the topic of Jesus' 2nd Coming—i.e. the time of Earth's regeneration back to its peaceful, restful, Garden-of-Eden-like conditions—through the ancient stories (parables) of Noah, Lot, and Joshua, God had secretly completed an extremely accurate picture of the Messiah's 2nd Advent. In other words, by 1294 BC God had revealed HOW and WHEN this sinful age on Earth would come to an end through the meaningful details of these 3 stories. The only hitch…<u>NO ONE</u> understood it!!! Yet the 3 stories clearly revealed in the end, only <u>1</u> house of resurrected righteous souls will be saved on Earth by rising up off of it, carried by angels to meet the Lord Jesus in the air after the sound of a trumpet and a shout, during mankind's 6,000[th] year from Creation, while simultaneously ALL of planet Earth's surface and wicked, godless people are destroyed by fire! To understand God had clandestinely foretold <u>that</u> much information concerning Jesus' 2nd Coming over 1,000 years before the Messiah (Jesus) was ever born on Earth is downright astonishing!

Even so, God did not stop prophesying about the event! For once Israel became established as a nation in Canaan land, God rose up prophets among them who began prophesying <u>directly</u> about what would become known as the *"great day of the Lord's wrath"*. For instance, in the 7th century BC, Zephaniah proclaimed: *"<u>The great day of the LORD is near…That day is a day of WRATH</u>, a day of trouble and distress, a day of wasteness and desolation, a day of darkness and gloominess, a day of clouds and thick darkness, <u>**a day of the TRUMPET**</u>…Neither their silver nor their gold shall be able to deliver them in the day of the LORD'S WRATH; <u>but the WHOLE LAND shall be devoured by the FIRE of his jealousy: for **he shall make even a speedy riddance of ALL them that dwell in the land**</u>" (Zephaniah 1:14-18)*. Notice, in this Scripture passage, how God now began referring to the day of the Lord's 2nd Coming as the *"day of the Trumpet"*! God would continue prophesying clearly and openly of Christ's return (many times noting a Trumpet's involvement). Listen to the Apostle Paul in the 1st Century AD: *"In a moment, in the twinkling of an eye, <u>**at THE LAST TRUMP**</u>: <u>for the trumpet shall sound, and the dead shall be raised incorruptible, and we shall be changed</u>" (I Corinthians 15:52)*.

Keep this "trumpet-involvement during Christ's 2nd Coming" in mind now as we revisit God's baffling (seemingly pulled out of nowhere!) 7 Holy Feasts He appointed with the Israelites to keep (celebrate) yearly, immediately after their divinely-led escape from the Egyptians. Do you remember them? The 7 yearly Feasts were given to Moses while he was on Mount Sinai during the Israelites first year in the wilderness (1334 BC); therefore, it was still 40 years before the prophetic story (parable) of Joshua played out, secretly describing in detail Jesus' 2nd Coming. (Remember, also, the Messiah, Jesus Christ, fulfilled the first 4 Feast IN SUCCESSION on there <u>VERY</u> monthly day(s) during his last year on planet Earth—mankind's 4,000th year!—during his 1st Coming: They were the Feast of Passover, Unleavened Bread, First Fruits, and the Feast of Weeks or Pentecost.) Well, stunningly (as I told you in the *Moses* chapter), the final 3 Feasts God instituted with the children of Israel were to be prophetic shadows of Christ's 2nd Coming, just like the first 4 were prophetic shadows of his 1st Coming!!! Do you see? This is what Paul meant when he wrote: *"Let no man therefore judge you in meat, or in drink, or in respect of an HOLYDAY, or of the new moon, or of the (HIGH) SABBATH DAYS: **WHICH ARE A SHADOW OF THINGS TO COME**" (Colossians 2:16, 17).* Friend, Paul wrote this Scripture AFTER Christ's ascension, which proves some of the holydays (or Feast days) were/are still prophecy for the future!!! And yes, without question, Christ will fulfill the last 3 Feasts IN SUCCESSION on their VERY monthly day(s) during mankind's 6,000th year. Are you shocked? Well, let us take a look at them.

The 5th Holy Feast God established was—get this!—the **Feast of Trumpets** to be observed on the 1st of Tishri [See Figure # 5, page 182]. "Tishri" was the Israelite's 7th lunar month of the year. Listen to God: *"In the SEVENTH month, in the FIRST DAY of the month, shall ye have a (high) sabbath, a **memorial of BLOWING of TRUMPETS**, an holy convocation" (Leviticus 23:24).* Are you kidding me? Friend, I cannot make this "stuff" up!!! God instituted an entire holyday for the Israelites to observe about nothing but *"blowing of trumpets"*!!! This must have seemed ridiculous to the Israelites in 1334 BC, but once God began prophesying through the 1st millennium BC prophets about the coming *"Day of the Lord's wrath"* and calling it the *"Day of the Trumpet"*, maybe they started putting two and two together. But most people today have NO CLUE about this prophetic Feast day and how it pinpoints the time (during a solar year) of Jesus Christ's return to planet Earth!

Notice, God picked the first day of the 7th month of the Jewish lunar calendar for this Feast day! Friend, God could have picked any month—like the 3rd, 4th, 6th, 9th, or whatever. So WHY did God choose the 1st day of the 7th month for the "Feast of Trumpets"? Because it, too, prophetically verifies God's 7 day (7,000 year) plan!!! Take note, the "Feast of Trumpets" occurs at the VERY BEGINNING of the 7th lunar month, because Jesus' 2nd Coming will happen at the very beginning of the 7th millennial day (or year 6,000). Interestingly, of the 7 Holy Feasts day(s) this is the ONLY one that occurs at the beginning of a lunar month—i.e. at a new moon when the night sky is completely dark, bereft of any moonlight. So, even the moon's phase in its monthly cycle around Earth verifies the "Day of the Lord" will certainly be a *"time of darkness"* for that portion of the Earth experiencing nighttime when he returns! But, without a doubt, Jesus Christ will return to Earth around the start of the Fall season (probably in September or October) on Tishri 1 (during a new moon) to the sound of a great trumpet blast and a shout, perfectly fulfilling Israel's 5th Feast, the "Feast of Trumpets"! Zechariah prophesied: *"And the LORD shall be seen over them, and his arrow shall go forth as the lightning: and **the LORD God shall BLOW the TRUMPET**, and shall go with whirlwinds of the south" (Zechariah 9:14).*

The 6th Holy Feast God established was the **Day of Atonement** to be observed on the 10th of Tishri. In other words, 10 days after the Feast of Trumpets was/is to be the "Day of Atonement". God told Moses: *"Also on the TENTH DAY of this SEVENTH month **there shall be a DAY of ATONEMENT**: it shall be an holy convocation unto you; and ye shall afflict your souls" (Leviticus 23:27).* This was the ONLY day each year the high priest would enter the Holy of Holies in the Temple, where the Ark of the Covenant was kept, to sprinkle blood and make atonement (a covering) for Israel's sins. So, surely, THIS will be the day when God officially applies the sin-cleansing blood of the ONLY true and righteous sacrificial Lamb of God (Jesus) to make atonement for all the repented sins of the resurrected righteous, casting them into the sea to remember no more!

Around 600 BC, the prophet Jeremiah wrote about the coming Day of God's Atonement and the new Covenant He will established with His people (the righteous): *"But this shall be the covenant that I will make with the HOUSE of Israel; After those days, saith the LORD, **I will put my law in their inward parts, and write it in their hearts; and will be their God, and they shall be my people**. And they shall teach no more every man his neighbour, and every man his brother, saying, Know the LORD: FOR THEY SHALL ALL KNOW ME, from the least of*

389

*them unto the greatest of them, saith the LORD: for **I will forgive their iniquity, and I will remember their sin no more**" (Jeremiah 31:33, 34)*. Wow, what a day on Earth it will be when <u>everyone</u> KNOWS God (love), meaning everyone will have a heart bubbling full of God's Spirit of love, which translates to God's Law of Love (the 10 Love Commandments) will be divinely knitted *"in their inward parts"* to be automatically and continually kept! THAT, my friend, is what you have to look forward to on Earth during the millennial reign of Jesus Christ and forevermore, provided you make it into his Kingdom! (By the way, remember <u>anyone</u> who repents of sin and follows God's Way of Love is a spiritual *"child of Abraham"* and <u>OF</u> the spiritual *"House of Israel"*)

The 7th and final Holy Feast God established was the **Feast of Tabernacles** to be observed from the 15th to 21st of Tishri. God told Moses: *"<u>The FIFTEENTH DAY of this SEVENTH month shall be **the FEAST of TABERNACLES for seven days unto the LORD**</u>" (Leviticus 23:34)*. This came to be a 7 day long celebration of rejoicing over the fall harvest, which prophetically symbolized the joyful celebration the <u>harvested</u> <u>righteous</u> will experience after being resurrected at Christ's 2nd Coming and having their sins atoned. Remember, Jesus often spoke in parables about the last day *"harvesting of the saints"*! One time Jesus said, *"Lift up your eyes, and look to the fields; for <u>they are white already to HARVEST</u>" (John 4:35)*. At that time, Jesus was talking about all the righteous souls who lived and died during the first 4,000 years of mankind's history. But, now, there is almost 6,000 years worth of righteous souls ready for the final harvest!

During the 7 day "Feast of Tabernacles" the Israelites lived in temporary shelters called "booths" or "tabernacles". This was a picture of the coming day when God (love) will "tabernacle" with all the forgiven righteous after the final harvest! Listen to John the revelator: *"I John saw the holy city, new Jerusalem, coming down from God out of heaven, prepared as a bride adorned for her husband. And **I heard a great voice out of heaven saying, Behold, the TABERNACLE of GOD is with men**, and <u>he will dwell with them, and they shall be his people, and God himself shall be with them, and be their God. And God shall wipe away all tears from their eyes; and there shall be no more death, neither sorrow, nor crying, neither shall there be any more pain:</u>*

390

for the former things are passed away" (Revelation 21:2-4). What an amazing day of rejoicing that will be! Surely, the day(s) the Lord God Almighty celebrates His wedding (union) with the resurrected righteous (and then tabernacles with them forever) will be from the 15th to 21st of Tishri, fulfilling the Feast of Tabernacles.

Well, my dear friends, there you have it: The completed prophetic significance behind all 7 of God's Holy Feasts He instituted with the Israelites in the wilderness in 1334 BC. Make no mistake about it; Jesus Christ will return to Earth during the lunar phase of a new moon on the VERY (yearly celebrated) day of the Israelites "Feast of Trumpets" during mankind's 6,000th year. So why is it impossible to pinpoint the EXACT day and hour? Because there are approximately 12.4 lunar months in a solar year, which caused the ancient Israelites to occasionally have to add an extra lunar month to their 12 month yearly calendar to keep the months (and Holy Days for that matter) from drifting throughout the seasons; thus, it is impossible to pinpoint the correct fall month for the Feast of Trumpets. Do you understand? Eventually, in the 4th century AD, the Israelites were able to mathematically calculate a method of adding the 13th lunar "leap month" on specific years of a repetitive 19 year cycle, which continually realigned their lunar calendar to the solar calendar [See Figure # 9]. But even though the Israelites may celebrate the "Feast of Trumpets" on a particular new moon date in the fall of AD 2028, it may not be the correct new moon! It could be the new moon that occurs the month before or after the date they have set for the Feast of Trumpets. Do you understand? In other words, ONLY God knows the precise "new moon date and exact time" Jesus will return to Earth on during mankind's 6,000th year!!!

Ok, let me switch gears here slightly and ask you…Is there more Biblical evidence supporting the fact Jesus Christ will return to Earth during mankind's 6,000th year besides just the prophetic 7 day Creation story and Noah's story where he was 600 years old when Earth's surface was destroyed? Of course!!! God continually hinted throughout the Bible that the number "6" was man's number—meaning some specific "length of time" multiplied by 6 would be ALL the time mankind would be allowed to self-govern himself on planet Earth. Or you can think of it like this; God will allow mankind to "labor under sin's curse" for

Figure # 9
Jewish Monthly Lunar Calendar

#	Name	Length	Gregorian Equivalent
1	Nissan	30 days	Mar-Apr
2	Iyar	29 days	Apr-May
3	Sivan	30 days	May-Jun
4	Tammuz	29 days	Jun-July
5	Av	30 days	July-Aug
6	Elul	29 days	Aug-Sep
7	Tishri	30 days	Sep-Oct
8	Cheshvan	29 or 30 days	Oct-Nov
9	Kislev	30 or 29 days	Nov-Dec
10	Tevet	29 days	Dec-Jan
11	Shevat	30 days	Jan-Feb
12	Adar I	30 days	Feb-Mar
		(added only in leap years)	
12	Adar	29 days	Feb-Mar
		(called Adar Beit & month 13 in leap years)	

Note: In 4th century AD, a 19 year cycle was established to know exactly when to add the leap month (Adar I) to continually realign the Jewish lunar calendar with a solar year. It is as follows:

Adar I is added: 3rd, 6th, 8th, 11th, 14th, 17th, & 19th years.

a total of 6 days (which is 6,000 years) until He steps in and "*makes and end to His Creation*", ushering in the peaceful, restful (Sabbath) millennial reign of His son (Jesus Christ the Messiah) on a gorgeous, newly-regenerated planet Earth! Consequently, God created mankind on the 6th day of Creation, and the "number" of the antichrist's name will be precisely 6-6-6: "*Here is wisdom. Let him that hath understanding count the number of the BEAST: for it is the number of a MAN; and his number is SIX HUNDRED THREESCORE and SIX*" (Revelation 13:18).

392

God's 6,000 year time limit for mankind's rule on Earth was also confirmed in the 6th century BC when Nebuchadnezzar, king of Babylon, made an IMAGE of Gold for ALL mankind to worship: *"To you it is commanded, O people, nations, and languages...ye fall down and worship the golden image...And whoso falleth not down and worshippeth shall the same hour be cast into the midst of a burning FIERY furnace" (Daniel 3:4-6).* Friend, Nebuchadnezzar's golden image was a prophetic picture of the coming Antichrist's reign on Earth, when he will demand ALL peoples, nations, and tongues worship his beastly image!!! And just think; this prophetic "event" was happening in Babylon over 600 years before God gave John the Revelator the book of "The Revelation" which describes the coming Antichrist's reign. So, what was the dimensions of Nebuchadnezzar's golden statue image? Listen to the record: *"Nebuchadnezzar the king made an image of gold, whose height was THREESCORE (60) cubits, and the breadth thereof SIX cubits" (Daniel 3:1).* See, the prophetic truth is in the details!

Amazingly, over 400 years earlier in the 10 century BC, God had already played out a prophetic vision of the Antichrist's reign on Earth through the story of David slaying Goliath. Goliath was a giant who was/is a picture of the beastly Antichrist, and David was a picture of the coming King of Kings, the Messiah Jesus Christ. You know the story, as Goliath lumbered towards David: *"David put his hand in his bag, and took thence a STONE, and slang it, and smote the Philistine in his forehead; and he fell upon his face to the earth. So David prevailed over the Philistine with a sling and with a STONE" (I Samuel 17:49, 50).* Friend, this is a prophetic picture of the triumphal victory Christ will win over the Antichrist (beast) at his 2nd Coming. Jesus (the rock) will kill the beast! So how tall was Goliath, and what was the weight of his spear's head? Listen to the Biblical record: *"Goliath, of Gath, whose height was SIX cubits and a span...and his spear's head weighed SIX HUNDRED shekels of iron" (I Samuel 17:4, 7)*! Our enemy, Satan, is said to throw *"fiery darts" (Ephesians 6:16)* at us; thus, Goliath's spear represented the 6,000 years Satan (the antichrist) would be allowed to deceive mankind into disobeying God's 10 Love Commandments.

Furthermore, the prophetic story (parable) of David (Jesus) & Goliath (Satan) paralleled a prophetic dream God would also later give

Nebuchadnezzar of a great image in the form of a man. The image symbolized and foretold of Earth's coming <u>world</u> powers until the time of the end. Hear how the image was brought to an end: *"<u>Thou sawest till that a STONE was cut out without hands, which smote the image upon his feet...and brake them to pieces.</u> Then was the iron, the clay, the brass, the silver, and the gold, broken to pieces together, and became like the chaff of the summer threshing floors; and the wind carried them away, that <u>NO place was found for them</u>: **<u>and the STONE that smote the image became a great mountain, and filled the whole earth</u>**"* (Daniel 2:34, 35). God would later articulate it like this in "The Revelation": *"And <u>the seventh angel sounded</u>: and there were great voices in heaven, saying, <u>The kingdoms of this world (earth) are become the kingdoms of our Lord, and of his Christ; and he shall reign for ever and ever</u>"* (The Revelation 11:15).

So, what does the "<u>STONE</u> killing Goliath" and the "<u>STONE</u> demolishing Nebuchadnezzar's man-image" foretell? Well, it is evident throughout Scripture that Jesus Christ is known as the stone: *"For <u>Jesus the Messiah is (the one referred to in the Scriptures when they speak of) a 'STONE discarded by the builders which became the capstone of the arch</u>"* (Acts 4:11, Living Bible). Subsequently, the "stone" symbolizes Christ annihilating Lucifer's reign on Earth in the above stories. But I believe there could be more to it, for it is likely that these divine prophetic stories will be fulfilled even more LITERALLY at Jesus 2nd Coming by a massive meteorite (*"stone cut out without hands"*) violently striking Earth and setting its entire surface on FIRE!!! Listen to "The Revelation": *"And <u>the seventh angel poured out his vial into the air</u>; and there came a great voice out of the temple of heaven, from the throne, saying, **<u>IT IS DONE</u>**. <u>And there were voices, and thunders, and lightnings</u>; **<u>and there was a GREAT EARTHQUAKE, such as was not since men were upon the earth,</u>** <u>so mighty an earthquake... the cities of the nations fell...every island fled away, and the mountains were not found. And there fell upon men a great hail out of heaven, every STONE about the weight of a talent</u>"* (The Revelation 16:17-21). Friend, this sounds like a detailed description of the result of a massive meteorite colliding with planet Earth! And that is all I am going to say about that.

Well, my friend, I have provided extensive Biblical evidence in this book supporting the fact God has determined a 7,000 year plan for mankind's time on planet Earth, because I have revealed many Biblical secrets—given to me by God!—maintaining the Messiah (Jesus Christ) died on Earth during mankind's 4,000th year and will return to Earth during mankind's 6,000th year. Thus, <u>the eye-catching Title to this book is Truth: Jesus Christ WILL return to planet Earth exactly 2,000 years after the year of his death</u>!!! But, as I said in the *Introduction*, what is the point in comprehending this amazing revelation if you are not properly prepared to meet the Christ? Then, it is useless! Consequently, the most important information to gain from this book is the crystal-clear Biblical knowledge of EXACTLY what you MUST **<u>DO</u>** to please God and obtain eternal life. THAT knowledge is priceless! And I pray THAT wisdom is what you hold near and dear to your heart long after you put this book down.

In that regard, God has furnished me with one final parable to help you distinguish the correct relationship between God's part and mankind's part in the salvation equation. In other words, through careful consideration of the following analogy, you will be able to rightly discern (keep in place) the Messiah, Jesus Christ's roll and <u>YOUR</u> <u>ROLL</u> (or mankind's roll) in obtaining eternal life for your soul. Then, and only then, can you truly become a witness for God (love), for you will know precisely what you MUST <u>DO</u> and what you must instruct others to <u>DO</u> to obtain eternal life (or to be saved).

So, here it is: There is a car a soul <u>MUST</u> drive on a journey through a dark and evil world to reach and enter the Promise Land (or to obtain eternal life in the Kingdom of God). There is only <u>ONE</u> car that can take you there! Its make: JEHOVAH (the one true God that exists), its model: SALVATION. Now, since a car needs an engine to move (or to go), this car has a unique, special engine that was built by the Creator God, through Jesus Christ, and it runs on the blood of the Lamb. You never have to fill the tank with fuel, for there is an inexhaustible supply of righteous blood. <u>ALL</u> you have to **<u>DO</u>** is DRIVE THAT CAR, and you will reach the Promise Land and obtain eternal life!!!

So HOW do you drive the car? Well, it has an instruction manual for that called FAITH! Specifically, here is what the manual says to <u>DO</u>:

1. You MUST open the car's driver side door by <u>making God (love) first in your life</u>; 2. You MUST get in the car and sit down in the seat by <u>worshipping no idols</u>; 3. You MUST put the key in the ignition and turn it on by <u>not blaspheming God's name (Holy Spirit)</u>; 4. You MUST click on the headlights by <u>keeping the Sabbath day holy</u>; 5. You MUST engage the transmission into drive by <u>honoring your father and mother</u>; 6. You MUST step on the accelerator pedal by <u>doing no murder</u>; 7. You MUST steer the wheel by <u>committing no adultery</u>; 8. You MUST watch for turns and danger ahead by <u>not stealing</u>; 9. You MUST look for danger behind you in the rearview mirror by <u>not lying</u>; 10. And, finally, you MUST continue in that manner by <u>not coveting dirt</u>.

How about that? But what are these 10 things? They are the 10 Love Commandments!!! They are how you LOVE God with all your heart and LOVE your neighbor (God, too) as yourself!!! Remember, Faith in God (love) only works (or is proved) by DOING the DEEDS of LOVE: *"faith which worketh by love" (Galatians 5:6)*. So, if you willingly <u>DO</u> those 10 things, THE "Jehovah Salvation" CAR WILL GO!!! In other words, you WILL reach the Promise Land and obtain eternal life. Do you see? It is that simple! That is <u>ALL</u> anyone has EVER had to <u>DO</u> to obtain eternal life.

Now, let me ask you a question…when you drive a car, do you need to know anything about the engine to make the car go? NO!!! All you have to <u>DO</u> is drive the car. As long as the car <u>has</u> an engine under the hood, it will go. Do you see? THIS is <u>exactly</u> how it is with the "Jehovah Salvation" car that leads to eternal life: **YOU DO NOT NEED TO KNOW <u>ANYTHING</u> ABOUT THE ENGINE TO MAKE THE CAR GO!!!** So, let me make the comparison: A traditional car has an "internal-combustion engine" which provides power to move the wheels by sucking a mixture of air and gasoline into a cylinder block, igniting it with a spark, propelling pistons up and down, turning a crankshaft, etc., etc, etc; but the car that leads to eternal life has a "forgiveness-for-sins engine" which provides power to move a soul back to God! The nuts and bolts of <u>this</u> engine is the story of how God <u>FREELY</u> sent His son into the world in human form, how he lived a sinless life, how he willingly chose to die (separate his spirit from God's) and pay the required death penalty (or ransom price) for all mankind's sins, etc.,

396

etc., etc. Do you see? Look, learning this information and "believing it happened" is like learning how the internal-combustion engine operates and "believing it works": NONE of that information, or your thoughts (beliefs) about it, will move the car!!! ONLY <u>DRIVING THE CAR</u> WILL MOVE IT.

Incidentally, the "forgiveness-for-sins engine (motor)" in the "Jehovah Salvation car" was/is God's <u>free gift</u> to mankind! Do you understand? Look, one of the key parts required to build that motor was a SINLESS human being. And mankind could not provide that, because ALL mankind had sinned! Therefore, salvation (or obtaining eternal life) can NEVER be attributed to mankind's "works" alone, because <u>GOD had to build the engine in the car that would take mankind back to God</u>. In another words, "*NO man can boast*" that his salvation is because of himself—save Jesus Christ! But at the same time, mankind must DO works—"*<u>WORK</u> <u>out</u> his salvation*" by obeying the 10 Love Commandments—to DRIVE the "Jehovah Salvation car". In other words, mankind MUST <u>REPENT OF SIN</u> to obtain eternal life.

Friend, this is NO small revelation, for it fully refocuses the light of TRUTH (love) onto EXACTLY what you MUST <u>DO</u> to obtain eternal life! So keep thinking about the analogy and many of your Biblical questions will be answered. Like, this is why God could wait 4,000 years to fully reveal to mankind the internal workings of the "forgiveness-for-sins engine" He would build in the "Jehovah Salvation (or eternal-life) car": Because mankind's <u>knowledge</u> of THAT motor just did/does not matter with regards to them obtaining eternal life! On the other hand, God <u>did</u> provide every soul who ever lived on planet Earth the instruction manual for how to DRIVE the "eternal-life car", for EVERYONE has known the difference between good & evil—which is obeying or disobeying the 10 Love Commandments, respectively. Do you see? Thus, EVERYONE has had a choice as to whether they wanted to drive the car that leads to eternal life or not! And the same is true for all mankind, today. It is your choice.

From the "car analogy", you can now also understand why people all over the world (from all different backgrounds and religions) have a shot at obtaining eternal life. Do you see? It is because they KNOW WHAT TO <u>DO</u> to drive the "eternal-life car", for <u>all</u> mankind knows what "love is" and what "love is not". See, it is alright if people never hear the story of the Messiah (Jesus Christ), for again THAT is just the nitty-gritty of how the eternal-life car's engine works! Many people on Earth will obtain eternal life without ever having seen or read a Bible because they made a choice to "live a life of love"—obey the 10 Love Commandments—during their Earthly lifetime, but when their spirit transitions into the spirit world I promise you they will then hear, learn, and know the story of Jesus. They will find out THEN that HE is the reason they are in heaven, for anyone who makes it there will HAVE HAD TO HAVE there sins—which again we ALL have committed!—forgiven through Christ.

Alright, let me take this parable's revelation one step further and really jar the minds of some of you folks (who hold incorrect beliefs about what a soul MUST know and DO to obtain eternal life) by informing you of the following truth: God NEVER had to tell mankind the story of Jesus Christ! Chew on that fact awhile!!! See, the resulting atonement of Jesus' Earthly ministry would be just as binding whether mankind knew/knows about it or not. Do you see? Listen, as long as Christ came to Earth in human form, lived a sinless life, and died and rose again, mankind's spirits would be free from the death penalty of the Law of sin! In other words, the "forgiveness-for-sins engine" in the "eternal-life car" would be built!!! The only difference…mankind would not know about it! And oh how sad, terrible, and tragic that would be for us today!!! If there was no Bible (with the Messiah's Old Testament, prophetically fulfilled, New Testament salvation story contained in it) mankind would have little reason or hope to believe in God (love) today. Do you see? Moreover, this book you are reading right now would not have been written, for without the Bible I would have had NOTHING to talk about to convince you that God exists and that heaven and hell are real.

And yet, God declared in the Bible that ALL the evidence mankind needed to possess to KNOW the Creator God exists and to follow after His Way of Love is the following: "*For the invisible things of him (God) from the creation of the world are clearly seen, **being understood by the things that are made**, even his eternal power and Godhead; SO THAT THEY (WE) ARE WITHOUT EXCUSE*"

(Romans 1:20). Wow! Therefore, look around at God's creation—i.e. the stars, planets, animals, etc—for that is ALL GOD EVERY HAD TO PROVIDE MANKIND as evidence He (love) exists!!! Think about that; God says "experiencing His creation" is reason enough for you to: "***DO for others what you want them to DO for you****. This is the teaching of the laws of Moses in a nutshell" (Matthew 7:12, Living Bible).* Now you should realize today why Satan is directly attacking God's claim to be the "Creator of ALL things in the universe" by proposing the absurd theory of macroevolution. Satan is trying to undermine the ONLY evidence God declared mankind needed to encounter to KNOW there is a God and that they will face judgment for their deeds. (By the way, Satan is REALLY cackling, to the point of tears, at the people who are buying this science fairytale!!!) But even so, no matter what you want to believe about the universe, God NEVER had to write the Bible (or the story of the Messiah) for mankind!

So WHY did God write the Bible? It was for one purpose only my friend: In order that you and I would have further reason (evidence) to BELIEVE in God (love). God knew Satan's deception in the "end times" would be so great, concerning the reality of Him, that He worked on writing the Bible from Creation in a "prophetic manner" to later be able to reveal the hidden meaning behind the Bible's stories to provide further evidence of His actuality. Do you understand? (I should say a secondary purpose for God writing the Bible was for mankind to have a written record of the difference between good & evil; therefore, folks with Bibles will have NO argument with God on Judgment Day for NOT following His WAY of love—i.e. obeying the 10 Love Commandments, which is driving the "eternal-life car"!) Thus, God wrote the Bible out of love for mankind! And it is amazing, wonderful, and precious. You should idolize, cherish, and thank Him for every word!

The first major prophetic Biblical revelation God provided mankind (as additional evidence of His existence) was the Old Testament fulfillment of the Messiah's work. It is the amazing revelation I have disclosed to you in this book. It is the nuts and bolts of how the "forgiveness-for-sins engine" in the "eternal-life car" was built. It is the contents of the message Jesus divulged to his Disciples after his resurrection: *"And he said unto them, These are the words which I spake*

399

unto you…that ALL things must be FULFILLED, which were written in the law of Moses (first 5 books of the Bible), and in the prophets, and in the psalms, CONCERNING ME. Then opened he their understanding, that they might understand the scriptures, And said unto them, Thus it is written, and thus it behoved Christ to suffer, and to rise from the dead the third day: And that REPENTANCE for the REMISSION (forgiveness) of SINS should be preached in his name among all nations" (Luke 24:44-47).

Listen, once a person grasps the incredible, prophetic nature of the Scriptures—for no one, EXCEPT A GOD, can accurately foretell the future thousands of years in advance by secretly directing and controlling certain detailed events in mankind's history—they will absolutely know the Bible is TRUTH; thus, everything in the Bible (God, Satan, Heaven & Hell, etc.) must be truth. THIS then will give them an ironclad reason to WANT TO DRIVE the "eternal-life car"!!! And the "decision made to drive the car (obey the 10 Love Commandments)" is called REPENTANCE. When someone repents (willfully stops sinning) they activate the "forgiveness-for-sins engine" and begin driving (or moving) the car that leads to eternal-life. Is that not awesome? If you die in that state (mode), you WILL obtain eternal life. But, if you ever willfully stop doing the things you MUST DO to drive the "Jehovah Salvation car", the car will stop and you will not obtain eternal life: *"For if we sin WILLFULLY…there remaineth NO MORE sacrifice for sins" (Hebrews 10:26).*

You can go back to each of the 10 things you MUST DO to drive the "eternal-life car" and see how the car will stop in each case. I will give you some examples: If you let off the accelerator pedal by willingly "hating someone"—which is murder (or unforgiveness) in the heart and disobedience to the 6th Love Commandment—the car will stop and you will not journey to the Promise Land. In other words, your soul will perish! If you let go of the steering wheel by willingly "committing sexual immorality"—which is adultery and disobedience to the 7th Love Commandment—the car will stop by crashing. If you turn the headlights off by willingly "not keeping God's Sabbath day holy"—which is disobedience to the 4th Love Commandment—you will be driving in the dark and will almost surely wreck! If you turn the key

400

off by willingly "blaspheming God's name"—which is disobedience to the 3rd Love Commandment—the engine will quit and the car will stop. If you stop looking for trouble ahead by willingly "stealing"—which is disobedience to the 8th Love Commandment—you will eventually hit something and the car will stop! I think you get the point. You MUST willingly continue to DO all the things that keep the "eternal-life car" moving to obtain eternal life. Never, for any reason, quit driving the car!!!

Listen to God speaking through the 6th Century BC prophet Ezekiel: *"When the righteous turneth away from his righteousness, and committeth iniquity (sin), and DOETH according to all the abominations that the wicked man doeth, shall he live? ALL his righteousness that he hath done shall NOT BE MENTIONED: in his trespass that he hath trespassed, and in his sin that he hath sinned, in them SHALL HE DIE"* (Ezekiel 18:24). Wow, how about that? In other words, you can live righteously for 60 years of your life and DO all kinds of good, but if you willfully start living a life of sin (disobeying the 10 Love Commandments) God will forget all the good you have done and your soul will perish in the lake of fire on Judgment Day! Now you know why Satan never stops tempting and tricking you into sinning against God; he knows as long as you are still living on Earth he has a shot at deceiving you into "disobeying the 10 Love Commandments" in order to kill your soul for all eternity! THAT is why I plead with you: You MUST repent of sin and then NEVER return to the WAY of sin (evil) if you plan on obtaining eternal life.

Listen to Ezekiel: *"IF the wicked will turn from ALL his sins that he hath committed, and keep ALL my statues, and DO that which is lawful and right, he SHALL SURELY LIVE, he shall not die"* (Ezekiel 18:21). Do you see? This is a guarantee from God! Listen to Him: *"When the wicked man turneth away from his wickedness that he hath committed, and DOETH that which is lawful and right, HE SHALL SAVE HIS SOUL ALIVE. Because he CONSIDERETH, and turneth away from ALL his transgressions (sins)"* (Ezekiel 18:27, 28). God cannot be any more transparent about what a soul MUST DO to obtain eternal life. Friend, this is the most wonderful (good) news in the world! It does not matter how much evil or wickedness you have done towards

401

God and other people in your lifetime up until this point: If you are still breathing on planet Earth, you have hope and a chance at winning (obtaining) eternal life for your soul! You just have to REPENT—turn from your wicked ways and begin living a life of love towards God and your neighbor by obeying God's 10 Love Commandments—and God will forgive all your sins (evil) and reward you with eternal life in His Kingdom.

My great concern today is that the Biblical message of "*repentance* FOR the *forgiveness* of sins" is almost non-existent in organized religion!!! Today, if someone asks a church "minister" what they MUST DO to obtain eternal life, they will likely hear the ambiguous expression, "You need to accept Jesus into your heart." But friend, do you know this "phrase" does NOT exist in the Bible? Oh I know it has a nice religious ring to it, but what on Earth does it mean? A person recites a few words and then goes on there merry sinful way! Are you kidding me? Are you not dumbfounded that this VERY QUESTION was asked of Jesus in Scripture (several times!) and his words do NOT come out of "ministers" mouths today? I have mentioned them in this book…Christ answered if you want to obtain eternal life "*Obey the 10 Love Commandments*" or "*Love God with all your heart and your neighbor as yourself*". In other words, if the car-parable God gave me above had been told by Christ back then, he would have said, "You MUST DRIVE the 'eternal-life car'!" Do you see?

So, who do you think is behind the invention of this nebulous "religious phrase"? Friend, I am convinced it is Satan! What is his motive? He wants to remove ALL the importance of "having to live a righteous life to obtain eternal life" and make people believe "obtaining eternal life" can be accomplished through some one-time prayer, followed up by church attendance. But THAT is NOT the Bible's message!!! I am sternly warning you to not listen to Lucifer, for he is out to deceive the entire world! Meanwhile, he never stops tempting people to live in sin (fueled by greed) because he KNOWS full-well the end result of "*willful sin*" is eternal death. Try and understand "sitting in a church building once a week" does not count towards righteousness! You MUST willfully stop sinning, which means you MUST REPENT of sin. It is the only WAY to obtain eternal life. Jesus Christ even said

402

so himself; to obtain eternal life you MUST willfully choose to live your life in OBEDIENCE to the 10 Love Commandments! Rebuke all voices to the contrary!!!

Amazingly, when doing a study of the word "*accept*" in the Bible, one finds it is ALWAYS used in regards to "GOD ACCEPTING US"! How about that? In other words, when we choose to stop willfully sinning (disobeying the 10 Love Commandments) then GOD ACCEPTS US. Now honestly people, who do you know that likes to twist God's Holy Word? SATAN, my friend, the old snake himself!!! He has been doing this to God's words ever since that catastrophic day in the Garden of Eden. He is the most subtle of all creatures, and he loves to distort, alter, misrepresent, and change God's Word! And he has disgustingly warped Scripture to say "mankind accepts Jesus (God)", but listen to God: ***"But in every nation he that FEARETH him (God), and WORKETH RIGHTEOUSNESS, is ACCEPTED with him"*** *(Acts 10:35)*. Paul wrote: *"that we may lead a quiet and peaceable life in all GODLINESS and HONESTY. **For this is GOOD and ACCEPTABLE in the sight of God our Saviour**." (I Timothy 2:2, 3)*. Do you see? After you stop sinning and start obeying the 10 Love Commandments ("*work righteousness or godliness!*"), God will ACCEPT you!!! THAT is what the Bible teaches is the WAY to obtain eternal life. I assure you, YOU are in NO position to accept God, for YOU ARE NOT GOD!!! So screw your head on right, detest Lucifer's empty rhetoric, and then "man-up" to your responsibility of what you MUST DO to please God and be accepted by HIM—which is to REPENT of sin by obeying His 10 Love Commandments!

But today "ministers"—Lucifer's agents!—are preaching sermons and writing books on "how to love your life in this world" filled with self-love and greed for money and possessions (dirt)—the VERY ideology Christ said will produce ALL of sin (evil) and ultimately send a soul to hell! Then they like to end their selfish, sin-producing doctrine by offering you a chance to "accept Jesus (God)". Are you kidding me? Friend, there is NO message of sin, repentance, or hell! Can you recognize deceit? Can you perceive trickery? Friend, Lucifer is having a heyday downplaying (hiding) all of mankind's responsibility of having to "turn from sin and repent" to obtain eternal life! Do you not see it? He is masking the truth! He wants you to believe "obtaining eternal life" is easy. He wants you to think you can simply babble some words in a "sinner's prayer" and guarantee yourself entrance into the Kingdom of God. He wants you to forget the Biblical *"work out your OWN salvation with fear and trembling"* process! Wise up, reader, and have no part in the Devil's deception.

Look, if Satan can get you to not worry about the sin in your life (by believing in his concocted lies) he knows the consequence will be disastrous for you on Judgment Day: For the Law of sin and death is still binding! Listen to James eloquent words. *"Let no man say when he is tempted, I am tempted of God: for God cannot be tempted with evil, neither tempteth he any man: But every man is tempted, when he is drawn away of his own lust, and enticed. Then when lust hath conceived, it bringeth forth sin: **and sin, when it is finished, bringeth forth death**"* *(James 1:13-15)*. I will not deceive you my friend! I will not sugar coat the truth! I am here to call Satan out on his lies! You MUST stop your "willful sinning"—your non-loving ways—if you want to obtain eternal life, which means you MUST "CHANGE YOUR LIFE" and start living a life of love towards God and your fellow man as outlined by obedience to the 10 Love Commandments!

Actually, right from the beginning in the story of Cain and Abel, God revealed ALL mankind ever needed to know and <u>DO</u> to obtain eternal life. God noticed Cain coveted the acceptance Abel's lamb offering had received, and Cain's jealousy turned to hatred. So God asked Cain: *"<u>Why art thou wroth</u>? And why is thy countenance fallen? **If thou DOEST WELL, shalt thou not be ACCEPTED**? And **if thou DOEST NOT WELL, sin (death) lieth at the door**"* *(Genesis 4:6, 7)*. The word "well" is from the Hebrew word *"yātab"* meaning: <u>to do good, right</u>. Can it be any simpler? God knew Cain recognized good from evil (right from wrong). He did not have to explain it to Cain, because the *"knowledge of good & evil"* was now part of mankind's spirits! Thus, this little story proves if we <u>DO</u> good (well), which is to love, God will <u>ACCEPT</u> US on Judgment Day, but if we continually choose to <u>DO</u> evil (not well), which is to NOT love, God will turn us away! In other words, obtaining eternal life is a daily fight! It is work! And it has a cost! You MUST conquer sin by forsaking yourself of its pleasure. Thus, Paul wrote: *"follow after righteousness, godliness, faith, love, patience, meekness.* ***FIGHT the good fight of faith****, (and) lay hold on eternal life" (I Timothy 6:11, 12).*

Here is another falsehood purported by "minister" today: They will claim some number of people—like one million or so—have been "saved by accepting Jesus" from their ministry. Are you kidding? Do you really believe this? Friend, no one knows how many people will "obtain eternal life" from a particular ministry, because no one knows if these people have <u>returned</u> to a life of sin. Do you see? They could have had "stony hearts" or "thorny hearts" and after sometime of believing in God (love)—by obeying the 10 Love Commandments—they may have returned to a life of willful sin (evil)—by disobeying the 10 Love Commandments—and are now on their way to hell! Shoot, some of them may NEVER have quit sinning in the first place because they were not told they MUST repent! So, do not believe these misguided preachers claims, for they are deceived about the Bible's true message of what a soul MUST <u>DO</u> to obtain eternal life.

Alright, let me conclude this book: Friend, there is a heaven and there is a hell, and the sobering fact is one of them is in your soul's future! The Bible was/is written in a prophetic manner (specifically the story of the Messiah's 1st & 2nd Comings) solely to increase your FAITH (belief) in God (love), so that you will rightly FEAR God and make the decision to REPENT of evil (sin) to obtain eternal life. See, "believing in God (love)" is not some crap shoot. It does not require "blind faith" as many people think today! The Bible (God's prophetic written word to mankind) verifiably <u>proves</u> God and His Word are NOT some manmade hoax. Consequently, if after reading this book you still think the Bible is just a book written by a bunch of men making up stories, then I do not know what else to say to you! But if you now believe, I humbly urge you to cry out to your heavenly Father. If you care at all about your soul's eternal destiny, I beg you to fear God and follow after His WAY of love (righteousness).

He is asking you to "forsake the pleasures of sin" for the tiny season of your life down here in this age on Earth to reap eternal life with pleasures evermore! If you do this, it means you will live a life of "sacrificial love" towards God and your fellow man, as outlined by obeying the 10 love Commandments. Do not delay in your decision to REPENT of your sins. <u>DO</u> it NOW!!! <u>DO</u> it TODAY!!! Now is the time for salvation. If you keep on willfully sinning, you are like a man playing Russian roulette with his soul, for at any minute your life on Earth could end. Listen to Jesus: *"<u>But if that evil servant shall say in his heart, My lord delayeth his coming; and shall begin to smite his fellowservants (disobey the 10 Love Commandments), and to eat and drink with the drunken;</u> **<u>The lord of that servant shall come in a day when he looketh not for him, and in an hour that he is not aware of, and shall cut him asunder, and appoint him his portion with the hypocrites: there shall be weeping and gnashing of teeth</u>"** (Matthew 24:48-51).* Please do not make this mistake!

Kill your greedy desire for money and possessions (the root of all evil). Rid your life of sexual immorality. Spend the Sabbath day forgetting about work and money and get to know God! Get radical about God (love)! Get militant about it! Get serious about your soul's eternal destiny. Hate evil (sin) and love good (love): *"Beloved, <u>follow NOT that which is evil, but that which is good.</u> **<u>He that DOETH good is of God</u>: <u>but he that DOETH evil hath not seen God</u>"** (III John 1:11).* I am just a voice of one crying out in the wilderness, "Repent my brothers and sisters, so you might receive God's forgiveness for all your sins!" I love you with all my heart. I love you with a deep, grinding love that churns in the core of my soul, fearing for your eternal destiny.

One day soon, God is going to judge every one of us for how we chose to live. Listen to Ezekiel: *"<u>Therefore I will judge you...every one according to his WAYS, saith the LORD GOD.</u> **<u>REPENT, and TURN yourselves from ALL your transgressions (sins); so iniquity (sin) shall not be your ruin. CAST AWAY from you ALL your transgressions, whereby ye have transgressed; and MAKE YOU A NEW HEART and a NEW SPIRIT; for why will ye die</u>**...<u>For I have no pleasure in the death of him that dieth</u>, saith the LORD GOD: **<u>wherefore TURN YOURSELVES, and LIVE YE</u>"** (Ezekiel 18:30-32).* Do you see? I am begging you to make yourself a new heart (thoughts, desires, & emotions) with respect to right living, for God will have NO pleasure in seeing any of His spirit children perish on Judgment Day.

With the Promise Land attainable before them, God spoke

406

the same words of advice to the Israelites in the wilderness through Moses: *"I command thee this day to love the LORD thy God, to walk in his ways (love), and to keep his (10 Love) commandments and his statues and his judgments, THAT THOU MAYEST LIVE...But if thine heart turn away, so that thou wilt not hear, but shalt be drawn away...I denounce unto you this day, that YE SHALL SURELY PERISH...**I call heaven and earth to record this day against you, that I have set before you LIFE and DEATH, blessing and cursing: therefore CHOOSE LIFE**"* (Deuteronomy 30:16-19). Friend, God is setting this same choice before you today! Choose this day in whom you will serve: Follow God's WAY of love (obey the 10 Love Commandments) and live by obtaining eternal life for your soul, or follow Satan's WAY of sin (disobey the 10 Love Commandments) and die by driving your soul into hellfire. THINK long and hard about it, my friend, for your soul's ETERNAL destiny rests on your decision!

Planet Earth is barreling towards some very dark days in the not too distant future. So terrible and horrible that I dare not mention them. The prophetic stories (parables) of Noah, Lot, and Joshua are about to be intricately fulfilled, for Jesus is coming with his angels to put an end to Earth's wickedness by consuming its surface and godless inhabitants with a raging fire. Listen to the Holy Spirit prophesying through Paul: *"And to you who are troubled REST with us, **when the Lord Jesus shall be revealed from heaven with his mighty angels, IN FLAMING FIRE taking vengeance on them that KNOW not God, and that OBEY NOT the gospel of our Lord Jesus Christ:** Who shall be punished with everlasting destruction from the presence of the Lord, and from the glory of his power"* (II Thessalonians 1:7-9).

But that is not the end of the story! For a few short days after the *"Day of the Lord's wrath"* God will regenerate planet Earth into a glorious paradise. It will be so wonderful that you cannot possibly imagine it. Please do not miss it: *"Watch now,"* the Lord Almighty declares, *"the DAY of JUDGMENT is coming, burning like a furnace. The proud and wicked will be burned up like straw; like a tree, they will be consumed—roots and all. **But for you who FEAR my name, the Sun of Righteousness will rise with healing in his wings. And you will go free, LEAPING for JOY like calves let out to pasture.** Then you*

407

will tread upon the wicked as ashes underfoot," says the Lord Almighty. ***(SO) REMEMBER TO OBEY THE (10 LOVE COMMANMENT) LAWS I GAVE ALL ISRAEL THROUGH MOSES MY SERVANT"*** *(Malachi 4:1-4, Living Bible).* Amen.

Afterword

Friend, it took me 20 months to write (and edit countless times) this manuscript. It was a massive undertaking and an arduous process, one that consumed almost all my time and mental energy. But I have done what the Lord has asked me to DO: I have written down the Biblical revelation He gave me. The work was completed in October of AD 2009 during the Feast of Tabernacles, and I am very thankful it is finished.

Most of you would benefit immensely by turning right around and rereading this entire book again, for I struggled greatly in finding the correct order in which to divulge all the intricately related information. But now that you have a general overview of the revelation under your belt, I believe the second time through the material would REALLY hit home! It would be like watching a movie the second time…when you can fully understand and appreciate all that happened. So please consider doing this. Then I encourage you to read the Bible through from front to back cover, and I believe you will be in awe of God.

I want you to understand that I have <u>NO</u> desire in my heart to profit monetarily from this book! I only possess an intense yearning to get this book into as many people's hands as possible, for I wish that all souls would obtain eternal life and that none would perish. THAT is my passion. Therefore, I am going to make this book available to you for as cheap as I possible can. (In fact, I will be giving many of them away for free!!!) To attain this goal, I must purchase 5,000 books to get a very reasonable printing cost. And this I will do! But I need your help in getting this message out. So I am asking you (as God leads) to help purchase these books to give out to your family, friends, church members, or just whomever you meet walking the street.

The book's official website is UndeniableBiblicalProof.com, and you may go there (and direct other people there) to learn about and purchase the book. Realize, there is substantial cost to creating and maintaining a website, fulfilling orders, etc.; thus, purchasing 1 book will be at retail price, but purchasing in multiplies will be extremely discounted. And for those of you without computer access, you may purchase 10 or more books directly from me using the order form at the back of this book.

I want to leave you with a spiritual dream the Lord gave me a little over 2 years after my dad's profile appeared on my refrigerator door. For the dream's significance neatly wraps up this books most important message concerning what you MUST <u>DO</u> to obtain eternal life! After months of aligning my life up totally and completely in accordance to God's 10 <u>Love</u> Commandments (e.g. making God first in my life, giving up my idol aspirations to be a country music star, selling all my country CD's, keeping God's Sabbath day holy, forgiving those who hurt me, sponsoring 7 poor children through Children International, giving thousands of dollars to other Christian charities, eliminating all sexual immorality, etc.) the Lord furnished me with the following dream on Friday May 25, 2007—yes, just 4 days before my 40 day fast began!—during the 1 a.m. hour.

In the dream I was standing in my very own, real-life, one bedroom apartment, when suddenly I began hearing noises coming from under my house. As I bent down to listen, I was somehow able to see through an aperture to the outside of my house. Then (I do not know how) but I slid through the opening and landed on the ground around the foundation of my house. What I saw next shocked and perplexed me.

I was standing in the dirt on the bottom of an approximately 5 feet deep and 5 feet wide tunnel dug around my house's foundation. There was a metal chain-link fence enclosing in the tunnel which extended overhead and attached to the house. It was like the fence built over a sidewalk along a skyscraper building in a big city (that is being worked on above) providing a safe walking place for pedestrians below. It did not take me long to realize…I was in a construction zone! Since it was dark there were yellow floodlights hanging around, and there were men with hardhats walking everywhere. They were going in and out from underneath my house's foundation. No one seemed to notice me, so I hunkered down and glanced through an opening in the cinderblock (like a vent opening) and noticed people cleaning and removing debris from my approximately 4 feet tall crawlspace. Then I saw some men laying new pier blocks, strengthening and reinforcing the girders holding up my house! I could see and hear there trowels spreading the gritty cement. It was a flurry of activity.

I was dumbfounded! I thought, "What on Earth are these people doing under my house? And where did they come from?" Right about then I heard a voice yelling out instructions for the work taking place. His authoritative voice boomed above the droning chitchat of the workers, and I turned to see the man. And there he was…he had a white hardhat on his head, clip board nestled in his left arm, and he was gesturing and pointing with his right hand. It was James Robison!!! He is a TV minister who helps the poor all over the world (e.g. drilling water wells, feeding starving children, etc.) and one of the ministries I had been giving generously to in previous months! At that moment I woke up and it was precisely 2:00 a.m. on my digital alarm clock.

I felt the Lord's warm presence in my room—or possibly an angel sent by Him, I do not know. But within minutes I knew the interpretation of the dream, for the words of Christ were brought into my mind: "*Not all who sound religious are really godly people. They may refer to me as 'Lord,' but still won't get to heaven. For the DECISIVE question is whether they OBEY my Father in heaven. At the Judgment many will tell me, 'Lord, Lord, we told others about you…' But I will reply, 'You have never been mine. Go away, for your deeds are evil.'* **All who listen to my instructions (to obey the 10 Love Commandments) and FOLLOW THEM are WISE, like a man who builds his house on solid rock. Though the rain comes in torrents, and the floods rise and the storm winds beat against his house, it won't collapse, for it is built on rock.** *But those who hear my instructions (to obey the 10 Love Commandments) and IGNORE THEM are FOOLISH, like a man who builds his house on sand. For when the rains and floods come, and* *storm winds beat against his house, it will fall with a mighty crash"* *(Matthew 7:21-27, Living Bible)*. Wow!

Do you understand my dream? My apartment (house) represented my body (or temple) where my soul dwells. The decision I made to <u>repent</u> of my sins by <u>DOING</u> the things on the "do side" of the 10 Love Commandment chart and <u>NOT DOING</u> the things on the "do not side" literally had my soul's foundation being fortified against the coming Day of Judgment! How awesome is that? Friend, you too can have this "spiritual house construction" taking place in your own soul: All you have to <u>DO</u> is repent of your sins by conscientiously following after God's WAY of Love as outlined by the 10 Love Commandments. Doing THOSE deeds will prove your faith in God (Love), and that faith will land you inside the pearly gates!

Well, I wish I could get this book into the hands of every person living on the face of Earth—certainly, everyone with a Bible should have it as an adjunct—for the message contained in this book has the power to change a person's life (since it fully and irrefutably explains the Bible's true meaning and intent) and win them eternal life. Therefore, if you care about your family and friends, please provide them with this book!

Thanks so much,

Gabriel Ansley

Order Form

Gabriel Ansley
P.O. Box 814
Hermitage, Tennessee
37076

Date _____

Name _____

Street Address _____

City _____

State _____ Zip _____

Email _____

Quantity	Title	Price	Total
10	Undeniable Biblical Proof	$ 5.00	$ 50.00
	Undeniable Biblical Proof	$ 5.00	

 * Minimum order of 10 books

Sub-Total _____

Shipping (10%) _____

Total _____

Make check to: Gabriel Ansley
Send to: address above

Author may also be contacted at above address
Or: gabrielansley@gmail.com

Order Form

Gabriel Ansley
P.O. Box 814
Hermitage, Tennessee
37076

Date _____

Name _____

Street Address _____

City _____

State _____ Zip _____

Email _____

Quantity	Title	Price	Total
10	Undeniable Biblical Proof	$ 5.00	$ 50.00
	Undeniable Biblical Proof	$ 5.00	

  * Minimum order of 10 books

Sub-Total _____

Shipping (10%) _____

Total _____

Make check to: Gabriel Ansley
Send to: address above

Author may also be contacted at above address
Or: gabrielansley@gmail.com

Order Form

Gabriel Ansley
P.O. Box 814
Hermitage, Tennessee
37076

Date _____

Name _____

Street Address _____

City _____

State _____ Zip _____

Email _____

Quantity	Title	Price	Total
10	Undeniable Biblical Proof	$ 5.00	$ 50.00
	Undeniable Biblical Proof	$ 5.00	

* Minimum order of 10 books

Sub-Total _____

Shipping (10%) _____

Total _____

Make check to: Gabriel Ansley
Send to: address above

Author may also be contacted at above address
Or: gabrielansley@gmail.com